Reproductive Health Management

Edited by
DR. SIBNATH DEB

AKANSHA PUBLISHING HOUSE
NEW DELHI-110002 (INDIA)

AKANSHA PUBLISHING HOUSE
4649-B/21, Ansari Road
Darya Ganj, New Delhi - 110 002
Ph.: 23263193 / 9811582579 / 09435116718
Telefax: 011-23263193
Email: ektabooks@yahoo.com
www.akanshapublishinghouse.com

Reproductive Health Management

First Published 2009
ISBN 978-81-8370-191-4

PRINTED IN INDIA

Published by Akansha Publishing House, New Delhi and Printed at Aryan Enterprises, Delhi.

Contents

Foreword

Although the field of Reproductive Health is still relatively new, this book titled *'Reproductive Health Management'* clearly illustrates that it is both an integrated academic domain and a distinct professional career pathway. As a university lecturer I am excited by this volume because it achieves something highly valuable: it provides a rich vein of raw material that can be used by teachers and students to give life to concepts and theory.

Dr. Deb and colleagues have structured this book very well. The first four chapters define the field, show how RH articulates with other domains of sexual health, psychology and biomedicine, and discuss the significant achievements to date and the difficult challenges ahead for India. The three main sections on adolescent health, HIV/AIDS and Family Planning provide evocative accounts of cultural traditions and recent changes in personal behaviours and informal and formal care that directly impact upon mortality, morbidity and quality of life.

Some of the authors make explicit the links between human rights and reproductive health, but between the lines it is clear that all contributors are driven by the desire to alleviate the indignity and suffering of the many millions of people disempowered by poverty, personal stigma and discrimination. The chapters that report survey data and health statistics confirm what many who work in this field would expect to find in their local regions, but the real benefit of this book is that the collective contributions from diverse regions lead to powerful generalisations which, we hope, can be applied to effective system-wide management.

Overall, this book gives us good grounds for optimism. The various local studies and the broader comparisons of waves of national statistics reveal solid, if sometimes slow, progress toward better reproductive health outcomes. The work described here should contribute to training of the next generation of professionals in many disciplines. I for one will be drawing from this valuable resource for my International Health class, and I strongly encourage others to do so.

Dr. Michael P Dunne
Professor of Social Epidemiology
Queensland University of Technology
Brisbane, Australia

Preface and Acknowledgements

The Government of India has taken various measures from time to time to address some very pressing and emerging problems, such as overpopulation, teenage pregnancy, infant mortality, maternal mortality, morbidity, and STDs including HIV/AIDS; the outcomes of these efforts, although encouraging are not necessarily satisfactory in relation to the magnitude of the issues at hand.

During the 8th plan, the Government of India adopted an integrated Child Survival and Safe Motherhood (CSSM) programme. The process of integration of related programmes initiated with the implementation of the CSSM programme was pushed a step further in 1994 when the International Conference on Population and Development in Cairo recommended that the participant countries implement unified programmes for Reproductive and Child Health (RCH).

Hence, after Cairo Conference, the Government of India integrated all the health related programmes of the 8th plan under one banner titled *'Reproductive and Child Health (RCH)'* in the 9th plan with a view to providing need-based, client-centered, demand-driven, high quality and integrated RCH services to the beneficiaries.

The RCH approach has been defined as follows:

'People have the ability to reproduce and regulate their fertility, women are able to go through pregnancy and child birth safely, the outcome of pregnancies is successful in terms of maternal and infant survival and well-being and couples are able to have sexual relations free of fear of pregnancy and of contracting diseases.'

This concept is in keeping with the evolution of an integrated approach to the ongoing programmes in the country aimed at improving the health status of young women and children.

Under the RCH programme, all aspects of women's reproductive health across their reproductive cycle, from puberty to menopause, are covered. The RCH programme addresses the needs that have emerged over years of implementing the Family Welfare Programme. As opposed to the Family Welfare Programme, the RCH programme aims to be more in tune with the ground realities concerning overall health needs of women and children, implementation needs of health workers and local demographic needs and conditions. The components, which are covered under the RCH, include

- Effective maternal and child health care;
- Increased access to contraceptive care;
- Safe management of unwanted pregnancies;
- Nutritional services to vulnerable groups;
- Prevention and treatment of RTI/STI;
- Reproductive health services for adolescents;
- Prevention and treatment of gynaecological problems;
- Screening and treatment of cancers; especially uterine, cervical and breast cancers.

The RCH programme was launched in India on 15th October 1997. Meanwhile, the researchers and academics have carried out a number of studies on different dimensions of the issue and/or implemented different intervention programmes for improving the situation. A natural outcome of these efforts is the felt need at many circles that the rich experiences and the lessons learnt should be compiled into a document to guide and benefit future inquiries. In the product that has thus been compiled, three broad dimensions of reproductive health are emphasized - adolescent care/health, HIV/AIDS and family planning methods, each addressed by leaders in their respective fields.

Psychological sciences alone have trained and qualified individuals to deal with and manage stress and modify behavior. The service of a psychologist as a counselor is an important aspect of reproductive health and HIV/AIDS intervention. For delivering effective counseling services to the victim and/or a person with high-risk behaviour, a counselor should be sensitive to the cultural diversity of his or her clientele and should incorporate those aspects in the practice to facilitate successful intervention. In the beginning of HIV/AIDS pandemic, the important role that a counselor could play in the prevention and management of the problem was not given serious attention by the authorities in India. It was, however, Dr. Sushma Mehrotra, who joined the National AIDS Control Organization (NACO) as a consultant (counseling) and played a significant role in convincing the authorities that counseling is an important aspect of reproductive health in general and HIV/AIDS in particular and that this service should be delivered by the mental health professionals. She was instrumental in brining out the curriculum for training of the HIV/AIDS counselors for which NACO and WHO extended full support to the idea. A group of highly experienced and dedicated professionals worked very hard in developing and finalizing the curriculum for training of HIV/AIDS counselors. I was fortunate to be one of the resource persons in this curriculum development. Afterwards, NACO also helped the academic institutes to receive Global Funds grant to strengthen the capacity of academic institutes for training of HIV counselors across the country.

Institutions, which have taught me a lot of lessons on reproductive health, include the Community Health Research and Training Unit (CHRTU), the University of Western Australia, Australia and MODE – one of the leading professional research companies in India. In the CHRTU, I was trained in the field of reproductive health and qualitative research in 1994, while in MODE, I was involved in a number of research projects on different aspects of reproductive health funded by the national and international agencies and gained professional experience, knowledge, and insightful understanding about the issues. I am especially indebted to Prof. Peter Underwood, Director of CHRTU, The University of Western Australia, Australia and D.P. Basu, Managing Director of GFK MODE Private Limited for their significant contribution in my professional career and for giving me exposure in the said field. I worked in MODE for three years with a group of dynamic researchers and learnt a lot from all of them. The late Prof. B.N.Ghosh, former Director of All India Institute of Hygiene and Public Health, Abhijit Dasgupta, Maitreyee Ghatak and Ruma Banerjee are among some of them. I am grateful to all of them for their role in encouraging, sustaining and facilitating my interest in the field of reproductive health.

I am grateful to all the resource persons for their spontaneous response and contribution in this document. The resource persons who contributed in this document are from different leading and creditable academic and research institutions in India, namely, The National AIDS Research Institute (NARI), Pune (under Indian Council of Medical

Research), National Institute for Research in Reproductive Health, Mumbai (under Indian Council of Medical Research), International Institute for Population Sciences (IIPS), Mumbai, National Institute of Health and Family Welfare, Delhi, Indian Institute of Technology Kanpur, Kanpur, All India Institute of Hygiene and Public Health (AIIHPH), Kolkata, Calcutta School of Tropical Medicine, Kolkata, Institute of Public Health, Bangalore, Population Research Centre of the Institute of Economic Growth, University Enclave, Delhi, Medical College, Thiruvananthapuram, Kerala, Medical College, Kolkata, Department of Psychology, Andhra University, Andhra Pradesh, Department of Applied Psychology, Calcutta University, Kolkata, Department of Sociology, Madurai Kamaraj University, Tamil Nadu, Department of Sociology and Population Studies, Bharathiar University, Coimbatore, Tamil Nadu, Department of Health and Family Welfare, Government of Orissa, Orissa and GTZ Health Sector Support, GTZ India. Other independent researchers, some of whom are associated with various institutions have also made their contribution. All the resource persons are among the leaders in their respective fields.

The rich experience of the knowledgeable and experienced academics and researchers would be immensely beneficial for other researchers, programme planners and policy makers in developing evidence-based intervention programmes in the field of reproductive health, for taking course corrective measures in case of on-going intervention programmes and for efficient management of the same. I express my sincere gratitude to Prof. Michael Dunne, Social Epidemiologist, School of Public Health, Queensland University of Technology, Australia for reviewing the document and writing the 'Foreword' for the same despite his busy schedule. Special acknowledgement is due to Bishakha Majumdar, Ruhi Sinha and Anindita Chaudhury for their special and professional assistance in brining out this document. An effort has been made to produce an error-free document. However, if there is any typing and/or printing error, the same is regretted.

DR. SIBNATH DEB
Faculty Member, Department of Applied Psychology
Calcutta University
92, A.P.C.Road, Kolkata-700 009
E-mail: sibnath23@rediffmail.com / sibnath23@gmail.com

Profile of Contributors

Prof. Archana Shukla, Ph.D. in Psychology teaches Clinical and Counseling Psychology and Motivation and Affective Processes at Lucknow University, Lucknow. She is a consultant to various organizations such as NCERT, IGNOU, NIPCCD, NABARD, UPSC, National AIDS Control Organization (NACO), and Staff Selection Commission (SSC). Prof. Shukla is widely known for the workshops that she conducts on communication skills, emotional intelligence, happiness, personality growth, stress management etc. for various public and private sector organizations. She is a master trainer on HIV/AIDS counseling for prevention, care and support. She has published 35 articles in various National and International Journals and has several chapters in books on Psychology.
E-mail: prof.a.shukla@gmail.com

Ashutosh Srivastava is currently working as Senior Project Officer, GFATM-7 project, Lucknow University, Prior to that he was working as Curriculum Design and Development Manager with Mind Edutainment, a company working on the thinking skills among children. He also worked as a lecturer of Psychology and Behavioral Sciences with Amity University and also an International Program Manager with The Cognition Group, USA. He is also associated with various organizations as a Consultant Psychologist for training and counseling, including HIV/AIDS counseling.

Prof. Madhumita Dobe, MBBS, DCH, MD, MCH, FIPHA, is the Head of the Department of Health Education, All India Institute of Hygiene and Public Health. She is involved in post graduate teaching, training and research activities in Public Health and has to her credit over 20 publications in peer reviewed bio-medical journals and books and over 200 invited lectures/editorials in scientific meetings/journals. She is Co-author of the training manual for health professionals on RCH prepared by Indian Public Health Association used for training health care providers. She has received several Fellowship awards including GOI Fellowship under Colombo Plan, Fellowship by American Cancer Society at 13th World Conference on Tobacco or Health, P.C. Sen Award for the best paper in Rural Public Health Research in the National Conference of the IPHA 2002. She is the Secretary General of Indian Public Health Association (H.Q.), Secretary of the West Bengal Chapter of South East Asia Regional Bureau of the International Union for Health Promotion, Chairperson: Manpower Resource Development Committee- International Union for Health Promotion and Education- South East Asia Regional Bureau, Joint Secretary: Breast Feeding Promotion Network of India (BPNI), West Bengal.

Dr. B. Nalini is the Professor of Sociology in Madurai Kamaraj University, Madurai, Tamilnadu. Her specialization areas are Sociology of Health and Social Gerontology. She has published many articles in these subjects in national and international journals. She has authored three books. Dr. B. Nalini has undertaken many research projects sponsored by the UGC, Ministries and ICMR. She has visited many foreign countries. Address for Correspondence: Dr. B. Nalini, Professor, Department of Sociology, Madurai Kamaraj University.

Dr. Vandana Bhattacharya, Research Officer, Department of Social Science, National Institute of Health and Family

Welfare, Delhi has long research experience in the field of reproductive health. She was involved in a number of studies on the same subject and published a number of papers in the journals. Her current areas of research interest are adolescent reproductive health and HIV/AIDS.
E-mail: vandanabhattacharya@rediffmail.com

Prof. A. Sheelamoni, Department of Obstetrics and Gynaecology has been working in the field of adolescent pregnancy for the last ten years. Prof. Sheelamoni has published a number of research papers in the reputed medical journals. His current areas of research interest include adolescent health.

Prof. M.K.C. Nair, Professor of Pediatrics and Director, Child Development Centre, Medical College, Thiruvananthapuram, Kerala. Prof. Nair was the former President of Indian Academy of Paediatrics. He has more than 20 years of research and teaching experience. He has published more than 30 research papers in the national and international journals in addition to producing a lot of educational materials on adolescent health and development.

Dr. N. Audinarayana is currently Professor and Head, Department of Sociology and Population Studies, Director, School of Social Sciences, Bharathiar University, Coimbatore, Tamil Nadu. After completing M.A., M.Phil., and Ph.D. Degrees in Population Studies from Sri Venkateswara University, Tirupati, he worked as Technical Assistant / Research Officer at the International Institute for Population Sciences, Mumbai during 1982-1987 and later joined the Bharathiar University as Lecturer. He has 21 years of teaching and 28 years of research experience in the fields of specializations like Nuptiality (Marriage and Related Aspects), Fertility, Women's Health Issues, Ageing and Reproductive / Sexual Health Issues of Young Men. He has published / edited 6 books and about several papers in various International

and National refereed Journals and Edited Volumes and completed 13 Minor/Major research projects (as Principal / Co-investigator) funded by the IIPS, Mumbai, UGC, UNDP, PIP, UK, Welcome Trust, UK, Ford Foundation and McArthur Foundation, USA, and the Ford Foundation, USA. He has participated and presented a large number of papers in International and National Conferences/Seminars/ Workshops. Visited countries like Singapore, France (Tours and Paris), South Africa (Durban and Johannesburg), Italy (Rome), Switzerland (Zurich) and Kenya (Nairobi) for participating and presenting papers at the International Conferences. He is member in several Professional Bodies like IASP, IASSH, IUSSP, ISMS, ISA and APA. Currently, extending services as Secretary to the Bharathiar University Teachers' Association (BHUTA).
Phone: 0422-2424862, 2428451, Mobile: 09443154366, E-mail: audi_bu@yahoo.co.in

Dr. C.P. Prakasam is a retired Professor from Department of Public Health and Mortality Studies, International Institute for Population Sciences, Deonar, Mumbai. He holds Ph.D. degree in Demography from University of Mumbai. After his post graduation he did Certificate and Diploma in Population Sciences with Government of India fellowship at IIPS. He is author/co-editor of many books. His research specializations include Biostatistics, Epidemiology, Mortality and Computer Applications to demographic data analysis. He also worked as Associate Professor at the Demographic Training Research Centre, Addis Ababa University, Ethiopia. Besides teaching demography, he has wide experience in several research projects, organized national and international seminars and published research papers.
Address for Correspondence: Dr. C.P.Prakasam, C2-5/2:3, Sector-4, Vashi, New Bombay-400703, Maharashtra, India, E-mail: c_prakasam@yahoo.com

Prof. M.V.R. Raju PhD, Head, Department of Psychology, Andhra University, is the Director, Centre for Psychological Assessment and Counseling, Andhra University. He has 23 years of teaching and research experience. His areas of Specialization are Health, Counseling and Organizational Behavior. He has been involved in national and international organizations like, Council Member of Indian Association of Applied Psychology, Member, Andhra Pradesh Academy of Psychologists, Editor and Scientific Board Member, European Journal of Intellectual Disability Switzerland, Editor for Preston Journal of Social Sciences, Pakistan and Consulting Editor Journal of Indian Applied Psychology. He has authored 11 books in English and Telugu and edited two books. He attended 32 national and international conferences and presented research papers. And also he published 33 research articles in national and international journals. He has been awarded Psychometric Testing Services Award. 2007 at the 10th National Conference, Applied Psychology, 2008, Pondicherry for his outstanding contribution in Human Resource Development, Best Academician 2007 Andhra University, and Dr. Sarvepalli Radhakrishnan Best Researcher Award, Andhra University 2006. He is a Resource person and trainer in major public and private sector organizations like HPCL, Visakhapatnam Steel Plant, Visakhapatnam Port Trust, NTPC, NMDC, Regency Ceramics Ltd, Central Prison, Police Department, and Revenue Department etc.

E-mail:mraju14@rediffmail.com, mvrraju.psychology@gmail.com

Dr. N.D.S. Naga Seema is working as a Teaching Associate in the Department of Psychology, Andhra University, Visakhapatnam. She has presented 7 papers in national and international conferences and seminars. Attended more than 12 national and international conferences and workshops. She had worked as a Lecturer in Psychology in Govt. Degree College for Women, Visakhapatnam for 3 years. As a Co-

author, she published 7 papers in various journals.
E-mail: nagaseemavsp@yahoo.com

Dr. Roy Amrita, M.B.B.S. has been working in the field of adolescent health for the last two years. Her main areas of research interest are risk behaviour among adolescents and their social networking system.

Prof. Dipankar Guha Roy, M.B.B.S., Department of Forensic Medicine and Toxicology, Medical College, Kolkata, has 15 years research and teaching experience. Prof. Guha published a number of research papers in the journals and guided a number of students for Masters' Dissertation in the field of teenage pregnancy and Forensic Medicine.

Prof. Tapas Kumar Bose, Head, Department of Forensic Medicine and Toxicology, N.R.S. Medical College, Kolkata, has 20 years research and teaching experience. Dr. Bose has published about 10 research papers in the reputed journals in addition to attending a number of national and international conferences. He has guided a number of students for Masters' Dissertation.

Dr. Ruby Alambusha, MA., MPS, Ph.D., Project Associate at IIM, Ahmedabad and has five years of research experience.
E-mail: rubyalambusha@gmail.com,alambusha_iips@ rediffmail.com.

Prof. Sulabha Parasuraman, M.Sc., C.P.S., Ph.D., Professor and Head, Department of Population Policies and Programmes at International Institute for Population Sciences. One of the Co-ordinators of the National level project titled 'National Family Health Survey', has 18 years research and teaching experience.
E-mail: sulabhap@iips.net, Sulabhap@rediffmail.com.

Dr. Rahul Sen, MBBS (Cal), DGO (Cal), MRCOG (London), MRCP (Dublin), is a member of the Royal College of Obstetricians and Gynaecologists, London, and the Royal

College of Physicians of Ireland. He has worked for four years in the departments of Obstetrics and Gynaecology in several renowned hospitals in England. At present he is working as a Consultant Obstetrician and Gynaecologist in Bhagirathi Neotia Woman and Childcare Centre, and Peerless Hospital and B. K. Roy Research Centre, Kolkata. Several of his articles pertaining to health have been published in the reputed daily, '*The Statesman*'. He has lectured on several occasions on adolescence in several schools in Kolkata. Dr Sen has a website, www.docsen.com, through which he attempts to spread health awareness. Dr. Sen is also very much involved in creative writing. His first novel, 'The Noah' has been appreciated by readers across the globe. It is tale about cloning of human beings. His second novel, 'The Sequel', got published in June, 2008. Dr. Sen is an obsessive traveller, and loves to trek in the Himalayas.

Dr. (Ms.) Ranjana Kar, M.Sc. in Statistics followed by Master Degree in Population Science from IIPS, Mumbai and Ph.D. She has also completed a certificate course on 'Epidemiology in Action' from the Liverpool School of Tropical Medicine, U.K. She has 24 years of research and teaching experience and she has started her carrier in the H and FW Department, Government of Orissa under DFID Project as Monitoring and Evaluation Office, also worked as Lecturer in Statistics at Rural Health Training Centre, Jagatsinghpur and now working as an Assistant Director, Statistics in the State Institute of Health and Family Welfare, Government of Orissa. Her responsibilities included teaching in training programmes and undertaking different studies for the Institutes. She has also expertise in the field of Health and Management Information System and Policy and Planning and also completed training from the Administrative Staff College of India, Hyderabad and Indian Institute of Health Management, Jaipur. Very recently, she has also completed the National Family Health Survey-3 for the State of Orissa as the Coordinator besides other research studies at national significance such as CAN Approach, use of Iodized Salt, KAP for Iodine Deficiency Disorder, use of Acceptability of the Indian System of Medicine in Orissa and evaluation of Kishori Shakti Yojana in Orissa and West Bengal.

Prof. Bibhuti Saha, M.B.B.S., D.T.M. & H., M.D., is Professor and Head, Department of Tropical Medicine, Calcutta School of Tropical Medicine, Kolkata-700073. Prof. Saha has been in the teaching profession since 1988 and has guided many dissertation works on various tropical diseases for M.D., Diploma, M.Sc. courses of University of Calcutta and West Bengal University of Health Sciences. Prof. Saha is course co-ordinator, Convener, Board of Studies and Examiner for M.D. (Tropical Medicine), D.T.M.H. courses of West Bengal University of Health Sciences. Prof. Saha acted as a Trainer for the Training of Trainers programme for Physicians Training Initiative in HIV/AIDS of Clinton Foundation/Indian Medical Association/NACO for West Bengal and Orissa. He is a core member of Fellowship in HIV Medicine course of Calcutta School of Tropical Medicine and Medical College, Kolkata in collaboration with Christian Medical College, Vellore. He is also a senior faculty member of National AIDS Control Organisation (NACO), Antiretroviral Treatment Training Centre of Calcutta School of Tropical Medicine, Kolkata. Prof. Saha has published more than 23 articles in national and international journals.

Dr. Ayesha Chowdhury, D.G.O, M.D. (Gynae and Obs), is a Consultant Gynaecologist and Senior Medical Officer, ART Centre, Calcutta School of Tropical Medicine, Kolkata.

Dr. Seema Sahay is currently working as Assistant Director, Scientist D at the National AIDS Research Institute, Pune, India. She completed her graduation in Botany from the Hindu College, Delhi University. She did her post graduation and received doctorate from Department of Anthropology,

University of Delhi. She has been an ICMR and Fogarty fellow. She was conferred the Fogarty fellowship for Leadership program, Women's Global Health Scholars program at the University of California, San Francisco, USA. Dr. Sahay has published over 25 papers in national and international journals and she has presented over 50 abstracts at national and international conferences. Her major areas of work are: experimental study on anxiety and depression in HIV infected individuals, intervention education study on adolescents, social and behavioral aspects of human clinical trials on prevention of secondary transmission, microbicides and HIV vaccines, observational studies on cancer of service screening using (VIA), observational studies, cohort studies and descriptive epidemiological studies. She has conducted qualitative studies on standard of care for microbicide trials and care and support. In the clinical trials, she has played a major role in recruitment and retention of the clinical trial participants; planning, developing and implementing the community involvement plan of NARI that aims at educating the community, identification and training of peers, tracking of community based referrals and involving Community Advisory Board (CAB) and local NGOs in NARI research. In the first HIV phase-I vaccine trial in India, she was the principal recruiter and responsible for developing a 3-tier strategy of community contact and education program.

Dr. Sushma Mehrotra, MPhil and PhD in Clinical Psychology, was associated with SNDT Women's University Mumbai as a faculty member in the Department of Psychology from 1990-2004. She has 15 years experience in HIV prevention field developing guidelines and protocols, counseling manuals, conceptualizing, planning, managing, monitoring and implementing policies and programs nationally and internationally. Dr. Mehrotra was the first psychotherapist in India who brought trauma therapy Eye

Movement Desensitization and Reprocessing (EMDR) to India. She led the team of 40 trained EMDR practitioners from Mumbai to Gujarat in Western India after the devastating earthquake in 2001 to work with 16,000 children and adults for overcoming PTSD. She is a qualified MBTI practitioner and conducts workshops and seminars for personality development, creativity, interpersonal communication and dealing with stress. Her important assignments have been with National AIDS Control Organization, Ministry of Health, Government of India as a National consultant to develop Voluntary Counseling and Testing strategies and practices across India and with CARE, India as a Project Director for implementing HIV prevention program supported by Bill and Melinda Gates Foundation. She is also a consultant for WHO South East Asia Regional Office.

Prof. A. K. Sharma is the professor of Sociology in Humanities and Social Sciences Department of Indian Institute of Technology Kanpur. He has guided a large number of doctoral and post-doctoral students and produced several books and articles in reputed academic journals in India and outside. He is actively associated with a couple of NGOs, which have conducted studies in the field of education, rural development, health, and HIV/AIDS in different states of India. His areas of interest are child mortality, sociology of health, and HIV/AIDS.

Dr. Suresh Sharma M.Sc., M.P.S. (Demography), Ph.D., Faculty Member in Population Research Centre, Institute of Economic Growth (IEG), Delhi, has 18 years of research experience. He specializes in epidemiology, reproductive and child health, public health, gender issues among adolescents and youth, population projections, and mathematical demography. He has authored three books '*Health Problems of Rural Population in India*'; '*Reproductive Health in Delhi Slums*' and '*Growing Rural-Urban Disparity in Uttarakhand*' (forthcoming). He has published several monographs and

contributed several articles in national and international journals on population and health issues. He has coordinated several projects for the World Resources Institute (WRI) Washington, World Bank (WB), the United Nations Population Fund (UNFPA), the National Commission for Population (NCP) and Ministry of Health and Family Welfare (MoHFW), Government of India. He is the executive member of the Indian Association for the Study of Population (IASP). He was the Member of Board of Trustee of the Indian Association for the Study of Population (IASP) 2004-06. He has visited a number of countries like Austria, Nepal, Singapore, Norway, Denmark, France, Italy, Thailand, Hungary, Sweden and so on for academic and research purpose. He was involved in two major research projects on Reproductive and Child Health (RCH) and National Family Health Survey (NFHS) at the IEG, Delhi.
E-mail: *suresh@iegindia.org / suresh_prc@ yahoo.com*

Dr. Balaiah Donta, Ph.D., a biostatistician, is Scientist F, National Institute for Research in Reproductive Health, Indian Council of Medical Research (ICMR), Mumbai has 20 years research experience in the field of family planning and reproductive health.

Dattaram D Naik, MA, MPS, DPM, a sociologist and demographer, is a Social Worker, National Institute for Research in Reproductive Health, ICMR, Mumbai.

Dr. Saritha Nair, PhD, a demographer, is Scientist B, National Institute for Research in Reproductive Health, ICMR, Mumbai.

Umesh Iddya, BSc, a statistician, is Technical Officer, National Institute for Research in Reproductive Health, ICMR, Mumbai.

Dr. Anil Bandivadekar, MBBS, DPH, a public health physician, is Deputy Health Executive Officer, Municipal Corporation of Greater Mumbai (MCGM), Mumbai.

Dr. J. N. Pandit, MBBS, DPH is at present working as the Senior Technical Expert in the Health Sector Support of German Technical Cooperation (GTZ), Kolkata providing technical support to the Department of Health and Family Welfare, Government of West Bengal since 2004. Prior to joining GTZ, Dr. Pandit worked with an international NGO titled CINI-Child in Need Institute as Deputy Director and also worked with the Department of Health and Family Welfare, Government of West Bengal for 26 years in various capacities starting from the Medical-Officer of BPHC, District Family Welfare Officer of two districts. He worked in the Family Welfare Department for seven years as Assistant Director of Health Services and handled UIP, CSSMP and RCH at the state level. While in government service Dr. Pandit worked on lien with the World Health Organization on the National Polio Surveillance Programme in Bihar. While in Government Service Dr. Pandit underwent several training programmes on different aspects of health. He attended training on "Project Management and Evaluation" organized by Management Training and Development Institute of Washington DC, USA. held at Florida, USA. GTZ sent Dr. Pandit to Heidelberg University, Germany, for training on 'European Foundation for Quality Management (EFQM) Assessor Training'. He has also undergone a training organized by National Accreditation Board for Hospital and Health Care Providers (NABH) under the Quality Council of India. At present he is working on Quality Assurance Programme. He has facilitated the development of a Strategy for Bio-Medical Waste Management for the Basic Health Care facilities and a Standard Treatment Protocol for the Medical Officers working in the BHC level facilities for the Department of Health and Family Welfare, Government of West Bengal.

Dr. N. Devadasan, MBBS, MPH, is a medical graduate from CMC Vellore who served the tribals of Gudalur, Nilgiris District for more than 10 years. Working with an NGO,

ACCORD, he and his wife were instrumental in setting up an entire health system for the tribals including village health workers, nurse practitioners and a 30-bed hospital. This entire health system was partially funded by a community health insurance scheme. After this, he joined the WHO at the country office and was in charge of the communicable disease cluster. Among other activities, he was instrumental in developing the integrated disease surveillance Programme for the Government of India. During the three years, he had investigated many rare outbreaks, including the Nipah virus outbreak in Siliguri, and the Plague outbreak in Himachal. However, WHO was too far removed from his first love – the field and the people of India. So he returned to Bangalore and along with some well wishers founded the Institute of Public Health. This is basically a centre for training and research, focusing on the middle and senior level officers in the government services. During his tenure there, he has been extensively researching health insurance in India. Today he is considered one of the key authorities on health insurance and is on various state and central government committees. IPH organizes various courses ranging from short term ones to a Ph.D. programme. He is also a visiting faculty at the Sree Chitra Tirunal Institute of Medical Sciences and Technology (SCTIMST), Kerala.

Swarn Lata is currently pursuing her Ph.D., as SRF, on Social Skills Training from Psychology Department, Lucknow University, Lucknow. She has to her credit three chapters in books, and four published articles. She is actively involved in HIV/AIDS Counseling.

I. Reproductive and Sexual Health: General

1

Reproductive and Sexual Health: Problems, Provisions and Possibilities

Prof. Archana Shukla & Ashutosh Srivastava

Summary

The paper presents a conceptual clarification of various reproductive and sexual health (RSH) domains and issues. It highlights the differences between family planning and reproductive and sexual health concerns. Next, an effort is made to identify some current reproductive health needs particularly among displaced populations and young girls. The importance of the RSH can be gauged by the fact that it is a human right. Various RSH services in emergency versus longer term stable settings are then enumerated. Finally, an effort is made to generate awareness toward constraints to providing quality comprehensive reproductive and sexual health care so that the same could be overcome. The paper concludes by suggesting that men's participation in reproductive and sexual health is a necessary precondition to achieving the targets.

Introduction

> *'The Millennium Development Goals, particularly the eradication of extreme poverty and hunger, cannot be achieved if questions of population and reproductive health are not squarely addressed. And this means stronger efforts to promote women's rights and greater investment in education and health, including reproductive health and family planning.'*
>
> *—United Nations Secretary-General Kofi Annan, July 2005*

'Reproductive health is a state of complete physical, mental and social well-being and not merely the absence of disease or infirmity, in all matters relating to the reproductive system and to its functions and processes. Reproductive health therefore implies that people are able to have a satisfying and safe sex life and that they have the capability to reproduce and the freedom to decide if, when, and how often to do so. Implicit in this last condition are the rights of men and women to be informed and have access to safe, effective, affordable and acceptable methods of family planning of their choice. It also includes the right of access to other methods of their choice for regulation of fertility which are not against the law, and the right of access to appropriate health-care services that will enable women to go safely through delaying pregnancy, conceiving, and child birth and provide couples with the best chance of having a healthy infant. Also included is sexual health, the purpose of which is the enhancement of life and personal relations, and not merely counseling and care related to reproduction and sexually transmitted diseases' (*Definition of reproductive health adopted in the Program of Action of the International Conference on Population and Development, ICPD, and endorsed by the United Nations General Assembly in its resolution 49/128, 1994*).

As outlined by the International Conference on Population and Development (ICPD) reproductive and sexual health (RSH) is thus not merely about reproduction. RSH must be viewed as a set of three interconnected domains that include universal rights, women's empowerment, and health service provision. Firstly, RSH promotes a universal understanding that is premised on the fact that RSH as a basic human right is to be fulfilled by all governments. Secondly, RSH seeks to address the underlying causes of gender inequality and inequity to promote women's empowerment. Thirdly, the provision of universal access, utilization, and quality of RSH services addresses issues related to sexual and reproductive ill-health, and possibly death. The three domains of rights, women's empowerment and equality, and services must work in unison in order for individuals to achieve healthy reproductive and sexual lives and thus overall health and wellbeing.

The first domain of RSH is based on a rights-based approach. Everyone is entitled to the rights and freedoms set out by the Universal Declaration of Human Rights, which includes the right to health and education without distinction based on race, sex, religion, etc. Universal reproductive and sexual rights are expected to be supported and upheld by governmental policies and laws, specifically the right for couples and individuals to decide if, when, and how many children they would like to have, as well as access to information to enable them to make these choices; the right to attain the highest standard of sexual and reproductive health; and the right to make RSH decisions without discrimination, coercion or violence (ICPD, Programme of Action, 7.3).

The second domain of RSH, women's empowerment, emphasizes the fact that norms, values, and laws create an environment that influences the extent of women's equality and power within a society. Broadly, this means (1) addressing issues of gender inequality and empowering women, (2) ensuring that males understand their responsibilities and participate in these decisions, (3) eliminating various obvious as well as subtle forms of discrimination against the girl child (e.g. female genital cutting, forced early marriage, compulsive child bearing, etc.), and (4) accessing education. This second arena of RSH thus addresses how social and sexual inequities lead to power imbalances in relationships causing unsatisfying sex lives and ill-health. Furthermore, RSH does not affect women alone and must not be solely promoted as a women's issue. Men not only also have their own reproductive health needs, but are also very likely to get affected by women's reproductive and sexual health. Therefore, the involvement of men becomes an integral and essential part of protecting women's RSH.

In promoting women's empowerment and addressing issues of equality, relationships must not only be viewed in the context of those between men and women, but also of the surrounding psycho-socio-cultural environment. Attitudes and norms about sexuality and gender carry profound meanings in every community. The knowledge of power dynamics and decision-making in sexual relationships, between service providers and clients, and between community leaders and citizens - all affect an individual's social status and thus reproductive and sexual health.

The final domain of RSH deals with service provisions. That women's utilization of health services is very dismal is a common knowledge. Enhanced service provisions refer to the ability of public and private service providers to address factors that may inhibit an individual from accessing and utilizing these services besides providing a variety of quality RSH services. This may include ensuring widespread information on services and methods of not only family planning and safe sex but also affordability, confidentiality, convenience, availability and attract-ability of supplies.

Difference between RSH and Family Planning

The concept of reproductive and sexual health differs from

the existing family planning (FP) and maternal and child health (MCH) programs. Programmes dealing with various components of reproductive health exist in some form almost everywhere. But they have usually been delivered in a separate unconnected manner. For example, the objectives, design and evaluation of family planning programs have hitherto been largely driven by a demographic imperative, without due consideration to related health issues such as maternal health, family well-being, STD prevention and management, etc. Evaluation too was largely in terms of quantity rather than quality - numbers of contraceptive acceptors as opposed to the ability and opportunity to make informed decisions about reproductive health issues. In general, such programmes exclusively targeted women, taking little account of the social, cultural and intimate realities of their reproductive lives and decision-making powers. Moreover, these tended to serve only married people. Services were rarely designed to serve men even though they have reproductive health concerns of their own, particularly with regard to sexually transmitted diseases. Yet, the involvement of men in reproductive health is important because they have an important role to play as family decision-makers with regard to family size and family planning and as encouragers and support givers to women's use of health services.

A reproductive health approach thus differs from a family planning approach in several ways. It aims to build upon what exists and at the same time to modify current narrow and vertical programmes to ones in which every opportunity is taken to offer a full range of reproductive health services in a linked way to both women and men. The underlying assumption is that people with a need in one particular area (say treatment of a sexually transmitted disease) also have needs in other areas (family planning or antenatal/ postpartum care). It is now increasingly recognized that dealing with one aspect of reproductive health can have synergistic effects in dealing with others. For example, management of infertility is difficult and expensive but it can be largely prevented through appropriate care with early diagnosis of symptoms of abnormality and prevention and management of STDs. Promotion of breast-feeding similarly influences reproductive health in many ways - it helps to prevent certain postpartum problems, delays return to fertility, may help to prevent ovarian and breast cancer, and improves neonatal health, as well as attachment between mother and the newborn child.

Another important difference between the existing programmes and those related to the new concept of reproductive health is the way in which people, particularly women and young people who are the most affected by reproductive health concerns, are involved in development, implementation and evaluation of a programme. As women become more involved in programmes it leads to (1) a profound rethinking of the behavioural, social, gender and cultural dimensions of decision-making which affect women's reproductive lives and (2) thus dealing with reproductive health in newer ways.

Reproductive Health Needs and Concerns

Reproductive health affects, and in turn, gets affected by the broader context of people's lives including their economic circumstances, education, employment, living conditions, family environment, social and gender relationships, and the traditional and legal structures which decide the extent of permissiveness vs. restrictiveness of the communities in which they live. Sexual and reproductive behaviours are governed by a complex juxtaposition of biological, cultural and psychosocial factors. Therefore, the attainment of reproductive health is not limited to interventions by the health sector alone. Most reproductive health problems cannot be significantly addressed without a collaboration and a proactive involvement among social scientists, health professionals, and policy makers on the one hand, and the families and communities on the other.

The precise configuration of reproductive health programs and policies thus ought to take into account each country's specific socio-cultural situations and the availability of appropriate interventions. Thus, such programmes are likely to vary from country to country. Globally, however, both the epidemiological data and the expressed wishes of diverse communities indicate that effective RSH interventions are most likely to include attention to the issues of nutrition, hygiene, family planning, STD prevention and management, and, prevention of maternal and prenatal mortality and morbidity. To facilitate this, gender atypical socialization is a must.

Reproductive health should also address issues such as harmful practices, unwanted pregnancies, unsafe abortions, reproductive tract infections including STDs and HIV/AIDS, gender-based violence, infertility, malnutrition and anemia, and reproductive tract cancers. Appropriate services that must be made accessible include information, education, counselling, prevention, detection and management of health problems, care and rehabilitation.

Reproductive health strategies should be founded first and foremost on the health of individuals and families. Such strategies must ensure accessibility to quality-care, respect for the individual, freedom of choice, informed consent, and confidentiality and privacy in all reproductive matters. Special attention must be focused on meeting the reproductive health needs and concerns of adolescents, particularly the young girls.

The status of girls and women in a society, and how they are treated or mistreated, is a crucial determinant of their reproductive health. Educational opportunities for girls and women powerfully affect their status and extent to which they have control over their own lives and their health and fertility. The empowerment of women is, therefore, an essential prerequisite to RSH.

Women bear by far the greatest burden of reproductive health problems. Women are at risk of complications from pregnancy and childbirth; they also face risks in preventing unwanted pregnancies, suffer the complications of unsafe abortions, bear most of the burden of contraception, and are more exposed to contracting, and suffering the complications of reproductive tract infections, particularly sexually transmitted diseases (STDs). Among women of reproductive age, 36.0% of all healthy years of life lost are due to reproductive health problems such as unregulated fertility, maternal mortality and morbidity and sexually transmitted diseases including HIV/AIDS. By contrast, the equivalent figure for men is 12.0%.

Biological factors alone do not explain women's disparate burden. Their social, economic and political dependence and disadvantages have a detrimental impact on their self-esteem and reproductive health. Young people of both sexes are particularly vulnerable to reproductive health problems because of a lack of information, power of decision-making, and access to services.

A number of countries have expressed the desire to move forward with a new and comprehensive approach to reproductive and sexual health. Support to national authorities in carrying out a systematic review of reproductive health needs at country level should focus on the importance of adding innovative and participatory approaches to more familiar epidemiological methodologies in which the process tends to be directed by experts and framed by biomedical approaches and indicators. The identification of reproductive health needs, the determination of priorities and the development of programmatic responses to those needs should be conducted through an inclusive process, soliciting the perspectives of a range of groups concerned with reproductive health including, for example, women's health advocates, youth groups, health care providers at the periphery as well as at the central level, health planners, researchers, and non-governmental organizations.

Several instruments have already been developed for situation analysis and needs assessment in different components of reproductive health, for example, family planning and safe motherhood. However, in the context of the new approach to reproductive health, it is necessary to ensure that assessment and prioritization reflect people's concerns as agreed at national and local levels and not the priorities of agencies or donors. It is important to avoid duplication and to develop tools that are appropriate for the social-cultural realities of a country. A number of such instruments already exist and are widely used. However, it is important to ensure psychometric worth of the various instruments currently available.

Similar considerations apply to the selection of priorities for action in reproductive health. Criteria for identification of priority problems should include not only importance - prevalence, severity, public concern, government commitment, impact on family, community and development - but also the feasibility of addressing them - known interventions, cost-effectiveness, availability of financing, human resources and adequate equipment and supplies.

The operationalization of the new concept of reproductive health will mean changes in skills, knowledge, attitudes and management. People will have to work together in innovative ways. Health care providers will have to collaborate with others including psychologists, sociologists, NGOs, women's health advocates, religious leaders and young people. Managerial and administrative changes will also be needed because integrated services can impose, at least initially, greater burdens on already over-stretched staff and require attention to motivating, planning and logistics in order to ensure availability, continuity and quality services.

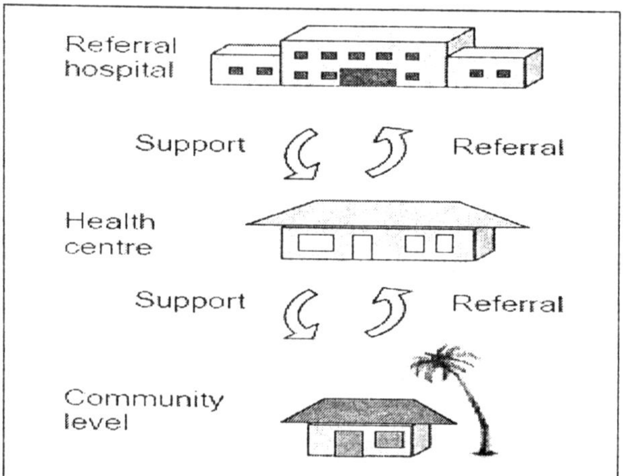

Figure 1. Strong links needed between levels of health care service delivery

Training for reproductive health workers will need to focus on improving both technical and interpersonal skills. Additional training, particularly in counselling skills and in ways of reaching out to under-served groups could be essential elements of such training. The back-up and support of referral systems functioning in a given area will be essential, if the full range of reproductive health concerns is to be adequately addressed.

Reproductive Health as a Human Right

A healthy reproductive and sexual life is now considered to be a basic human right for all, including refugees and other forcibly displaced persons, and is protected by three bodies of law: human rights law, refugee law, and humanitarian law. The foundations for reproductive rights were first established in the two fundamental human rights treaties: the United Nations Charter, adopted in 1945, and the Universal Declaration of Human Rights, adopted in 1948, which ensured an individual's right to health. In 1949, the Geneva Convention on the Protection of Civilians in Times of War provided the basis from which reproductive health was addressed under humanitarian law. Although not addressing reproductive health specifically, it made reference for protection and special assistance to 'maternity cases' as well as protecting women 'against rape, enforced prostitution, or any form of indecent assault'.

In 1951, refugee law came into effect with the efforts of the United Nations Convention Relating to the Status of Refugees. Its 1967 Protocol specified refugee rights to be granted by all signing states. This means that all signing parties must grant refugees who are lawfully staying in the country the same rights as its citizens, including rights to the provision of social security, maternity, and sickness. But, it also means that those refugees, who are illegally within the county, are not often given the same rights; and these people may have difficulty accessing health and reproductive health care and services.

In 1976, the international community agreed on an additional covenant that provided more detail to the rights embodied in the Human Rights Declaration and the Convention of the Status of Refugees, with implications for issues of gender, reproductive health, and refugees including those individuals not lawfully within a host county. The International Covenant on Economic, Social and Cultural Rights (ICESC), Article 12, goes beyond the Universal Declaration's right to health. This Article proclaims 'the right of everyone to the enjoyment of the highest attainable standard of physical and mental health' and then outlines steps to the realization of this goal. While there is no specific mention of reproductive health rights, some of its provisions, such as Articles 10(2) and 12(2a), address reproductive health issues (UNHCHR, 1976).

In 1979, The Convention on the Elimination of All Forms of Discrimination against Women (CEDAW) set clearer definitions and standards than the earlier covenants with respect to gender equality. It expanded the protections against discrimination and called for increased attention to vulnerable groups including refugees and migrants. CEDAW is the only human rights treaty that addresses women's reproductive health rights through acknowledgement of pervasive social, cultural, and economic discrimination against women. In particular, Article 12 of the Convention requires states to 'eliminate discrimination in access to health services throughout the life cycle, particularly in the areas of family planning, pregnancy and confinement, and the post-natal period' (CEDAW, 1979). In 1999, CEDAW made further recommendations emphasizing that 'access to health care, including reproductive health, is a basic right under the Convention on the Elimination of All Forms of Discrimination against Women (CEDAW Article 12, 1999). It comprehensively addresses violence against women, STIs and HIV/AIDS, female genital mutilation (FGM), unwanted pregnancies, safe motherhood, provision and access to services, and quality of services provided, and declares that all of these are to be addressed by the participating states as provision of basic human rights.

The 1989 Convention on the Rights of the Child (CRC), similarly guarantees that children have access to basic human rights including health and access to RSH information and services. The 2002 Optional Protocol of the CRC was extended to prevent the sale of children for prostitution, because it endangers their RSH status.

Framed within human rights and refugee law, a Humanitarian Charter and Minimum Standards of Care in Disaster Assistance were developed by a large group of agencies in 1997. This Charter describes core principles of humanitarian actions in order to reaffirm the rights of affected populations, as well as pointing out responsibilities of warring parties or states. The Charter formed the basis of the Sphere Handbook, which sets out minimum standards of care for multi-sectoral disaster responses. In 2004, an updated version came into effect, which, in addition to other crosscutting themes, addresses RSH related issues of protection, gender, children, HIV/AIDS, and people living with HIV/AIDS. Chapter Five of the Sphere Handbook outlines the minimal standards in health provision with a specific section addressing issues of RSH.

Finally, the most detailed documents and powerful agents of change, which draw on previous human rights treaties and various conventions, but do not have any legally binding recourse, are the ICPD and FWCW (Fourth World Conference on Women, 1995) documents. These documents are based on international consensus decisions supporting gender equality, rights, and women's empowerment, and clearly set out the concepts of sexual and reproductive rights including refugee reproductive rights.

RSH Services in Emergency versus Longer-Term Settings

Emergency RSH services target displaced populations, often living in some kind of make shift arrangements like camps. Populations who undergo emergencies like forced migration are not a homogeneous group, and this fact impacts upon service delivery, as do the length of time a camp has been established and the range of services provided. Services provided during an acute emergency phase will be somewhat different from those required in stable refugee or other camp settings. While a standard set of specific services has been developed for emergency settings, as the situation stabilizes, comprehensive RSH services must be tailored to meet the general needs.

Emergency RSH Services

Policy on reproductive health has been the last to come on board in emergency settings. Traditionally, food, shelter, sanitation and basic health care were among the first set of priorities. Where RSH services were seen as a priority, the emphasis was on maternal and child health care (MCH) or STI services as part of the general health care (Palmer, 1998). However, RSH needs of displaced populations were recognized in the early 1990s (Wulf, 1994). The Inter-Agency Field Manual highlighted the fact that specific RSH services needed to be delivered in acute emergency settings till the time the situation stabilized and full RSH services could be implemented. It was recognized that not providing emergency RSH services resulted in severe adverse consequences such as maternal and infant deaths, unwanted pregnancies often resulting in unsafe abortion, and the transmission of STIs or HIV- all of which are preventable.

However, it has been documented that in most post-emergency camps, the reproductive health outcomes are better than in their respective host country and country of origin (Hynes et al., 2002). This evidence demonstrates that quality RSH services can be provided in difficult settings with positive outcomes. Yet, despite improved awareness and mounting research, RSH service delivery has been and to a large extent remains inconsistent and insufficient. It is perhaps a reflection of donor and/or head office commitments and coordination (RHRC, 2003).

The Minimal Initial Service Package (MISP) provides the basic standard of reproductive health care that must be delivered together with all other basic services during the initial days of an emergency setting. The priority is to reduce both short and long-term RSH ill-health and mortality, with the aim that additional funding will be provided for continuation of services once the situation has stabilized

(Krause, Jones, and Purdin, 2000). Implementation of MISP does not require the additional assessments that longer-term services do, since documented evidence has already justified the use of MISP. MISP is a package of kits and supplies together with activities to be put in place by trained staff. The reproductive health kit is designed for the basic emergency phase and is made up of twelve different sub-kits to be ordered and used according to the level of care provided. Depending on the setting, some components of the MISP kits will be more relevant to a particular situation, and assessment must be made to determine the capacity of the organizations to implement them as well as the needs within the target community. One obstacle to providing MISP in emergencies is that like any other service, all components must be planned for together with having trained staff right from the onset; otherwise, fragmented and less robust service provision can occur as the situation develops (RHRC, 2003).

In emergency settings, the core components of MISP to be planned for and delivered include: (1) The co-ordination and implementation of MISP by identifying a lead agency and a reproductive health coordinator; (2) Prevention and management of the consequences of sexual violence by enhancing physical security in the camps, ensuring availability of female protection and health staff, incorporating issues of sexual violence into health meetings, making information available and widely delivered to refugees, and ensuring medical response including the availability of emergency contraception; (3) Reduction in transmission of HIV both in terms of safety procedures for medical staff as well as the availability of free condoms; (4) Prevention of excess neonatal and maternal morbidity and mortality through the provision of clean delivery kits for mothers and birth attendants besides midwife delivery kits to assist with basic obstetric emergencies (but not surgical), and a referral system in place to provide essential obstetric care that can only be managed at hospital level; (5) Plans for comprehensive RSH services to be integrated into primary health care to affect the power balance in the relationship as soon as possible (UNHCR 1999).

One of the more controversial components of MISP is the provision of emergency contraception (EC). EC is one method used to prevent unwanted pregnancy as a result of sexual violence, which often accompanies conflict and displacement. It is available either in the form of a pill or a copper intrauterine device (IUD). The pill can prevent unwanted pregnancy, if used within seventy-two hours, and should under no circumstances be regarded as a method of contraception. Technically, it is an easier method to administer than the copper IUD. However, EC pills are a contentious issue as they have inappropriately gotten linked with the abortion debate. Some view it as an abortive method rather than a preventative measure against unsafe abortion. The key problems hindering effective implementation of EC pills are the lack of appropriate training for staff on how to administer the pill and attitudes towards the pill, women's awareness of EC, and funding (Goodyear and McGinn, 1998). Due to the fact that sexual violence in emergencies now plays a major role in RSH, it is imperative that EC can be provided in a timely manner and that the health staffs as well as women are aware of its existence.

Longer-Term RSH Services

Once an emergency situation has stabilized, there are some specific RSH concerns that must be taken into consideration and tailored for to suit the population's needs. Long-term planning includes integrating RSH services into the set of ongoing services. Longer-term RSH services even in a camp setting must evolve to meet the changing RSH needs of the population including psychological and chronic problems (Hynes et al., 2002). However, there comes a point when it is not financially or politically sound to continue providing parallel services for refugees (WHO, 2000). There are several challenges involved in this process: One, standards of RSH services and care have to be ultimately transferred to local NGOs and/or service providers in the host area or area of return; Two, it must be ensured that women are enabled to take active control in matters related to their health and can maintain access to family planning methods (condoms, pill, IUDs, etc.) and health services.

Some of the major long-term RSH services are briefly discussed below:

Safe Motherhood

Safe motherhood includes antenatal care, safe delivery, and post-natal care. It is an umbrella service under which other services can be integrated, such as family planning, STI and HIV/AIDS prevention and management, female genital cutting (FGC) and other RSH concerns. Averting maternal death and maternal morbidity is paramount to safe motherhood. However, statistics reveal that much work still needs to be done in this area. Globally, 600,000 women die from pregnancy-related causes each year (UNHCR, 1999) and for each woman who dies, 30–100 other women will suffer from maternal morbidity (UNFPA Fast Facts).

Although precautions to avert maternal death and disability are known, however, they are not always available to women in developing countries and forcibly displaced populations. It is known that approximately 15.0% of all pregnant women including refugees develop unforeseen complications that require essential obstetric care. Yet, both obvious and subtle obstacles prevent women from accessing this care. For example, displaced populations have little access to transportation to hospitals, in addition to the fact that timely referrals are difficult to make, if traditional midwives are unskilled and referral facilities are unavailable. Therefore, in order to avert maternal death and disability, the following minimum services are required: ante-natal services, minimally skilled assistance for proper delivery care (both traditional birth attendants and midwives), established referral systems and timely access to these facilities, and post-partum care for the assessment of mother and child health, particularly if a woman is alone as head of family.

Other related issues that may increase in unstable migrant settings and thus need to be targeted include miscarriage (spontaneous abortions) and peri-natal and neo-natal mortality. An estimated 3.4 million out of 8 million infant deaths per year result from poor maternal health and inadequate delivery care. Both are characteristic of displaced environments (UNFPA Fast Facts). The most important factors leading to mortality are infections, birth asphyxia, and low birth weight resulting in difficulties keeping the new born alive? Key contributors (which are typical to forcibly displaced persons) are a change in lifestyle including maternal deficiency in specific nutrients, lack of ante-natal care and improper care during delivery, failure to provide immediate care for the baby and appropriate post-partum care (Save the Children).

Family Planning

Family planning (FP) services are necessary both to persons not wanting a pregnancy and to those who desire pregnancy, but want to ensure adequate spacing. There is no conclusive evidence to specify whether fertility rates increase or decrease during displacement. There have been arguments for both, but the most convincing is that fertility rates resemble those of pre-migration settings in stable or longer-term refugee/displaced conditions (McGinn, 2000). However, it is imperative that migrant populations are provided with effective, safe, and culturally appropriate methods of family planning. The most basic form of FP should be condoms, not only to assist with family planning decisions, but also to protect against STIs and HIV/AIDS.

Gender-sensitive intervention is essential to address the dynamics of knowledge, power, and decision-making in sexual relationships, between service providers and clients, and between community leaders and citizens. Men must be recognized as having reproductive health needs together with the fact that the involvement of men is an essential part of protecting women's reproductive health. The other related issue that may increase in unstable migrant settings and must be targeted is unsafe abortions. They are an outcome of unwanted pregnancies (often the result of sexual violence, especially in conflict situations). There are an estimated 20 million unsafe abortions each year, and 19 million of these occur in developing countries, of which many do not legally allow abortion for rape cases. Approximately one-third of women undergoing unsafe abortions experience serious complications and approximately one in eight women who die each year from pregnancy-related causes do so due to abortion complications (Guttmacher Institute, 1999).

While in no cases should abortion be promoted as a method of family planning (ICPD para. 8.25), post-abortion care (PAC) services are necessary to mitigate maternal mortality and morbidity due to incomplete or septic abortions. This means that referral systems must be established, and existing facilities must be able to manage minimum complications and take prompt referrals when required. To be effective, PAC services must be linked to other FP and RSH services, rather than exist as stand-alone services, in order to avoid repeat abortions (Post-abortion Care Consortium, 2002). Whether or not abortion is legal in the host country, PAC must be included in comprehensive RSH services.

STIs and HIV/AIDS

Poverty, powerlessness, and social instability increase the

transmission of STIs and HIV/AIDS (Krause et al., 2000). The disintegration of family and other stable relationships and norms regarding sexual behaviors accelerate transmission of STIs and HIV/AIDS. This makes refugees and displaced populations a particularly vulnerable group, more so if they are women and adolescents, due to their disadvantaged socio-economic status. Often sex is used as a form of currency in exchange for goods/services such as food, security, shelter, and other basic needs and condoms are not always used, thus increasing possible transmission of STIs and HIV.

A controversial view is that refugee HIV rates are higher than a host population's. Perpetuation of this view only further marginalizes a displaced population and can lead to discrimination and stigmatization. A recent study by the UNHCR and their partners has revealed that the prevalence of HIV in three out of four refugee populations was lower than in the host country (UNHCR, 2003). A study of Rwandan refugees in Tanzania revealed that HIV rates remained lower and more stable in official camp settings than rates among Rwandans living outside of camps within the host population (Mayaud, 2001). There is certain to be some mixing between the host and displaced groups, and the mixing of these low- and high-prevalence populations (of both migrant and host populations) can increase transmission of STIs and HIV through increased sexual networks and risky behaviours. In instances of military presence, STIs and HIV transmission is accelerated due to the fact that the military often has a higher prevalence of these diseases than civilians, and the soldiers' movements contribute to the spread.

Controlling the transmission of STIs not only helps to reduce long-term reproductive morbidities such as ectopic pregnancy and infertility, but also reduces the likelihood of HIV transmission; thus, it is an important strategy for preventing the spread of HIV/AIDS. The syndromic approach endorsed by WHO/UNAIDS has become the standard of care in many countries for management of the most common STIs. By directing treatment against the common causes of easily identified STIs, primary healthcare workers can achieve high rates of cure without the delay and cost involved with laboratories, which is not always feasible in camp settings. Contact tracing of partners should always be part of the STI treatment; however, in an unstable environment it may not always be possible.

Another main mode of transmission is mother-to-child transmission (MTCT) or vertical transmission. Integrating HIV services into general RSH care can reduce transmission to children since the spread of HIV from an infected mother can occur during pregnancy, during labour, or after delivery through breast milk. Therefore, attempts to reduce chances of vertical transmission must be tackled at multiple points.

Integrating HIV management into RSH care is an important way to avoid MTCT. The addition of voluntary HIV testing into antenatal care can help reduce the spread of disease to the child at birth through antiretroviral (ARV) medicine. The WHO estimates that 15.0 –30.0% of HIV-infected mothers transmit HIV during pregnancy and delivery without ARVs (WHO). Post-natal care targeting breast-feeding is an extremely important part of general RSH care, but especially with HIV-positive women. The WHO estimates that 10.0 –20.0% of mothers with HIV will transmit it through breast milk.

For forcibly displaced populations, the Inter-agency Field Manual advocates standards on HIV and infant feeding established by UNAIDS, UNICEF, and WHO. These include the possibilities of avoiding breast-feeding and using formula or an HIV-negative wet nurse, or exclusive breast-feeding for a short period of time and then weaning abruptly. However, in unstable situations some or all of these may be impractical. Especially, if formula cannot be correctly stored and prepared, the infant may be at greater risk of infections, illness and death than the transmission of HIV (UNHCR, 1999). Healthcare providers must be properly trained in post-natal care to provide the best possible counselling to all mothers, especially HIV-positive mothers by taking their socio-cultural-financial contexts into account. Constant research is being conducted, and UNICEF/WHO should be contacted for any updates.

Sexual and Gender-Based Violence

Gender is a prescribed set of roles assigned to men and to women that is defined and upheld by learned societal norms and constructs. Gender roles can vary according to different cultures, and fundamentally define status, identity, and power relations in almost every society. Gender differences between women and men can place burdens on women's health. The roles, rights, responsibilities, and status assigned to women by society leave women vulnerable to poor nutrition, physical and mental abuse and unwanted and unprotected sexual intercourse. They can also limit women's access to health care and attaining good RSH.

Gender-based violence is violence against a particular group based on their gender or sex, rather than indiscriminate violence. It includes physical, mental, sexual, verbal, and psychological abuse. While rape and sexual assault are most commonly known, it also includes marital rape, domestic violence, sexual exploitation, sexual harassment, physical assault, verbal abuse, confinement, female genital mutilation, forced marriage, early marriage, infanticide, socio-economic discrimination, and social exclusion (UNHCR, 2003). Violence against girls and women throughout the world causes more death and disability among women aged 15–44 than cancer, malaria, traffic accidents, and even war (UNFPA Fast Facts). It fundamentally stems from unequal power relations and most often the powerless are the women and children.

Sexual and gender-based violence (SGBV) can happen in all settings; however, displacement and its associated stressors can exacerbate the frequency or magnitude with which it happens. This includes the breakdown of social structures, poverty, socio-economic discrimination, psychological strains of refugee life, and powerlessness. It can happen at any stage of displacement, and thus, prevention and responses must be tailored to the different circumstances of each phase, from initial conflict, to flight, to place of asylum, and to reintegration (UNHCR 1999 and 2003). There can be fatal results of SGBV, including homicide, suicide, and infant mortality. More common are non-fatal consequences including reproductive ill-health, physical disabilities, emotional and psychosocial disorders, negative social outcomes, and trauma (UNHCR, 2003). Stigma, shame, and silence are inextricably linked to this issue, which can lead to under-reporting of the crime. Therefore, preventive measures should be set up on the assumption that it is a problem to be tackled with coordinated medical, psychosocial and legal responses (UNHCR 1999; Ward 2002), as only one of these is not an effective intervention without the others.

Commitment to SGBV is improving, but it is not widely implemented as a core feature of humanitarian interventions yet, despite standards and protocols (Ward, 2002). A multi-sectoral intervention including the health sector, social workers, psychologists, law enforcers, and legal/policy systems must work in a coordinated effort.

Reproductive and Sexual Health among Adolescents

Adolescence and youth is defined as the period between approximately 10–20 years of age. It is a time of continuous change physically, mentally, and socially. This age group faces social pressures and expectations that can affect their reproductive health status. Young people, therefore, require information about how best to handle these changes in order to make decisions that can prevent sexual ill-health and also enhance their self-esteem. Parents can be valuable sources of information and counselling to their children, as are other well meaning adults in and out of the family, who as role models have a great deal of influence on changing social attitudes (UNFPA 2000). However, while intending to protect young people, some adults may limit young people's access to information and health services due to the fear that imparting information may promote curiosity and exploratory behavior related to sex. Yet, information is the greatest tool young people have to empower themselves and to protect themselves from reproductive and sexual ill-health.

Displacement accentuates the turmoil typical of this period. The breakdown of family, community, social norms, loss of parental supervision, lack of schooling and recreational activities, frustration, boredom, insecurity of refugee life, and uncertainty about the future may lead adolescents to experiment with risky behaviours, including violence, drug abuse, and unprotected sex (UNHCR, 2000). Some may have already gone through traumatic experiences such as armed conflict, sexual abuse, violence, and/or loss of family members, and many have to deal with these issues alone. Therefore, RSH services must target the unique needs and circumstances of this group.

Working with young people to address their reproductive and sexual health requires special skills of service providing. Being culturally sensitive while providing information and services to young people, confidentiality, a non-judgmental attitude, a non-threatening environment, easy accessibility to health care, and a service provider of the same sex are all extremely important to attracting young people to accept services (UNHCR 1999). Integrating adolescent RSH services into mainstream health care may not be a good idea as it may ostracize young people from seeking services due to fear of reprisal, shame, or embarassment.

Disseminating information to young people can be difficult. In stable settings, education systems are a popular means of providing information to a large number of young people. Because education services can be limited within displaced settings, or many young people may leave school during this time, displaced young people are less likely to access health-related information through schools. Other means must be devised to ensure that appropriate messages are being delivered. One common method to ensure participation of young people is to work through peers. Young people often have a culture of their own, with their own norms. Working with peer educators helps to break down the adult–young person barriers, and allows young people access to information regarding the basic changes in their bodies and emotions; ways to avoiding pregnancy, STIs and HIV/AIDS, as well as issues that may be especially pertinent to their circumstances, such as forced sex or selling sex for survival. All of this information must be accompanied with instructions on how and where to access services.

Men's Participation in Reproductive and Sexual Health

In the past, the principle objection to male participation in sexual and reproductive health has been that adding male services will damage the quality of women's services and create additional competition for already scarce resources. However, we know now that information and services must be integrated in a way that is beneficial to both men and women (Wegner, 1998). For example, men who are educated about reproductive health issues are more likely to support their partners in decisions on contraceptive use and family planning, be supportive during pregnancy, and if obstetric complications arise, they will know how not to delay getting the appropriate assistance. Men's education on the protection, testing, and treatment of STIs, as well as stressing partner notification, can assist in reducing HIV transmission. Getting men to share the responsibility of good reproductive and sexual health can help to prevent disease, as well as to share the benefits of contraception decisions and avoid the risks which are otherwise present.

At the same time, service providers must be aware of the gender dynamic within a couple. A woman may be fearful of losing her partner or be threatened with violence if he knows she is positive for a STI or HIV. Women may feel their husband is not supportive of birth spacing or longer-term contraception and may want use it without the partner's knowledge (Ringheim, 2002). Programs that support a couple approach must be careful not to jeopardize a woman's right to decision-making. Gender-sensitive programming is essential to address the dynamics of knowledge, power, and decision-making in sexual relationships.

In this context, one has to acknowledge the consequences of the still rampant gender typical socialization and ideologies of 'early marriage', 'bear children soon after the marriage', 'must have a son', 'daughter is a burden and a shame', 'why educate a daughter', etc. Perpetuation of such discriminating attitudes and behaviors is so subtle that often people fail to even realize how they contribute to it. It is no wonder then that so very frequently we come across the problems of poor self-concept, powerlessness, school dropout, symptoms of ill health such as anemia and other nutritional deficiencies, too many children in the hope of getting that illusive male child, and poor health services utilization in the context of young girls and women. It is wastage of almost 50.0% of the population. Voluminous work will have to be done with both men and women to erase such ideologies if one even wants to dream about a just and egalitarian social scenario.

Sex-based socialization thus lead to harmful traditional practices that are endorsed and practiced by various cultures causing lasting adverse biological and psychosocial effects on the individuals (Toubia, 1995). Included in these practices are female genital cutting (FGC), early marriage, female infanticide, etc. Reproductive and sexual health services seek to eliminate these practices while at the same time approaching them with sensitivity. Changing attitudes and values and challenging beliefs require long-term, ongoing, multidisciplinary action.

It is very important, therefore, that RSH service providers are sensitive to the special needs facing young girls. While the girls are still adolescents, they may require information relevant to their age group, but at the same time they also require access to information that prepares them to handle specific reproductive issues relating to their future marital status such as family planning, birth spacing, and delaying conception. It is a common knowledge that young girls receive little or no RSH education upon their entrance into marriage from elder female relatives in the family. If elder females have died or become separated from them during displacement, it is important that these young girls receive the necessary RSH education from other concerned authorities.

Constraints to Providing Quality Comprehensive Reproductive and Sexual Health Care

Ensuring access to and availability of quality reproductive and sexual health care in the various stages of forcibly displaced situations technically seems straightforward: needs can be identified and services can be fitted to suit these needs. However, there are a few key obstacles that prevent the care from being accessed by individuals who are most in need of these services.

The 'Global Gag Rule'

Anti-abortion proponents in the USA have supported the

Mexico City Policy, also known as the 'Global Gag Rule' by those who oppose it, since the Reagan administration. It was dropped during the Clinton administration but continues to be strongly enforced under the current Bush administration. The rule prohibits federal funding to overseas organizations for family planning, if they use any of their non-US funds to provide abortion-related activities, including providing information about abortion through counselling or advocacy. While the rule is promoted as anti-abortion in attempts to reduce the incidence of abortions, and calls for a separation between family planning services and abortion-related activities, the reality is not so clear-cut when providing comprehensive RSH services, as these two often overlap. Furthermore, evidence from The Centre for Reproductive Rights and Population Action International shows that the Global Gag Rule is detrimental to women's lives (Cohen 2003). Studies show that providing comprehensive RSH services that include post-abortion family planning services are more effective at reducing abortion rates than not providing information or access (Cohen, 2001).

Even in countries where abortion is broadly legal, the USA maintains its anti-abortion stance and is able to control and prohibit necessary funds to indigenous organizations that support all types of reproductive and sexual healthcare services including family planning, ante-natal and post-natal care, not only pro-abortion related activities. The rule forces indigenous NGOs who provide reproductive health care to choose between providing legal abortion-related services in their own country and stopping unsafe, illegal abortions, or foregoing eligibility for US funding to provide desperately needed family planning services (US-based intermediaries are themselves not subject to the restrictions but are responsible for their overseas partners' compliance). Fundamentally, it means that millions of women in developing countries are denied access to essential RSH care.

However, a turn for the opponents of the Gag Rule occurred when the rule was attempted to apply to the US President's US$15 billion global HIV/AIDS initiative. It was found that the Gag Rule could not be applied without hindering other components of RSH service provision linked to HIV prevention and management services. Therefore, the Gag Rule does not apply to organizations that legally support abortion-related activities and receive funding for HIV/AIDS activities, yet it remains in place if the same organization applies for USAID's family planning funding (Cohen, 2003).

It is easy to see how this legislation can affect reproductive and sexual health services for forcibly displaced populations. For example, while President Bush promoted his five-year, US$15 billion anti-AIDS initiative, his administration and members of Congress successfully de-funded the United Nations Population Fund (UNFPA) for the second year, depriving developing nations of US$34 million for family planning (UNFPA, 2003). The other blow was delivered by the US State Department to the RHRC, who planned to deliver a programme to young people displaced by armed conflict in Angola and the Congo. Due to the fact that one of the Consortium's partners, Marie Stopes International (MSI), continues to provide safe abortions and is therefore ineligible for US family planning funds, the entire Consortium has been penalized (Cohen 2003). As a direct consequence to MSI, a loss of more than US$3 million to the MSI Partners in Africa has resulted in the closure of three centers in Kenya, an outreach programme servicing poor communities in Ethiopia, and other centers in Tanzania.

Monitoring and evaluation of reproductive health takes place at two levels - the country and the global level. Globally, the international community has already defined a number of indicators relevant to reproductive health, including maternal mortality (percentage of pregnant women who have at least one antenatal visit, percentage of pregnant women who have a trained attendant at delivery, and percentage of pregnant women immunized against tetanus) contraceptive prevalence rates, and a newborn indicator that reflects maternal reproductive health (percentage of infants weighing less than 2500g at birth).

WHO is working on additional indicators for global monitoring in reproductive health, including indicators on incidence and prevalence of sexually transmitted diseases, quality of family planning services, access to and quality of maternal health services, prevalence of female genital mutilation and prevalence and nature of obstetric and gynecological morbidities.

Table 1
Selected Reproductive Maternal and Infant Health Indicators (UNFPA, UNICEF, UNAIDS 2006)

Country	Contraceptive prevalence - modern methods	Total fertility rate (2006)	Maternal mortality ratio	Antenatal care coverage %	% births with skilled attendants	Infant mortality per 1000 live births	HIV prev adults 15-49, 2005 (UNAIDS)
East Asia							
China	83	1.72	56	89	83	32	0.1
Korea DPR	53	1.95	67	-	97	43	-
Mongolia	54	2.28	110	94	99	53	<0.1
South and South East Asia							
Afghanistan	4	7.18	1900	16	14	144	<0.1
Bangladesh	47	3.04	380	49	13	52	<0.1
Bhutan	19	4.00	420	-	24	50	<0.1
Cambodia	19	3.85	450	38	32	90	1.6
India	43	2.85	540	86	43	62	0.9
Indonesia	57	2.25	230	92	66	36	0.1
Lao PDR	29	2.25	650	27	19	82	0.1
Malaysia	30	2.71	41	74	97	9	0.5
Myanmar	30	2.17	360	76	56	69	1.3
Nepal	35	3.4	740	28	11	58	0.5
Pakistan	20	3.87	500	43	23	73	0.1
Philippines	33	2.94	200	88	60	25	<0.1
Sri Lanka	50	1.89	92	95	97	15	<0.1
Thailand	70	1.89	44	92	99	18	1.4
DR Timor-Leste	9	7.64	660	61	24	85	-
Viet Nam	57	2.19	130	86	85	27	0.5
Oceania							
Melanesia		3.59		-	61	57	Fiji (0.1)
Papua New Guinea	20	3.74	300	78	53	66	1.8

Reproductive health indicators should thus cover not only the quantitative indicators such as those listed above, but also some qualitative indicators, such as women's satisfaction with services, perceptions of quality, maternal discomfort and dissatisfaction, perceived reproductive morbidities, opportunities for choice, and enabling environments. Particular attention will be paid to indicators that identify disparities within countries – between population groups and/or regions, for example.

Data collection should be seen as a means towards an end rather than an end in itself. It will, therefore, be necessary to focus increasingly on performance-based measures such as maternal audit, surveillance and other process measures. Such program indicators should be useful for policy-making and be generated through data collection procedures that are useful for programme management at the level at which the data are collected. All data collection efforts should be sustainable by the national authorities and able to take into account new developments in terms of strategic thinking and implementation. In addition, all indicators should be valid, objectively measurable and reliable.

REFERENCES

CEDAW (1979). Convention on the Elimination of All Forms of Discrimination against Women - http://193.194.138.190/html/menu3/b/e1cedaw.htm

Cohen, S. (2001). 'Global Gag Rule: Exporting Antiabortion Ideology at the Expense of American Values'. *The Guttmacher Report on Public Policy* (4)3 - http://www.guttmacher.org/pubs/journals/gr040301.html

Cohen, S. (2003). 'Global Gag Rule Revisited: HIV/AIDS Initiative Out, Family Planning Still In'. *The Guttmacher Report on Public Policy* (26)4 - http://www.globalgagrule.com

Goodyear, L., and Hynes, M. (2001). Integrating Reproductive Health into Emergency Response Assessments and Primary Health Care, *Prehospital Disaster Med.* 16(4):223-30.

Goodyear, L., and McGinn, T. (1998). Emergency Contraception among Refugees and the Displaced, *The Journal of the American Medical Woman's Association* 53(5) Suppl. 2:266–70 - http://jamwa.amwa-doc.org/vol53/pdf/53_5_8.pdf

Guttmacher Institute, 'Reproductive Health Kits Provided by UNFPA to Kosovar refugees', *Guttmacher Rep Public Policy*, 2(3):12-13, 1999.

Hynes, M., Sheik, M., Wilson, H., and Spiegel, P. (2002). Reproductive Health Indicators and Outcomes Among Refugee and Internally Displaced Persons in Postemergency Phase Camps, *The Journal of the American Medical Woman's Association,* 288(5):595–607.

International Conference for Population and Development - http://www.iisd.ca/Cairo/program/p07000.html

IWHC and WHO. Creating Common Ground. Geneva, WHO, 1991.

John Hopkins University (1996). Population Reports, Chapter 2. Population Information Program, Centre for Communication Programs. Series J, No. 45 - http://www.infoforhealth.org/pr/J45/j45chap2.shtml

Krause, S., Jones, R., and Purdin, S. (2000). Programmatic Responses to Refugees' Reproductive Health Needs, *International Family Planning Perspectives* 26(4):181–7. http://www.rhrc.org/pdf/agi-usa-org2618100.pdf

Mayaud, P. (2001). The Challenge of Sexually Transmitted Infections Control For HIV Prevention In Refugee Settings: Rwandan Refugees In Tanzania', *Transactions of the Royal Society of Tropical Medicine and Hygiene* 95:121–4.

McGinn, T. (2000). Reproductive Health of War-Affected Populations: What Do We Know?' *International Family Planning Perspectives* 26(4):174–80 - www.agi-usa.org/pubs/journals/2617400.html

Palmer, C. (1998). Reproductive Health for Displaced Populations, RRN Network Paper 24. London: Relief and Rehabilitation Network, Overseas Development Institute.

Post-Abortion Care Consortium (2002). Essential Elements of Post-Abortion Care: An Expanded and Updated Model - http://www.pac-consortium.org/Pages/pacmodel.html

RHR Emergency Contraception Section - http://www.rhrc.org/media/rhr_basics/ec/index.html.

RHRC (2003). Global Decade Report - http://www.rhrc.org/pdf/Global_Decade_Report.pdf

RHRC: RHR basics section - http://www.rhrc.org/media/rhr_basics/misp/index.html

Ringheim, K. (2002) 'When the Client Is Male: Client-Provider Interaction from a Gender Perspective'. *International Family Planning Perspective* 28(3):170-5, 2002 http://www.guttmacher.org/pubs/journals/2817002.html

Toubia, N. (1995). *Female Genital Mutilation. A Call for Global Action*. New York: Rainbow.

UNAIDS - http://www.unaids.org/

UNFPA - www.unfpa.org

UNFPA (2000). State of the World's Population 2000. Lives together, worlds apart: men and women in a time of change, Chapter 6 - http://www.unfpa.org/swp/2000/english/ch06.html

UNFPA (2000). State of the World's Population 2000. Lives together, worlds apart: men and women in a time of change - http://www.unfpa.org/swp/2000/english/ch02.html

UNFPA Fast Facts - http://www.unfpa.org/rh/mothers/facts.htm

UNHCHR (1976). International Covenant on Economic, Social and Cultural Rights - http://www.unhchr.ch/html/menu3/b/a_cescr.htm

UNHCR - www.unhcr.org

UNHCR (1999). *Reproductive Health in Refugee Situations: an Inter-agency Field Manual*, Chapters 2 and 4.

UNHCR (1999). Reproductive Health in Refugee Situations: an Inter-agency Field Manual, Chapter 3 - http://www.unhcr.org/cgi-bin/ texis/vtx/protect/opendoc.pdf?tbl=PROTECTION&id=403a0f6c8

UNHCR (2000). *Action for the Rights of Children Resource Pack: Sexual and Reproductive Health*. Geneva, Switzerland.

UNICEF - http://www.unicef.org/

United Nations High Commission for Refugees (UNHCHR) - http://www.unhcr.org/

Ward, J. (2002). If Not Now, When? Assessing Gender-Based Violence in Refugee, Internally Displaces and Post-Conflict Settings: A Global Overview - http://www.rhrc.org/resources/gbv/ifnotnow.html

Wegner, M. N. et al., (1998). 'Men as Partners in Reproductive Health: From Issues to Action'. *International Family Planning Perspective* 24(1) http://www.guttmacher.org/pubs/journals/2403898.html

WHO - www.who.org

WHO (2000). Reproductive Health during Conflict and Displacement: a guide for program managers, Chapter 9 - http://www.who.int/reproductive-health/publications/RHR_00_13_RH_conflict_and_displacement/RH_conflict_chapter9.en.html

World Health Organization. Achieving Reproductive Health For All. The Role of WHO. WHO/FHE/95.6. Geneva, WHO, 1995.

World Health Organization. Care of Mother and Baby at the Health Centre: A Practical Guide. WHO/FHE/MSM/94.2. Geneva, WHO, 1994.

World Health Organization. *Health, Population and Development*. WHO/FHE/94.1. Geneva, WHO, 1994.

World Health Organization. Mother-Baby Package: Implementing Safe Motherhood in Countries. WHO/FHE/MSM/94.11. Geneva, WHO, 1994.

World Health Organization. Women's Health: Improve our health - improve the world. WHO/FHE/95.8. Geneva, WHO, 1995.

Wulf, D. (1994). 'Refugee Women and Reproductive Health Care: Reassessing Priorities', Reproductive Health for Refugees Consortium.

2

Reproductive and Child Health in India: Achievements and Challenges

Prof. Madhumita Dobe

Summary

Despite impressive achievements, the challenges in the field of reproductive health include high female mortality rates, high maternal mortality ratio and slow decline in fertility. Numerous pregnancies and closely spaced births along with unwanted pregnancies terminated by unsafe abortions negatively affect maternal health. Although more than half of currently married women use contraception, unmet need for contraceptives exists. While the knowledge of family planning is nearly universal, less than 50.0% of married women (13 – 49 years) currently use modern contraception. Marriage before 18 years is still common and the median age at first birth has increased marginally. Only 50.0% of the pregnant women have at least three antenatal check ups. In the field of child health, infant mortality continues to decline but child immunization rates are not encouraging, with small improvement in full vaccination coverage. Malnutrition continues to be a significant problem for children and adults, with increase in wasting among children and no change in the percentage of underweight children. There is remarkably high prevalence of anaemia in children age 6-35 months, and among women its prevalence has actually increased. Women and children remain underserved. India's RCH program needs to improve access to services along with facilitation of informed choice through dissemination of comprehensive and accurate information about reproductive and child health care and creation of a supportive environment through mother and child-friendly laws/regulations and adopting mother and child-friendly settings approach.

Introduction

India's basic health indicator has improved dramatically over the past 50 years, with significant improvement in the Infant Mortality Rate (IMR), Maternal Mortality Rate (MMR) and life expectancy. However, over the 90's, progress on child health has stagnated and MMR remains unacceptably high at 437 along with an increasing polarization of health conditions. Overall, the poorest 20.0% of Indians have more than twice the rates of mortality, malnutrition and fertility than that of the richest 20.0%.

In order to effectively improve the health status of women and children especially the poor and underserved by reducing infant, child and maternal mortality and morbidity and to fulfill the unmet need for Family Welfare Services in the country, the Government of India, during 1997-98, launched the RCH Programme for implementation during the 9th Plan period by integrating Child Survival and Safe Motherhood (CSSM) Programme with other reproductive and child health (RCH) services. In addition, new components for management of Reproductive Tract Infection (RTI) and Sexually Transmitted Infection (STI) have also been incorporated. Reproductive and Child Health is currently operational in the entire country, encapsulating a range of essential services and delivery agents, which are both cost-effective and technically appropriate for maternal and child health outcomes, although there is much scope for greater responsiveness to the demands of the population, particularly the poor and marginalized. The Government of India Population Policy (2001) embodies the Cairo principles and its outcome objectives are consistent with the MDGs.

Table 1
Important Maternal and Child Health Goals

Indicator	*2010*	*MDG*
IMR	<30	<30
NMR	<20	<20
MMR	<100	<100
Institutional Delivery	80%	

Life Expectancy

India is one of the few countries in the world where women and men have nearly the same life expectancy at birth. The fact that the typical female advantage in life expectancy is not seen in India suggests there are systematic problems with women's health in India. Indian women have high mortality rates, particularly during childhood and in their reproductive years. In other words, there is a deficit of several million girls/ women who should be part of the population but are not. This deficit of females- 'missing women'- is due to higher female than male mortality rates for every age group up to age 30 (IRG, 1996a). This could be attributed to differential treatment of girls and boys in terms of feeding practices and access to health care. As a consequence of their overall lower status, women experience discrimination in the allocation of household resources, including food and access to health services. Boys are breast-fed longer than that of girls. Boys who are ill are more likely to be taken for medical treatment than are girls (Bhalla, 1995; Jejeebhoy and Rao, 1995).

Causes of death for children aged 1 to 4 show girls dying at a higher rate than boys from accidents and injuries, fever, and digestive disorders—all causes that are related to living conditions and negligence (Government of India, 1995).

Declining Fertility

Many of the health problems of Indian women are related to or exacerbated by high levels of fertility. More than 50 years ago, India became the first country in the developing world to initiate a state-sponsored family planning programme with the goal of lowering fertility and slowing the population growth rate. Since the 1960s, however, the Indian population has continued to grow by approximately 2.0% annually. The population is expected to grow beyond 1.5 billion before it stabilizes. Overall, fertility has continued to decline since NFHS-2, dropping to 2.7 children from 2.9 children. Ten states have reached the replacement level or the below replacement level fertility. However, there are large differences in fertility levels by state, education, religion, caste and place of residence. Research on women's status has found that the contributions Indian women make to their families often are overlooked, and instead they are viewed as economic burdens. There is a strong preference for the male child in India, as male children are expected to care for parents as they age. This preference for child children, along with high dowry costs for daughters, lead to women bearing large numbers of children in an attempt to have a son or two survive to adulthood. While this remains a barrier to more rapid decline in fertility, an increasing number of women who have only daughters say that they want no more children. In NFHS-3, 62.0% of the women with two daughters and no sons say they do not want more children, compared with 47.0% in NFHS-2.

Maternal Mortality and Morbidity and Its Relation to Fertility

Research has shown that numerous pregnancies and

closely spaced births erode a mother's nutritional status, which can negatively affect the pregnancy outcome (e.g., premature births, low birth-weight babies) and also increase the health risk for mothers. India still has a high maternal mortality ratio—approximately 300 deaths per 100,000 live births. The level of maternal mortality varies greatly by state, with Kerala having the lowest ratio, states like Uttar Pradesh and Rajasthan reporting ratios over 500, and Madhya Pradesh and Bihar reporting ratios over 450. This differential maternal mortality is most likely related to differences in the socioeconomic status of women and access to health care services among the states.

The high levels of maternal mortality are especially distressing because the majority of these deaths could have been prevented if women had access to and existing health services could utilize (either proper prenatal care or referral to appropriate health care facilities). In fact, the leading contributor to high maternal mortality ratios in India is lack of access to health care (The World Bank, 1996).

Unwanted pregnancies terminated by unsafe abortions also have negative consequences for women's health. One of the most extreme manifestations of preference for male children is gender-selective abortion. The use of medical technology to determine the sex of a foetus is rampant in India, and over 90.0% of the foetuses that are aborted are female (The World Bank, 1996). In all countries, more boys are born than girls, with a sex ratio at birth around 105 boys per 100 girls. Data on hospital births from various parts of India show that sex-selective abortion has increased the sex ratio at birth to 112 boys per 100 girls (Das Gupta, 1994).

Increasing Usages of Contraceptives for Reducing Fertility

Reducing fertility is an important element in improving the overall health of Indian women. Declining fertility is due in large part to women's increased use of contraception. More than half of the currently married women use contraception, and their use of modern methods has increased from 43.0% to 49.0% between NFHS-2 and NFHS-3. Despite a large increase in the number of women using contraceptives and limiting their fertility, there is still unmet need for contraceptives in India. Most of the unmet need among younger women is for spacing births rather than limiting them. Contraceptive choice and quality of care within the RCH program remain problematic.

While health care is important, there are several other factors that influence maternal mortality and health. Medical research shows that early age at first birth and high numbers of total pregnancies take their toll on a woman's health. While the knowledge of family planning is nearly universal in India, less than 50.0% of the married women aged 13 to 49 currently use modern contraception and female sterilization remains the main form of contraception;

Increasing Average Marriage Age

Forty-five percent of women aged 20-24 were married before the legal age of marriage at 18 years, compared with 50.0% seven years earlier. This shift in age at marriage also influences the median age at first birth, which increased by six months to 19.8 years.

Lack of Proper Care During Pregnancy and Delivery

More than three-quarters of the pregnant women in India receive at least some antenatal care (ANC), but only half of the pregnant women make at least three visits to health practitioners during their pregnancy, as recommended. Most women who did not receive health care during pregnancy reported that they thought it was unnecessary (IIPS, 1995). Thus, there is a definite need to educate women about the importance of health care for ensuring healthy pregnancies and safe childbirths. Another reason for the low levels of prenatal care is lack of adequate health care centres. It is currently estimated that 16.0% of the population in rural areas live more than 10 kilometers away from any medical facility (Bhalla, 1995). The disparity between urban and rural women is especially pronounced, with 74.0% of the urban women having at least three ANC visits as compared to 43.0% of rural women.

Place of birth and type of assistance during birth have an impact on maternal health and mortality. Births that take place in non-hygienic conditions or births that are not attended by a trained medical personnel are more likely to have negative outcomes for both the mother and the child. Births assisted by a health professional has increased to 48.0% from 42.0%; with 75.0% of the urban women in comparison to only 39.0% of the rural women in NFHS-3 receiving professional assistance. Institutional births increased from 34.0% to 41.0%, but most women deliver their children at home. It is recommended that women receive postnatal care within two days of delivery, but only about a third reported receiving care during that critical period. The proportion of women receiving no post-natal care varied greatly in terms of educational level and place of residence.

Widespread Domestic Violence

Violence against women is a health problem that is often ignored by authorities, who view such behavior as beyond their purview. However, violence against women has negative consequences on physical, mental and social health of the women and adverse effects on the health of the children of the victims.

While violence is a serious health issue for the Indian women, it is difficult to say how widespread it is. The available data show an increase in the reported level of violent crime against women. However, such statistics do not reflect the actual levels of these crimes because many incidents, particularly domestic violence, go unreported.

The data that are available show that much of the violence to which women are subjected occurs in the home and/or is carried out by relatives. For instance, in majority of the reported rape cases, family members are the perpetrators. Many of the victims are young women. In the past few years, there has been an increase in the reported incidence of torture and cruelty by the husband and the husband's relatives.

The most media-sensationalized type of violence against women in India is the dowry death. Dowry-related violence rates are higher among the poor and the lower castes. Alcoholism is also associated with increases in violence against women. Victims of domestic violence remain in abusive situations, since the Indian women have low levels of education and formal labor force participation. They typically have little autonomy, living under the control of first their fathers, then their husbands, and finally their sons.

Decline in Infant Mortality

Infant mortality continues to decline, dropping from 68 to 57 per thousand births. There were particularly notable drops in the infant mortality rates in Bihar, Goa, Haryana, Jammu and Kashmir, Meghalaya, Orissa, Punjab, Rajasthan, Tamil Nadu, and Uttar Pradesh.

Little Progress with Full Immunization

The situation regarding child immunization rates is not encouraging. By the time they are one year old, children are supposed to have received a BCG vaccination against tuberculosis, a measles vaccination, and three doses each of polio and DPT vaccines. Overall, there was only a small improvement in full vaccination coverage, with 44.0% of the children ages 12-23 months receiving all recommended vaccinations, up from 42% seven years earlier. Substantial improvements in coverage have been made in all vaccinations except DPT, which did not change at all between NFHS-2 and NFHS-3. Gains are particularly evident for polio immunization coverage, but nearly one-quarter of children age 12-23 months have still not received the recommended number of polio doses.

Progress in vaccination coverage varies markedly among the states. In 11 states, there has been a substantial deterioration in full immunization coverage in the last seven years, due to a decline in vaccination coverage for both DPT and polio. On the other hand, there was major improvement in full immunization coverage in Bihar, Chhattisgarh, Jharkhand, Sikkim and West Bengal. Other states with marked improvements in full immunization coverage were Assam, Jammu and Kashmir, Madhya Pradesh, Meghalaya, and Uttaranchal.

Diarrhoea in Children

Diarrhoea continues to be a major health problem for children. Although knowledge about Oral Rehydration Salts (ORS) for the treatment of diarrhoea is widespread among mothers, only 26.0% of the children who had had diarrhoea received a solution made from ORS packets, a figure virtually unchanged from the 27.0% in NFHS-2. Further, only 58.0% of the children with diarrhoea were taken to a health facility, in comparison to 65.0 % seven years earlier.

Malnutrition

Malnutrition continues to be a significant problem for children and adults in India. While there have been some improvements in the nutritional status of young children in several states, nutritional deficiencies are still widespread. Most striking has been the increase in wasting, or weight for height, among children. NFHS-3 found 19.0% of children wasted up from 16.0% seven years earlier. At the same time, there has been virtually no change in the percentage of children who are underweight (47.0% in NFHS-2 and 46.0% in NFHS-3). According to the NFHS, Indian children suffer from the highest proportions of malnourishment in the world. More than half (53.0%) of all girls and boys under 4 years of age were malnourished, and a similar proportion (52.0%) was stunted (i.e., too short for their age). Other studies show that many women never achieve full physical development (The World Bank, 1996). This incomplete physical development poses a considerable risk for women by increasing the danger of obstructed deliveries.

Mother's education, according to the NFHS, is highly correlated with the level of malnutrition among children. Children of illiterate mothers are twice as likely to be undernourished or stunted as children whose mothers have completed at least high school. The differentials are even larger when severely undernourished children are considered. Children of illiterate mothers are three times as likely to be severely undernourished as children of mothers with at least high-school education.

Adult women and men suffer a dual burden of undernutrition and overnutrition. One third of the married women are too thin, while 15.0% are overweight or obese. In all, nearly half of the married women are either underweight or overweight. Among married men, 28.0% are too thin and 12.0% are overweight. The states with the largest percentage of overweight women and men are Delhi, Kerala, and Punjab. Overweight prevalence is more among the highly educated.

The negative effects of malnutrition among women are compounded by heavy work demands, by poverty, by childbearing and rearing, and by special nutritional needs of women, resulting in increased susceptibility to illness and consequent higher mortality. Poor nutrition among women begins in infancy and continues throughout their lifetimes. Women and girls are typically the last to eat in a family; thus, if there is not enough food they are the ones to suffer most (Horowitz and Kishwar, 1985).

Widespread Anaemia

NFHS-3 also found a remarkably high prevalence of anaemia – 79.0% in children age 6-35 months. The prevalence of anaemia is even worse than it was in NFHS-2 (74.0%) and is primarily linked to poor nutrition. Anaemia is also very common among adults, and among women its prevalence has actually increased over the past seven years - from 52.0% to 56.0% among married women and from 50% to 58.0% among pregnant women. Studies have found that between 50.0% and 90.0% of all pregnant women in India suffer from anaemia. Severe anaemia accounts for 20.0% of all maternal deaths in India (Source: The World Bank, 1996). Severe anaemia also increases the chance of dying from a hemorrhage during labour. Even though men are much less likely than women to be anaemic, anaemia levels in men are still quite high (24.0%).

Challenges Ahead

(i) Expanding Need-based Services

Women remain one of the most underserved segments of the Indian population. An expanded reproductive health programme must include access to safe, effective and affordable methods of family planning, for both women and men, informed choice in contraception and high-quality supplies. It also must promote safe motherhood and the prevention of sexually transmitted diseases, and make efforts to reduce violence against women. It must provide access to safe and affordable abortion services, as well as services for the infertile, and provide comprehensive and accurate information about reproductive health care, including the risks and benefits of different contraceptive methods. Programmes must have well-trained service providers with good interpersonal communication and counselling skills, and must offer appropriate follow-up care and regular monitoring and evaluation of performance, incorporating the perspectives of clients and beneficiaries.

An expanded programme also must offer services to a wide range of clients, not just to married women of the childbearing age. Unmarried women, adolescent girls and boys, and postmenopausal women all have distinct needs for information and services. Perhaps most important, an expanded reproductive health programme must address men, both in terms of their own health needs and in terms of their role in ensuring reproductive health and choice for their wives.

These changes cannot be accomplished without major shifts in the delivery of services. Strategically placed emergency obstetric services and access to specialists will be required, as will attention to overcoming obstacles to accessing facilities, such as transportation to and from remote locations. In addition, counselling capacity and referral chains also need to be strengthened.

(ii) Informed Choice

Although the target-free approach espouses informed choice in contraceptive selection, the experience of programme planners, health care workers and clients indicates that there is still little choice among contraceptive acceptors in method selection, e. g., a woman who reports that she does not want any more children but would prefer a nonpermanent method, would still be offered sterilization. While some health workers reportedly have taken a more client-centered approach to their work, the needs-assessment tool provided in the manual does not address which method a woman intends or prefers to use, nor does it request information regarding a woman's preference for switching methods. Provision must be made for the collection of information on women's actual contraceptive preferences. Moreover, women who accept sterilization, particularly those living in rural areas, often do so having only minimal information about the procedure, about after-care and about possible complications.

(iii) Women's Access to Quality Care

More attention has been paid in the past to physical infrastructure, personnel and equipment than to standards of care. In addition, expanding the scope of services is a necessary but not sufficient step toward improving women's access to quality health services. The health-care delivery system has been largely insensitive to the needs of women and the constraints they face in expressing their needs-let alone the obstacles they face in obtaining services. Outreach services, essential for secluded women, are deficient and health workers are poorly informed about reproductive morbidity. There is little understanding of the perceptions, beliefs and attitudes that workers may need to address in order to enhance clients' compliance and confidence.

Service delivery strategies have not addressed the serious constraints that women face in acquiring good health care. Vulnerability, lack of autonomy, unequal social status and limited access to economic resources inhibit a woman's capacity to seek health care and may even limit her ability to recognize that she is in need of services. Even when a problem has been identified, women may not be able to obtain proper treatment because accessing the service is too difficult or because the expense is deemed unnecessary. Constraints on women, and therefore on their health-seeking behaviour, operate through social beliefs, norms and practices that are dismissive of women, through segmented markets for land, labor, credit and technology that deprive them of independent resources, and through discriminatory legal practices and government insensitivity that limit their rights.

The empowerment of women to gain greater control over the circumstances of their own lives is a necessary condition to overcoming these obstacles. Full access to appropriate care for women requires the creation of an environment that supports women's efforts towards self-determination.

(iv) Training

The mode of training and the focus of the training curriculum provided to the health providers must be appropriate, women-sensitive and need-oriented in order to equip workers to communicate better with clients and address motivational issues.

(v) IEC

The new reproductive health orientation requires major changes in both the content and delivery of information, education, and communication programmes. Messages communicated to the public about family planning and reproductive health must go far beyond raising awareness about contraception and the small family norm. Local norms, perceptions and beliefs in the area of reproductive health need to be assessed, with messages tailored to differences in culture, language and community needs. The challenge lies in reorienting communication and education activities to incorporate this wider interpretation of reproductive health; to focus attention on the varying information needs of women, men and youths and to utilize the media as the most suitable to convey information to these diverse groups. This kind of reorientation requires a fresh look not only at messages and media, but also at the training of communicators.

(vi) Monitoring and Evaluation

It is essential to develop a simplified monitoring and evaluation system that is useful to both service providers in the field and to those who are concerned with the overall performance and impact of the programme. Unfortunately, the existing system has not succeeded in condensing unwieldy data requirements. Providers are required to record a wide variety of unnecessary data on programme achievement and provider performance, an exercise that is cumbersome, time-consuming and unproductive. In addition, the health workers are required to keep identical client information in different registers, a futile exercise that requires extensive copying. Every day, workers spend an average of two hours on record maintenance, which often requires the help of family members or supervisors. Not surprisingly, health workers may not comprehend the need for all of the collected information, which may have little or no relevance for their ability to reach or understand the needs of their clients. There is an urgent need to understand the demands on and the conditions of the grassroots workers, and to develop a more reasonable schedule. The recording system should be completely reorganized so that workers only collect information relevant to the health needs of the women and men in the communities they serve.

The impact of the programme should be measured through periodic population-based surveys, using quantitative research methods. However, the performance of health care providers should be measured not only in terms of quantitative indicators, but also in terms of the quality of care they provide and of their clients' satisfaction.

Conclusion

India has shifted its priorities from a narrow family planning focus to a broader reproductive health orientation in which quality and informed choice are prominent features, and the tasks that lie ahead in making this shift a reality have been identified. Altering the perspective of stakeholders to accept the new approach remains an overarching challenge. Clients need to understand that reproductive and child health is their rights and therefore to demand accountability from the health system. It is critical that the changes in priorities and programmes be translated and communicated effectively and convincingly. The RCH programme is underpinned by the 10th Plan strategy for addressing poverty, with a focus on the poorest states, and has ambitious targets for reducing IMR and MMR. The

Government of India expects to 'increase access and utilization of quality Reproductive and Child Health services by the poor'.

REFERENCES

Bhalla, A. S. (1995). *Uneven Development in the Third World: A Study of China and India*, Basingstoke, United Kingdom.

Das Gupta, Monica, Lincoln, C. Chen and Krishnan, T.N. (eds.) (1995). *Women's Health in India: Risk and Vulnerability*, Mumbai.

Horowitz, Berny and Kishwar, Madhu (1985). '*Family Life–The Unequal Deal*,' in Madhu Kishwar and Ruth Vanita, eds., *In Search of Answers*: Indian Women's Voices from Manushi, London.

Health Watch (1997). Overview of the Issues That Emerged in The Regional Consultations, *Health Watch Activities 1996–; 97: Summary Reports*, Ahmedabad, India: Gujarat Institute of Development Research.

India National Family Health Survey Reports (1992-93; 1998-99; 2005-06) I, II and III; International Institute for Population Sciences, Mumbai.

India Registrar General (1996). Final Population Totals SRS Based Abridged Life Tables Fertility and Mortality Indicators Sample Registration Bulletin, 30, 1, New Delhi.

Jejeebhoy, Shireen J. and Saumya Rama Rao (1995). '*Unsafe Motherhood: A Review of Reproductive Health*,' in Monica Das Gupta, Lincoln C. Chen and T.N. Krishnan, eds., *Women's Health in India: Risk and Vulnerability*, Bombay.

The World Bank (1996). *Improving Women's Health in India*, Washington DC. The World Health Organization, 1996. mohfw.nic.in/dofw%20website/Child%20healthrti.pdf.

3

Social Components and Cultural Practices Influencing Motherhood in Rural India

Prof. B. Nalini

Summary

The study aims to bring to light the relationship between reproductive behaviour and the social factors. In rural areas the decision-making power of women on their own reproductive activities is influenced by the family which may be due to their limited knowledge on this matter and also economic dependency. The second half of the research describes how the culture of rural India takes better care of pregnant women indirectly. The study suggests that more knowledge on reproductive health should be imparted to rural girls even before child bearing. The cultural practices relating to pregnancy should be preserved because they extent care to the mothers.

Introduction

Health sciences have recognized the direct relevance of social and personal components in medical problems. Now, it is the responsibility of the social scientists to investigate into these aspects and report their relevance. Health issues and their treatment can be made complete only if these components are studied fully and understood with a holistic approach. Specially, in the consideration of the health status of women these factors play a crucial role and hence, have to be comprehended well. The health behaviour of women in India is unique. Although women, mostly mothers, play a vital role in the therapeutic process of their family members, they tend to neglect their own health. They hesitate to come out with their illness, specially their problems relating to reproduction. As a result of this there is a delay in medical treatment.

There are many cultural and familial factors that contribute towards the illness of women. Women are referred to the physician very late at an advanced stage of the disease either because the family has neglected their health or women themselves report their illness late, for various reasons like economic priority to children's health and education.

In the developing countries there were almost 2.4 million deaths among women in the reproductive age group; and of those, more than 500000-almost one-fifth –were ascribed to maternal causes, most of which are easily preventable. Chief among the causes were haemorrhage, sepsis, hypertensive disorders of pregnancy and obstructed labour. Each year millions of children are left without mothers, thus imperiling their own immediate safety and leaving them vulnerable to psychological and social burdens in the future.

Haemorrhage caused about 130000, with an estimated 14 million cases annually. Indirect causes during pregnancy, such as anemia and malaria, resulted in 100000 deaths. Hypertensive disorders of pregnancy, including pre-eclampsia and eclampsia, took the lives of about 60000 women. There were an estimated 140 unsafe abortions for every 1000 live births in 1990. Globally it is estimated that in more than half of the number of pregnant women were anemic, a threat not only to mother's health, but also a contributing factor to low birth weight. Low level of resources and skills and insufficient infrastructure make access to health difficult. In addition, women's inferior socioeconomic status, lack of resources and decision making power and low level of education hinder their use of appropriate health services. Premature death and sufferings relating to childbearing are not inherent in the human condition-they are rooted in the social, cultural and economic settings of the countries where they are prevalent. Something can be done about them.

The mother-baby package is based on the following principles considered to be the four pillars of safe motherhood that would address to the actual social conditions of the people. This package introduced:

1. To ensure that individuals and couples have the necessary family planning information and services to plan and space pregnancies;
2. To provide proper antenatal care so that complications of pregnancy are detected as early as possible and correctly treated;
3. To give all birth attendants the necessary knowledge, skills and equipment to perform a clean and safe delivery and provide postpartum care to the mother and baby; and
4. To make essential obstetric care available to all high-risk cases and emergencies.

By and large, the real decision makers continue to be the husband or mother-in-law; even educated women are often not the main decision-makers when sick (Ganatra and Hirve, 1995). In the slums of Delhi, as many as 82.0% of pregnant women reportedly required the permission of other family members to avail of antenatal or delivery care; even in an emergency, 81.0% indicated that they would have to wait for their husband and mother-in-law to make a decision (Bhandari and Mayank, 1999). The Harayana and Punjab study supports this finding. Results indicate that even more educated women, if the health worker recommends a referral for an obstetric emergency, the husband, mother-in-law or community elders can override the decision. The study also shows that although the importance of providing special food for sick and lactating cows is recognized in these agricultural settings, pregnant and lactating women have little say in accessing appropriate diets or health care.

True that the efforts made by WHO and the Governments of different Developing Nations have enhanced the health status of women, but not to the extent of the expectations. The maternal deaths are still high and require concern by these Nations. The efforts prove to be unfruitful because of poverty, ignorance among women and insufficient infrastructure facilities. WHO* reports that 72.0% of maternal deaths are due to the causes of haemorrhage (55.0%) sepsis (75.0%) eclampsia (65.0%) obstructed labour (80.0%) and unsafe abortion (75.0%). These deaths can be prevented with proper approach of the health care systems.

Objectives

The present research proposes to study these determinants of health with the following objectives.

1. To study the knowledge and decision-making power of women regarding their own reproductive health.
2. To find out whether married women have sufficient information on important reproductive matters prior to conception.
3. To describe the antenatal and postnatal care given to mothers, in the cultural context of their area.

---

* The World Health Report 1995. *Bridging the Gap*. WHO, Geneva.

Method

This is a descriptive study covering Madurai District in Tamilnadu. The study has two types of analysis. The first two objectives are explained with the help of data colleted from women through an interview schedule. This primary data was collected from a Multi Speciality hospital in Madurai City. The second part of the research describes the cultural factors peculiar to the study area that contribute for the reproductive activities of women. There are many cultural practices and customs in Indian culture that make child bearing an important event both socially and personally. These practices possess strong implications on the reproductive behaviour of women. This is covered under the third objective. The information regarding the cultural practices was obtained from elderly and experienced women living in this area. As far as the sampling was concerned hundred patients were interviewed who visited the hospital during the study period. Although it appears to be a conveniently designed one, it was difficult to convince the institution and also the sick patients for an interview. The major variables taken for analysis are residence, age, marital status, educational background and religion. This is elaborated in the second part of the work.

Description of the Sample

The sample consists of 72.0% of women in the age group of 20 to 30 years, 8.0% between 30 to 40 years and the rest above 40 years. The age at marriage is 15 to 20 years for 54.0% of the sample and 20-25 for 40.0% and 4.0% above that age group. The sample consists of 53.0% of employed women and 60% of the sample are from urban background. The age at 1st child is below 25 years whereas the age at bearing the last child spread over between 20 to 40 years. (16.0% in 15-20 year, 34.0% in 20-25 years, 32.0% in 25-30 years 10.0% in 30 to 35 years and 8.0% in 35-40 years). The respondents seem to live in both joint (52.0%) and nuclear families (48.0%). The educational background of the respondents is low because 80.0% are educated up to school level, 12.0% illiterates and only 8.0% have completed college education. The religious composition of the sample is as follows 84.0% Hindus, 14.0% Christians and 2.0% Muslims. Majority of the respondents (84.0%) belong to the backward caste, while 6.0% upper caste and 10.0% scheduled caste.

Knowledge and Decision-Making Power of Women on Health Matters

Earlier studies* reveal that the knowledge of Indian girls on reproductive health is very poor. The social factors like early marriage; low educational and social status and seclusion of girls from social activities are some of the reasons attributed for low level of knowledge of girls about reproductive health. To talk or discuss about sexual matters are always a taboo for women. The study shows that 50.0% of the women were ignorant of the process of conception till their marriage. The same percentage of women is found to be ignorant of the use of contraceptive methods at the time of their marriage. They state that they slowly got informed of these things only after their marriage. Another 16.0% of the respondents came to know about contraceptives only after they delivered their first child. Only the rest 34.0% had knowledge on these matters before marriage. The knowledge on contraceptives seems to be less among the sample till their marriage. It is found that they collect information on these subjects through their doctors (60.0%), neighbours (25.0%) and media (15.0%).

---

* Radhika, Ramasubban and Shireen, J. Jejeebhoy (eds.) (2000). *Women's Reproductive Health*. Rawat Publications, Jaipur.
Prakasam, C. P. and Siva Raju, S. (2006). *Adolescents Reproductive: Health Perspective* (Ed.). B.R. Publishing Corporation, New Delhi.

The investigation shows that the decision to consult a particular doctor is made by the husbands of 86.0% of the respondents and his family members. But the decision on the number of children to bear is jointly taken by the couple themselves (40.0%), while women decide it solely (22.0%) and 38.0% the husband takes the decision. This is certainly a change in the trend of decision making shifting from the husbands dominating the decision making process to the couple together determining it. This might be due to the reasons like a) the changing social and culture context that demand careful decision making, b) women being employed and contributing to the family income, c) the broader perspectives of modern men to accept the decisions their wives and d) probably the high medical cost.

The sample of the study consists of majority of employed women. But the analysis of data discloses that 80.0% of them dependent on their husbands for financial support medical treatment. At the same time, 52.0% for moral support and 42.0% for physical support the role of the husbands become very less. It is 52.0% and 42.0% respectively. The dependency of women on their parent on all other matters seems to be high.

The knowledge level of the sample of the study on contraceptives in the earlier analysis was found to be very low. Corresponding to that, as per the data, the adoption of contraceptives is also very poor. It is only 10.0% of the sample that adopts some kind of devise while the rest does not go for any. The data reveals that mostly the samples in the age group upto 25 years of age do not adopt any device. Those above 30 years of age have either gone for sterilization or use 'copper T'. One important factor to be noted here is that the husbands never prefer to go either for sterilization or use condom. It is only the wives who take precaution to prevent early conception or postpone the next one.

Cultural Practices relating to Child Birth

The traditional health practices that prevail in the rural pockets of India form a separate cultural entity by itself. Rural societies prescribe and proscribe specific diet habits, behavior patterns and celebrations that occupy essential part of their life. One such activity that bears both cultural as well as medical significance is pertaining to child bearing and delivering. The Indian attitude towards bearing a child and delivering it to the world has a cathectic value rather than just a biological activity. While the modern treatment applies new techniques to make the delivery easier, the rural people possessed faith in midwives who conducted deliveries in a traditional manner. They waited for natural delivery. Thus delivering a child to the world involved great risk in villages. Although changes have taken place in villages on midwifery, adoption of improved methods is not yet common due to several reasons. At present in rural areas although Primary Health Centers are available, many pregnant women do not go for regular antenatal check ups in institutions during their pregnancy. During the field work it was narrated that sometimes-pregnant women return from work, complete their household work including cooking, washing and grinding with labour pain after which, they lie down and deliver the baby on their own. Some incidents are narrated on how sometimes, the fetus slips down even while they are doing the work or before lie down. For them bearing and delivering a child is part of natural course of life (unlike the urban women to whom it has become a kind of sickness and medical treatment altogether).

The Indian society as a whole considers bearing and rearing children as a totally feminine role. The matter of conception and rituals that follow it predominantly involve the fair sex. Carrying a baby is the *only stage* in a woman's life when special care is given to her with respect to their diet and compassion is shown. In the case of rural women, in spite of such compassion shown they are normally directed to do work that requires bending and walking because there is a belief that such activities make the hip bone (pelvis) flexible and hence the delivery easier.

Motherhood elevates the status of a woman in Indian society. A barren woman is always subject to criticisms and curse form the family member. She is blamed as 'maladi' (infertile women) and is always perturbed with the risk of being divorced by her husband or thrown out by the husbands' family. Hence, the conception of a baby assures her a definite and confirmed status in her family.

Indian society celebrates motherhood. There are a number of rituals and ceremonies pertaining to pregnancy. Pregnancy of a girl, specially the first child, is taken as a jubilant message in the family. The ceremonies conducted during the last quarter of pregnancy are of great importance, like marriage, in the family. The antenatal and postnatal care given to the mother in rural areas is one of cultural significance than medical importance. From an outsiders point of view the practices may be unscientific and crude but for the rural people the procedures are easier and normal that go along with their day-to-day life style at home. Local untrained but experienced midwives called 'dais' perform delivery. They adopt a traditional mode of delivery and administer herbal medicine. (These daises were the people who were trained by the Government latter.) Midwifery has cultural, social and medical implications. The present investigation describes midwifery in rural India. It should be noted that delivery by traditional dais is not the regular practice in these villages but there are case of it occurring at times

This portion of the study focuses on midwifery practiced in South India. Three villages located in three different districts of Tamil Nadu are selected for the study. The names of the Districts are Madurai, Tirumangalam and Usilampatty. The literacy rate of these villages is very low, while female literacy is still lower. It is also found that their maternal mortality rate is high and the infant mortality rate is still higher.

The data are gathered from the traditional midwives who are living in the sample villages and are the natives of that place. Focused interviews were carried out to collect the required information. As each village has only one midwife at present she was interviewed. The study considers each midwife as a case. The description is made on the basis of the narrations of the dais.

Case I: Village 'A' of Madurai District

> *This village 'A' is located in Madurai district. This is a dry land area depending mainly on seasonal rainfall for cultivation. The midwife of this village belongs to a caste group called 'Thevar' which is considered to be a Most Backward Caste in South India. She has learnt the skill of midwifery from her mother who also practiced midwifery in the same village. She has not undergone any formal training in midwifery in the same village or under the government programs. Her family possesses a small piece of agriculturist land. She has four sons and three daughters. This midwife has not acquired even basic school education. Traditional midwifery is not practiced as an occupation in villages; they feel that this is a calling or a service to the society. The midwife accepts neither money nor material gifts for herself in return. Normally the midwife abstains from consuming food or water from the house in which she attended delivery. Only after 30 days she eats food in that house probably due to 'pollution' resulting from delivery.*

The Rituals

Like marriage, pregnancy is also celebrated with joy by the family members. The girls in India enjoy an enhanced status, privileges and additional care when they conceive a baby. The whole family showers love and care during this period. They feed the girl with good nutritious food, make her to take rest and put her in good comforts, both mentally and physically. Usually at the seventh or ninth month of pregnancy, the family celebrates, a function called 'Valaikappu' or 'Seemandham'. In this ceremony the girl is dressed like a bride with silk saree and flowers. This function is performed in the husband's family and the parents bring a specific kind of food called 'variety' rice* to the whole family. All the relatives are served with the food. When the feast is over, the bangle ceremony is performed. She is made to sit up on a plank and in front of her a plate full of glass bangles and a cup full of sandal paste and 'cumcum' are placed. The relatives of her mother's family and her husband's family then come one by one apply sandal paste to her forearms and each one help her wear a pair of bangles. Then they apply vermillion (cumcum) on her forehead bless her and gift her some cash, folded in betel leaves with betel nuts. As the married women perform this ritual, widows are not entertained to participate in this ritual. After the ritual is over, the guests are fed with the 'variety' rice. Then the girl accompanies her parents to her natal family where she will stay till the delivery.

In Indian culture usually the life cycle ceremonies have the galore of gift exchange, presentations and reciprocal rituals between affinal kin groups. After a few days from bangle ceremony, the woman folks of the boy's family visit the girl with raw rice, gingelly oil and black jaggery. On

---

* It is a custom to prepare five or seven types of rice – rice with tamarind pulp, tomato rice, sweet rice, coconut rice, curd rice and vegetable rice.

reaching the house, they prepare a pastry out of the above ingredients in a specific procedure. They make a temporary hearth outside the house using dried palmary leaves as fuel. All the ingredients are mixed together to which they add mixing it will with the help of coconut tree stem as a spatula. When this item is cooked, it is served in seven palm leaves on a winnowing pad. Prayers are offered to the Gods after which they eat the prepared food. In one of the leaves it is reserved for the pregnant girl while the rest is consumed by important family members. It is a custom to prepare five or seven types of rice – rice with tamarind pulp, tomato rice, sweet rice, coconut rice, curd rice and vegetable rice.

The pregnant girls are advised to eat good food with greens in plenty. In rural areas, they are expected to work well rather than to take rest, as they believe that physical exercise will make the delivery easier. There are certain restrictions placed on the pregnant girl. She has to avoid, going out after dusk. In rural areas there is a fear that wandering spirits might disturb the well being of the pregnant woman. It is a common observation is South India that the elders of the family keep on instructing the pregnant girls regarding the 'dos' and 'do not dos' like sitting or lying down in a specific fashion or not sitting on the entrance door. During pregnancy the women get additional care and attention by natal and conjugal family since she is carrying the progeny of the family.

Delivery Practices

With the onset of the pain, there is a general practice of checking whether the pain is false or real labour pain. False pain is referred to as 'Chootu Vali'* meaning pain (vali) due

* This jeera water is given to the girl to drink. If the pain subsides, it is taken as false pain. In case the pain continues, then it is labour pain and the girl is attended immediately. Then village folks adopt another method also to detect the real pain. 'Bull eye' egg is prepared with lots of caster oil and the girl is asked to consume it. In this method the real medicinal value is from the

to heat ('choodu'); Jeera (cumin seeds) is fried in mud pot and is soaked in the water of the 'watered rice'** of the previous day for a few minutes.

As the labour pain commences the girl is asked to walk here and there inside the room. When an intense labour pain start the girl is asked to sit on a sac filled with paddy husk with legs apart and is asked to push. It is learnt that delivery takes place either in sitting or lying down posture. The midwife helps the girl by holding the legs apart, assisted by an elderly female of the family gripping her hands tight. In some cases if the rupture does not take place easily, the plated hair of the girl is inserted into her own mouth. She is made to avert and starts vomiting. In that pressure it breaks and the delivery is made easier. As soon as the baby is out cold water is sprinkled with force on its face. This sprinkling is called 'thunukku thanni' meaning 'alert water' which only, they believe, makes the child alert and active in its future days otherwise the child will be dull headed. When the baby is delivered, the girl is asked to stand up. The midwife applies lot of caster oil on her own head, presses and rotates her head on the girl's stomach. This forces the remaining placenta and waste expel out quickly and thoroughly. The umbilical cord is cut with the sickle*** leaving two inches from the child's naval. A bed is prepared with hay stock for the new mother to lie down.

She is expected to rest for three days, after which she has to remove the hay stock bed herself, take it outside and

---

caster oil. As caster oil is not palatable, it is given with egg. In the Indian culture the health conditions are always differentiated on two conditions of the body – the heat or cold status of the body. The belief is the pain other than labour pain occur due to heat of the body.

** In rural families the rice is cooked once a day in the evening and the left over is watered in order to keep the rice fresh and fermented. This rice is consumed the next day.

*** Nowadays the trained dais in rural areas are supplied with a kit consisting of proper equipments. But still traditional dais during interviews, reported the use of sickle.

burn it later. She takes head bath and now she is permitted to move inside home as normal as others. Till three days, she and the materials she was using are considered to be polluting, this is, 'theetu', that is pollution.

Placenta Disposal

The way placenta is disposed off follows a ritualistic pattern. A temporary bathing hut is constructed in front of the house with coconut or palm leaves. A pit is dug out in one of the corners. The placenta is thrown inside the pit and a big boulder in placed on it, on which branches of neem leaves are kept. The boulder is kept so that dogs do not snatch the placenta out. The neem leaves keep branch the bad spirits away. This hut is used as toilet and bathing place for the girl till the pollution period is over. On sixteen day flimsy construction is removed. By this time placenta decomposes.

Diet after Delivery

Although the mother is fed with normal diet after delivery there is certain special preparation of medicinal / curative value, to be consumed by her every day. A 'laygiyam' (a semi solid pastry) is prepared with pepper, jeera, cumin seeds, fried garlic and tailed pepper (all these incredients are powdered). It is added to powdered black jaggery and placed on fire. The jaggery melts and mixes with the powder. It is taken from fire and small balls are made. The girl is advised to eat it frequently. The ingredients of the 'laygiyam' have medicinal value and it has the effect of expelling the waste that might remain inside the womb completely. Apart from this the girl is fed with ragi and malt porridge regularly, which aids her, regains her stamina. Another special item given to the delivered mother is chicken soup or gravy, garlic gravy and fenugreek gravy in tamarind pulp.

The ritual proceeding childbirth is that the relatives of the conjugal family are expected to visit the girl with certain number of chicken, gingely oil and jaggery. Other relatives also bring these items as they are considered to be essential items* of diet for the girl. The mother is advised to feed the child with breast milk immediately. The rural people believe that the breast milk for the first few days (which they call as 'cheembal') is rich in 'nutrients'.

The rural women when compared to the urban women regard conceiving a baby and delivery it to the world as normal course of life. Their day-to-day activities, work time, household tasks are not interrupted just because they are carrying a baby. There are two reasons for it. Firstly, as they are daily wagers working on the agricultural field, they have to earn their daily bread by the wage. Secondly, they are not fussy about pregnancy as their counterparts in the cities. The midwife reports several incidents of carrying mothers delivering the baby within a few minutes of the onset of the pain. There is a case of a girl who delivered the baby in standing posture before she could lie down. She narrated another case that washed the house** , hand pounded ragi and lied down to deliver the baby within a minute or two before the elders came for assistance. Usually rural women work till they get pain and even after it till they deliver. They believe that such works make delivery easier.

Children are considered to be God's gifts in Indian culture. But there are certain social and economic factors that lead to the killing of the babies soon after their birth. Village A is a place that is dominated by a particular caste group among whom infanticides is common due to poverty and the practice

---

* These three items (chicken, oil and jaggery) are considered to be 'hot food stuffs' that keep the girls body warm. The folk belief is that the delivered girls are likely to suffer from 'fits' as a result of chilliness of their body. The oil cures the inflammation in the womb and the passage while jaggery expels the remaining waste form the womb.

** Washing the house thoroughly with water ones in a week on a Fridays or Tuesdays is a ritual. Bringing pots of water from outside house and cleaning is a strenuous task.

of dowry. This killing is performed by midwives only. The midwife stated that she too had to perform some such killings. The female babies are killed by letting a few drops of *Kallipal –cactus milk*-into its mouth, or putting a grain of the paddy into baby's nose or by feeding the baby with spicy chicken soup. The midwife, who is kind enough to assist the mother to bring the baby out, also knows the way to kill it if parents do not wish to have it.

Case II: Village 'B' from Usilampatti

> *Case II is another tiny village in Usilampatti District. The midwife of this hamlet belongs to 'Paravar' caste. She is married and has eight children. She learnt the 'art' from her mother who is also a traditional midwife. By accompanying her mother she learnt it on her own. Her husband is a cooley. She is an illiterate woman. The midwife would not receive money or gift for assisting the girls in delivery. She says that it is the service she renders to her own people in the village. The villagers usually inform the midwife of the conception in the third month itself. But she will not make any visits to the girl till she is called for to attend when the pain starts.*

The Ceremony

The ceremony called 'Valaikappu' or 'seemandham' is performed in the seventh or ninth month. Usually this ceremony is preformed only in odd month. The rituals are the same as followed in village A. The preparation of rice and wearing of glass bangles to the girl are similar. The diet prescribed for the carrying girl consists of good nutritious food with frequent consumption of lime with honey.

The Labour

The midwife is called when the labour pain starts. The

midwife while starting from her home offers prayers to Lord Alagar, her deity. She brings a small quantity of castor oil and gives it to the priest of the nearly temple who in turn places it at the foot of the God and prays. The oil gets consecrated. On reaching home, the consecrated castor oil is poured by the midwife on the labouring girl from her chest to flow down on her belly. If the oil flows down faster, it is indicated that the delivery will be quick and easy.

The process of assisting labour is found to be different in this village. A saree of a mother, who had delivered a child without many pains, is borrowed and tied at the roof of the room. The delivery posture varies. The midwife sits on a stool at about 50 cms high, stretching her legs. The labouring mother sits on the feet of the midwife. A helper, usually a relative, stands at the backside of the labouring girl supporting her back. The delivering girl is now asked to hold the edge of the saree hanging from the roof and is asked to (push) strain. During labour time, cold water is poured on the labouring mother now and then. The midwife keeps her palm on the stomach of the girl and slightly twists in a specific fashion to turn the baby to the correct position and make the delivery easier. When the baby is born, the cord is cut around two inches from the body of the child with a blade. In their own linguistic expression around the breadth of 4 fingers it is 'Naalu veralkadai alavu' meaning length of four fingers. The cord then is dragged till the forehead of the delivering girl and severed. This length, as they understand, indicates the point up to which it should to be out.

The placenta is removed and is put into a pit dug for this purpose to decompose. The people of this village believe that if the placenta has red knots on it, the next child will be a girl and if it is white then it will be a boy. If there are no knots on placenta, they guess that there is no more childbirth for the girl. There is another belief pertaining to the sex of the child. If the fetus in the mother's womb kicks all the sides, it is believed to be a girl baby. In case the kick falls only on the left side, then the child is a boy. The baby is fed with mother's milk immediately. The special diet for the mother includes fried garlic mixed with black jaggery, and chicken dishes every day.

Abortions

Although child bearing and rearing are considered to be a great blessings, there are occasions during which, the mother wants to abort the fetus. When the mothers does not want to carry the child due to reasons like illegal contacts or 3rd or 4th child or early pregnancy, the woman approaches the midwife for aborting it. The folk practice is to soak in and place the kallipal, that is, cactusmilk inside the genital for 2 hours after which the blood oozes out with the aborted fetus. Even 4-month-old fetus is aborted this way. Another method of aborting the child is to burn woolen blanket fully and the ash is mixed with black jiggery. Three small balls of this mixture are swollen by the conceived girl in empty stomach. This causes over bleeding and fetus is mistreated.

Case III: Thirumangalam District Village

> *This village is located in Thirumangalam district of Tamil Nadu. The midwife of this village is from Piramalai Kallar caste. She is educated up to eighth standard. Her husband is an employee of Government Hospital. They have one daughter and two sons. The information furnished by the midwife is almost similar to the earlier two cases. This is probably due to the proximity of the districts. Hence the study gives references only to the practices that vary from the previous cases.*

The rituals on 'seemandham' are the same as in other cases. In this village the wife of the maternal uncle' of the girl is asked to put the first set of bangles to the girls.

Instruction is given not to break the glass bangles, while wearing it, as it is a bad omen. The diet prescribed for the carrying girl is normal rice meals with plenty of moringa leaves, and dates fruits. The girl is advised to drink plenty of water during pregnancy period. The delivery is conducted in lying posture. After the delivery the girl is made to lie down on the bed made out of old cloths. The dhobi of the village only has to wash the clothes of the girl after delivery. The girl is not permitted to do it. At the end of the month, the dhobi is given a set a new cloths, oil, black jiggery and cash for the task she did.

The placenta expelled at the time of delivery is dumped and closed in a pit dug outside the house. The umbilical cord is cut in "four finger space" from the child's body. The cord is thrown into the well nearby. The belief is that as the cord swells in size, the baby will put up weight and grow. The special diet after delivery includes chicken, fish and dried fish. It is believed, that the dried fish stimulates location. A 'laygiam' is prepared with jiggery, ginger, dry ginger, garlic, cardamom. The new mother has to eat it regularly for the whole month. This will heal the wound inside the body and also expels the waste from the womb thoroughly. The baby is fed with the mother's milk immediately. The village people advise the pregnant girls to sleep turning to one side and not upwards since it will lift the baby to the chest of the girl and hurt her. The pregnant girls should not sit on the main entrance door, which will make the head of the fetus will grow bigger in size.

Discussion on Child Birth Practices

The practice of traditional midwifery in rural India may be commented as unscientific but it is highly dependable and approachable for the rural folks. The Government may extend training to midwives. But still the traditional practices persist. That is the reason why the traditional 'dais' are given training with better obstetric methods and provided with a kit. But it is learnt that at present only a very few deliveries in rural areas are performed at home with the help of the traditional midwives. The origin of midwifery can be traced back to the occupation of 'ambattachi' who are the wives of the barbers of the village. They were considered to be the experts in assisting deliveries. But the rituals relating to pregnancy are still followed with great care.

The midwives performed this task as their obligation to the society and received only in kind. This is part of the occupational structure of castes in rural areas. The so-called polluting caste women abet the act of delivering the child to the world the process of which is 'polluting'. But these midwives acquired this skill from their mothers by being with them during deliveries. The traditional midwives, as per the information gathered, are called in only at the onset of pain. She is not consulted either in initial stages or even periodically during the pregnancy. She has the skill only in getting the child out. In case the pregnant girls have some complication during pregnancy they will approach PHC for treatment.

They do not anticipate any money for the service. For them the skill is a 'gift by God', 'obligation to the family' and an 'essential role' in the community life. This is the reason why the traditional midwives happily respond when called and the needy spontaneously approach them. The midwives are being consulted for aborting the fetus. In villages (also in cities) a great number of abortions are performed for reasons like illegal or premarital conceptions, unwanted pregnancy and earlier pregnancy after delivery. These abortions done by midwives are not recorded. Sometimes women undergo such abortions without the knowledge of their husband and family members.

The social status enjoyed by women in rural areas is comparatively lower in many aspects. But the recognition and status accorded to a pregnant girl is superior to than an unmarried girl and a barren girl. After marriage the girl joins the household chorus and starts playing the role of a devoted wife and then a 'responsible mother'. Her own wishes and needs are of secondary importance. It is at this period of pregnancy that the girl is shown extra care, given additional food/diet proper rest. Since the custom says that the delivery has to be conducted in mother's house, the girls all emotions and physical needs are taken care of. She is only a 'loving daughter' with a simple role to play. Moreover the observance of 'pollution' (theettu) also in a way helps in the girl taking rest even if she stays back at husbands house (may be for the third or fourth delivery). During pollution period she has to abstain from moving all over the house and touching article. Hence she does not participate in household activities because it is a rest period for her.

Discussion on Safe Motherhood

The study has focused on four major aspects of maternal health. They are a) knowledge about conception b) use of contraceptives for safe motherhood c) women's power to decide on their own motherhood d) the kind of post natal care of women receive in their cultural background.

a) There are barriers to information* on maternal health, pregnancy and delivery to Indian women. It is a taboo for girls to talk about like sex and related matters prior to marriage. There are lot of misconceptions about pregnancy and related health practices the belief system sometime mislead women to follow wrong methods. The present study confirms this fact. The sample is found to possess scanty knowledge regarding conception and also contraception. They admit that they either know it after marriage or only after the birth of the first child.

* Sugathan, T.N. and B.B.L. Sharma, "Clinical Services and Follow up of oral Pill acceptance", *Journal of Population Research* 1, 1 : 59-69.

A complete knowledge could facilitate women to plan for safe motherhood.

b) In order to achieve demographic goals, Indian Government has implemented a number of Family Planning Schemes. Specially, the awareness camps on contraceptives aim to enhance the level of awareness among the eligible couples. In spite of such efforts, it is found that the adoption depends on a number of personal factors.** The fear of side effects, desire for a male child and husband's likeness are some factors influencing the use of contraceptives. Indian men normally do not prefer the use of condom and other methods. They consider contraceptives are only for women to adopt. The analysis reveals that majority of young women do not adopt any device. Women above 30 years of age are careful in the use of contraceptives. The low percentage of adoption of contraceptives among the age group between 15 and 25 years in this study is due to the reasons like ignorance on this matter.

c) In Indian rural cultural set up, by and large, the decision-making on matters relating to pregnancy and delivery is influenced by the husbands and mothers-in-law. The young girls/mothers often leave the decisions on conception and number of children to their husbands voluntarily in order to avoid family conflicts. They are powerless even if they are earning members. The cultural practices and socioeconomic conditions constrain women from seeking healthcare. The present work comes out with the earlier findings that the husbands' decide on conception and the number of children. There is a small change, if not

** Ganatra, B.R. and S.S. Hirve, "Unsafe Motherhood : the determinants of material morality", *Journal of the Indian Medical Association*, 93, 2 : 34 – 35.

remarkable, that the couples together decide on this matter. But the decision on the institution to be admitted is decided by the husbands and in-laws, probably due to other factors like the economic consideration, convenience and to consult the family consultant. A few more findings relating to these aspects are the certain percentage (8.0%) home deliveries are undergone by the respondents and 30.0% of the respondents are married to their relatives as the choice is made by their parents.

d) It is quite unique in Indian context that the cultural components play a vital role in the health of an individual. Rituals and practices that are followed in the tradition are found to be beneficial in certain respects. Women, who are usually accorded a low status in the social life, enjoy a relatively better status under the cultural canopy of motherhood. They are bestowed with extra care and food during motherhood. Especially at the post partum period, the diet and rest that are due for women at their mother's house are cultural advantages for them. These practices are part and parcel of the social life that it has to be described as a folk practice. Since, the cultural prescription is to deliver the child in mother's place (the place of origin of the girl), the girl takes sufficient rest till she gets well and her mental well-being is quite fine and free from disturbances.

REFERENCES

Bidarakop, G.S. (2000). *Mother and Child in India.* Reliance Publishing House, New Delhi.

Digumarthi Bhaskara, Rao and Digumarthi Pushpalatha, Rao (1999). *Women and Family Health.* Discovery Publishing House, New Delhi.

Haradahan, Mandal (2006). *Reproductive Behaviour and Health Care Practices*. Rajat Publications, New Delhi.

Imrana, Qadeer, Kasture, Sen and K.R. Nayar (eds.) (2001). *Public Health and Poverty of Reforms*. Sage Publications, New Delhi.

Prakasam, C.P. and Siva Raju, S. (2006). *Adolescents Reproductive: Health Perspective* (Ed.). B.R. Publishing Corporation, New Delhi.

Radhika, Ramasubban and Shireen, J. Jejeebhoy (eds.) (2000). *Women's Reproductive Health*. Rawat Publications, Jaipur.

Vatsala, Samant (ed.) (2000). *Health Awareness for Women*. Gyan Publishing House.

Saswata, Ghosh (2008). Fertility Transition in West Bengal: Revisiting Basu and Amin's (2000) Diffusion Hypothesis. *Social Change*, 38, 1, 110-116.

The World Health Report 1995. *Bridging the Gap*. WHO, Geneva.

4

Socio-Cultural Determinants of Reproductive Health among Urban Poor Women

Dr. Vandana Bhattacharya

Summary

The broad objective of the present study was to understand the role of socio-cultural and psychological factors in reproductive health of women. The study was carried out in the slum areas in Delhi covering a group of 59 women from Govind Puri slum area in Delhi. The woman who were in reproductive phase and completed at least 10 years after marriage and having at least one child were selected purposively for the present study. Data were collected with the help of a specially designed Semi-structured Questionnaire. These apart, four focus groups discussion (FGDs) were conducted with women. Findings revealed that most of the women (66.1%) got married below 18–21 year of age while about 27.1% women married between 21-23 years of age. About 59.3% of the women had 4 to 6 conceptions while about one-third (33.0%) had even 6-8 pregnancies, which indicates the vulnerabilities of Delhi slum women towards anaemia, malnutrition and reproductive tract infections with frequent pregnancies. Majority of the women reported that they did suffer from some sort of gynecological problems in the past like menstrual irregularity (25.4%), pregnancy related complications (22.0%), RTIs/UTIs (15.3%), prolapsed uterus (6.8%), vaginal discharge (3.4%) and so on. FGD reveled that women in slum areas have little choice sexual activity. They were subjected to coercion, abuse and/or unable to negotiate safer sexual practices. As a result, they are more vulnerability to sexually transmitted diseases.

Introduction

Women's health needs differ from those of men because of their biological differences, and also as a result of gender differentials (Arber et al., 1991). Unlike men, women need health services even when they are not ill to prevent unwanted pregnancies, to carry wanted pregnancies to term, and to deliver safely. Women are also biologically more vulnerable than men to a number of reproductive health problems, including reproductive tract infections and sexually transmitted diseases. While women in India face many serious reproductive health problems, the study under reference focuses on the issue of psychosocial effects on reproductive morbidities among married women.

The right to reproductive health is a key component of women and men's reproductive and sexual rights. Moreover, the achievement of reproductive health is inextricably linked to women's and men's ability to exercise reproductive and sexual rights, which includes, besides the right to reproductive health, the right to:

1. Reproductive decision-making including voluntary choice in marriage, family formation and determination of the number, timing and spacing of one's children; and the right to have access to the information and means needed to exercise voluntary choice;

2. Equality and equity for men and women to enable individuals to make free and informed choices in all spheres of their life, free from discrimination based on gender; and

3. Sexual and reproductive security including freedom from sexual violence and coercion, and the right to privacy.

There are also substantial data to show that Indian women bear a high burden of reproductive ill health (Bagchi, 1997, Bali, 1999; and Rao, 2002). Studies show that the heavy load of reproductive morbidity among Indian women is an outcome of their poverty, their powerlessness, low social status, malnutrition, infection, high fertility and lack of access to health care. Thus, socio-economic and biological determinants operate synergistically throughout the lives of poor women to undermine their health, resulting in high levels of morbidity and mortality. There is, therefore, an urgent need to design and implement services to address women's reproductive health needs. Women centered, gender-sensitive services must be organized and implemented.

Most government programmes have generally ignored the fact that reproduction takes place through sexual relations, which are conditioned by broader gender relations. A review of conventional demographic and family planning literature illustrates that the population field has neglected issues related to sexuality, sexual decision-making, gender roles and relationships, and has focused largely on outcomes such as fertility decline, unwanted pregnancy, and more recently on infection. Clearly, social constructions of sexuality and gender relations impact on reproductive health. Although these issues are considered to be politically sensitive, in reality these issues have been neglected.

Poor reproductive health has repercussions not only for women but also for their family members. Women in poor reproductive health are more likely to deliver babies with low weight or infants with various morbidities. They are also less likely to be able to provide food and adequate care for their children. Finally, a woman's reproductive health affects the household economic well being, as a woman in poor reproductive health will be less productive in the labor force.

The prevention and control of reproductive morbidities have become a national priority. Research and programmatic efforts have been significantly enhanced over the last decade; however, the epidemic continues to spread widely and remains a public health as well as a development challenge.

Reproductive health gynecological morbidity includes any condition, disease or dysfunction of the reproductive system which is not related to pregnancy, abortion or childbirth, but which may be related to sexual behaviour. Assessing the dimensions and causes of gynecological morbidity is as challenging a task as measurement of maternal morbidity and mortality. In India, Pakistan and Bangladesh women are said to suffer from a Triple Burden i.e. i) Demographic because of the heavy child rearing responsibilities accompanying high fertility rates, ii) Gastronomic (because of the constraints of poverty and traditional style and methods of cooking and eating), and iii) Geneotological (because of the traditional 'elders').

Burden of the Disease

Reproductive Tract Infections (RTIs) refer to three different types of infections viz., endogenous, iatrogenic and sexually transmitted infections, which affect the reproductive tract:

i) Endogenous Infections are probably the most common RTIs worldwide. They result from an overgrowth of organisms normally present in the vagina. Endogenous infections include bacterial vaginosis and candidiasis. These infections can be easily treated and cured.

2) Iatrogenic Infections occur when the cause of infection (a bacterium or other microorganism) is introduced into the reproductive tract through a medical procedure such as menstrual regulation, induced abortion, and the insertion of an IUD or during childbirth. This can happen if surgical instruments used during the procedure have not been properly sterilized, or if an infection that was already present in the lower reproductive tract is pushed through the cervix into the upper reproductive tract.

3) Sexually Transmitted Infections (STIs) are caused by viruses, bacteria, or parasitic microorganisms that are transmitted through sexual activity with an infected partner. About 30 different sexually transmitted infections have been identified, some of which are easily treatable, many of which are not. HIV, the virus that causes AIDS, is perhaps the most serious sexually transmitted infection as it eventually leads to death. STIs affect both men and women, and can also be transmitted from mothers to children during pregnancy and childbirth.

RTIs result in numerous serious consequences, particularly in women. Pregnancy-related complications, as well as congenital infections, can result from RTIs. Pelvic inflammatory disease (PID) can develop, and can cause infertility, ectopic pregnancy, and chronic pain. Recently, it has been shown that certain infections can increase the chances of HIV transmission. Unfortunately, symptoms and signs of many infections may not appear until it is too late to avoid such consequences and damage to the reproductive organs.

RTIs affect more than health. The morbidity associated with RTIs also affects the economic productivity and quality of life of many individual women and men, and consequently, of whole communities.

Prevalence of RTI/STI in India

It is difficult to estimate precisely the prevalence of RTIs/STIs in the Indian context. Current surveillance systems for STIs/HIV do not provide a complete picture of the incidence of these infections or trends over time. Moreover, data from population-based and facility or convenience-based studies are variable and cannot be compared since different sampling methods, laboratory procedures and criteria were used for diagnosis (Hawkes and Santhya, 2001).

In the early 1990s, the annual incidence of STIs was estimated at around 5.0% of the adult population, which implies that about 40 million new STI cases are occurring annually in the country (NACO, 1998). This is possibly a conservative estimate of the actual number of cases as it is based on surveillance data from public sector STD clinics, which are mainly located in urban areas and utilized by only 5.0% – 10.0% of patients with STIs (NACO, 1998). Reported prevalence rates of bacterial, protozoal and viral infections among women in facility and community-based studies are reflected in Table-1. Figures reveal that the prevalence of RTIs/STIs is high not only among high-risk population groups but also among low-risk groups in many parts of the country, including rural areas.

Clinic-based data indicate that genital ulcer diseases, particularly syphilis, predominate among both men and women. Further, the review indicates that the incidence of viral infections is increasing and, in recent years, has grown from around 3.0% to nearly a fourth of all infections seen at sexually transmitted disease (STD) clinics, in some cases outstripping rates of bacterial infection; endogenous and iatrogenic infections contribute significantly to the high prevalence of RTIs among women in India. For example, community-based studies among women in different parts of the country report a prevalence of bacterial vaginosis and candidacies ranging from 14.0% to 62.0% and 1.0% to 34.0% respectively (Aggarwal et al., 1999; Bhatia et al., 1997; Garg et al., 2002; Oomman, 1996).

This qualitative study aims to illustrate the process of identifying how social factors influence a community's experience with self-reported gynecological morbidities. Therefore, the objective of the present study was to understand the role of socio-cultural and psychological factors in reproductive health of women. The study also explored issues like gender, migration, and prevailing misconceptions about reproductive morbidity in greater detail.

Method

This exploratory study was carried out in the slum areas in Delhi. Fifty nine women were selected purposively from Govind Puri slum area in Delhi for collection of data with the help of a specially designed semi-structured questionnaire. Women who were in reproductive phase and completed at least 10 years after marriage and having at least one child was considered for the present study. These apart, four focus groups discussion (FGDs) were conducted with women, 12 in each group.

Results

Data in Table 1 shows that most of the women (66.1%) got married below 21 years of age. As a result, their reproductive phase in life was longer. About 27.1% of the women got married between the age group of 21-23 years.

Table1
STI Rates among Women in India

Study Population	Prevalence e Ranges (%)							
	GC	*CT*	*Syphilis*	*TV*	*HSV*	*HPV (Clinical Diagnosis)*	*HBV*	*HIV*
1	*2*	*3*	*4*	*5*	*6*	*7*	*8*	*9*
Community-based								
Ever/ currently married women 1	0.0 - 4.2	0.5- 28.7	0.2- 8.8	4.3- 27.4	—	11.8	4.8	2.0 – 2.1
Unmarried & married women 2	0.3- 3.9	1.4 - 5.2	0.2-10.5	0.8- 14.0	1.4	—	—	—
Symptomatic women 3	—	—	—	16.8	—	—		
Pregnant women 4	0.3	4.3	1.2-11.0	10.0	—			
Facility-Based and Convenience Samples								
STD clinic patients5	1.3- 20.0	—	29.3-43.3	—	4.0-15.4	6.7-15.6	—	1.2
Wives of STD patients6	2.4	20.3	7:4	3.3	—	—	2.0-12.0	13.6

(Contd...)

1	*2*	*3*	*4*	*5*	*6*	*7*	*8*	*9*
Commercial Sex Workers 7	0.5- 19.1	4.6 –22.9	4.3-63.0	8.8-54.1	7.5-20.0	0.5	—	—
Gynecological OPD patients 8	—	0.2-31.3	4.4-17.0	0.4-26.0	0.3-25.0	0.6-42.4	—	2.6
Antenatal patients9	0.0 - 5.5	2.3	0.9-6.2	17.8	—	—	—	49.9
Gynecological patients with virginities complaints10	0.0-2.6	2.6-20.0	2.2	1.6-17.6	12.0	—	—	0.0
Gynecological patients with 'cervical erosion'11	—	3.0	—	—	—	—	—	—
Infertility and PID patients12	0.1-11.0	0.5-24.2	0.5	0.5	—	—	—	—
Women with obstetric complications13	—	18.8	—	—	—	—	—	—
Acceptors of tubule ligation 14	0.1-2.2	0.0-02	0.5-7.0	0.9	—	—	—	

Sources: Table 1: STI rates among women in India

1. Aggarwal et al., 1999; Bhatia et al., 1997; Chhabra et al., 1991; Garg et al., 2002; Parikh et al., n.d.; Prasad et al., 2000; Santhya, 1999

2. APAC, 1998a, Bang et al., 1989; Oomman, 1996; Thomas et al., 2002

3. Chopra et al., 1990; Kamat and Banker, 1993; Nandan et al., 2001; Singh, Joshi and Bajaj, 1990

4. DFID et al., 2001a; 2001b; 2001c; 2001d; 2001e; 2001f; Mayank, Bahl and Bhandari, 2001

5. Bhatnagar et al., 1991; Chaudhary et al., 1988; Chopra et al., 1990; Gangakhedkar et al., 1997; George et al., 1997; Kamat and Banker, 1993; Mali et al., 1991; Misra et al., 1992; Misra, Das and Chandrawati 2001

6. Divekar et al., 2000; Malathi et al., 2002; Parashari et al., 1994; Singh, Joshi and Bajaj, 1990; Sinha, 1994

7. Divekar et al., 2000; Desai et al., 2003; DFID et al, 2001a; 2001b; 2001c; 2001d; 2001e; 2001f; Gangakhedkar et al., 1997; Jana et al., 1998; Urmil et al., 1989

8. Bhatnagar et al., 1991; Chaudhuri and Iyengar, 1994; Dhall et al., 1990; Gogate et al., 1990; Jayarao et al., 1989; Joshi et al., 1994; Mali et al., 1991; Mishra, Singh and Sharma, 1988; Misra et al.,

1992; Misra, Das and Chandravati, 2001; Pal et al., 1993; Parashari et al., 1994; Sinha, 1994; Vajpayee et al., 2000

9. Gupta, Thergaonkar and Chawla, 1998; Hira, 1991; Kunte et al., 1999; Pal et al., 1993; Rowley and Berkley, 1998; Singh et al., 1992; Vajpayee, Seth and Malhotra., 2001

10. Aggarwal et al., 1999; Chhabra et al., 1993; Deb et al., 1989; Kar et al., 1988; Mania-Pramanik et al., 2001; Pandit et al., 1993

12. Bhujwala et al., 1988; Brabin et al., 1998; Chhabra and Fali, 1992; Kushtagi et al., 1991; Mania-Pramanik et al., 2001; Vishwanath et al., 2000

13. Mania-Pramanik et al., 2001

14. Brabin et al., 1998; Char and Vaidya

Table 2
Age at Marriage (Sexually Active) (N=59)

Age-Group	*Frequency*	*Percent*	*Cumulative Percent*
<18 – 21 years	39	66.1	66.1
21-23 years	16	27.1	93.2
23-25 years	3	5.1	98.3
25-27 years	1	1.7	100.0

Age at Marriage (Sexually Active)	*Test Value = 0*					
	t	*df*	*Sig. (2-tailed)*	*Mean Difference*	*95% Confidence Interval of the Difference*	
	16.207	58	.000	1.424	1.25	1.60

The average age of the marriage among the respondents was16.2 with an interval of difference of 1.25 to 1.60

Table 3
Total Number of Conceptions Attained by the Women during the Active Reproductive Span (N=59)

	Total Number of Conceptions (Completed at least First Trimester)	*Frequency*	*Percent*
1	2-4	4	6.8
2	4-6	35	59.3
3	6-8 and above	20	33.9

Data in Table 2 clearly shows that 59.3% of the women living in a slum of Delhi had 4 to 6 conceptions. About one-third (33.0%) were the women who had even 6-8 pregnancies. These figures show that how prone can be these women to anaemia, malnutrition and reproductive tract infections with frequent number of pregnancies.

Table 4
Mean of Age at Marriage, Conceptions, Live Births, Abortions Undergone by Women (N=59)

Age at Marriage (Sexually Active) Total	*Total No. of Conceptions*	*Total No. of Live Births*	*No. of Abortions (Induced and Spontaneous)*
Mean	3.27	2.68	.59
N	59	59	59
SD	.582	.706	.722

The Table 4 gives average number of total conceptions, live births and the abortions experienced by the women under study. These women were either working at home (preparing papads for the company) or as maidservants in nearby localities. In one way or the other they were earning money for the family in addition to daily household work. The FGD reflected the fact that bearing a child in her womb was not an easy task for them.

Table 5
Suffered from any Gynecological Problem (N=59)

	Gynecological Problem	*Frequency*	*Percent*
1	Yes	42	71.2
2	No	17	28.8

Reply to a question whether the women suffered from any gynecological problem at any point of time in life, 71.2% women reported 'yes'. Findings reveled from the FGDs also corroborate the quantitative data in regard to the said issue (Table 5).

Table 6
Type of Problems (N=59)

	Problems	*Frequency*	*Percent*
1	Genital tract infections	10	16.9
2	Vaginal discharge	2	3.4
3	Menstrual irregularity	15	25.4
4	Pregnancy complications	6	22.0
5	Prolapsed uterus**	4	6.8
6	Any other-fibroid/ surgery done /cancer etc.	13	10.2
7	RTI/ UTIs *	9	15.3

**- Pain in iliac fossa or lower abdomen with associated vaginal discharge and with or without fever.*

- *Vaginal discharge with associated itching or irritation, white or colored discharge with or with out foul odour.*
- *Recurrent disuria with fever, back pain, with or without high coloured urine.*

***A feeling of something coming out. Only symptoms suggestive of second or third degree prolapse were taken into consideration.*

Further, the women who reported suffering from gynecological problems were asked to state the nature of the problem. Findings revealed that maximum number of them suffered from menstrual irregularity (25.4%), followed by pregnancy related complications (22.0%), genital tract infections (16.9%), RTIs/UTIs (15.3%), prolapsed uterus (6.8%), vaginal discharge (3.4%) and other problems like fibroid/surgery done and/or cancer (Table 6).

From informal interviews with some of the women, it was revealed that white discharge for many women was a normal phenomenon and they do not feel like to report about the same during any quantitative study. Therefore, slum women are more prone to serious gynecological and related morbidities in near future.

Table 7
Treatment Taken for any Reported Reproductive Illness

	Treatment	*Frequency*	*Percent*
1	Self	37	62.7
2	Allopathic	11	18.6
3	Surgery	6	10.2
4	Homopathy/Ayurvedic	5	8.5

The above table shows that what kind of treatment they opted an average 1.5 to 3 years of attaining menopause phase) while women undergoing various physical and mental problems (Table 2). About 62.7% did self-medication, 18.6% visited nearby allopathic doctor/RMP in severe problems while 10.2% did undergo surgery. These are the women who are aware with the fact that in this transition also women need medical help. They had undergone the treatment from the nearby Govt. hospital 8.5% are the women who did other medication.

Table 8
Attitude of the Husband towards the Reproductive Problem

Attitude of Husband	*Frequency*	*Percent*
Very Cooperative	9	15.3
Cooperative	13	22.0
Neutral	9	15.3
Somewhat uncomfortable	15	25.4
Very uncomfortable	13	22.0

When asked about the attitude of the husbands regarding the illness of women, 15.3 and 22.0% of the women stated that their husbands were very cooperative and cooperative respectively. Rest of the women reported that husband was either neutral (15.3%), somewhat uncomfortable (25.4%) and/or very uncomfortable (22.0%).

Focus Group Discussion illustrates the process of identifying as to how social factors influence a woman's experience with self-reported gynecological morbidities. Gender, migration, and prevailing misconceptions about reproductive morbidity are discussed below in greater detail.

The detail FGDs were conducted in the same area with the four groups taken of 12 women in each group. The summary of the findings are as follows.

Sociogramme of One Focus Group Discussion

This sociogramme is a graphical representation of social links and line of communication that the women had during the discussion among themselves on the specific issue. On seeing it, one can easily comment upon the kind of interaction among the participants. Facilitator was a catalyst to carry out the discussion to gather the need-based information from the group through discussion. Stars were the number of participants and a facilitator. Two recorders were also there to write the verbatim and draw the sociogramme.

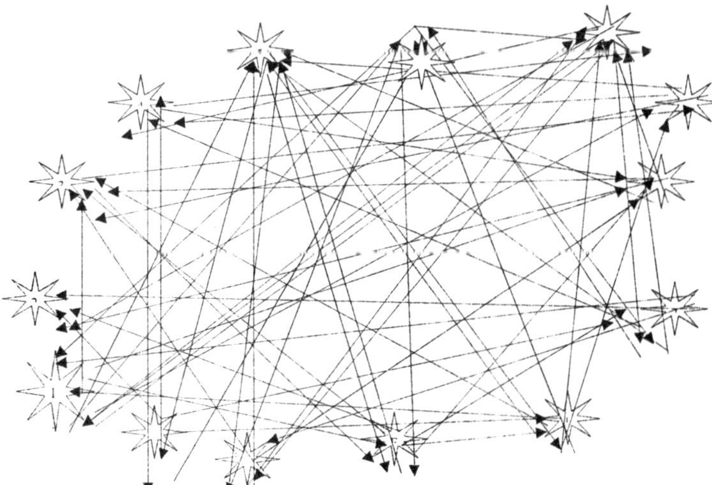

Gender refers to the different social identities, roles, and responsibilities of men and women in their society. Differences in behavior and the level of power between men and women could have an important impact on the risk of contracting RTIs and STIs.

The women discussed in detail about the possible reasons for getting reproductive infection. Almost all the women in two different FGDs and 59 in-depth interviews were unanimous about the following issues:

- Almost all said, women have little choice in, when, and with whom sexual activity occurs. They may be subjected to coercion and abuse, or unable to negotiate safer sexual practices. As a result, their physiological vulnerability to infections is higher. *'Aaj Kal Kucch pata nahin kya ho jae'.*
- Sixty five percent of the respondents said that differing standards of behavior may mean that while men can seek sexual experience outside of marriage, women were expected to remain monogamous. *'Admi kya karta hai kahan jata hai humko kya pata, aurat to kuch galat nahin karke bhi fasti hai'*. Thus, even if their own behaviour is not risky, women may be exposed to infections through their husband's behavior.
- *'Admi kam nahin karta teen bacche hain, main to ma hoon'* i.e., "If women do not have easy access to financial resources, they may be economically bound to risky partnerships or pressured to exchange sex for money or goods. Around 25.0% of the women supported the fact. This shows that this behaviour may increase their exposure to infection.
- Most of the respondents stated that physical consequences of infection, such as infertility, are punished more severely in women, such as through

loss of social status, abandonment or divorce. Women may also be blamed as carriers of sexually transmitted infections and suffer physical violence as a result.

Migration

The group also came out of the fact that mobility of populations, whether voluntary or forced, brings individuals and groups in contact with infections to which they may otherwise not have had exposure. The women being in Delhi were well aware of the mode of transmission of sexually transmitted diseases. The group came out with the following facts:

- Long term or cyclical labour migration that takes men or women away from their families often results in new infections returning with the workers to their families and home communities.
- Trade routes can bring mobile people into contact with one another and with each other's infections.
- Forced migration, such as in the cases of refugees, also brings populations with different disease prevalence together. Many refugee populations are composed of mainly of women and children. Sexual assault, unwanted pregnancies, and commercial sex are increasing, which can raise the risk of infections.

Misconceptions

It was found that RTIs, particularly those related to sexuality and sensitive issues receive les attention and women take it less seriously. There were a lots of myths attached with the issue. The major myths and misconceptions were as follows:

1. Women believed that endogenous infections are a normal part of the 'female experience' and not realized that they were carrying health risks for which treatment was available.

2. Endogenous infections were misinterpreted as sexually transmitted diseases, causing embarrassment, shame, and fear of seeking treatment.
3. Masturbation leads to weakness and going to sex-worker is a way out to avoid masturbation.
4. Spouses in general felt that having relations with many partners will lead to vitality.
5. Misconceptions relating to HIV/AIDS transmission were widespread.
6. Even where accurate information on HIV transmission is available, people refuse to acknowledge their behavior as risky and deny personal vulnerability.
7. Most of the husbands did not want to use condoms out of feeling that it might deprive maximum sexual pleasure.

Discussion

Risk Factors for RTI/STI Transmission: Reliable data on the factors (proximate as well as background) placing men and women at risk of acquiring infection and the constraints they face in accessing appropriate and timely care are limited.

Factors Related to Sexual Behaviour: Several factors related to sexual behaviour have led to a widespread and sustained epidemic of STIs, including HIV/AIDS in India. Sexual activity outside marriage is generally proscribed, but there has always been considerable laxity in favor of men. Several avenues, primarily commercial sex networks, are available for men seeking premarital and extramarital sexual relations. Cultural taboos on open discussion of sexual matters have constrained avenues for acquiring knowledge about safe sexual practices and the means for practicing safe sex.

Sex Workers: Several factors including high rates of partner change, early initiation into commercial sex, exposure to multiple STIs, non-use or limited use of condoms, and non-treatment or delayed or faulty treatment of STIs make sex workers a core group for the transmission of STIs, including HIV.

A substantial proportion of female sex workers are young—one in three is below 25 years of age and almost one in ten is adolescents. The vast majority are ever married, but often not currently living with their husbands. High partner change (three to five clients a day) characterizes the sexual practices of sex workers. Studies show that men, particularly young men, often go to sex workers in groups and in such situations, the average number of penetrative episodes per sex worker may be even higher .Given these high-risk practices, it is not surprising that the prevalence of STIs among sex workers is estimated to be high, ranging from 36.0% to 81.0%. Studies show that HIV prevalence rates are also high; for example, 24.0% in Goa and 55.0% in Mumbai.

Clients of Sex Workers: The respondents feel that male clients of sex workers constitute a critical bridge population in spreading the infection from the core group to the general population. A substantial proportion of clients are below 25 years (two in five), ever married (more than one in two), and currently married and living with their spouse (two in five) (NACO, 2001). By age 21, three-fourths had had their first sexual experience, with 7.0% reporting sexual experience before 16 years. One in three reported sexual initiation with a sex worker. On an average, these men reported having sexual contact with 3.9 sex workers and 1.5 nonregular partners in the three months prior to the survey. These sexual contacts, particularly those with non-regular partners, are often unprotected. Mobile population groups such as truck crews are recognized as playing a major role in transmission. A behavioural surveillance indicates that one-third of truck drivers and nearly one-half of helpers reported contact with sex workers in the year prior to the survey. Small scale studies report over 80.0% of truckers visit sex workers regularly (two-seven times a week) and a substantial proportion engage in homosexual activities. As may be expected, the prevalence of STIs among truckers is high, ranging from two-fifths to almost three-fourths.

Even though acknowledged as a potential bridge population, there has been little research on the social context or sexual behaviour of migrant groups in India (Available evidence, however, reveals a serious lack of understanding of STI/HIV prevention and transmission, and high-risk practices including sexual contact with sex workers. More than one in ten clients of sex workers, for example, stays away from their regular residence. These men run a high risk of spreading the infection to their sexual partners.

Low-risk Population

The study through the FGDs reflects the fact that extramarital relationships due to one or the other reason exist in the community. The reported Premarital or Extramarital relationships are very less in the community. Though premarital chastity and marital fidelity are still valued, a number of small-scale studies have observed comparatively high (at least, higher than culturally perceived) levels of premarital and extramarital sexual activity in the general population. A review of studies among young people reveals that fewer than 10.0% of young women and 15.0% - 30.0% of young men report premarital sexual experiences .Sexual relations among young people tend to be characterized by early debut (particularly among women in the context of marriage), multiple partner and casual sexual relations, and visits to sex workers (particularly among young men), and lack of condom use. Not surprisingly, between 7.0% and 22.0% of male patients (the majority of whom were unmarried) and between 12.0% and 44.0% of female patients (the majority of whom were married) attending STD clinics were reported to be adolescents. The extent of reported extramarital sexual activity (i.e., non-spousal sex reported by married people) is relatively low - 2.0% – 6.0% among women and 4.0% - 12.0% among men, although studies of STD clinic patients suggests that extramarital sexual activity may be higher in this group

Limited Use of Condoms

About 76.0% of the respondents said their spouse's don't want to use condom. In 45.0% cases (as reported by the respondents in FGDs) use of condom become the reason of coercion and violence within the couple. Nationally, only 3.1% of married couples were currently using condoms as a method of family planning in 1998-99. Consistent use of condoms in non-marital sexual liaisons was also negligible among both high- and low-risk groups. Studies on premarital sexual behaviour among school- and college-age boys in India show that the vast majorities are engaged in unprotected sex, even with commercial sex workers. In a study among sexually active unmarried and married men and women, but predominantly young, middle class, unmarried men in Mumbai, only 27.0% reported always using condoms. Unmarried men and women are more likely to use condoms than their married counterparts. Studies also show that condom use 80 among young people is primarily motivated by the desire to prevent pregnancy rather than to prevent both STIs and pregnancy. For example, in a study among unmarried and married men in Orissa, 19.0% of sexually active unmarried men reported condom use during the last sexual act, and among those who reported condom use, 61.0% reported pregnancy prevention as the main reason for use.

Studies among adults also show that 50.0% – 88.0% of men who reported a non-marital sexual experience never used condoms during such encounters and a small proportion (4.0% – 13.0%) reported that they always used condoms during non-marital sexual liaisons. Consistent condom use among perceived or known high-risk groups was also low. For example, a behavioural surveillance survey of sex workers indicates that only half reported consistent condom use with paying clients in the one month prior to the survey. The vast majority (80.0%) of sex workers did not use condoms consistently with non-paying clients.

Endogenous and Iatrogenic Factors

White discharge or irritation/ itching in vital parts are common and normal for 43.0% of the respondents. The general perception of the women is that it is a normal symptom related to sex. The women as are from low economic group have poor personnel hygiene. Studies documenting the role of endogenous and iatrogenic factors in causing RTIs are few in India. Evidence from these studies, though not definitely conclusive, indicates an association between the role of poor genital/personal hygiene and symptoms of RTIs.

Among iatrogenic causes of infections, the use of IUDs has been reported to be a significant risk factor for pelvic inflammatory diseases in some facility-based studies. Sterilized women are more likely to report experiencing lower or upper RTIs compared to non-users or users of reversible contraceptive methods. Studies also report that women, who have undergone other invasive surgical procedures, including dilation and curettage, are more likely to experience pelvic inflammatory disease

Perceptions/misperceptions often rooted in cultural and ethno-medical beliefs may also place men and women at risk of engaging in high-risk behaviors or not adopting protective behaviors. Explorations of young men's sexual anxieties and health problems in Gujarat indicate that most perceive semen loss through masturbation and nocturnal emissions as dangerous, leading to weakness and impotence. Some young men feel that they must seek out sexual partners, including sex workers, to avoid the debilitating effects of semen loss.

Gender Inequalities and Norms

Gender inequalities and women's relative lack of autonomy in matters relating to their lives influence their risk of acquiring infections in several ways; Women under study were uneducated, having low economic strata, supporting family income by doing various works at home or outside. The FGD discovered that these women were not at all empowered to take decisions related to their reproductive Health. The elderly in the family decide over whether or not to have a child; when to go for it ; use of contraception; immunization of the child and use of family income .There is no or very less interspousal communication among the couple. '*Admi bat kya karega, usko to apne kam se matlab hay*'. Women believe that whatever spouses ask them to do they are supposed to do.

Women who are socially, culturally and economically dependent and subordinate to their sexual partners may find it difficult to make decisions on whether or not to have sex, or to negotiate and convince partners to have safe sex within and outside of marriage. A community-based study reports that two-thirds of symptomatic women who requested their husbands not to have sex were either verbally abused or physically abused. Sex workers were also constrained from exercising their sexual and reproductive rights.

Lack of intimacy or partner communication which makes talking about sex, pregnancy and safe practices extremely difficult may also make sexual partners particularly female partners vulnerable to infections .Several studies show that women and men often do not inform their spouses about their gynaecological symptoms A study among married women and men in rural Tamil Nadu reported that slightly more than one-third (37.3%) of women with symptoms of possible RTIs and one-fifth (19.9%) of symptomatic men informed their spouses about their illness experience. Prevailing norms of masculinity and femininity may reinforce risk behaviours. Dominant ideologies of masculinity may prevent boys and men from seeking information on sex for fear of appearing ignorant and therefore unmanly, and at the same time, may condone gaining sexual experience through liaisons with girlfriends and sex workers. In contrast, dominant ideologies of femininity may silence the voices of women, who could be fearful that their reputation is at stake if they appear too knowledgeable about sexual matters or play an active role in sexual relationships.

Treatment Seeking Behaviour

There are wide variations in patterns of treatment seeking for RTIs/STIs. However, a common observation is that a significant proportion of symptomatic do not seek treatment. Majority of women don't take any treatment for the reproductive problems. *'Admi ka kya hay bataินge to hum per hi shak karega'*. Theses women feel insecure in telling to their husbands about their reproductive problems. It came out of the discussion that they hide their problems and indulge themselves in vulnerable conditions.

Studies report that between one-third and two-third of women suffering from symptoms suggestive of RTIs/STIs do not seek treatment .When care is sought, it tends to be after some delay Women often seek medical intervention only when they find they are too weak to work or experience problems in their sexual relationships. Even when treatment is sought, women tend to follow a sequence of options, ranging from self-treatment or home remedies to visiting traditional healers, unqualified practitioners or qualified allopathic providers; Non-compliance with the recommended treatment regimen is not uncommon. Adolescent girls tend to be even more reluctant to seek treatment for symptoms suggestive of RTIs/ STIs.

Access to Services

Access to RTI/STI services is grossly inadequate, particularly in urban slum areas. With the shift in the reproductive health paradigm, there have been efforts to integrate services for the treatment of RTIs/STIs at all levels of health care, including at the primary health care level. However, primary health care facilities are currently inadequately equipped to offer effective diagnosis and treatment for RTIs/STIs. For example, a recent survey of health facilities across the country reports that RTI/ STI services are provided by only one-sixth of primary health centers as most lack trained staff and facilities. Only 46.0% of these centers have a laboratory and in several states, less than one-fifth have a laboratory. The survey also indicates that there is a mismatch between the availability of laboratory facilities and laboratory technicians—for example, in Maharashtra, while 97.0% of the primary health centers have laboratories, only 24.0% have a laboratory technician on the staff. In West Bengal, in contrast, while only 4.0% of primary health centers have a laboratory, 20.0% have a laboratory technician.

Additionally, only 25.0% of primary health centers have at least one medical officer trained in RTI/STI treatment. Moreover, most primary health centers (82.0%) do not have a female medical officer, which may severely constrain women's ability to access RTI/STI services, even if made available at the primary health center level. Facilities for the diagnosis and treatment of RTIs/STIs are far from adequate even at the level of community health Centers. Districts hospitals are expected to function as first referral units for further treatment in community centers.

Conclusion

The reproductive and sexual rights are laid in our RCH

programme as discussed in the review and introduction. The present qualitative with quantitative data clearly shows the analytical situation of the urban slum.

The women even supporting family income cannot adhere to Reproductive decision-making including determination of the number, timing and spacing of one's children; and the right to have access to the information and means needed to exercise voluntary choice; they do not have the resources to make free and informed choices in all spheres of their life, free from discrimination based on gender; neither do they possess the sexual and reproductive security including freedom from sexual violence and coercion, or the right to privacy. Bounded within these circumstances their vulnerable conditions lead to various kinds of reproductive health problems.

The reproductive morbidities have implications that extend beyond their effects on health. Numerous social factors play a role in determining the risks, reactions, and prevalence patterns in any population. These social issues differ between socio-cultural environments and therefore need to be identified and taken into account if education, prevention, and treatment programs are to achieve sustainable success.

REFERENCES

Arber, Sara, and Ginn, Jay (1991). *Gender and Later Life*. London: Sage.

Aggarwal, A.K., Kumar, R., Gupta, V. et al., (1999). Community-based Study of Reproductive Tract Infections among Ever Married Women of Reproductive Age in a Rural Area of Haryana, India. *Journal of Communicable Diseases*, 31(4): 223-28.

Bagchi, Kalyan (1997). Introductory Address. In the Plight of Elderly Females in India. Report of the National Seminar on the Need for Focusing Attention on the Plight of Elderly Females, December 20-22, 1996, New Delhi: Society for Gerontological Research, 4-6.

Barai, Daksha C. (1996). Integrated Health Care and Allied Services for the Elderly: Some Perspective. In Vinod Kumar (ed.). *Ageing: Indian Perspective and Global Scenario*. New Delhi: AIIMS, 102-104.

Bali, Arun P. (1999). *Ageing and Social Care: Trends and Policies*. In Ramachandran, C.R. and Shah, Bela (ed.), *Public Health Implications of Ageing in India*. New Delhi: ICMR, 195-204.

Bhatia, J.C., Cleland, J., Bhagavan, L., et al., (1997). Levels and Determinants of Gynaecological Morbidity in a District of South India. *Studies in Family Planning*, 28(2): 95-103.

Garg, S., Sharma, N., Bhalla, P. et al., (2002). Reproductive Morbidity in an Indian Urban Slum: Need For Health Action. *Sexually Transmitted Infections*, 78(1): 68-69.

Hawkes, S. and Santhya, K.G. (2001). Diverse Realities: Understanding Sexually Transmitted Infections and HIV in India. *Population Council Working Paper No. 15*. New Delhi.

Report of National AIDS Control Organisation (NACO), 1998; 2001.

Nandan, D., Gupta, Y.P., Krishnan V., et al., (2001). Reproductive Tract Infection in Women of Reproductive Age Group in Sitapur/Shahjahanpur District of Uttar Pradesh. *Indian Journal of Public Health*, 45(1): 8-13.

Rao, Venkoba A. (2002). The Frail Elderlies – Coping with their Needs. In Vinod Kumar (ed), *Aging: Indian Perspective and Global Scenario*, New Delhi: AIIMS, pp. 45-46.

Oomman, N. (1996). Poverty and Pathology: Comparing Rural Rajasthani Women's Ethnomedical Models with Biomedical Models of Reproductive Morbidity: Implications for Women's Health in India. Ph.D. Thesis, Johns Hopkins University, Baltimor.

II. Adolescent Health

5

Unmarried Adolescent Pregnancy

Prof. A. Sheelamoni & Prof. M.K.C. Nair

Summary

Unmarried adolescent pregnancy still remains a medical and social problem in many developed as well as developing countries. In India, as abortion among unmarried women is a highly sensitive issue, no data/ information are available exclusively on adolescent unmarried pregnancy and their risk factors. A summary report shows that 20.0% of the women seeking abortion in India are unmarried teenagers. The changing social environment, increasing nuclear families, more opportunities of social interactions amongst adolescents, less supervision, family problems, permissive attitude of the society, influence of media and changing moral norms have resulted in an increase in sexual activity amongst youngsters and a rising incidence of pregnancies among adolescents and young adults. Unmarried girls usually report much later when compared to married women, and the majority resort to illegal abortion, which may lead to complications like septic abortion that not only endanger their life, but also may lead to future fertility problems.

Introduction

Adolescents and young adults constitute an extremely important group that can shape the future of the world. Of the six billion-world population, more than one-fourth, i.e. 1.7 billion, are young people between the age of 10 to 24, and 86.0% of them live in the developing countries (Source: Population Reference Bureau, 2000). India, the second most populated country of the world, with a population of more than a billion, adolescents (10 – 19 years) and young adults (10 – 24 years) represent around 30.0% of the population. (NFHS, 1998).

Adolescents: A Neglected Group

In India, even though adolescents form one-fourth of the population they have been recognized as an underserved section, perhaps because as a group they are relatively disease free. Though this situation has been changing over the past two decades, young people still seem to be remaining a marginalized social group, both in terms of their access to health care and their relative neglect by policy makers (Mann and Tarantola, 1996). Only in last three to four years, there has been a growing concern for this age group, especially after International Conference on Population and Development at Cairo, and the Government of India's recent approach to implement Reproductive and Child Health (RCH) Programme under National Rural Health Mission (NRHM).

Concerns about Unmarried Adolescents in India

- Adolescents become sexually mature approximately 4 to 5 years before they reach emotional maturity (Tomar, 1998).
- As a stage of transition from childhood to adulthood, adolescence is a time of self-discovery and considerable risk-taking, and is susceptible and vulnerable to external influences. The socio-cultural environment has

an impact on their health, development, security and dignity. At this stage, media and peers exert a powerful influence (Elder, 1992).

- During adolescence, individuals develop sexual interests and may begin to establish intimate relationships.
- Decline in family values, earlier puberty and later marriage extend the risks of unprotected sex among unmarried adolescents.
- Since the subject of adolescent sexuality remains taboo in most societies, education about responsible sexual behaviour and specific and clear information about the consequences of sexual intercourse (including pregnancy and sexually transmitted diseases) are frequently not offered in the home, at school, or in other community settings. Therefore, much of the 'sex education' that adolescents receive is from media and misinformed peers.
- Myths/misconceptions concerning sexual matters are prevailing among the majority of adolescents.
- Taboos on open discussion of sexual matters have constrained the avenues for acquiring knowledge about safe sexual practices and the means for practicing safe sex.
- A large proportion of adolescents in many parts of the world, therefore, are engaging in premarital sexual activity with little use of contraception, without realizing the consequences of unprotected intimacy, until it is too late (Tomar, 1998).
- As a result, they may be susceptible to unwanted pregnancies, unsafe abortions, sexually transmitted infections and HIV/AIDS.

Consequences of Early Sexual Activity

Although sexual development is an integral part of adolescence, early sexual activity can have a number of negative consequences. Data available globally suggests that unprotected sexual activity in adolescence increases the risks of too-early and/or unwanted pregnancy, health complications from pregnancy and child birth, unsafe abortions, cervical cancer, social rejection and STIs including HIV/AIDS, with long-term physical and social consequences (Population Studies, 1989; Singh and Wulf, 1990). According to estimates, one in 20 adolescents contract sexually transmitted infections every year and half of all new cases of HIV/AIDS occur among 15–24 year-olds (Joint UN Programmes on HIV/AIDS, 2001)

Magnitude of the Problem of Unmarried Adolescent Pregnancy

Most reports on adolescent pregnancy refer to women aged 15 – 19 years. Nevertheless, many girls reach puberty at a younger age and therefore, are susceptible to become pregnant earlier. The earliest age of pregnancy had been reported in girls aged 8–10 years. Adolescent pregnancy may occur in married or unmarried teenagers (13–19 years) and can be intended or unintended. Globally, most adolescent pregnancies occur within marriage, but the problem in unmarried teenagers should not be ignored (UNICEF, 2001). Unmarried adolescents may conceive accidentally as a consequence of sexual abuse, unsafe sexual activity; they may see also motherhood as a way to achieve adult status or as a strategy to get sexual partner to care for or marry them.

Incidence of Unmarried Adolescent Pregnancy: Global Scenario

Data on the numbers of adolescent abortions are scarce, but estimates for those in developing countries range from 1 to 4.4 million (McCauley, 1995). Though official statistics on unmarried adolescent pregnancy is not available, the situation is common and its incidence may well be showing an upward trend, because of modernization and globalization. The proportion of teen births to unwed mothers seems to be rising at least in some countries. For instance, teen births to unwed mothers have risen by almost 70.0% in Kenya during the 1980s and by 50.0% in the US since 1980. Teenagers make up a quarter of all mothers in Transkei, South Africa, and well over 75.0% of them are unmarried. Such a high rate of teenage pregnancy is indicative of a high level of unprotected adolescent sexual activity. A hospital-based cross-sectional study of adolescent post-abortion patients, in Blantyre, Malawi, showed that unmarried adolescents comprised 9.0% of the patients and out of these students constituted 38.6%. (Archibong, 1991).

Adolescent sexual behaviour and reproductive health risks in Cameroon were investigated using data from the 1996 Adolescent Reproductive Health Survey. It was observed that 9.0% of the females aged 15-17 years and 20.0% of the females aged 18–22 years had had an abortion (Meekers and Calves, 1999). A study in a rural area of southeast Nigeria on reproductive tract infections and sexual health among 458 unmarried teenagers 12-19 year old revealed that at least 24.0% had undergone an induced abortion. (Brabin et al., 1995).

Incidence of Adolescent Abortion: Indian Scenario

In India, after the liberalization of Medical Termination of Pregnancy (MTP) Act in 1972, adolescent abortions have shown a steady increase (MTP Act, 1971). Being a highly sensitive topic, there is no clear data available regarding prevalence of pregnancy among the teenagers in our country. The trivial proportions of abortions reported in surveys clearly indicate a large extent of under-reporting with respect to induced abortions. Illegal abortions to terminate pregnancies resulting from pre-marital sexual relationship may be carried out in the private sector and hence never come on record. India's actual abortion rate may probably be about two to five times the reported rate of 3 abortions per 1000 women. (Barreto et al., 1992).

Studies Exclusively on Unmarried Adolescent Pregnancy in India

In India, as abortion among unmarried women is a highly sensitive issue, no official surveys or studies are available exclusively on unmarried adolescent pregnancy. The few descriptive studies available on adolescent pregnancy include few unmarried pregnancies also. The majority of these studies have been hospital-based rather than community-based and have been conducted among the urban rather than rural young women. The available literature in India reflects a teenage pregnancy rate between 8.0 - 14.0% among the females of 15-19 years age. There are hospital-based studies on abortion, which suggest that adolescents constitute a significant proportion of abortion seekers, as high as one in every three, and the typical adolescent abortion seeker is unmarried (Chhabra et al., 1988). For instance, a study in rural Maharashtra, India, indicates that while spacing and sex selection were the main reasons for married adolescents to seek abortion, pregnancies resulting from non-consensual sex mainly accounted for abortions among the never-married (MacArthur Foundation India Programme, 2003-2007).

A summary report shows that 20.0% of the women seeking abortion in India are unmarried teenagers (MacArthur Foundation India Programme, 2003-2007). A report from Delhi indicates that at least 8.0% of the 3,700 abortions conducted by a chain of abortion clinics during a four-month period earlier in the year 2003 were on adolescents (Chhabra, 2003). It is reported that almost 10.0% to 15.0% of the cases of medical termination of pregnancy

(MTP) in public hospitals in Mumbai involve young, unmarried girls. A cross-sectional study in Chandigarh among adolescent girls (10-19 years) seeking abortion services showed that out of the total of 83 adolescent girls, 75 were unmarried; moreover, contraceptive awareness among the girls was low (Trikha, 2001).

Factors Enhancing the Risk of Pregnancy among Unmarried Adolescent Girls

Unmarried adolescent pregnancy is a negative outcome of unprotected sexual activity. Various factors have been pointed out by different authors as contributing to increased sexual activity and unwanted pregnancy. For example,

(i) **Changing Social Context:** The impact of the changing social context in shaping the sexual behavior of young people has been pointed out by studies in India as well as those in other countries (Speizer et al., 2001). The impact of the traditional value system that used to influence the sex-related behavior of individuals is waning because of certain new trends in social development, such as urbanization with its widespread impact on human life, migration to slums in the cities and the changing lifestyles.

(ii) **Low Educational Level**: Various studies showed association between low educational level and unmarried adolescent pregnancy (Lammers et al., 2000).

(iii) **Lack of Productive Engagement:** The close relation between scarcity of employment and adolescent pregnancy has been mentioned in a few studies.

(iv) **Rising Age at Marriage Coupled with Declining Age at Menarche:** Since the average

age at marriage is increasing and the age of menarche is declining, the young people have a longer interval between their sexual maturity and marriage. This situation has increased the possibility of them being engaged in premarital sexual relationships (Kanjilal, 1999).

(v) **Lack of Parental Supervision and Control:** Parental level of attachment with the adolescent girls and supervision of their behaviour are important factors for protecting adolescents from unsafe sexual relations.

(vi) **Poor Intra-family Relationship:** When teens live with both parents in a stable family environment and have close relationships with them, they are less likely to engage in unprotected sex and become pregnant (Thomas, 1999).

(vii) **Problem Family:** Children hailing from problem family were found to be more prone for adolescent sexual activity.

(viii) **Peer Group Influence:** Friends play a crucial role in shaping the characters of young people. Peer influence is often cited as predictor of early sexual activity. There is evidence that young people are affected by the sexual attitudes and behaviours of their friends (Monika, 2000).

(ix) **Effect of Media**: Mass media can have a profound impact on young people. While on one hand, these channels of communication offer great opportunities, on the other hand, much of what is currently conveyed may put young people at odds with the value systems of their own family and culture.

(x) **Lack of Sexual and Reproductive Health Knowledge:** Data from various studies revealed lack of proper knowledge regarding safe sexual behaviour, pregnancy, and STDs/HIV, as risk factors for adolescent pregnancy (MHFW, GOI, Country Paper, 1998).

(xi) **Child Sexual Abuse:** Sexual abuse in childhood can lead to high-risk behaviour later in life including early onset of consensual sexual activity and unwanted pregnancy.

(xii) **Victim of Rape or Incest:** Adolescent pregnancy can also result from rape or incest. A study reports that in India there is an alarming increase in the number of rape cases. In India, the incidence of reported adolescent rape cases (10–16 years) increased by 26.0% between 1991 and 1995(SACA, UNFPA CST for CASA, 1999). It is reported that 20.0% of the pregnancies of adolescent abortion seekers in Mumbai were due to rape and incest.

Although data are sparse, there is evidence that a disturbingly large number of adolescent girls are subjected to rape or forced prostitution. It has been estimated that 25.0% of rape victims are young adolescents less than 16 years of age and 20.0% of all sex workers are adolescents (MacArthur Foundation India Programme, 2003-2007). Due to societal pressures of stigma and bad name to family, these cases are generally not reported, specially the cases of incest.

Consequences of Unmarried Adolescent Pregnancy

Of widespread concern are the problems related to pregnancies occurring outside a socially sanctioned union - which include reduced educational opportunities for young women, unsafe abortions, high-risk deliveries, poor economic outcomes and compromised social status. Early pregnancy contributing to long-term poor social, economic, and health outcomes for the mother and child have been noted by a number of researchers. (Westall, 2003).

(i) **Unsafe Abortions:** As pregnancy before marriage is considered immoral and highly condemned, unmarried girls go for termination (abortion) even at the cost of their lives (Bennett, 2001). Due to social stigmatization, they often have to depend on unskilled practitioners for termination of pregnancy and hence most often end up in unsafe abortion and not reporting to higher centers even after complications have developed. Unsafe abortion has been defined as the termination of a pregnancy either by persons lacking the necessary skills or in an environment lacking the minimal medical standards, or both. (Olukoya et al., 1996).

Incidence: In many developing countries induced abortions tend to be unsafe. It has been estimated that 2 million unsafe abortions are performed in the developing countries alone (Population Reference Bureau, 1997). Young women aged between 15 and 19 years account for at least one fourth of the estimated 20 million unsafe abortions performed each year, resulting in some 78,000 deaths (CHARCA, 2002). Data on abortions occurring outside the legal framework is rare and unreliable. The estimates for non-legal/unsafe abortions are largely speculative and range from 2 – 5 to 10 – 11 illegal abortions for every legal abortion. (Chhabra and Nuna, 1994).

(ii) **The Health Risks of Unsafe Abortion:** *The health risks of unsafe abortion include sepsis (infection) caused by unsanitary instruments, incomplete abortion, hemorrhage, injuries to genital organs (such as cervical laceration and uterine perforation, vesico-vaginal fistula) and toxic reactions to chemicals or drugs used to induce abortion (Elder, **1992**). Unsafe abortions put many women at grave risk of lifelong disability, infertility or death (Sing et al., 1997).*

(iii) **Maternal Mortality Due to Unsafe Abortion**: Research on induced abortions shows evidence indicating that induced abortions have been a major cause for maternal deaths in the developing world, with abortion-related complications accounting for nearly half of all maternal deaths (Dixon-Muller, 1993). High levels of maternal mortality and other complications from induced abortions have been brought out by studies from different settings (Gogna et al., 2002; Van den Broek, 1998). Though official statistics are not available, these situations are common, and their incidence may well be in an upward trend. In India, even when the abortion laws are less restrictive, procuring an abortion seems to be difficult for any woman and even more difficult for an unmarried adolescent. Both socio-cultural and financial factors were perceived to be encouraging the practice of unsafe abortions. The major socio-cultural factor in question is the stigma attached to unwed pregnancy and abortion, considering it as highly immoral (Khan et al., 1996). As a result, many women remain vulnerable and end up risking their lives by going to untrained local practitioners (Ganatra, 2002). Inadequate and untimely access to good quality health services and reproductive healthcare are a major factor affecting maternal mortality (MacArthur Foundation India, 2003).

(iv) **Pregnancy in Unmarried Adolescents and Adult Women: Different Situations**

- Adolescents have less access to the information about available health services and safe modes of abortion.
- They are unlikely to get support from parents, partners and society.

- Adolescents and their parents may not recognize pregnancy at the earlier stage.
- Fear of stigmatization, discrimination, financial constraints and negative attitude of care providers prevent them from visiting the qualified caregivers.

That is why they go for alternative modes of abortions, leading to incomplete, unsafe abortion and complications.

(v) **Delayed Health Seeking Behaviour:** It has also been noted that adolescents are considerably more likely than older women to delay seeking abortion services and hence undergo second trimester abortion, which carry a higher risk of complications (Johnston and Hill, 1996). Various hospital-based studies reveal that the risk of abortion-related complications is 12 times higher for second trimester abortions than for first trimester ones (ICMR Task Force Study, 1989). The reasons for this delay were lack of awareness of pregnancy, ignorance of services, fear of social stigmatization, absence of family support and cost considerations.

Health Risks of Continuing the Pregnancy

(i) **Too Early Pregnancy and Child Bearing:** Young people, who become pregnant, face serious health risks, as they may not be physically mature to handle the stress of pregnancy and childbirth. Women aged between 15 -19 years are three times more likely to die from complications of pregnancy than women aged between 20-24 years, especially if they are unmarried and thus less likely to receive prenatal care (Creastsas, 2002). Creatsas has pointed out the prevalence of anaemia among adolescent mothers even in the developed countries like

England. Pregnancy-related complications are among the main causes of death of 15-19 years old women worldwide (World Development Report, 1993). Infants born to adolescent mothers are more likely to be born before term and have low birth weight. They have than normal infants have 24.0% higher risk of dying in the first month of life and this risk continues during early childhood (WHO Report, 1995).

Social Problems

Women who experience unplanned premarital pregnancy face personal and familial shame, compromised marriage prospects, abandonment by their partners, single motherhood/ undesired motherhood, a stigmatized child, early cessation of education and an interrupted income or career. Furthermore, children born to single women often are neglected or abandoned (WHO and UNICEF Report, 1995; Gorgen et al., 1993). Abortions, forced marriages, adoptions and emotional problems that can lead to depression and suicide are also common. Young unmarried mothers in some countries seem to have been forced to turn to prostitution to support themselves and their children.

Social Problems for the Mother

- Personal and familial shame
- Compromised marriage prospects
- Abandonment by their partners
- Single motherhood/undesired motherhood
- Early cessation of education, interrupted income or career
- Spread of STIs-HIV/AIDS
- Abortions

- Forced marriages
- Depression
- Suicide
- Prostitution

Social Problems for the Baby

- Neglected/abandoned child
- Low birth weight
- Neonatal, infant and early childhood death
- Malnutrition
- More likely to have developmental delays
- Adoptions
- Child abuse
- Involvement in anti-social activities
- Ill-treatment by the society

Pregnancy Prevention Programmes

Although we may believe that the best way to guarantee a reduction in unmarried adolescent pregnancy would be to achieve a reduction in premarital sexual activity, in reality, prevention of teenage pregnancy requires a multi-pronged approach. We should be addressing education of adolescents both in and out of schools, counselling of parents, comprehensive sex education – more appropriately called family life education, creating opportunity for employment, improving physical and mental health of adolescents, along with change in cultural behaviour of the society.

Many kinds of adolescent pregnancy prevention programmes have been implemented in India in recent years. Experience has proven that sex education programmes are poorly researched, hastily implemented and annoyingly short-lived, contributing to confusion rather than clarity. The 'Adolescent Education Programme' being implemented at the National level by the NCERT and proposed by the UNICEF was withdrawn following criticism, that the module followed an approach that was against our culture and had explicit contents and expressions, which could make it difficult for teachers to explain it in the class and parents to clarify it at home. On the other hand, Child Development Center, Kerala had a very positive experience of conducting family life and life skill education among 11,000 adolescents in 102 higher secondary schools and nearly 15,000 out-of-school adolescents. The difference was made by the fact that a team of male and female teachers representing all the schools scrutinized the module prepared by an expert committee and the parents' teachers' association's representatives again approved the same.

Various WHO studies have shown that sex education does not increase sexual activity and can, in fact, lead to postponement of sexual initiation and protective behaviour once sexual activity begins. Carefully constructed education programmes that address the needs of young people, gain their trust and correct their misconceptions and fears and would be more successful than the present state of silence. Research evidence has also shown that the dual message encouraging adolescents to delay intercourse, but to use contraception if at all they have to have sex, is more effective than approaches that focus solely on abstinence or solely on contraception.

Out-of-School Adolescent Girls

Out-of-school adolescent girls constitute a sizeable proportion of the female population and it is extremely difficult to reach them. They are particularly vulnerable and neglected, by government programmes that are solely focused on reproductive health of married women. As a result, general knowledge among out-of-school adolescents on the most basic aspects of sexuality and reproductive health is limited and is often shaped by inaccurate information from peers and the media. Family life education classes could be given at the Anganwadi for out-of-schoolgirls.

Adolescent Health Education and Life Skill Training Programme

As our society today is not ready to accept sex education in schools, more acceptable names like Family Life Education (FLE) or Adolescent Education Programme (AEP) can be used instead of calling it sex education.

Family Life Education

- Family Life Education for young unmarried population (in and out of schools) be strengthened and adolescents' clinics should provide more information about the benefits of abstinence, delayed sexual activity relevance of contraception if and when they have sex, emergency contraception and consistent safe sex practices.
- Training by medical professionals for teachers, anganwadi workers and NGOs to impart family life education.
- Bring outside faculty to give sexual and reproductive health education, as their own teachers may not be acceptable for children.
- Teen clubs and adolescent clinics for in and out-of-school adolescents.
- Adolescent care, counselling, empowerment and support services (ACCESS) units at Taluk hospitals and major private hospitals
- Peer educators for designing and periodical evaluation of the functioning of adolescent clinics

- Family counselling centres to be attached to PHCs and district hospitals
  - For counselling parents with marital disharmony and improve intra-family relationship
  - Counsel parents to give children correct information on sexual issues so as to prevent rape and sexual exploitation.
  - Advice regarding proper parental supervision and control.
- Empowerment and self-employment for out-of-school adolescents.
- Mass media campaign against rape and other sexual abuse.

Role of Health Systems

Health system, social system and the legal system should be more gender-friendly towards adolescent girl's issues, and they should give a supportive and non-judgmental environment to them, so that girls would fearlessly approach authorities for solving their problems.

Recommendations

With half the population in the developing countries comprising of individuals below the age of 24 years, the problem of teenage pregnancy looms large and therefore urgent efforts are necessary to tackle the situation through a holistic approach. Adolescent sexual and reproductive health clinic with supportive counselling services may be started at the Taluk hospitals under the National Rural Health Mission (NRHM).

REFERENCES

Adolescent Reproductive Behaviour: Evidence from Developing Countries (1989). *Population Studies*, New York, UN, 2: 109/ (Add.1.).

Adolescent Health and Development: The Key to the Future, Paper Prepared for the Local Commission on Women's Health, World Health Organisation 1995(G). WHO, 1995b.

Archibong, E.I. (1991). Illegal Induced Abortion—A Continuing Problem in Nigeria. *International Journal of Gynaecology and Obstetrics*, 34: 261–265.

A Picture of Health: A Review and Annotated Bibliography of the Health of Young People in Developing Countries, WHO and UNICEF, Geneva, 1995.

Barreto, T., Campbell, O.M.R., Davies, J.L., Fauveau, V., Filippi, V.G.A., Graham, W.J., Mamdani, M., Rooney, C.I.F., and Toubia, N.F. (1992). Investigating Induced Abortion in Developing Countries: Methods and Problems. *Studies in Family Planning* 1992; 23, 159-170.

Bennett, L.R. (2001). Single Women's Experiences of Premarital Pregnancy and Induced Abortion in Lombok, Eastern Indonesia. *Reproductive Health Matters*, 9,37-43.

Brabin, L., Kemp, J., Obunge, O.K. et al., (1995). Reproductive Tract Infections and Abortion among Adolescent Girls in Rural Nigeria. *Lancet*, 345 (8945), 300-4.

Chhabra, S., Gupte, N., Mehta, A., and Shende, A. (1988). Medical Termination of Pregnancy and Concurrent Contraceptive Adoption in Rural India. *Studies in Family Planning*, 19, 244-247.

Chhabra, Rahul (2003). *Times News Network*, December 2003.

Chhabra, R., and Nuna, S.C. (1994). *Abortion in India: An Overview*. Veerendra Printers, New Delhi, 63.

CHARCA (2002). Coordinated HIV/AIDS Response Through Capacity-Building and Awareness Duration 3 Years. Start Date 01 January 2002.

Creatsas, G. and Elsheikh, A. (2002). Adolescent Pregnancy and Its Consequences. *European Journal of Contraception and Reproductive Health Care*, 7, 167-172.

Dixon-Mueller, R. (1993). The Sexuality Connection In Reproductive Health, *Studies in Family Planning*, 24, 269-282.

Elder, Glen H, Jr. (1992). "The Life Course." In the Encyclopedia of Sociology. Edited by E.F. Borgatta and M.L.Borgatta, New York: Macmillan, 1120-1130.

Ganatra, B. and Hirve, A. (2002). Induced Abortions among Adolescent Women in Rural Maharashtra, India. *Reproductive Health Matters*, 10, 76-85.

Grant Making Strategy. The Macarthur Foundation India. Population and Reproductive Health Area Summary of 2003 - 2007 Work Plan.

Gogna, M., Romero, M., Ramos, S., Petracci, M., and Szulik, D. (2002). Abortion in a Restrictive Legal Context: The Views of Obstetrician-Gynaecologists in Buenos Aires, Argentina. *Reproductive Health Matters*, 10,128-137.

Görgen, R., Maier, B., and Diesfeld, H.J. (1993). Problems Related To School Girl Pregnancies in Burkina Faso, *Studies in Family Planning*, 24, 283-294.

Indian Council of Medical Research (ICMR). *Illegal Abortion in Rural Areas: A Task Force Study*. New Delhi: ICMR 1989.

Johnston, H.B. and Hill, K.H. (1996). Induced Abortion in the Developing World: Indirect Estimates. *International Family Planning Perspectives*, 22, 108-114 and 137.

Joint United Nations Programme on HIV/AIDS 2001.

Khan, M.E., Barge, S., and Philip, G. (1996). "Abortion in India: An Overview," Paper Presented at the IUSSP Seminar *on Sociocultural and Political Aspects of Abortion from an Anthropological Perspective*, Trivandrum, India, 25-28.

Kanjilal, Barun. (1999). Young Women's Sexual and Reproductive Lives. *Journal of Health Management,* 1(1): 143-149.

Lammers, C.M., Ireland, M. and Resnick, R Blum (2000). Influences on Adolescents' Decision to Postpone Onset of Sexual Intercourse: A Survival Analysis of Virginity among Youths Aged 13 To 18 Years. *Journal of Adolescent Health*, 26, 42-48.

Mccauley, A.P., and Salter, C. (1995). Meeting the Needs of Young Adults, Population Reports. Baltimore: John's Hopkins School of Public Health, *Population Information Program*, Series J, 41, 6.

Meekers, D., and Calvès, A.E. (1999). Gender Differentials in Adolescent Sexual Activity and Reproductive Health Risks in Cameroon. *African Journal of Reproductive Health*, 3(2), 51-67.

Medical Termination of Pregnancy Act, Act No. 34 of 1971, 3(2), Explanation I, Reprinted in *International Digest of Health Legislation* 1971, 22, 965.

Mann, J.M., and Tarantola, D.J.M. (Eds.) (1996). AIDS in the World, *Oxford University Press*, II, New York.

Monika Ardelt Laurie Day (2000). University of Florida. Parents, Siblings and Peers: Close Social Relationships and Adolescent Deviance. *Journal of Early Adolescence*, 22(3), 310-349

Ministry of Health and Family Welfare, Country Paper, 1998.

National Family Health Survey India, 1998 -1999; 14.

Olukoya, A.A., Kaya, A., Ferguson, B.J., and Abouzahr, C. (1996). Unsafe Abortion in Adolescents. Special Communication from the World Health Organisation. *International Journal of Gynaecology and Obstetrics*, 75, 137-147.

Population Reference Bureau, 2000. The World's Youth.

Population Reference Bureau. Chart of the World's Youth 1996. PRB Washington 1997.

Singh, S., and Wulf, D. (1990). *Today's Adolescents, Tomorrow's Parents: A Portrait of the Americas*. New York: Alan Guttmacher Institute.

Sing, U., Porter, F.D., and Thilakavathy, S. (1997). Knowledge of HIV Transmission and Sexual Behaviour of College Students in Pune, India (Letter) *AIDS*, 11, 19-20.

Speizer, I.S., Mullen, S.A., and Amegee, A. (2001). Gender Differences in Adult Perspectives on Adolescent Reproductive Behaviours: Evidence From Lome, Togo. International Family Planning Perspectives, 27, 178-185.

The South Asia Conference on Adolescents, UNFPA CST for CASA, 1999.

Thomas, Gary (1999). "Where True Love Waits." Christianity Today 1999; 43: 40-45. Vogt, Nancy R. "Correlates of Adolescent

Sexual Activity in the Family: A Religious Group. *Unpublished Doctoral Thesis*. Fuller Theological Seminary School of Psychology.

Tomar, Anjul (1998). Teen Pregnancies, Back-Street Abortions Seen Rising. *Indian Express Newspapers* (Bombay), Wednesday, June 10, 1998.

Trikha, S. (2001). Abortion Scenario of Adolescents in a North Indian City: Evidence from a Recent Study. *Indian Journal of Community Medicine*, 26(1), 48-55.

UNICEF. Early Marriage: Child Spouses. *Innocent Digest*, Italy 2001.

Van Den Broek, N.R. (1998). Adolescent Reproductive Health: Observations in a Hospital Setting. *Transactions of the Royal Society of Tropical Medicine and Hygiene*, 92: 554-555.

Westall, J. (2003). Poor Education Linked with Teen Pregnancies. *British Medical Journal*, 314: 537.

World Development Report (1993). World Bank. *Investing in Health*. Washington DC.

(Ref: Grant Making Strategy, The MacArthur Foundation, India Population and Reproductive Health Area Summary of 2003 - 2007 Work Plan).

(Special cases in Obstetrics practice/ Manual of Obstetrics Shirsh N Daffari Sandeep Chakravarthi Adolescent and teenage pregnancies page- 362).

6

Adolescent Health Issues in the Western States of India

Prof. N. Audinarayana

Summary

In the Indian context, examining the adolescent health issues is the recent phenomenon. The recent large-scale surveys, like National Family Health Surveys and Reproductive Health Survey efforts have explored selected health issues of married adolescent women (15-19 or 13-19 years). Using such data, as well as other published sources, an attempt is made here to examine the health issues of the adolescent married women (including pre-marital sexual behaviour of adolescents/youth) for the three western states of India viz., Gujarat, Maharashtra and Rajasthan on a comparative basis. Adolescent unmarried boys and girls appear to be vulnerable to pre-marital sexual activity, mostly unprotected, whereas married adolescent women are well noted for early marriage, early initiation to sex and motherhood, poor nutritional status and thereby, come across unsafe reproductive health outcomes. Gujarat appears to be better, in terms of majority of the indicators of adolescent health viz., higher mean age at marriage and cohabitation, age at first birth, better utilization of maternal health care aspects and need (both met and unmet) for family planning, than Mahararashtra and Rajasthan. Conversely, married adolescent women living in the states of Rajasthan and Maharashtra seem to fare better in nutritional aspects like height, Body Mass Index and anaemia than those who reside in Gujarat. Policy implications include effective management of RCH programme, introduction of sex education component in school curriculum and management strategies to improve iron status among adolescents.

Introduction

Adolescence, the transitional stage of life between childhood and adulthood, is a relatively new concept in India. As a result, the relationships between the physical, social and psychological changes that are specific to adolescents, and their vulnerability to health problems, have remained largely unrecognised and unexplored. In the Indian context, adolescent health is important, especially in case of girls who generally tend to be neglected during their childhood in matters related to food, education and health care. On the other hand, they are burdened with early marriage, early sexual initiation, and early child bearing and rearing, in addition to homemaking and participation in economic activities. In the process, their health deteriorate and consequently they face a lot of general as well as reproductive health problems during the adolescence years, which, if not properly treated, carry over to the later stages of their life. It is rightly mentioned that 'adolescents are adults of future years'. If adolescents carry any disability or if their needs are not addressed, the infirmities will show up in the adult population in future. This involves large cost, not only to the individuals but also to the country. In India, it is even more critical to address the needs of adolescents because a large number of adolescents particularly, in rural areas, get married and become mothers' (Department of Family Welfare, 1997).

In India, the adolescent population is gradually growing, both in absolute terms as well as relative to other age groups.

Like many other groups, adolescents have specific health issues and problems. However, in the Indian context, examining the adolescent health issues is the recent phenomenon. In fact, the credit of stressing the need for looking into the reproductive health needs of adolescents as a separate group goes to the International Conference on Population and Development (ICPD, Cairo, 1994) and later, the Beijing Women's Conference held in 1995. In line with these, the Government of India launched the Reproductive and Child Health Programme in 1997 whereby it aimed to expand services to meet the needs of hitherto under-served and neglected population sub-groups, including adolescents. Later, while adopting the National Population Policy, 2000, special attention was also given to this group especially in preparing the strategies and programmes for improving their reproductive health and nutrition. Thus, there appears to be an increasing recognition among policy makers about the need to address adolescents beyond the family planning framework. But public sector programmes on the ground are relatively few and there remains a dearth of information (Mamdani, 1999; Jothimani, 2004). With this background, an attempt was made in this paper to review some of the basic health issues of adolescents, especially reproductive health of married women (age 15-19 years), mainly based on the recent large-scale surveys conducted in the western states of India, in addition to a few micro-level studies conducted among unmarried adolescents (age 10-19 years).

Earlier Research on Adolescent Health Issues

As noted earlier, in India, only recently researchers have started to focus on adolescents' health issues and therefore, research in this line is at the infancy stage. Moreover, among the studies conducted so far, majority dealt with only small samples drawn from adolescent boys and girls. There too, ample importance was given only to girls, especially to those who live in urban areas and slums, focussing on their knowledge about menstruation, human reproduction, sexuality and sexual behaviour. Some of the works have tried to explore the menstrual hygienic practices. nutritional aspects like growth pattern and anaemia among girls, and pre-marital sexual behaviour (for a critical review one can see Jejeebhoy, 1996; Jothimani, 2004). However. as a part of National Family Health Surveys and Reproductive and Child Health Surveys, some valuable information is being collected from married adolescents of age 15-19 years (13-19 years in the case of NFHS-I). The health issues of adolescents from these surveys include maternal care, reproductive health problems and nutritional health related issues, in addition to marriage and cohabitation patterns, pregnancy outcomes, etc.

Methods

For the present paper, most of the data (depending upon the availability and limitations) has been elicited from the published sources of both large-scale as well as micro-level studies conducted in three major states of western India, viz., Gujarat, Maharashtra and Rajasthan. The major sources are NFHS-I (1992-93) and II (1998-99) reports (PRC, Pune and IIPS, 1994; PRC, Vadodara and IIPS, 1995; PRC, Udaipur and IIPS, 1995; IIPS and ORC Macro, 2001a; 2001b; 2001c) and RHS-RCH, Round I (Phase I, 1998 and II, 1999) data for the concerned states (Data in CD from RCH, IIPS) and a critical review of selected studies conducted in these states. Simple frequencies have been compiled and/or computed for various indicators of adolescent health issues from these sources and presented the same on comparative basis across the three states under consideration.

Results and Discussion

Adolescents' Pre-marital Sexual Behaviour

One of the major adolescent health aspects that has

caused much concern among researchers and policy makers in the recent past is the pre-marital sexual behaviour, as such experience is mostly unplanned and unprotected. Several critical reviews made on this aspect have clearly indicated that a substantial proportion of boys (about 20.0-30.0%) and girls (about 10.0%), from urban areas and/or slums, is sexually active during adolescence before marriage. A few have ardently argued and in fact, there is ample evidence that sexual activity among unmarried adolescents is increasing (Jejeebhoy, 1996; Khanna, et al., 2002; Audinarayana, 2005). Given the sensitivities involved in the topic, majority of the studies have been conducted among small and convenient samples till recently, but in the recent past a few attempts have been made to elicit information from comparatively larger samples (Table 1).

Table 1

Prevalence of Pre-Marital Sex among Adolescents / Youth in Selected Western States of India

Author(s) and Year of Publication	*Location and Year*	*Sample*	*Age (in Yrs.)*	*Ever Had Pre-Martial Sex*	
				Boys	*Girls*
Studies from Maharashtra					
Rangaiyan, 1996	15 Colleges in Mumbai, 1995	College Students 1408 Boys	18-22	15	
Abraham and Anil Kumar, 1997	4 Colleges of Low Income Students, Mumbai, 1995	College Students 613 Boys 335 Girls	14-23	26	3
Verma et al., 1998	Slums of Mumbai, 1996	1344 Men	16-49	20 (16-20 Yrs.)	

(Contd...)

Author(s) and Year of Publication	Location and Year	Sample	Age (in Yrs.)	Ever Had Pre-Martial Sex	
				Boys	Girls
Mawar et al., 1999	Colleges in Pune, 1996-98	College Students 825 Boys 996 Girls	15-22	37	12
Mutatkar and Apte, 1999	Two villages in western Maharashtra	Adolescents 500	14-22	10	
Ghule, 2004	4 Colleges in Ahmednagar Dt., Maharashtra	College Students 1456	16-21	29	
Studies from Gujarat					
Sharma and Sharma, 1997	Rural and Urban and Colleges in Gujarat, 1994	College Students 368 Boys	16-21	25	
Rajgopalan et al., 1998	Schools in Vadodara, 1997	School Students 387 Boys 338 Girls	12-15	7	2
Patel et al., 2000	Slums of Ahmedabad, 1999	Adolescents 151 Boys 93 Girls	10-19	24	12
Daftuar and Biswas, 2000	Slums of Anand 1999	Adolescents 300	15-19	55	38
Studies from Rajasthan					
Verma and Lhungdim, 2004	Rural Jalore District, Rajasthan, 2000	559 Un-married 2351Currently Married Men	<=24 <=24	32	16

Source: Khanna et al., 2002; Audinarayana, 2005

The age at which adolescents become sexually active varies according to the socio-cultural setting where they live. Moreover, young boys report sexual activity earlier than young girls because pre-marital sex is, to a certain extent, socially acceptable for boys in India, whereas girls are expected to postpone intercourse until they get married. Results provided in Table 1, by and large, suggest that most of the studies cited here were conducted among college students of urban areas and adolescents of urban slums of Maharashtra and Gujarat. Two studies dealt with rural samples, one in Maharashtra and another one in Rajasthan. On the whole, a modest proportion of adolescent/young boys have ever participated in sexual intercourse, ranging between 15.0-55.0%, whereas the corresponding proportions for girls range between 3.0-38.0%. Such proportions appear to be somewhat higher among adolescents residing in slums. Though majority of these studies did not explicitly collect and report data about the use of condoms during pre-marital intercourse, it is surprising to note that among those who ever participated in sexual intercourse before marriage, only a few used condoms; as low as 5.0% among slum-dwellers of Gujarat to a maximum of 18.0% and 20.0% among college students of Mumbai and rural married and unmarried men of a rural district in Rajasthan. These figures suggest that the adolescents are more vulnerable to STIs as well as HIV/AIDS, in addition to RTIs and teenage pregnancies before marriage, which may end up in abortions and its related complications among girls.

Marriage, Cohabitation and Childbearing of Married Adolescents

In the Indian context, in addition to participation in sex at early ages by adolescents, there is social sanction to initiate sex during adolescence after marriage. Early marriages are greatly supported by socio-cultural and economic factors, especially for girls. But in case of men, marriage during adolescence is not customary, largely because a man's eligibility as a groom is dependent on his being able to earn and support a family. Overall, in India, nowadays, marriages during adolescence are less common than they were one or two generations ago. Data from NFHS and RCH surveys (Table 2) clearly suggest that women in Rajasthan, closely followed by those in Maharashtra, by and large, get married much early than their counterparts in Gujarat. Obviously, a large number of adolescents as well as women of 20-44 age group start to live with their husbands below 18 years in that order and thereby, the median ages of women at cohabitation are also much lower in the former states compared to the latter (Gujarat). Interestingly, the percentage of women who begun childbearing during adolescence (13-19 years) is higher in Maharashtra closely followed by Rajasthan. Such proportion is comparatively less in Gujarat. Thereby, the median age at first birth is closer to the upper bound of adolescence in Maharashtra, whereas it has crossed this age by about one year in the other two western states. All these data support the fact that a modest proportion of the female adolescents in western states of India, especially those in Rajasthan and Maharashtra, get married during their teenage and thus become sexually active very soon (with husband) and thereby, fall prey to teenage childbearing. Such childbearing is one of the ways for a young woman to ensure stability of her marriage and acquire a high status within her family and community (Alan Guttmacher Institute, 1998).

Maternal Health Care of Adolescent Married Women

Till the implementation of Reproductive and Child Health (RCH) programme in India, the Maternal and Child Health (MCH) and/or Child Survival Safe Motherhood (CSSM) components under the family welfare programme mostly targeted married adult women, and thereby, married adolescents were mostly neglected. This is because health workers mostly face difficulties to contact and motivate the

Table 2

Marriage, Cohabitation and Childbearing of Adolescents in Selected Western States of India

Marriage, Cohabitation and Childbearing Aspects	*Gujarat*	*Maharashtra*	*Rajasthan*
1 % Currently Married			
- 13-14 years-			
NFHS – I	0.2	6.6	1.8
NFHS – II	0.3	2.8	1.3
- 15-19 years - NFHS – I	21.6	35.6	39.6
NFHS – II	21.0	28.0	27.3
2. Age at Marriage - Females			
- SMAM – NFHS – I	20.2	19.3	18.4
NFHS – II	20.2	19.8	18.3
- Median – NFHS – I	18.2	16.4	15.2
NFHS – II	17.9	16.7	15.3
3. Girls Married (Since January 1996) At Age below 18 Yrs.			
RCH-I – Phase 1	44.2	30.0	59.7
4. Age at First Cohabitation- Females			
- Median - NFHS – I	18.6	16.6	16.4
NFHS – II	18.4	17.6	16.5
5. Respondent Started to Live with Husband < 18 Yrs.			
- 15-19 years -			
RCH-I – Phase 1	73.4	76.2	83.3
RCH-I – Phase 2	77.1	72.3	83.5
- 20-44 years -			
RCH-I – Phase 1	49.0	62.8	64.4
RCH-I – Phase 2	46.3	59.1	80.3
6. Women of age 13-19 who have begun Childbearing			
– NFHS-I	8.9	19.9	13.0
Median Age at First Birth			
NFHS – I	20.0	18.9	20.3
NFHS – II	20.1	18.9	19.5

Source: NFHS – I and II and RHS-RCH – I, Phase 1 and 2 Reports of the three states under consideration.

latter group for utilising various maternal care services, as the latter do not know the importance of such services - since they are yet to start childbearing. Among all the maternal care aspects, antenatal care for adolescent married women is important, as most of them do not have prior knowledge of pregnancy and its related aspects. In addition, majority of them are either suffering from anaemia or malnutrition (details are discussed in the later part of this paper). Data provided in Table 3 suggest that a large per centage (about 36.0 - 68.0%) of married adolescent women in Rajasthan did not receive any antenatal check-up (either at home or at a health facility), whereas the corresponding proportions were moderately low (18.0 - 36.0%) in Gujarat and the lowest in Maharashtra (9.0 -19.0%). In case of TT injections and IFA tablets received during pregnancy also, married adolescent women in Rajasthan are at a greater disadvantage than that of their counterparts in Gujarat and Maharashtra.

Even in the case of natal and postnatal care aspects, married adolescent women appear to be very poor. In Rajasthan, as many as 75.0 - 90.0% of all births by adolescent married women took place at home rather than at health institutions compared to about 60.0 - 66.0% in Gujarat and 49.0 - 63.0% in Maharashtra. Consequently, for a larger number of births (59.0 - 78.0%) in Rajasthan, health personnel did not assist during delivery, as compared to other states under consideration (38.0 - 59.0% in Gujarat and 39.0 - 54.0% in Maharashtra), whereby there is higher risk of maternal and infant mortality in Rajasthan. Another worrisome fact is that for about 60.0-67.0% of deliveries by adolescent women in Rajasthan, Disposable Delivery Kit (DDK) have not been used, whereby the possibility of infection for mother and child is more. The corresponding percentage is moderately high in Gujarat (50.0-52.0%), but is recorded to be comparatively lower in Maharashtra (21.0-31.0%). Even in the case of post-partum check-ups by

Table 3
Maternal Health Care of Adolescents (<20 years) in Selected Western States

Maternal Health Care Indicators	*Gujarat*	*Maharashtra*	*Rajasthan*
1. Have Not Any Antenatal Check-ups			
NFHS – I	24.7	18.7	67.8
NFHS – II	18.0	9.3	52.3
RCH-I – Phase 1	29.1	12.5	47.4
RCH-I – Phase 2	35.7	15.1	35.8
2. Have Not Taken at least One Dose of TT Injection			
NFHS – I	30.7	20.7	67.7
NFHS – II	25.2	11.7	38.5
RCH-I – Phase 1	31.9	14.2	40.7
RCH-I – Phase 2	30.1	11.1	37.2
3. Have Not Received any IFA Tablets			
NFHS – I	30.1	29.2	67.8
NFHS – II	28.9	14.4	59.6
RCH-I – Phase 1	37.4	26.1	69.1
RCH-I – Phase 2	44.6	23.4	51.9
4. Have Home Deliveries			
NFHS – I	64.7	63.1	90.5
NFHS – II	60.1	55.9	76.5
RCH-I – Phase 1	64.3	57.8	78.3
RCH-I – Phase 2	66.3	49.1	75.7
5. Have Not Had Health Personnel Assistance at Delivery			
NFHS – I	59.5	54.3	76.0
NFHS – II	53.1	47.6	59.3
RCH-I – Phase 1	37.9	39.2	62.7
RCH-I – Phase 2	44.6	40.6	78.2
6. DDK Not Used			
RCH-I – Phase 1	51.6	20.6	66.8
RCH-I – Phase 2	50.2	31.0	59.8
7. Have Not Had Postpartum Check-up <2 Months			
NFHS – I	90.5	72.2	95.1
RCH-I – Phase 1	72.5	71.4	84.7
RCH-I – Phase 2	81.1	77.3	90.6

Source: NFHS – I and II and RHS-RCH – I, Phase 1 and 2 Reports of the three states under consideration.

Auxiliary Nurse Midwife (ANM) within 2 months (in the case of NFHS-2) and/or 6 weeks (in the case of RCH), adolescent women in Rajasthan are at a great disadvantage closely followed by those in Gujarat and Maharashtra. All these figures suggest the fact that among the western states of India, maternal health care aspects among married adolescent women, by and large, are very poor in Rajasthan, whereas they are at a moderate level in Gujarat, but comparatively better in Maharashtra. Interestingly, with a few exceptions, within a short span of 6-7 years, there seems to be a slight progress in all the aspects, irrespective of the states under consideration, but the ranking of states have been maintained; Rajasthan is still at the greatest disadvantage followed by Gujarat and Maharashtra.

Counselling to Adolescent Girls and Prevalence of Anaemia

In the Indian context, with the implementation of the RCH programme, special attention has been given to taking care of the adolescent population, especially girls. Therefore, in RHS-RCH, an attempt was made to know whether any health professionals have counselled the unmarried adolescent girls (15-19 years) about their possible health problems. The information for the western states (Table 4) showed that during Phase I of Round I, about one-fifth of the unmarried girls in Gujarat and Maharasthra have been counselled by one or the other health professional, either at home or at the health centre, whereas proportion is much less in the case of Rajasthan (7.0%). On the other hand, the reverse pattern is noticed in this regard during RCH-Phase-II. When information was elicited about the prevalence of anaemia among these unmarried adolescent girls, though small proportions reportedly suffered from anaemia, such proportions appear to be comparatively higher in Maharashtra than in Rajasthan and Gujarat. However, the point to be borne in mind here is that though through RCH programme it is mandatory to provide services to adolescent girls, a large percentage of them were not counselled/contacted and/or had not sought such services. While lack of awareness could be the major reason for such pattern, one can't rule out the possibility that during the visits of health personnel (especially ANM) to the homes, the girls may not have been available because of attending school/college and/or working outside home for wages.

Table 4
Counselling to and Prevalence of Anaemia among Unmarried Adolescent Girls (15-19 years) in Selected Western States of India

Counselling to and Anemia among Adolescent Girls	*Gujarat*		*Maharashtra*		*Rajasthan*	
	%	*N*	*%*	*N*	*%*	*N*
1. Counselling to Unmarried Adolescent Girls						
RCH-I – Phase 1	18.9	95	17.5	97	7.2	111
RCH-I – Phase 2	8.0	75	7.8	90	19.0	126
2. Suffered from Anaemia						
During the last 3 Months						
RCH-I – Phase 1	3.2	95	13.4	97	7.2	111
RCH-I – Phase 2	0.0	75	7.8	90	2.4	126

Source: NFHS – I and II and RHS-RCH – I, Phase 1 and 2 Reports of the three states under consideration.

It is widely documented that, in India, adolescent girls are in greater need for extra nutritional intake, but they are poorly nourished; and because of this their body growth is less than the normal and a large proportion of them suffer from anaemia. In view of this, in NFHS-2, an attempt was made to collect information about the nutritional status and anaemia among currently married women of 15 - 49 years in a systematic manner. Data for western states of India (Table 5) suggest that about one-sixth of adolescent married women (15-19 years) in Gujarat are of below-normal height (145 cm.) closely followed by adolescents in Maharashtra, whereas such proportion is very less in Rajasthan. Likewise, the percentage of adolescent girls whose Body Mass Index (BMI) is below the normal level (18.5 kg/m^2) is found to be higher in Maharashtra, closely followed by Gujarat, whereas it is moderately less in Rajasthan. Thus, the average BMI for adolescent women is comparatively higher in Rajasthan than in Gujarat and Maharashtra. All these support the fact that about fifty percentage of the adolescent girls, by and large, are poorly nourished and therefore, they suffer from short body stature and lower BMIs; married adolescent women in Rajasthan are slightly better in these regard than the other two western states. In case of anaemia (Table 5), it is noticed that though more than 50.0% of adolescent married women is suffering from anaemia in the three states under consideration, such proportion is comparatively higher in Gujarat than in Rajasthan and Maharashtra. There is a clear pattern in the case of those who suffering from moderate/ severe anaemia, wherein such proportion is comparatively higher in Gujarat than in Maharashtra and is the lowest in Rajasthan. However, a few micro level studies conducted in these states around 1990s revealed that a large proportion (ranging from 75.0-98.0%) of unmarried adolescent girls as well as married adolescent women (ages 10/13-18/19) were suffering from anaemia (Mamdani, 1999; Jothimani, 2004). Generally, malnutrition results in stunting among adolescent girls and thereby, they tend to have small or deformed pelvis, which may prevent normal delivery. On the other hand, moderate or severe anaemia during adolescence or presents a serious risk; it is one of the most common causes of mortality during pregnancy.

Table 5
Nutritional Status and Prevalence of Anaemia among Married Adolescent Women (15-19 years) in Selected Western States of India, NFHS-II

Indicators of Nutritional Status	*Gujarat*	*Maharashtra*	*Rajasthan*
1. Height, % below 145 cm.	15.6	11.5	4.5
2. Mean Body Mass Index	18.8	18.7	19.5
3. % below BMI below 18.5kg/m^2	48.7	49.8	32.3
4. % of women with any Anaemia	57.7	51.7	53.9
5. % Suffering from Anaemia –			
Mild	33.4	30.6	35.5
Moderate / Severe	24.3	21.1	18.4

Source: NFHS – I and II and RHS-RCH – I, Phase 1 and 2 Reports of the three states under consideration.

Domestic Violence, Contraceptive Use and Unmet Need for Family Planning

Domestic violence against women is one of the major problems in India especially in the family where women lack education and economic autonomy. Married adolescents are likely to face this problem to a greater extent since they are mostly emotionally immature and new entrants at their husband's (in-laws') home. Such violence not only affects women's physical health directly, but also affects their social and mental health indirectly. In fact, in the recent past, it has been widely acknowledged that violence against women has become not only a human rights concern but also a public health concern in both the developed and developing countries. Data from NFHS-II highlight that about 16.0% of ever-married adolescent women had been beaten or mistreated physically since their age 15 either by husbands or in-laws/ parents/brothers, whereas the corresponding proportion is comparatively less in Gujarat and still less in Rajasthan (Table 6).

Table 6
Domestic Violence, Use of Contraception and Unmet Need for Family Planning among Adolescent Women (15-19 years) in Selected Western States of India

Reproductive / Urinary Tract Infections	*Gujarat*	*Maharashtra*	*Rajasthan*
Ever-married women reporting Beaten or Mistreated Physically since age 15			
NFHS - II	10.1	15.8	5.7
Use of Contraception			
- ***NFHS-I*** **- Spacing**	1.8	3.4	1.3
Limiting	1.4	5.7	0.7
- NFHS-II - Spacing	7.4	2.4	3.6
Limiting	2.2	4.0	0.5
Unmet Need for FP			
- NFHS-I - Spacing	27.0	21.8	27.7
Limiting	1.8	6.2	4.3
- NFHS-II - Spacing	17.7	29.8	29.8
Limiting	0.4	1.5	2.5

Source: NFHS – I and II and RHS-RCH – I, Phase 1 and 2 Reports of the three states under consideration.

Use of contraceptive methods, by and large, is lower among adolescent married women as they are expected to produce children and prove their fertility immediately after marriage. Among the western states, the percentage of married adolescent women who are using one or the other method of contraception ranges between 2 and 10 only.

However, such proportion is considerably higher in Gujarat than in Rajasthan and Maharashtra. Interestingly, the percentage of adolescent girls using contraceptive methods to limit childbearing is higher in Maharashtra, which is more closely followed in this by Gujarat than by Rajasthan. Another pertinent fact noticed here is that a substantial proportion of the adolescent married women (about 30.0-32.0%) in the western states under consideration has reported their desire to delay the next birth or limit childbearing, but is not using any contraceptive method (unmet need). Such proportion is the highest in Rajasthan, closely followed by Maharashtra and then Gujarat (Table 6). The major reasons for such rates are: till recently, the family planning programme has aimed to achieve demographic goals in specified time periods and, moreover, targeted at older married women who have two or three children. The focus is mostly on permanent family planning methods, especially female sterilization, and thereby, even the availability of spacing methods through the public health services is very limited. Further, though condom is available to adolescent boys, adolescent married men mostly underutilize it, since it is poorly promoted. However, with the implementation of the RCH programme, there is a slight improvement in the situation and thereby, the figures appear to be slightly better in the latest round of NFHS.

Pregnancy Wastage and Infant and Child Mortality

In the earlier lines, it has been clearly brought out that many adolescent girls enter married life early and thereby, sexual activity would be initiated early, which would result into early/teenage childbearing. The consequences of early childbearing are severe not only to mothers, but also to the pregnancies they bear and to the children to whom they give birth. RCH data for western states (Table 7) suggest that about one-sixth of the deliveries by adolescent mothers are not normal; inter-state differentials are not that clear in this case. With regard to pregnancy wastage, data from NFHS-I revealed that about 6.0% of all pregnancies in married adolescents, irrespective of their state background, resulted in spontaneous abortions or stillbirths, whereas the corresponding percentages in Phase 1 and 2 of RCH-I was reported to be somewhat higher, about 9.0 -1.0%. By and large, with a few exceptions, the proportion of pregnancy wastage appears to be marginally higher among the married adolescents of Rajasthan and Maharashtra than their counterparts in Gujarat. Curiously, NFHS-I data highlights that about a small percentage of all pregnancies to married adolescents ended up in induced abortions; this is comparatively much higher in Rajasthan than Maharashtra and Gujarat. However, in case of Phase 1 and 2 of RCH-I, such proportions range between 0.5 and 1.5, and appears to be inconsistent across the states under consideration. It is also interesting to note that the rates of infant and child mortality for those mothers whose age at birth is below 20 years are highest in Rajasthan, followed by Gujarat and then Maharashtra. Moreover, all these rates are much higher for adolescent mothers than their counterparts at higher ages in the three states and time periods under consideration (NFHS-I and II Reports of three states under consideration).

Reproductive Tract Infections (RTIs)

Adolescents, by and large, are unaware of the reproductive process and contraception and therefore, they may not know the importance of preventive and/or curative aspects of reproductive tract infections. So also is the case with sexual vulnerability of newly married adolescents, who are equally ill informed and, therefore, are mostly unprepared for sexual intercourse and its consequences. All these make them suffer from RTIs and sexual intercourse problems. Data from NFHS-II (Table 8) highlight that about 27 percent of adolescent ever-married women, irrespective of the state under consideration, reported of suffering from any abnormal

Table 7
Pregnancy Outcomes and Rates of Infant / Child Mortality among Married Adolescent Women (15-19 years) in Western States of India

Pregnancy Outcomes and Infant / Child Mortality	*Gujarat*	*Maharashtra*	*Rajasthan*
Delivery Not Normal			
- RCH I – Phase 1	7.1	17.8	12.4
–RCH I – Phase 2	16.9	14.4	15.9
Outcome of Pregnancy			
NFHS – I –Spontaneous Abortions	5.0	4.1	3.2
–Still Birth	1.2	2.0	2.6
–Induced Abortions	0.8	1.0	2.6
RCH-I – Phase 1 -			
–Spontaneous Abortions	7.5	8.8	9.0
–Still Birth	1.8	2.3	3.2
–Induced Abortions	0.4	1.5	1.1
RCH-I – Phase 2 -			
–Spontaneous Abortions	8.9	9.6	9.3
–Still Birth	2.3	2.4	2.5
–Induced Abortions	1.3	0.8	0.8
Rates of Infant / Child Mortality			
NFHS – I –Neo-natal Mortality	84.2	55.1	56.4
–Post-neonatal Mortality	36.4	23.3	43.3
–Infant Mortality ($_1q_0$)	120.6	78.4	99.8
–Child Mortality ($_4q_1$)	45.5	20.5	36.6
–Under-five Mortality ($_5q_0$)	160.6	97.3	132.7

(Contd...)

Pregnancy Outcomes and Infant/Child Mortality		*Gujarat*	*Maharashtra*	*Rajasthan*
NFHS– II	–Neo-natal Mortality	62.2	51.1	65.1
	–Post-neonatal Mortality	23.3	17.1	44.1
	–Infant Mortality ($_1q_0$)	85.5	68.2	109.2
	–Child Mortality ($_4q_1$)	29.5	21.6	39.9
	–Under-five Mortality ($_5q_0$)	112.5	88.3	144.7

Source: NFHS – I and II and RHS-RCH – I, Phase 1 and 2 Reports of the three states under consideration.

vaginal discharge. At the same time, around one-fifth of the adolescent women in Maharashtra are suffering from the symptoms of urinary tract infection (UTIs), whereas the corresponding proportions in Rajasthan and Gujarat are 13 and 10, respectively. On the other hand, among currently married adolescent women, more than one-third reported of suffering from any reproductive problem; this is somewhat higher in the case of Maharashtra than in Gujarat and Rajasthan. Another worrisome fact is that around one-fifth of the currently married adolescent women reported to be suffering from intercourse problems like painful intercourse (often) and bleeding after intercourse (ever); this appears to be marginally higher in Gujarat and Maharashtra than in Rajasthan. Another interesting point to be noted here is that the proportion of reporting RTIs/UTIs as well as sexual intercourse problems is higher among adolescent women than those belonging to higher age groups (NFHS-II Reports of concerned states). RCH data (Phase I and II) also revealed that a substantial proportion of the currently married adolescents reported of suffering from any RTIs/UTIs during the three months prior to the survey. Though the prevalence of such problems differs across the states between Phases II and I, adolescent women in Maharashtra, by and large, suffer less than their counterparts in Gujarat and Rajasthan.

Table 8
Reproductive / Urinary Tract Infections among Married Adolescent Women (15-19 years) in Western States of India

Reproductive / Urinary Tract Infections	*Gujarat*	*Maharashtra*	*Rajasthan*
NFHS - II			
1. Ever-married women reporting any abnormal vaginal discharge	27.6	26.6	26.3
2. Symptoms of a Urinary Tract Infection	9.7	20.1	13.4
3. Currently Married Women Reporting			
- Painful intercourse (often)	13.9	15.5	12.6
- Bleeding after intercourse (ever)	4.8	2.5	3.0
- Any Reproductive Health Problem	35.0	38.3	34.7
4. Currently Married Women Reporting			
Any RTIs/UTIs – RCH-I – Phase 1	40.3	30.3	36.6
RCH-I – Phase 2	34.7	30.4	47.1

Source: NFHS – I and II and RHS-RCH – I, Phase 1 and 2 Reports of the three states under consideration.

Conclusions and Policy Implications

On the whole, in India, adolescents (10-19 years old) have been recognized as a special and high-risk group only in the recent past. While unmarried boys and girls of this age-group appears to be vulnerable to pre-marital sexual activity, mostly un-protected, married adolescent women are well noted for early marriage, early initiation to sex and motherhood, poor nutritional status and thereby, coming across unsafe reproductive health outcomes. For instance, among the three western states of India under consideration, a modest proportion of the adolescents in Rajasthan and Maharashtra are entering into married life during their teen ages as well as become sexually active immediately (with husband); thereby, they fall prey to teenage childbearing. Maternal healthcare aspects among married adolescent women, by and large, are very poor in Rajasthan, at a moderate level in Gujarat, but comparatively better in Maharashtra. On the other hand, though about fifty percent of the married adolescent women are poorly nourished and thereby, suffering from short body stature and lower BMIs, adolescent women in Rajasthan are slight better in this regard than the other two western states. But in case of anaemia, though more than half of adolescent married women are suffering from it in the three states under consideration, such proportion is comparatively higher in Gujarat than in Rajasthan and Maharashtra. While less than 20.0% of married adolescents are using contraceptives, about one-third of them are reported to be in the state of unmet need.

With regard to the reproductive risk outcomes among adolescent married women, pregnancy wastage – spontaneous abortions and stillbirths, appears to be highest incidence (varies in the range of 6.0-12.0%). Infant and child mortality rates are also found to be high among adolescent married women whose age at birth is below 20 years. With a few exceptions, both these rates are highest in Rajasthan, whereas Maharashtra and Gujarat interchange their order in these regards. Moreover, all these rates are much higher for adolescent mothers than their counterparts at higher ages in the three states and time periods under consideration.

Based on the conclusions drawn from this paper, following policy implications are suggested for the better management of reproductive and sexual health of the adolescents.

1. First of all, effective management of RCH programme and training of doctors, paramedical personnel as well as Anganwadi workers of ICDS programme in various health issues of adolescents is an immediate and imperative task to be looked into earnestly. Allotment of sufficient funds by the Government has to be taken as a priority so as to improve the infrastructure. Emphasis should be given on appointment of more Lady Medical Officers, supply of medicines, conduct of school health programmes, conduct of meetings / camps at village / slum levels for unmarried and married adolescents, etc.

2. Introduction of sex education including information on human reproduction in the government school curriculum is another aspect to be looked into, through which one can cover a large majority of children. To gain acceptability within the community at large, sex education needs to be introduced into the school curriculum in a phased manner and possibly be incorporated into a broader curriculum on health education rather being in its own area of study. Teachers also need to undergo an intensive training programme so that they will be able to and will feel comfortable in providing such information to adolescents.

3. The government also needs to look into appropriate and feasible management strategies towards improving the iron status of adolescents with a more comprehensive approach than the present practice of distributing iron and folic acid tablets during the last trimester of pregnancy and, that too to a very limited extent for unmarried adolescents. Steps also need to be taken towards ensuring an adequate supply of good quality iron-folic acid tables. Educational

campaigns aimed at mothers, mothers-in-law and adolescents, emphasizing the importance of a diet, which includes information about iron-rich foods as well as foods that enhance iron absorption.

4. On research front, there is an urgent need for community-based studies on adolescents, both unmarried and married, focusing on their important needs, knowledge about reproduction, sexuality and reproductive/sexual health problems specific to them. Specific qualitative studies for in-depth understanding of the needs, perceptions and attitudes of the adolescents of different strata, like school/college going, working, as well as those residing in slum/rural/urban areas. Moreover, care must be taken to present disaggregated data by gender and various socio-cultural groups, in addition to slum/rural/urban populations so as to facilitate comparisons. In addition to these, a national adolescent database on various health aspects and their determinants should be created and maintained.

REFERENCES

Alan Guttmacher Institute (1998). *Into a New World Young Women's Sexual and Reproductive Lives.* Alan Guttmacher Institute, New York.

Audinarayana, N. (2005). *Correlates of High-risk Sexual Behaviour among Never-married male Industrial Workers in Tirupur City in Tamil Nadu.* AMCHSS, SCTIMST, Trivandrum.

Department of Family Welfare (1997). *Basic Guide to Reproductive and Child Health Programme: For Use of NGOs, Training Institutions and Health Functions.* Government of India, New Delhi.

International Institute for Population Sciences (IIPS) and ORC Macro (2001a). *National Family Health Survey (NFHS-2), India, **1998-99**: Gujarat.* IIPS, Mumbai.

International Institute for Population Sciences (IIPS) and ORC Macro (2001b). *National Family Health Survey (NFHS-2), India, 1998-99: Maharashtra*. IIPS, Mumbai.

International Institute for Population Sciences (IIPS) and ORC Macro (2001c). *National Family Health Survey (NFHS-2), India, 1998-99: Rajasthan*. IIPS, Mumbai.

Jejeebhoy, S. J. (1996). *Adolescent Sexual and Reproductive Behaviour: A Review of the Evidence from India*. Working Paper No. 3., International Center for Research on Women, Washington D.C., USA.

Jothimani, N. (2004). *Reproductive Health of Unmarried Adolescent Girls in a Rural Setting of Pollachi Taluk, Coimbatore District, Tamil Nadu*. Unpublished M. Phil Thesis. Bharathiar University, Coimbatore.

Khanna, R., Gurubaxani, S. and Sengupta, K. (2002). *Sexuality and Sexual Behaviour: An Annotated Bibliography of Selected Studies (1999-2000)*. WOHTRAC and CREA, New Delhi.

Mamdani, Masuma (1999). Management of Reproductive Tract Infections in Women: Lessons from the Field. In Saroj Pachauri (Ed.) *Implementing a Reproductive Health Agenda in India: The Beginning*. Population Council, New Delhi.

Population Research Centre, Gokhale Institute of Politics and Economics, Pune, and International Institute for Population Sciences (IIPS), Bombay. 1994. *National Family Health Survey (MCH and Family Planning), Maharashtra 1992-93*. IIPS, Bombay.

Population Research Centre, Mohanlal Sukhadia University (PRC, Udaipur) and International Institute for Population Sciences (IIPS). 1995. *National Family Health Survey (MCH and Family Planning), Rajasthan 1992-93*. IIPS, Bombay.

Population Research Centre, M.S. University of Baroda, Vadodara (PRC, Vadodara) and International Institute for Population Sciences. 1995. *National Family Health Survey (MCH and Family Planning), Gujarat 1993*. IIPS, Bombay.

7

Adolescents' Knowledge about HIV/AIDS in Southern States: NFHS-2 Data Analysis

Dr. C.P. Prakasam

Summary

The objective of the study was twofold. First, to know the knowledge, source of knowledge and ways to avoid AIDS (awareness about AIDS) among adolescent women (15-19, 20-24 age groups) in four high prevalence states viz., Andhra Pradesh, Karnataka, Maharashtra and Tamil Nadu. Secondly, to know the socio-economic variables influencing the knowledge and awareness towards AIDS. This was a secondary study based on report of National Family Health Survey two. Review of secondary data revealed that percentage of rural women who have heard of AIDS found to be more than urban in all these states except in Maharashtra. In case of Tamil Nadu, the awareness between adolescent and young women found to be very minimal. More than 90.0% adolescent and young women were heard of AIDS in Tamil Nadu may be attributed to the AIDS awareness and prevention campaign programs in Tamil Nadu. Television was the most important source of information about AIDS among adolescent and young women. Among women who have heard about AIDS, a large majority of women knew some ways to avoid AIDS

Introduction

Acquired Immune Deficiency Syndrome (AIDS) is an illness caused by the HIV virus. This virus transmitted through sexual contact, through contacts with contaminated needles or blood, or from an HIV infected mother to her child during pregnancy, delivery. Knowledge about transmission of HIV virus causing AIDS is an important phenomenon in the present situation, as India being ranked one of the HIV/AIDS affected country in the world. As a developing county, India with a wide base population susceptible for quick and high infection rate, when compared with other developing countries is still a low HIV-prevalence country with an adult prevalence rate at 0.8% as per NACO (2004). But, a low HIV-prevalence rate in a highly populated country can translate into a large absolute number of HIV cases, posing a high challenging task to public health personnel.

The first case of HIV/AIDS in India was detected in 1986 in Chennai, Tamil Nadu and the second in Mumbai. By 1994, NACO identified Maharashtra and Manipur as high prevalence states. Currently six states viz., Andhra Pradesh, Karnataka, Maharashtra, Manipur, Nagaland and Tamil Nadu are identified as high prevalence states. The moderate prevalence states are Kerala, Gujarat, Goa and Pondicherry. The states of Bihar, Rajasthan, Madhya Pradesh, Uttar Pradesh, Chhattisgarh, Jharkhand, Orissa and Assam are identified as highly vulnerable states (NACO 2003, PFI 2003). Going by the increasing number of cases in each four-year period from 1986 to 2002, it seems that the speed of invasion of the infection has slackened from 1998 to 2002. The number of people living with HIV/AIDS during 2002 was 4,580,000 and it was 5.206 millions by 31, July 2005. It is estimated that by 2010 the number of HIV infected persons would be 20 to 25 millions (Ojha and Pradhan, 2006). The unrefined increments in the new cases of HIV/AIDS from 1986 to 1998 can rightly be said to have been controlled by the improved awareness, knowledge among the population and the interventions from the Govt. of India and also different states.

HIV infections by state were found to be highest in the state of Tamil Nadu and Maharashtra (Table 1) in India. More than 55.0% of the total infections are from Tamil Nadu followed by Maharashtra contributing another 27.0% to the total. The other hard hit states are Andhra Pradesh, Karnataka, Manipur and Nagaland with the respective shares 9.8, 4.0, 2.8 and 0.8% respectively. Mumbai city is the most important financial, business and industrial center of India and it is a matter of great concern to find that the city's share is 4.7% of the total AIDS cases reported (Table 1).

In India, it has been observed that a shift of HIV infection from the high-risk groups to the general population, from urban to rural areas and an increasing number of women and youth being infected, from high prevalence states to all states, feminization, and youth vulnerability reaching high. Among youth in India, 35.0% of AIDS cases reported are below 25 years of age and 50.0% of the new infections in the age group 15-24 years.

The size of Indian youth population and their lack of knowledge towards HIV and AIDS is an important issue in reducing HIV infection. It has been observed that only 20.0% of young women aged 15-24 know two ways to prevent getting HIV infection and approximately 63.0% have not heard about AIDS (Bhardwaj, 2006, UNICEF, USAIDS, WHO, 2002), forecasts an alarming picture of the epidemic. For this vulnerable group (Adolescents), it is important to improve their knowledge and awareness towards HIV/AIDS.

Table 1
Percentage of AIDS Cases reported by State and share of AIDS Cases among Hard Hit States through August, 2003, India

Indian States	*Percentage of Reported Cases*	*Hard Hit States **	*Percentage Share Among Hard Hit States*
Andhra Pradesh	7.9	Andhra Pradesh	9.8
Delhi	1.5	Karnataka	4.0
Gujarat	6.5**	Maharashtra	26.8
Karnataka	3.2	Manipur	2.8
Madhya Pradesh	1.9	Nagaland	0.8
Maharashtra less Mumbai	16.7	Tamil Nadu	55.8
Manipur	2.2	All	100.0
Mumbai	4.7		
Nagaland	0.6		
Tamil Nadu	44.7		
West Bengal	1.7		
Others	8.4		
All	100.0		

Source: National AIDS Control Organization (2003)
* States where HIV infection has crossed 1 percent or more in antenatal Women.
** States where HIV infection has crossed 5 percent or more among high-riskGroups, but the infection is below 1 percent in antenatal women.

Keeping above points in view an attempt was made in this paper

1. To know the knowledge, source of knowledge and ways to avoid AIDS (awareness about AIDS) among adolescent women (15-19, 20-24 age groups) in four high prevalence states viz., Andhra Pradesh, Karnataka, Maharashtra and Tamil Nadu and

2. To know the of socio-economic variables influencing the knowledge and awareness towards AIDS.

Method

National Family Health Survey-2 collected data by asking questions on knowledge of AIDS and AIDS prevention. Ever married women aged between 15-49 years were asked initially, if they had ever heard of an illness called AIDS. Further respondents who had heard of AIDS were asked about their source of information on AIDS, and knowledge of ways to avoid AIDS. For the present study data were collected from the ever married adolescent women in the age group of 15-19 years and young women aged between 20-24 years who have ever heard of AIDS and if so, ways to avoid. Analysis has been done for the high prevalence states viz., Andhra Pradesh, Karnataka, Maharashtra and Tamil Nadu. To understand the relation between socioeconomic variables and awareness of AIDS, Logit regression has been used.

Results

Knowledge of AIDS

To assess the knowledge of AIDS, analysis has been made who have heard of AIDS by adolescent (15-19) and young married women (20-24) for the selected states. Nearly half of the adolescent women (Table 2) in Andhra Pradesh, 48.0% in Karnataka, 51.0% in Maharashtra and nearly 95.0% in Tamil Nadu heard about AIDS. Among the young women (20-24), 62.0% in Andhra Pradesh, around 57.0% in Karnataka, 70.0% in Maharashtra and 93.0% in Tamil Nadu heard about AIDS. There is substantial difference in awareness between adolescent and young women who have heard about AIDS and found to be more among young women (20-24) in Andhra Pradesh, Karnataka, and Maharashtra. In case of Tamil Nadu the awareness between adolescent and young women found to be very minimal (Table2). More than 90.0% of the adolescent and young women were heard of AIDS in Tamil Nadu may be attributed to the AIDS awareness and prevention campaign programs in Tamil Nadu.

Table 2
Percent of Ever Married Adolescent Women who have ever heard of AIDS in Andhra Pradesh, Karnataka, Maharashtra and Tamil Nadu, NFHS-2 Data

Ever Heard of AIDS		*Age Group*		
		15-19	*20-24*	*Total*
Andhra Pradesh				
	No	212 (50.4)	290 (37.6)	502 (42.1)
	Yes	209 (49.6)	482 (62.4)	691(57.9)
	Total	421 (100.0)	772 (100.0)	1193 (100.0)
	ψ^2=18.29**			
Karnataka	No	223 (51.9)	335 (43.1)	558 (46.2)
	Yes	207(48.1)	442 (56.9)	649 (53.8)
	Total	430 (100.0)	777 (100.0)	1207 (100.0)
	ψ^2=8.59**			
Maharashtra	No	203 (48.2)	285 (30.5)	488 (36.0)
	Yes	218 (51.8)	649 (69.5)	867(64.0)
	Total	421(100.0)	934 (100.0)	1355(100.0)
	ψ^2=31.79**			
Tamil Nadu	No	12 (5.2)	58 (7.5)	70 (7.0)
	Yes	217(94.8)	712 (92.5)	929 (93.0)
	Total	229 (100.0)	770 (100.0)	999 (100.0)
	ψ^2=1.79 N.S			

Adolescent and young women who have heard about AIDS by background characteristics in four states have been analyzed and the results are given in Table 3. The selected background characters are 1) Residence (Urban, Rural), 2) Education (No education, Primary, secondary, Higher), 3) Religion (Hindu, Muslim, Christian), 4) Caste (SC, ST, OBC and others), 5) Exposure to Mass Media (Read Newspaper, Watch TV, Listen to Radio). Considering these background characteristics it has been hypothesized as: .

- Urban, educated, Hindus, other caste, women and women who have been exposed media have hared about AIDS more than their counter part.

Percentage of ever married adolescent and young women who have heard about AIDS by background characteristics (Table 3) revealed percentage of rural women who have heard of AIDS were found to be more in rural areas than urban in all these states except in Maharashtra. Further, the percentage of the adolescent women (15-19) who have heard AIDS were found to be more than young women (20-24) except in Maharashtra. Awareness of AIDS among rural adolescent ever-married women were found to be three-fold in Andhra Pradesh, Karnataka and Tamil Nadu.

Comparison of adolescent and young women according to background characteristics shows (Table 3) that women with secondary education, Hindu, OBC and women exposed to watching TV found to have more aware of AIDS than other categories and there was no difference between adolescent and young women with respect to these background characteristics.

The Government of India has been using mass media, especially electronic media, extensively to create awareness to the general public about AIDS and its prevention. Hence, information about women who have heard of AIDS and their sources by states among adolescent and young women has been analyzed and the results are given in Table 4. The sources of information received about AIDS are viz., Radio, Television, Cinema, Newspaper/Magazine, Poster/Hording, Health worker, Friends/Relatives, School/teacher

Table 3
Percentage of Ever-Married Adolescent Women who have Heard About AIDS by Background Characteristics in Selected States: NFH-2

Background characteristics	*Andhra Pradesh*		*Karnataka*		*Tamil Nadu*		*Maharashtra*	
	15-19	20-24	15-19	20-24	15-19	20-24	15-19	20-24
Residence								
Urban	50 (23.9)	176 (36.5)	61(29.5)	183 (41.4)	76 (35.0)	328 (46.1)	116 (53.2)	435 (67.0)
Rural	159 (76.1)	306 (63.5)	146 (70.5)	259 (58.6)	141 (65.0)	384 (53.9)	102 (46.8)	214 (33.0)
Education								
No Education	52 (24.9)	131 (27.2)	46.9 (22.2)	96 (21.7)	36 (16.6)	128 (18.0)	33 (15.1)	78 (12.0)
Primary	63 (30.1)	90 (18.7)	31 (15.0)	48 (10.9)	56 (25.8)	178 (25.0)	44 (20.2)	109 (16.8)
Secondary	87(41.6)	201 (41.7)	117 (56.5)	211 (47.7)	112 (51.6)	303 (42.6)	130 (59.6)	322 (49.6)
Higher	7 (3.3)	60 (12.4)	13 (6.3)	87 (19.7)	13 (6.0)	103 (14.5)	111 (5.0)	140 (21.6)
Religion								
Hindu	175 (83.7)	398 (82.0)	175 (84.5)	384 (86.9)	199 (92.1)	617 (86.7)	161 (73.9)	471 (72.6)
Muslim	12 (5.7)	45 (9.4)	28 (13.5)	50 (11.3)	14 (6.5)	62 (8.7)	44 (20.2)	112 (17.3)
Christian	22 (10.5)	38 (7.9)	4 (1.9)	8 (1.8)	3 (1.4)	33 (4.6)	13 (6.0)	56 (8.0)

(Contd...)

Background characteristics	*Andhra Pradesh*		*Karnataka*		*Tamil Nadu*		*Maharashtra*	
	15-19	20-24	15-19	20-24	15-19	20-24	15-19	20-24
Caste/tribe								
Scheduled Caste	61 (29.2)	90 (18.8)	27 (3.2)	68 (15.5)	54 9 (24.9)	183 (25.7)	32 (14.7)	88 (13.6)
Scheduled Tribe	4 (1.9)	17 (3.5)	13 (6.4)	13 (3.0)	6 (2.8)	5 (0.7)	13 (6.0)	35 (5.4)
Backward caste	97 (46.4)	185 (38.6)	83 (4.0)	202 (45.9)	155 (71.8)	518 (72.8)	41 (18.8)	122 (18.8)
Other	47 (22.5)	187 (39.0)	81 (39.7)	157 (35.7)	2 (0.9)	6 (0.8)	132 (60.6)	403 (62.2)
Exposure to Mass Media								
Read Newspaper	74 (35.4)	198 (41.1)	81 (39.1)	197 (44.6)	50 (23.0)	226 (31.7)	80 (36.7)	335 (51.6)
Watch TV	154 (73.7)	373 (77.4)	150 (72.0)	345 (78.1)	158 (72.8)	517 (72.6)	159 (72.9)	525 (80.9)
Listen to Radio	94 (45.0)	228 (47.3)	156 (75.4)	327 (74.0)	127 (58.5)	390 (54.8)	86 (39.4)	304 (46.8)
Total	209 (30.2)	482 (69.8)	207	442	217	712	218	649

Table 4
Percentage of Ever-Married Adolescent Women who have Heard About AIDS by Source of Information Received In Selected States: NFHS-2 Data

Source of Information Received	*Andhra Pradesh*		*Karnataka*		*Tamil Nadu*		*Maharashtra*	
	15-19	20-24	15-19	20-24	15-19	20-24	15-19	20-24
Radio	65 (31.1)	162 (33.6)	145 (70.0)	310 (70.1)	109 (50.2)	416 (41.6)	43 (19.7)	171(26.3)
Television	156 (74.6)	379 (78.6)	170 (82.1)	366 (82.8)	176 (81.1)	587 (82.4)	167 (76.6)	524 (80.7)
Cinema	39 (18.7)	93 (19.3)	25 (12.1)	55 (12.4)	15 (6.9)	107 (15.0)	-	15 (2.3)
Newspaper/ Magazine	26 (12.4)	88 (18.3)	40 (19.3)	115 (26.0)	33 (15.2)	164 (23.0)	33 (15.1)	158 (24.3)
Poster/Hording	13 (6.2)	40 (8.3)	23 (11.1)	52 (11.8)	24 (11.1)	151 (21.1)	32 (14.7)	136 (21.0)
Health Worker	7 (3.3)	16 (3.3)	5 (2.4)	16 (3.6)	14 (6.5)	27 (3.8)	7 (3.2)	35 (5.4)
Friends/ Relatives	79 (37.8)	196 (40.7)	66 (31.9)	141 (51.9)	86 (39.6)	309 (43.4)	72 (33.0)	203 (31.3)
School/ teacher	3 (1.4)	6 (1.2)	2 (1.0)	3 (0.7)	4 (1.8)	7 (1.0)	9 (4.1)	14 (2.2)

Source of Knowledge about AIDS

Table 4 shows the percentage of ever-married adolescent (15-19) and young (20-24) women who have heard about AIDS from specific source in Andhra Pradesh, Karnataka, Tamil Nadu and Maharashtra. Television was the most important source of information about AIDS among adolescent and young women. More than 75.0% who know about AIDS received information from television in these four states. Among these four states (Table 4) more than 80.0% of women in Karnataka, Tamil Nadu and between 75.0 to 80.0% women in Andhra Pradesh and Maharashtra expressed that they knew about AIDS through Television. Other important source of information about AIDS was Radio and friends/ relatives. In Karnataka 70.0% of the women (Table 4) and in Tamil Nadu 40.0 to 50.0% women expressed Radio as a source of information about AIDS. Television, followed by Radio, was the most important source of information about AIDS for adolescent and youth women. However, friends and relatives were next most important source of AIDS information for illiterate and rural women who were not exposed to electronic media.

Knowledge of Ways to Avoid AIDS

Ever married adolescent and young women in these four states who have heard of AIDS were asked the way to avoid AIDS (Yes/No) and the results were given in Table 5. Further analysis was done for the responses given to 'what a person could do to avoid AIDS' and the results are given in Table 6.

Among women who have heard about AIDS, a large majority of women knew some ways to avoid AIDS (Table 5), only 17.2% adolescent and 15.6% youth in Andhra Pradesh, 16.8% and 16.1% in Karnataka and 12.4% and 10.9% in Maharashtra respectively do not know any way to avoid infection. Less than 4.0% of the adolescent and young women in Tamil Nadu Knew 'no way to avoid AIDS'. The low percentage in Tamil Nadu clearly indicates that knowledge of ways to avoid AIDS was very high than other states.

Among women who reported that something could be done to prevent AIDS, the most commonly mentioned ways of avoiding AIDS in Maharashtra was 'having only one partner' among adolescent (Table 6, 34.9, 37.6) and young women. In case of Andhra Pradesh, it was 'avoiding injections/using clean needles'. 'Ways to avoid AIDS' was found to be different in Karnataka and Tamil Nadu. Adolescent women in Tamil Nadu and Young women in Karnataka expressed same reason viz: 'avoid sex with commercial sex worker'.

Table 5
Percentage of Ever Married Adolescent Women who have Ever Heard of AIDS and Ways to Avoid AIDS In Selected States: NFHS-2 Data

States	*Ever Heard of AIDS*	*Ways to Avoid* AIDS	*Age* 15-19	*Group* 20-24	*Total*
Andhra Pradesh	Yes	No	36 (17.2)	74 (15.6)	110 (15.9)
		Yes	129 (61.7)	316 (65.6)	445 (64.4)
	DK	44 (21.1)	92 (19.1)	136 (19.7)	
	χ^2 NS	Total	209 (100.0)	482 (100.0)	691 (100.0)
Karnataka	Yes	No	52 (16.8)	71 (16.1)	123 (19.0)
	Yes	113(54.6)	290 (65.6)	403 (62.1)	
	DK	42 (20.3)	81 (18.3)	123 (19.0)	
	χ^2 =9.14,**	Total	207 (100.0)	442 (100.0)	649 (100.0)
Maharashtra	Yes	No	27 (12.4)	71(10.9)	98 (11.3)
	Yes	133 (61.0)	462 (71.2)	595 (68.6)	
	DK	58 (26.6)	116 (17.9)	174 (20.1)	
	χ^2 =8.64,**	Total	218 (100.0)	649 (100.0)	867 (100.0)
Tamil Nadu	Yes	No	6 (2.8)	26 (3.7)	32 (3.4)
	Yes	199 (91.7)	653 (91.7)	852 (91.7)	
	DK	12 (5.5)	33 (4.6)	45 (4.8)	
	χ^2 NS	Total	217 (100.0)	712 (100.0)	929 (100.0)

Table 6
Percentage of Ever-Married Adolescent Women who have Heard About AIDS by Ways to Avoid AIDS In Selected States: NFHS-2 Data

Ways to Avoid AIDS	*Andhra Pradesh*		*Karnataka*		*Tamil Nadu*		*Maharashtra*	
	15-19	20-24	15-19	20-24	15-19	20-24	15-19	20-24
Abstaining from Sex	3 (1.4)	14 (2.9)	3 (1.4)	6 (1.5)	4 (1.8)	13 (1.8)	1 (0.5)	11 (1.7)
Using Condoms	25 (12.0)	89 (18.5)	13 (6.3)	37 (8.4)	17 (7.8)	95 (13.3)	32 (14.7)	171(26.3)
Having only one Partner	53 (25.4)	176 (36.5)	48 (23.2)	104 (23.4)	161 (74.2)	555 (77.9)	76 (34.9)	244 (37.6)
Avoid Sex with Commercial Sex workers	58 (27.8)	114 (23.7)	64 (30.9)	175 (39.6)	84 (38.7)	320 (44.9)	70 (32.1)	246 (37.9)
Avoiding Sex with homosexual	1 (0.5)	11 (2.3)	28 (13.5)	60 (13.6)	2 (0.9)	14 (2.0)	3 (1.4)	11 (1.7)
Avoiding blood Transfusions	37 (17.7)	116 (24.1)	51 (24.6)	135 (30.5)	37 (17.1)	188 (26.4)	10 (4.6)	65 (10.0)
Avoiding injections/ using clean needles	79 (37.8)	204 (42.3)	68 (32.9)	168 (38.0)	47 (21.7)	239 (33.6)	45 (20.6)	199 (30.7)
Knows no way to avoid AIDS	36 (17.2)	74 (15.4)	32 (16.8)	78 (16.9)	6 (2.8)	26 (3.7)	27 (12.4)	71 (10.9)

Table 7

Ever Married Adolescent Women in Risk of Heard and Not Heard of AIDS in Selected States in India - Odds Ratio through Logit Regression Analysis, NFHS-2 Data

Explanatory Variables	*Andhra Pradesh*			*Karnataka*			*Maharashtra*			*Tamil Nadu*		
	15-19	20-24	15-24	15-19	20-24	15-24	15-19	20-24	15-24	15-19	20-24	15-24
Place of Residence												
Urban (Ref)												
Rural	3.220**	2.539**	2.885**	1.772NS	1.887NS	1.935**	2.086*	1.963**	2.132**	NS	10.24**	11.09**
Literacy												
Illiterate (Ref)												
Literate	0.138**	0.159**	0.155**	0.187**	0.132**	0.154**	0.213**	0.183**	0.191**	0.129**	0.171**	0.160**
Mass media												
Not Exposed (Ref)												
Exposed	0.368**	0.234**	0.283**	0.239**	0.165**	0.191*	0.293**	0.204**	0.229**	0.4[illegible]4NS	0.341*	0.350 NS
Ethnicity												
SC & ST (Ref)												
Non SC, ST	1.690 NS	0.930 NS	1.154 NS	0.790 NS	0.908 NS	0.856 NS	0.986 NS	0.981 NS	0.976 NS	2.81 NS	1.395 NS	1.550 NS
Constant	2.458**	5.568**	4.021**	2.724	4.681**	3.732**	2.023**	4.046	3.134	2[illegible].447	18.75**	20.74**
-2 Log likelihood	445.32	734.03	1199.08	452.74	724.15	1184.10	460.04	870.69	1344.97	6[illegible].647	311.571	384.972
100 * R^2	28.0	31.1	30.0	28.4	35.3	32.9	25.3	25.8	27.0	10.1	12.2	11.5

* P<. 05, ** P<. 001 NS= Not Significant Ref: Reference category

Knowledge of AIDS and knowledge of ways to avoid infection were very high among women in Tamil Nadu. However, only 7.8% of adolescent women (Table 6) and 13.3 young women knew 'using condoms' as ways to avoid AIDS. High percent young women (20-24) in Maharashtra and Andhra Pradesh expressed 'using condom' as a method to avoid AIDS. This implies that the AIDS prevention awareness programme in all these four states should have increased and efforts to educate adolescent and young women about condom use as a way to avoid infection.

LOGIT Regression Analysis

The explanatory variables viz., place of residence, literacy, exposed to mass media and ethnicity were considered for the analysis to understand the knowledge of AIDS in the selected states. The calculated odds ratio by adolescent (15-19), young women (20-24) and both the age groups (15-24) is given in Table 7. Results show that there was no significant effect by ethnicity on heard of AIDS (Knowledge of AIDS) in all these states. Place of residence, literacy, mass media showed significant impact on knowledge of AIDS in Andhra Pradesh and Maharashtra, among all women (Table 7). In Karnataka, literacy and mass media should have a significant impact on Knowledge of AIDS and in Tamil Nadu significant impact was observed with literacy variable among all women.

Summary and Conclusion

The knowledge and ways to avoid AIDS among adolescent (15-19) and young (20-24) women in four high prevalence states and the socio-economic variables influencing the knowledge of AIDS data were collected from NFHS-2. This secondary data analysis is based on the information collected through a nation-wide survey NFHS-2. Data analysis revealed that:

- There is substantial difference in awareness between adolescent and young women who have heard about AIDS and were found to be more among young women (20-24) in Andhra Pradesh, Karnataka, and Maharashtra.
- In case of Tamil Nadu the awareness between adolescent and young women were found to be very minimal. More than 90.0% of the adolescent and young women were heard of AIDS in Tamil Nadu may be attributed to the AIDS awareness and prevention campaign programs in Tamil Nadu.
- Percentage of the rural women who have heard of AIDS were found to be more than urban in all these states except in Maharashtra.
- Television was the most important source of information about AIDS among adolescent and young women. More than seventy five percent who know about AIDS received information from television in these four states.
- Among women who have heard about AIDS, a large majority of women knew some ways to avoid AIDS
- Knowledge of AIDS and knowledge of ways to avoid infection were very high among women in Tamil Nadu than other three states.

From the above analysis, it was evident that Television as a mass media played a major role in giving information about AIDS to women in rural areas in high prevalence states. Women in Tamil Nadu were aware of AIDS and ways to avoid AIDS better than other three states. Awareness programs about AIDS played a major role in enhancing knowledge of rural women about AIDS in Tamil Nadu. Other states should implement the same strategies adopted in Tamil Nadu in increasing knowledge of adolescent women about AIDS infection, which leads to better healthy state/s.

REFERENCES

Bhardwaj, Sanjana (2006). *Adolescents Reproductive Health Perspectives, The Young Faces of HIV in India,* in C.P. Prakasam, S. Sivaraju, (ed) BR Publishers, New Delhi.

NACO (2004). *Annual Report,* The Ministry of Health and Family-Welfare, New Delhi.

Ojha, V.P., and Pradhan, R.K. (2006). *The Macro-Economic and Sectoral Impact of HIV and AIDS in India: A CGE Analysis,* UNDP, NACO, NCAER, New Delhi.

Population Foundation of India (2003). *Fact Sheet HIV/AIDS,* New Delhi.

UNICEF, UNAIDS, WHO (2002). *Young People and HIV/AIDS,* Opportunity and Crises, July.

8

Reproductive and Mental Health of Married Adolescent Girls in Visakhapatnam

Prof. M.V.R.Raju & Dr. N.D.S. Naga Seema

Summary

Adolescent reproductive and sexual health issues are currently of great public health and social concern and marriage transforms virtually all aspects of girls' lives. Marriage marks the beginning of their sexual life and soon to become mothers. Marriage and childbearing bring new physical and mental health problems. The present study aimed at examining the biographical variables with regard to reproductive and sexual health awareness and to identify mental health problems of married adolescent girls. The sample of the study comprised of 181 married adolescent girls aged between 14-20 years in Visakhapatnam. A Semi-structured Questionnaire and the General Health Questionnaire were used in the present study. The findings revealed that a large proportion of the adolescent girls are married at the age of 19-21 years. Half of the married adolescents were educated below 10th standard. Most of them belonged to the Backward Caste communities and live in urban areas. Severe depression was experienced by tribal dwellers and scheduled castes. Majority of the respondents were not aware of reproductive and sexual health issues.

Introduction

Adolescent reproductive health always remained as a low priority area for health professionals and policy makers (Friedman, 1990; Serrano, 1990). However, adolescence is a vulnerable period, and the onset and pace of adolescence are changing, that often disproportionately affect them. Data gathered from the 1989 Bangladesh Fertility Survey indicate that a relatively large proportion (18.0%) of the adolescent marriages took place even before the onset of menarche and there was a clustering of majority of adolescent marriages immediately after the menarche period (Islam and Mahmud, 1996). India also shows a high rate of adolescent marriages especially among the women aged between 20-24 years, as high as 71.0% had already married by age 20.

In India, most adolescent girls of 15-19 years old are married. Adolescent girls aged between 15-19 constitute about 10.0% of the population. About 40.0% of adolescent girls are married before the age of 18, at a median age of 16, in contravention of the minimum legal age of (18 years) marriage.

When girls are married at a young age, it is often due to poverty, dowry pressures, parental concerns about premarital sex and pregnancy, and other economic or cultural reasons. For many, marriage marks the beginning of their sexual life and an increased social isolation, as girls typically leave their homes and natal villages, losing contact with friends and peers. Existing data cannot definitively show the causal links between early marriage, poverty, low educational attainment, and other social indicators, which are likely multi-directional. However, studies have found that married girls have many disadvantages related to health, social, and economic spheres, hampering their ability to negotiate their reproductive and broader lives, including the needs of their children.

Marriage transforms virtually all aspects of girls' lives. Typically, girls who marry are moved from their familiar home and village, lose contact with friends, initiate sexual activity with someone they barely know, and soon become mothers. While existing data cannot definitively show causal links, the literature suggests that young age and/or young age at marriage may be independently Correlated with low domestic authority, limited freedom of movement, and increased partner violence (Mason 1998; Jejeebhoy 2000; Kishor 2000; Kishor and Johnson 2004). Married adolescents comprise the majority of sexually active adolescent girls in most developing countries.

Rationale of the Study

Early marriage, that is, marriage below18 years of age, violates girls' rights, truncates their childhood and denies them a say in the choice of partner and timing of marriage. In India, despite several policy and programme efforts, early marriage persists with considerable variation between and within states. Unraveling the complex drivers of early marriage in particular contexts requires careful site-specific diagnostic research. Whether and how these downward pressures on age at marriage are ameliorated by India's national and state efforts to foster later marriage is not well understood. Research is required at the community level to understand the extent of actual implementation of various policies and programmes intended to prevent early marriage and the extent to which such efforts have found acceptability among parents and the community and to identify mental health problems and give proper interventions. To begin to fill this gap the present study was conducted.

Information about health issues among unmarried adolescents in India has recently been highlighted, but little is known about married adolescent girls and whether and how their reproductive health needs are met.

Adolescent Reproductive and Sexual Health

Adolescent reproductive and sexual health refers to the physical and emotional well-being of adolescents and includes their ability to be healthy and remain free from too-early or unwanted pregnancy, unsafe abortion, and sexually transmitted diseases including HIV/AIDS, and sexual violence or coercion (Sendorwitz, 1995; WHO, 1998).

In India, adolescent women, both married and unmarried, often lack even basic knowledge about HIV transmission and prevention measures. In addition, gender disparities in economic power and unequal social status affect their capacity to influence when, where and how sexual relations occur, rendering them vulnerable to coerced or unwanted sex, and placing them at high risk of exposure to HIV, which is becoming increasingly prevalent in India. Thus, in order to be effective, HIV prevention interventions must not only provide the information and tools that young women need to protect themselves from infection (but also help in empowerment of women in sexual matters.)

As marriage marks the initiation of sexual activity among an overwhelming majority of adolescents in India (Pelto et al., 2000) while there is growing evidence of premarital sexual activity among young men and women (Abraham and Kumar, 1999). Married adolescent girls experience parenthood even before their body is fully matured leading several biological risks. The experience of early and closely spaced childbearing is particularly risky for adolescents.

Access to knowledge and safe, non-judgmental, and supportive clinical and counseling services is essential, and due to existing social norms and gender biases these services are currently not accessible to married adolescent girls.

Further, because adolescent girls are an isolated and neglected population, little is known about their reproductive and sexual health (RSH) needs, status and outcomes, and the policies and guidelines around provision of RSH services to adolescents remain silent.

The objectives of the study are as follows:

- To examine the biographical variables of the married adolescent girls.
- To examine married adolescents reproductive and sexual health awareness.
- To assess mental health problems of married adolescent girls.

Method

Sample: The sample of the study comprised of 181 married adolescent girls whose age range was 14-22 years in Visakhapatnam.

Tools: The tools, which were used for collection of data, are as follows:

- The Biographical variables included age, education, income, caste, type of marriage, place of living.
- A semi structured interview schedule was used to assess reproductive and sexual health knowledge of the respondents.
- The General Health Questionnaire developed by David P. Goldberg (1979) is for measuring personal well-being and mental health. The GHQ included 28 items listed in the questionnaire. The four –point answers follow the pattern of 'more (or less) than usual', 'same as usual', 'less (or more) than usual', and 'much less (or more) than usual'. The four dimensions included somatic symptoms, anxiety/insomnia, social dysfunction and severe depression.

Results

The results of the present study are categorized in four sections:

Section I: Socio-Demographic Characteristics of the Respondents

The maximum number of married adolescent girls was found to be 109 under the age group of 19-21 years. This indicates that a large proportion of the adolescent girls are married at the age of 19-21 years.

Table 1 presents the educational status of respondents in the present sample. The percentage of girls who studied below 10th standard was 58.6. About 30.4% of the respondents completed 10th standard, 7.2% did their intermediate and only 3.9% of the respondents were graduates. The most significant findings in this study reveal that more than half of the sample had been educated up to secondary level or discontinued studies during secondary or primary level.

Table 1
Education-wise Distribution of the Sample

Education	*Number*	*Percentage*
Below 10th	106	58.6
10th Standard	55	30.4
Intermediate	13	7.2
Graduation	7	3.9

Monthly income of 49.2% of the respondents was less than Rs.2000 per month while 26.0%, 1.7% and 23.2% were earning Rs.3000, Rs. 4000 and Rs.4000 and above per month respectively. The monthly income below Rs 2000/- indicates poorer sections of the society, which is a major determinant of poor socio economical conditions of the respondents. These gives an indication of unaffordability and reduced accessibility to health related matters and issues.

Regarding type of marriage, it has been observed that in case of 68.5 % of the respondents it was arranged marriage while 31.5% married on their own i.e., love marriage. Though there is a shift in marriage practices, the results found highest percentage age of arranged marriage that strongly support early marriages, which are associated to the cultural and social expectations of the parents. It happens often due to poverty, dowry pressures, parental concerns about, premarital sex and pregnancy, or other economic or cultural reasons. A survey done in Lucknow, India, in 1985 revealed that most of the unmarried females (84.0%) favored their marriages being settled by their parents but with their own final approval and consent. Only 3.0% preferred a love marriage. Nearly 13.0% of these girls were of the opinion that their marriage should be settled entirely by their parents and that they need not be consulted (Kumari, 1985).

Table 2
Caste-wise Distribution of the Sample

Caste	*Number*	*Percentage*
Scheduled Caste	45	24.9
Scheduled Tribe	29	16.0
Backward Castes	92	50.8
Other Castes	15	8.3

Table 2 indicates the predominant feature of the Indian socio-cultural system i.e. the caste system. It was found that 24.9% of the respondents belonged to scheduled caste, 16.0% were Scheduled Tribe, and Backward Castes were about 50.8%, other castes of the respondents were 8.3%. This indicates that majority of the respondents belonged to Backward Caste.

Table 3
Place of Living-wise Distribution of The Sample

Place of Living	*Number*	*Percentage*
Rural	11	6.1
Urban	120	66.3
Tribal	50	27.6

Table 3 indicates that 6.1% of the respondents were from rural background, 66.3% were from urban and 27.6% were from tribal. The majority of the respondents belonged to urban dwellings.

Section II: Biographical Variables with regard to Mental Health Problems

Data in Table 4 indicates significant difference between biographical variable and type of marriage with regard to mental health factors. It was found that the respondents who had arranged marriage (mean =11.22) were significant on social dysfunction than those who had love marriage (m= 9.98). This is because once the parents get married to their daughters they feel that their responsibility is over. Now once they are married, they start their earnings and run family depending on their own earnings and living. There is a less involvement in social activities among the respondents who had arranged marriage. A study supported these findings that the married girls had less social mobility/freedom of movement than unmarried girls (Amin, Mahmud, and Huq 2002). Marriage during adolescence is common among those who are poor, less educated, and who observe more traditional customs and rituals. Early marriage can be seen as a means to financial security both for the family and the married adolescent to maintain economic, social, or political ties between families, castes, or tribes; or to protect young girls from (coerced or voluntary) premarital sex or pregnancy, both seen as dishonorable to the family (Mathur, 2003).

Table 4
Type of Marriage and Mental Health Problems

Sl. No.	*Factors*	*Group*	*N*	*Mean*	*SD*	*'t'-Value*
1.	Somatic symptoms	Love Marriage	57	9.64	3.17	0.976
		Arranged marriage	124	10.22	3.90	
2.	Anxiety/ Insomnia	Love Marriage	57	8.87	3.13	1.361
		Arranged marriage	124	9.55	3.11	
3.	Social Dysfunction	Love Marriage	57	9.98	3.30	2.169*
		Arranged marriage	124	11.22	3.70	
4.	Severe Depression	Love Marriage	57	8.29	3.01	1.246
		Arranged marriage	124	8.87	2.80	
	Total	Love Marriage	57	36.80	10.27	1.805
		Arranged marriage	124	39.87	10.79	

* *Significant at 0.05 level*

Data in Table 5 indicates that there is a significant difference (p<. 005) in the mental health problems between the respondents who were working and those who were housewives. Working women had less autonomy and command over household and reproductive decision- making. The overall mental health of working women is affected owing to the fact that they had to manage both the domestic responsibilities as well as work outside to financially support their family members/spouse. They expressed associated with anxiety and somatic symptom such as headache, insomnia, fatigue, and appetite disturbance as a result of being subjected to role-related limitations.

Table 5
Working Status and Mental Health Problems

Sl. No.	*Factors*	*Working status*	*N*	*Mean*	*S D*	*'t'-Value*
1.	Somatic symptoms	Housewife	158	9.87	3.61	1.578
		Working	23	11.17	4.10	
2.	Anxiety/ Insomnia	Housewife	158	9.17	3.04	1.878
		Working	23	10.47	3.51	
3.	Social Dysfunction	Housewife	158	10.64	3.56	1.851
		Working	23	12.13	3.78	
4.	Severe Depression	Housewife	158	8.58	2.61	1.253
		Working	23	9.39	4.26	
	Total	Housewife	158	38.29	10.38	2.063*
		Working	23	43.17	12.02	

* *Significant at 0.05 level*

It can be observed from the Table 5, that somatic symptoms are profoundly experienced by tribal married adolescents (m=11.50) as when compared to those living in rural (m=9.45) and urban areas (m= 9.49).

Table 6
Place of Residence and Mental Health Problems

Sl. No.	*Factors*	*Group*	*N*	*Mean*	*S D*	*ANOVA*
1.	Somatic symptoms	Rural	11	9.45	4.10	5.653**
		Urban	120	9.49	3.44	
		Tribal	50	11.50	3.84	
2.	Anxiety/ Insomnia	Rural	11	9.36	4.38	13.681**
		Urban	120	8.58	2.61	
		Tribal	50	11.16	3.25	
3.	Social Dysfunction	Rural	11	9.72	4.49	41.963**
		Urban	120	9.55	3.11	
		Tribal	50	14.14	2.23	
4.	Severe Depression	Rural	11	7.63	1.28	6.551**
		Urban	120	8.29	2.87	
		Tribal	50	9.88	2.81	
	Total	Rural	11	36.18	13.18	22.578**
		Urban	120	35.92	9.65	
		Tribal	50	46.68	8.57	

* *Significant at 0.05 level,* ** *Significant at 0.01 level*

It was also found that the tribal married adolescents were suffering greatly with anxiety/insomnia (m=11.16), social dysfunction (m=14.14) and severe depression (m=9.88). This indicates that those married adolescents who are living in tribal areas experience mental health problems. But the overall mental health problem was found to be high among those living in the rural areas (m=36.18). Presumably due to lack of educational opportunities, knowledge based information and traditional families in rural areas, the respondents lacked many opportunities and were restricted to the four walls of the house. They experience somatic complaints, anxiety, sleeplessness, stiffness in the head, severe headache, feeling of isolation and suicidal tendencies.

Table 7
Caste and Mental Health Problems

Sl. No.	*Factors*	*Group*	*N*	*Mean*	*SD*	*ANOVA*
1.	Somatic symptoms	Scheduled Caste	45	9.68	4.21	2.703*
		Scheduled Tribe	29	8.65	2.63	
		Backward Castes	92	10.41	3.68	
		Other Castes	15	11.53	3.04	
2.	Anxiety/ Insomnia	Scheduled Caste	45	9.46	3.03	1.599
		Scheduled Tribe	29	8.27	2.81	
		Backward Castes	92	9.47	3.19	
		Other Castes	15	10.20	3.32	
3.	Social Dysfunction	Scheduled Caste	45	10.08	3.36	6.503**
		Scheduled Tribe	29	8.89	3.29	
		Backward Castes	92	11.47	3.50	
		Other Castes	15	12.86	3.77	
4.	Severe Depression	Scheduled Caste	45	8.57	2.75	3.551**
		Scheduled Tribe	29	7.27	.99	
		Backward Castes	92	9.21	3.32	
		Other Castes	15	8.53	1.59	
	Total	Scheduled Caste	45	37.82	10.65	4.823**
		Scheduled Tribe	29	33.10	8.48	
		Backward Castes	92	40.58	10.95	
		Other Castes	15	43.13	8.91	

* *Significant at 0.05 level,* ** *Significant at 0.01 level*

Table 7 indicates the most unique feature of the Indian social system that is the caste system. It was found that scheduled caste married adolescents were experiencing somatic symptoms (m=9.68), social dysfunction (m=10.08) and severe depression (m=8.57).. Depression during adolescence was found to predict higher rates of marriage among younger women and subsequent marital dissatisfaction also. They felt that they had less cooperation, less emotional support, feelings of sadness, unhappiness, feelings of worthlessness or fatigue, poor self-esteem, difficulty concentrating or making decisions, and feelings of hopelessness). It was also found that the overall mental health of the Scheduled Caste, Scheduled Tribe are highly significantly experiencing mental health problems. This clearly indicates that these are socially disadvantaged people are at the same time less privileged to all sorts of needs and requirements.

Section III: Knowledge of Reproductive Health

Data in Table 8 indicate that the 70.2% of the respondents were aware of menstrual cycle while 25.4% of them did not know the same. The study also found that 4.4% of the respondents did not give any response to the item. It could be because of shyness or hesitation. Knowledge of menstruation seems to be adequate among the married adolescent girls. It is assumed that 25.4% of the respondents who had no prior awareness of the menstruation cycle either received no information about the same from their mothers or their mothers' hesitated from expressing their views to their daughters (Adhikary, 2007).

Table 8
Awareness of Menstrual Cycle

Sl. No.	*Menstruation Awareness*	*Number*	*Percentage*
1.	No answer	8	4.4
2.	Yes	127	70.2
3.	No	46	25.4

Table 9 indicate the findings related to whether there were restriction on the respondents with regard to Mobility, Discontinued school, talking to men and Food. It was found that 69.1% of the respondents had restriction with regard to mobility, 71.3% discontinued school, 71.3% were restricted from talking to other men, while 74.6% had restriction with regards to food. In almost all rural and urban societies there continues to exist sexual role and relationship expectations based on gender differences. The double standards are more evident for girls than for boys, girls face more risk than boys. Mobility and opportunity decreases for young women after reaching puberty owing to the fear of the family that she might either be sexually victimized or have consented intercourse which would bring dishonor to the family. Thus the role of women empowerment becomes very significant with respect to this.

Table 9
Restrictions of Living Conditions

Sl. No.	*Restrictions of*		*Number*	*Percentage*	÷^{2} *Value*
1.	Mobility	No	125	69.1	26.30**
		Yes	56	30.9	
2	Discontinued school	No	129	71.3	32.75**
		Yes	52	28.7	
3.	Talking to men	No	129	71.3	32.75**
		Yes	52	28.7	
4.	Food	No	135	74.6	43.76**
		Yes	46	25.4	

* *Significant at 0.01 level*

Table10 indicates the respondent's knowledge of reproductive system. About 97.2% of the respondents expressed correctly that the chance of becoming pregnant is not in the middle of the cycle. About 87.3% of the respondents expressed correctly that pregnancy couldn't take place during periods. About 76.8% of them stated that there is hardly any chance of conception right after the periods; almost all the respondents (100%) felt that pregnancy cannot take place just before the beginning of the periods. About 94.5% responded that there would be same chance all the time while 42.0% of them were aware of the point of highest likelihood of conception in the menstruation cycle

Table 10
Point of Menstruation Cycle with Greater Likelihood of Causing Conception

Sl. No	*Greatest chance of becoming pregnant*		*Number*	*Percentage*	*$\div^2$ Value*
1.	In the middle of cycle	No	176	97.2	161.55**
		Yes	5	2.8	
2	During her periods	No	158	87.3	100.69**
		Yes	23	12.7	
3.	Right after her period has ended	No	139	76.8	51.98**
		Yes	42	23.2	
4.	Just before her period begins	No	180	100.0	0.0
		Yes	0	0.0	
5.	Same chance all the time	No	171	94.5	143.21**
		Yes	10	5.5	
6.	Don't know	No	76	42.0	4.64**
		Yes	105	58.0	

***Significant at 0.01 level, * Significant at 0.05 level*

Table 11 shows a high level of variation with regard to becoming pregnant if the respondent has sex only once. About 61.3% of them didn't know, or rather felt there is a possibility of becoming pregnant. About 28.7% of them did not agree that a girl could become pregnant if she has sex only once while about 9.9% of the respondents believed that the girl could become pregnant. It indicates that most of the married adolescents were aware of getting pregnancy during a particular period.

Table 11
Chances of Pregnancy with One Time Intercourse

Sl. No	*Decision for Pregnancy*	*Number*	*Percentage*	*÷^{2} Value*
1.	Yes	18	9.9	73.40**
2.	No	52	28.7	
3.	Don't Know	111	61.3	

** *Significant at 0.01 level*

Table 12 provides the results towards negotiation of contraceptive use with their husband. About 89.5%, 86.7%, 93.4%, 84.5% and 77.9% of the respondents respectively did not have either low freedom of choice that is they cannot avoid or delay in sex, nor do they have proper ways to avoid pregnancy, knowledge about the use of condoms, avoiding HIV/AIDS and sexually transmitted diseases. This indicates that there is no awareness with regard to sexuality, sexual norms and decision- making. Since India is a male dominated country there is less chance of freedom of choice and decision making rights given to women.

Table 12
Negotiation of Contraceptive Use

Sl. No.	*Negotiation of Contraceptive Use*		*Number*	*Percentage*	*÷^{2} Value*
1.	Avoiding or delaying sex	No	162	89.5	112.97**
		Yes	19	10.5	
2	Ways to avoid pregnancy	No	157	86.7	97.72**
		Yes	24	13.3	
3.	Use of condoms	No	169	93.4	136.18**
		Yes	12	6.6	
4.	Avoiding HIV/AIDS	No	153	84.5	86.32**
		Yes	28	15.5	
5.	Avoiding sexually transmitted diseases	No	141	77.9	56.35**
		Yes	40	22.1	

** *Significant at 0.01 level*

Data in Table 13 indicates that 54.7% of the respondents were not confident to convince their partner to use a condom while 27.6% of them expressed average in their confidence in convincing their partners. On the other hand, about 11.0% stated that they could highly convince their partner to use condom. About 6.6% of the respondents did not answer this question, perhaps, owing to taboos attached with the issue and/or inhibitions.

Table 13
Level of Confidence to Convince Spouse to Use a Condom

Sl. No.	*Level of Confidence to Convince*	*Number*	*Percentage*	*$\div^2$ Value*
1.	No Answer	12	6.6	102.86**
2.	High	20	11.0	
3.	Average	50	27.6	
4.	No	99	54.7	

** *Significant at 0.01 level*

An overwhelming number of the respondents (86.2%) mentioned that their partners did not use condom during sexual intercourse while only 5.0% of them reported affirmative (Table 14).

Table 14
Does Your Partner Use a Condom?

Sl. No.	*Does your partner use a condom?*	*Number*	*Percentage*	*$\div^2$ Value*
1.	No Answer	16	8.8	227.94**
2.	Yes	9	5.0	
3.	No	156	86.2	

** *Significant at 0.01 level*

So far as decision-making process is concerned, data indicates that more than half of the couple (58.0%) took decision jointly for prevention of pregnancy. Surprisingly, most of the married adolescents (89.0%) were not aware of any methods of contraception, while only 8.3% of them reported having some knowledge about contraceptive methods.

Table 15
Reasons for Abortion

Sl. No.	*Reasons for abortions*		*Number*	*Percentage*	*χ^2 Value*
1.	For spacing	No Answer	72	39.8	91.30**
		Yes	106	58.6	
		No	3	1.7	
2.	Unwanted child	No Answer	106	58.6	91.30**
		Yes	72	39.8	
		No	3	1.7	
3.	Unmarried	No Answer	88	48.6	81.75**
		Yes	90	49.7	
		No	3	1.7	
4.	Gender	No Answer	123	68.0	115.17**
		Yes	52	28.7	
		No	6	3.3	

** *Significant at 0.01 level*

A number of reasons were found to be playing important role for abortion, which include spacing (58.6%), followed by pregnancy before marriage (49.7%), unwanted child (39.8%) and gender of the child (28.7%).

Replaying to a question whether married adolescent girls wish to become pregnant, 70.7% of them answered 'yes', which is very natural or biological phenomenon. On the other hand, about 16.0% of them did not want be pregnant. The study also revealed that majority of the adolescent girls (81.2%) did not try to end their pregnancy.

Table 16
Whether underwent Ultrasound Guided Scan

Sl. No.	Undergone ultra sound scan	Number	Percentage	χ^2 Value
1.	No Answer	7	3.9	99.64**
2.	Yes	63	34.8	
3.	Don't Know	111	61.3	

** *Significant at 0.01 level*

Data in Table 16 indicates the ultrasound scan awareness of the respondents. About half of the adolescents (61.3%) were not aware of the ultrasound-guided scan. It indicates how these individuals are managing when they are pregnant. In most of the poor and weaker sections of the society people never go to hospital for regular check ups and most of the delivery of the pregnant girls takes place at home. They have very limited knowledge about health related matters or the treatment. About one-third (34.8%) of them were aware of the ultrasound scan. It seems these individuals have already experienced during their health check ups.

Regarding gender determination of the child, most of the adolescents had no knowledge. Most of the respondents had adequate knowledge about HIV transmission and methods of prevention. Most of respondents reported that unsafe sex; blood transfusion and using non-sterilized needles are the means of HIV transmission.

Discussion and Conclusion

The present study aimed at assessing the knowledge about reproductive, sexual and mental health problems of married adolescent girls of Visakhapatnam. A large proportion of the adolescent girls are married, belonging in the age group 19-21 years. More than half of the married adolescents were educated below 10th standard. Major part of the respondents lie in the monthly income of below Rs. 2000. A large portion of the respondents had arranged marriage. Most of them belonged to the Backward Caste. The major %age of the respondents belonged to urban dwellings. Those living in Tribal areas and the scheduled caste experienced somatic symptoms. The respondents living in tribal areas were experiencing anxiety and insomnia Those living in tribal areas and belonging to the scheduled caste tribe, who had arranged marriage experienced social dysfunction as one of the mental health problem. Severe depression was experienced by tribal dwellers and scheduled castes. There was a significant difference in the mental health status between working and rural living married adolescents. Regarding knowledge about reproductive health, most of the respondents were aware of menstrual cycle. The respondents were highly restricted in terms of mobility, discontinued schooling, talking to men and choice of food. With regard to decision for pregnancy, most of them are aware of the chances of becoming pregnant. With regard to, sexual norms and decision making, it was found that they cannot avoid or delay sex, they do not have proper ways to avoid pregnancy, and they have insufficient knowledge about condoms, HIV/AIDS and sexually transmitted diseases. During negotiation of contraceptive use more than half of the respondents were not confident enough to convince their partner to use a condom. Large proportion mentioned that their partners did not use a condom. With regard to induced abortions it was found that more than half of the Couples decide to use some means to prevent pregnancy More than 80% of them did not answer whether they themselves, partner or other family members decide to use something to prevent pregnancy. Most married adolescents were not aware of any methods of contraception. It was found that one goes for abortion is due to spacing and if some one unmarried. Major part of the respondents had no role in the decision to terminate pregnancy half of the sample respondents were not aware of the ultrasound guided scan. Most of respondents reported that unsafe sex; blood transfusion and using non-sterilized needles are the means of HIV transmission. Inspite of having basic knowledge about the HIV/AIDS they have no awareness of the means of protecting oneself from the same. All these findings point to the overall negotiability over reproductive, sexual and mental health problems of the married adolescents. Access to knowledge, non-judgmental, supportive, clinical, counseling services, reproductive and sexual health awareness programmes is essential for married adolescent girls.

REFERENCES

Adhikari, P., Kadel, B., Dhungel, S.I., and Mandal, A. (2007). Knowledge and Practice Regarding Menstrual Hygiene in Rural Adolescent Girls of Nepal. *Katmandu University Medical Journal*, 5, 3, 19, 382-386.

Abraham, L. and Kumar, K.A. (1999). Sexual Experiences and Their Correlates among College Students in Mumbai City, India, *International Family Planning Perspectives*, 25 (3), 139-46.

Amin, S., Mahmud, S., and Huq, L. (2002). Baseline Survey Report on Rural Adolescents in Bangladesh, Dhaka: Ministry of Women's Affairs. Government of Bangladesh.

Friedman, H. (1990). Adolescent Health Promise and Paradox, In: H.M.Wallace and K.Giri (eds.), *Health Care of Women and Children in Developing Countries*, Oakland: Third Party Publishing.

Islam, M. and M. Mahmud (1996). Marriage Patterns And Some Issues Related To Adolescent Marriage In Bangladesh, *Asia-Pacific Population Journal*, 11(3), 27-42.

Jejeebhoy, S.J. (2000). Adolescent Sexual And Reproductive Behavior. A Review of The Evidence from India. In R. Ramsubban, and S. Jejeebhoy, (Eds), *Women's Reproductive Health in India*. Jaipur: Rawat Publications, New Delhi.

Kishor, Sunita (2000). 'Empowerment of Women in Egypt and Links to the Survival and Health of Their Infants,' in Harriet Presser and Gita Sen (eds.), *Women's Empowerment and Demographic Processes: Moving Beyond Cairo*. Oxford: Oxford University Press, 119–156.

Kishor, S, and Johnson, K. (2004). *Profiling Domestic Violence: A Multi-Country Study*. Calverton, MD: ORC Macro, 2004.

Kumari, R. (1985). Attitude of Girls Towards Marriage and A Planned Family, *Journal of Family Welfare*, 31(3), 53-60.

Mason, Karen Oppenheim (1998). 'Wives' Economic Decision-Making Power in the Family: Five Asian countries," in Karen Oppenheim Mason, Noriko O. Tsuya, and Minja Kim Choe (eds.), *The Changing Family in Comparative Perspective: Asia and the United States*. Honolulu: East-West Center, 105–133.

Mathur, S. (2003). *Too Young to Wed: The Lives, Rights and Health of Young Married Girls*. Washington, DC: ICRW.

Pelto, P.J., Joshi, A. and Verma, R. (2000). *Development of Sexuality and Sexual Behavior among Indian Males: Implications for Reproductive Health Programmes*. New Delhi: Population Council.

Serrano, C.V. (1990). Infant, Childhood and Adolescent Mortality in Developing Countries, In: H.M. Wallace and K.Giri (eds.). *Health Care of Women and Children in Developing Countries*, Oakland: Third Party Publishing.

Sendorwitz, J. (1995). Adolescent Health: Reassessing The Passage to Adulthood. World Bank Discussion Paper No.272.

World Health Organization. (1998). Overall Aims and Goals. Geneva: WHO.

9

Medical Termination of Pregnancy among Adolescent Girls in Kolkata

Dr. Amrita Roy, Prof. Dipankar Guha Roy
& Prof. Tapas Kumar Bose

Summary

The objective of the present study was to understand the socio-economic background of the pregnant adolescents in Kolkata along with medico-legal aspects. This hospital-based study was carried out in 2006 in the Eden Building of Medical College Hospital, Abinash Dutta Maternity Home and Lady Duffrin Queen Victoria Hospital, Kolkata. The study population comprised of 45 adolescent girls aged between 12 to 18 years, both married and unmarried. After the informed consent, they were interviewed according to the pre-designed pre-tested questionnaire. Findings revealed that majority of the adolescent girls who underwent MTP were aged between 16 to 18 years. Though the study was carried out in the urban area of Kolkata, more than half of them (53.3%) came from rural and suburban areas and mostly belonged to very poor socio-economic background. About 24.0% of the girls were illiterate while 44.4% studied up to the primary level. Most of the adolescent girls were housewives (58.0%) with one child. The unmarried adolescent girls (20.0%) were usually students and/or domestic assistants with a history of sexual promiscuity. This reflects the high rate of prevalence of early marriage (below 18 years) in the lower socio-economic strata. The subjects mostly belonged to Scheduled Caste Hindu community. About 60.0% of the girls did not use contraceptives or family planning methods. For most of the girls, it was their first abortion. The incidence of abortion was highest within the first trimester (95.6%). Social stigma was the chief cause of MTP (75.6%). However, two rape victims sought humanitarian abortion. Most of the girls (46.7%) had mild anemia at the time of examination. Dilatation and evacuation (80.0%) were the most popular methods of abortion.

Introduction

Medical Termination of Pregnancy (MTP) in adolescent girls presents as a matter of growing concern over the adverse social, health, economic and demographic effects of adolescent fertility. In the present pandemic of HIV/AIDS, adolescent pregnancy may help to analyze and interpret the sexual scenario among adolescent girls. In spite of an extensive study regarding MTP from its inception in India in April 1972, the actual incidence of abortion is not known (Mukherjee, 1994). In India, 6 million abortions take place every year of which 4 million are induced and 2 million are spontaneous (WHO, 1978). The practice of child marriage is still widely followed in India resulting in high adolescent fertility for which they are not prepared both physiologically and mentally. With greater permissiveness among the younger generation and due to rapid physical and sexual changes of the body during adolescence, which make them curious and impulsive, the adolescent population records a huge number of pregnancies ending in MTP. A pregnant woman less than 18 years of age is 2.5 times at risk for the complications of pregnancy than a pregnant woman between 18 to 25 years of age. Maternal mortality is 1-3.5 per 100,000 abortions in India (WHO, 1980). Seventh to eighth week of gestation is the optimum time for termination of pregnancy (Zimmerman, 1976). Studies indicate that the risk of death is 7 times higher for women who wait till 2nd trimester to terminate pregnancy (Tietze et al., 1969). Tietze and Lewitt noted that majority of women who patronize abortion are married. Simons (Simons, 1939) found that 25.0% of women in his study were married. An abortion may be sought by an unmarried woman from well-do-do family for protection of her image in the society and/or a married woman might go for abortion for keeping her family small. However, in the lower socio-economic group, such motivations are weak, or lacking. The poor classes want to have larger families and this account for a lower rate of abortions in this group (Singh et al., 2000). Adolescent pregnancy occurs in all societies but a very low rate of adolescent pregnancy is recorded in Netherlands (2/1000 adolescents) to extremely high rates in the Russian federation (more than 100/1000 adolescents) (Spitz et al., 1969). A New Zealand study shows that primi-gravida and nulliparous women were more significantly likely to choose first trimester MTP (Goodyear et al., 2006). A study in Norway showed that women who opted for abortions were more likely to be young, single and childless or have only one child. About 57.0% of these women were not using contraceptives at the time of conception (Skjeldestad, 1995). Another Norwegian study revealed that the prospect of single parenthood was the strongest determinant for choosing abortion independent of age and parity. Within all age groups of married women, the tendency to opt for abortion increased with parity rather than with age. Cohabitating and unmarried women chose abortion more often than married women. (Skjeldestad et al., 1994) A study conducted in San Francisco showed that 50.0% of the women were willing to consider abortion would do so during the first trimester (Learman et al., 2005). In Ohio, it was found that girls who had been pregnant also engaged in other risk behaviors including recent weapon carrying and cocaine use (Rome et al., 1998). A study in New York revealed that in 1992,112 pregnancies occurred per 1000 women aged 15-19 years of which 36 ended in abortions (Stock et al., 1997). In China, it was found that 28.2% of the women undergoing abortions were below 20 years of age and in case of unmarried abortion, patients appeared to be relying on abortion as a family planning method (Henshaw, 1992). A study conducted in 27 countries pointed out various reasons for induced abortion. These include (i) a desire to postpone childbearing (25.5%); (ii) wanting no (more) children (7.9%); (iii) not being able to afford a baby (21.3%); (iv) having a child will disrupt education or job (10.8%); (v) being too young; parent/s or others object to pregnancy (12.2%); (vi) risk to maternal health (2.8%), and risk to foetal health (3.3%) (Bankole et al., 1998). The major reason for unwanted conception among married women who were exposed to the risk of conception was contraceptive failure (WHO, 1987). In a study, the author showed that a large proportion of their acceptors were in their twenties (Sarkar, 1993). In another study in rural Maharashtra, adolescents constituted 13.1% of 1717 married women who had had MTP in 1996-1998. Most abortions were done in a private clinic. The married and separated adolescents sought abortion due to lack of family and partner support and social stigma (Gnatra et al., 2002). The age-specific fertility rate for married Indian women between 15 to-19 years was high. In 1981, 6.5% of the girls aged between 10-14 years married and among 15-19 years, 43.4% were married (48.8% in rural areas and 28.1% in urban areas). Young Indian married girls were pressurised for children by their husband's family, and without literacy there is not much choice. Since early 1900, mean age of marriage has risen from 12.77 years to 18.23 years in 1971-1981 (Goyal, 1994). A study in Tamil Nadu showed that unmarried women in India undergo induced abortions rather than reversible contraception to space or limit births. Consensual sex, sexual violence and women's inability to refuse their husband's sexual demands underlie the need for abortion among young women (Ravindran et al., 2004). The total potential for induced abortion is highest in Uttar Pradesh and lowest in Gujarat (Mishra et al., 1998). Analysis of 66 pregnancies in MTP Clinic, Eden Hospital, and Calcutta during 1976 – '77 showed that after introduction of MTP Act there has been an increase in sexual promiscuity. Although teenage pregnancy out-of-wedlock came from all segments of the society data showed that more came from the lower socio-economic group that has very little knowledge of reproductive biology and contraceptive practice (Chowdhury et al., 1979). A north-south comparison across India showed that women of southern India had relatively higher levels of literacy and lesser incidence of abortion (Bose et al., 2006). A study conducted in India over the period Jan. 1976 – Dec. 1978 revealed that among 100 unmarried women undergoing abortion, there were nine girls aged between 12 to15 years and 25 girls in the 16 to 19 years age group. Most of them were from nuclear families. About half of them (53.0%) were from the lower middle-income group. The largest (58.0%) reported they had had intercourse with known friends (Mandal, 1982). Among adolescents 15 to 19 years of age in U.S.A., Netherlands, Sweden, France, Canada and England, the high rates of abortion could be attributed to the lack of open attitude towards adolescent sexuality, lack of an easy approach for free and confidential family planning, and lack of a national policy promoting sex education in schools (Murray, 1986).

Objective

To find out the demographic and socio-economic factors as well as other socio-legal aspects which led to MTP.

Methods

A group of 45 pregnant adolescent girls, both married and unmarried, aged between 15 to 18 years, admitted to the Gynecology Ward, Eden Building of the Medical College Hospital, Kolkata for MTP were covered in the study with their consent. Data were collected with the help of a structured questionnaire.

The information, which were collected through the questionnaire, include demographic and socio-economic background of the girls like age, religion, place of residence, marital status, age at marriage, socio-economic status in relation to income, education and occupation. They were also questioned about relevant information like use of contraceptives, week of pregnancy when the abortion was done, history of previous abortion and their parity status. The reason for MTP was also explored during the study, in addition to exploring the various methods used for such MTP. In addition, data related to the mental and physical health of the subjects were also gathered to have a better picture about the issue.

Results

Findings revealed that most of the pregnant adolescent girls (95.6%) covered in the study belonged to 16-18 years age group. More than half of them came from the semi-rural and/or rural areas. Majority of the subjects were Hindus (57.8%) and mostly belonged to scheduled caste Hindu community, while the second largest number was (35.6%) Muslim girls.

Table 1
Educational Status and Occupation of the Pregnant Adolescent Girls (N=45)

Background	*Frequency*	*Percentage*
Educational level		
• Illiterate	11	24.4
• Primary (classes I-V)	20	44.4
• Secondary (classes VI-X)	14	31.1
Occupation		
• Student	3	6.7
• House-wife	26	57.8
• Worker	13	28.9
• Unemployed	3	6.7

Data in Table 1 shows that majority of the subjects was either illiterate (24.4%) or educated up to primary level (up to class V) (44.4%). Although more than half of them were housewives (57.8%), a large number of them were found to be working girls (28.9%).

Four-fifths of the subjects (80.0%) were married while one-fifth was unmarried (20.0%). So far as issue is concerned, the study found that 46.7% of the subjects had one child while 20.0% of them had two children.

Table 2
Marital Status and Number of Children

Marital Status	*Frequency*	*Percentage*
• Married	36	80
• Unmarried	9	20
No. of Children		
• 1 child	21	46.7
• 2 children	9	20.0
• No child	15	33.3

Data with regard to age at the time of marriage reveal that most of them were married at the age of 17 years (44.4%), while 25.0%, 16.7%, 11.1% and 2.8% were married at the age of 18 years, 16 years, 15 years and 14 years respectively (Table 3).

Table 3
Age of the Girls Studied at the Time of Marriage (N=36)

Age at the time of marriage (years)	*Frequency*	*Percentage*
• 14 years	1	2.8
• 15 years	4	11.1
• 16 years	6	16.7
• 17 years	16	44.4
• 18 years	9	25.0
Total	36	100

About 60.0% of the study girls did not use contraceptives at all, while only 4.4% regularly used the family planning methods. The rest 935.6%) used contraceptives irregularly. Replying to a query about awareness of family planning methods, 24.0% of them reported that they were not aware of the same while 9.0% of them stated that they were not tolerant of IUCD or oral contraceptive pills and developed side effects. Out of the 45 cases, 31 of them (68.9%) were having their first abortion while seven i.e., 15.6% of them had a previous history of abortion. About 4.0% of them reported that their present abortion was due to an accidental contraceptive failure (Table 4).

Table 4
Use of Contraceptives and History of Previous Abortion (N=45)

Use of Contraceptives	*Frequency*	*Percentage*
• Regular use	2	4.4
• Irregular use	16	35.6
• Do not use	27	60.0
History of Previous Abortion		
• Has history of previous abortion	7	15.6
• No history of previous abortion	31	68.9
• Did not answer	7	15.6

The main reason of MTP was social stigma attached with pregnancy among unmarried women as reported by 75.6% of the study subjects. About 9.0% of them had abortion on therapeutic grounds i.e., Rheumatic Mitral Stenosis, epileptic fits, manic-depressive psychosis and cervical malignancy. Eugenic abortion was done in case of infection by rubella virus in the first trimester. Four subjects did not answer this question. Most of the abortions were done within in the first 6 weeks of pregnancy (53.3%). Only 4.5% aborted after the first trimester.

Table 5
Cause of MTP and the Weeks of Pregnancy when the Abortion was Done (N=45)

Cause of MTP	*Frequency*	*Percentage*
• Social	34	75.6
• Humanitarian	2	4.4
• Therapeutic	4	8.9
• Eugenic	1	2.2
• Did not answer	4	8.9
Week of pregnancy when abortion was done		
• Bolow 6	24	53.3
• 7-12	19	42.2
• 12-18	2	4.5
• Above 18	0	0

About one-fifth (20.0%) of the subjects had either Dilatation - Evacuation (D/E) with copper T or Suction-Evacuation (S/E) with copper T, while about 80.0% did not use any contraceptive methods. The MTP was done following Dilatation and Evacuation or Suction and Evacuation only.

Table 6

Methods Employed for MTP (N–45)

Methods of MTP	*Frequency*	*Percentage*
• Dilatation and Evacuation or Suction and Evacuation with copper T	9	20
• Dilatation and Evacuation or Suction and Evacuation	36	80
Total	45	100

Further, the study revealed that majority (46.7%) of the girls had mild anemia while 31.1% of them had moderate anemia.

All the study subjects had either the consent of their family members or parents or their husbands for MTP. A few respondents were reluctant to answer a few questions due to sensitivity of the issue.

Discussion

Most of the pregnant adolescent girls in the study (95.6%) belonged to 16-18 years age group. This is because the girls, especially those from the lower socio-economic strata, are mostly pressurized by their family for early marriage. Two girls, aged around 15 years, were victims of rape and sought humanitarian abortion. According to the West Bengal Health Survey 2004-2005, there was no reported case of MTP below 15 years of age out of a total of 439 reported cases (Health on March, Govt. of West Bengal, 2006). Most of the cases came from rural and sub-urban regions (53.3%). The findings of the present study with regard to place of origin of the study subjects corroborate with the findings of another study carried out in the Medical College, Kolkata (Chakraborty, 1979). Since rural hospitals lack the minimum infrastructure facilities to terminate such adolescent pregnancies, teenagers come to the urban hospitals. Incident of teenage pregnancy before or after marriage in the urban area also take place. But, the people of the urban area, being better off in terms of income, may also choose to terminate their unwanted pregnancies in the private nursing homes. The highest incidence of MTP is in the lower socio-economic group (48.9%) (per capita income <Rs. 500/per month), the number of cases gradually declining with increasing income. Though it does not match with the observations of Spitz, Fisher-Med (1969), but the outlook of the present generation has changed i.e., the poor people also wish to restrict their family size.

Teenage pregnancy is also highly correlated with the educational background of the girl. Majority of the adolescent girls in the present study were either illiterate or studied up to primary level. This is because the practice of early marriage is still widely practiced in India and the expectation in Indian socio-cultural milieu is that after marriage a woman should become pregnant as soon as possible. In the present study, the adolescent girls from rural areas are mostly involved in cultivation and/or are working as daily labourers while most of the girls from urban areas are working as domestic assistants and/or ayahs and they mostly belonged to Hindu Scheduled caste communities. The second highest number of pregnant adolescent girls was from Muslim communities (35.6%).

Majority of the reported pregnant adolescent girls in the Medical College, Kolkata were married. Since less social stigma is attached with teenage pregnancy among married girls, they come to hospital without any inhibition and/or fear of disclosure of information. On the other hand, unmarried girls prefer to terminate the pregnancy by local non-medical professionals because of fear of social stigma and/ or social boycott (Chowdhury, 1979). The married women who had had two children underwent MTP because of their poor socio-economic condition, as they may not be able to bear any additional expenses in the family.

Findings of the present study further point out to the fact that early marriage is widely practiced in India, especially in the rural areas, and it happens mostly in case of people of lower social strata, which is against the Child Marriage Restraint Act 1978. In the Child Marriage Restraint Act 1978, it is clearly stated that a female less than 18 years of age and a male under 21 years cannot marry.

The study revealed that 60.0% of the girls did not use contraceptives. On the other hand, 36.0% of the girls used contraceptives irregularly and/or erratically mainly because their male counterparts frequently forgot to use the condom and/or did not like to use it. Surprisingly, 24.0% of the girls reported that they did not know about the family planning methods. Therefore, there is a need to create awareness among adolescent girls in the rural areas about family planning methods. About 9.0% of the girls stated that IUCD or oral contraceptive pills did not suit them and these had side effects.

Social stigma and medical complications were the main causes of MTP in case of most of the girls. Most of the abortions were done in the first trimester. According to Goodyear et al., (2006), mostly nulliparous and primi-gravida women were more likely to choose first trimester MTP.

In case of 80.0% of the MPTs, it was not done following proper methods, which could be harmful for the girl. Anaemia is the major problem affecting most of the girls and it is highly correlated with socio-economic condition of the adolescent girls. The prevalence of mild and moderate anaemia can also be justified by sudden growth spurt during puberty and due to the onset of menarche. Due to the rise in the age at marriage, there is more premarital sexual activity, fostered by the lengthening gap between puberty and marriage, and diminished parental and social controls. But in the present study, marriage at younger age or child marriage are still reported significantly especially in the rural areas. All the girls underwent MTP with the consent of their family members and/or guardians.

Conclusion

Adolescence being a time of exploration and impulsive behavior, it often culminated in sexual promiscuity and free mixing. This ended in abortion among rural unmarried adolescent girls. Another aspect, which became prominent in the study, is the practice of early marriage among girls in the rural areas. Then, they were pressurized for children by their husband's family. Being illiterate and having no and/ or negligible knowledge about contraceptive methods, they could not adopt precautionary methods to avoid pregnancy and/or could not insist on their partner to use condoms. This study shows the urgent need for introduction of reproductive health education in both rural and urban areas and in this regard both NGOs in the rural areas and schools in the urban areas should take special role to create awareness among adolescent girls about the issue. This study is based on a small sample. Another study with large sample covering a larger number of government and private health centres is recommended for better understanding of the issue.

REFERENCES

Bankole, Akinrinola, Singh, Susheela and Hass, Taylor (1998). Reasons Why Women Have Induced Abortions: Evidence from 27 Countries, *Int. Fam. Plann. Perspect.*, 24 (3).

Bose, S. and Trent, K. (2006). Socio-Demographic Determinants of Abortion in India: A North-South Comparison, *J. of Biosocial Sc.*, 38(2), 283.

Chowdhury, N.N., and Mukherjee, K. (1979). Sociological Implications of Pregnancy in Unmarried Teenagers, *J. Obstetrics. Gynae, India,* 29(2), 308-312.

Gnatra, Hirve (2002). Induced Abortions Among Adolescent Women in Rural Maharashtra, India, *Reprod. Health Matters,* 10 (19), 76-85.

Goodyear, Knowles, Masters (2006) First Trimester Medical Termination of Pregnancy-An alternative for New Zealand women, *Aust. N. Z. J. of Obs. Gynaecol.*, 46(3), 193-198.

Goyal, R.S. (1994). Dimensions of Adolescent Motherhood in India, *Soc. Biol.*, 41(1-2), 130-134.

Health on March 2006. State Bureau of Health Intelligence, Govt. of West Bengal, Swasthya Bhawan, 196-221.

Henshaw, S.K. (1997). Teenage Abortion and Pregnancy Statistics by State, 1992, *Fam. Plann.Perspect.,* 29(3), 115-122.

International Planned Parenthood Federation (1976). *People,* 3 (2), 27-42.

Learman, Dray, Gates, Kang Washngton et al., (2005). Abortion Attitudes of Pregnant Women in Prenatal Care, *Am. J. Obs. Gynecol.*, 192 (6), 1939-47.

Mandal, K.T. (1982). Problem of Unmarried Mothers (A Study of Socio-Psychological Aspects of 100 Women Seeking M.T.P.), *J. Indian Medical Assoc.*, 79 (5-6), 81-6.

Mishra,U.S., Ramanathan, M. and Rajan S.L. (1998). Induced Abortion Potential Among Indian Women, *Soc. Biology,* 45 (3-4), 278-288.

Mukherjee, J. B. (1994). *Forensic Medicine and Toxicology,* 2nd ed, I, 19-25.

Murray, J. (1986). Teen Pregnancy: An International Perspective, *Plan. Parent Rev.*, 6(1): 20-21.

Ravindran, T.K. and Balasubhramanian, P. (2004). 'Yes' to Abortion and 'No' to Sexual Rights: The Paradoxical Reality of Married Women in Rural Tamil Nadu, India, *Reprod. Health Matters,* 12(23), 88-99.

Rome Rybicki, Durant (1998). Pregnancy and Other Risk Behaviors Among Adolescent Girls in Ohio, *J. Adolescent. Health,* 22 (1), 50-55.

Sarkar (1993). Legally Induced Abortion in India, *Demography India*, 1st ed, 187-221.

Senderowitz, Paxman (1985). Adolescent Fertility: Worldwide Concerns, *Popul bull.*, 40(2), 1-51.

Skjeldestad, F.E. (1995). Using Induced Abortion To Measure Contraceptive Efficacy, *Fam. Plann. Perspect.*, 27(2), 71-96.

Skjeldestad, F.E., Borgan, J.K., and Dalveit, A.K. (1994). Induced Abortion. Effects of Marital Status, Age, and Parity on Choice of Pregnancy Termination, *Acta Obstet. Gynaecol. Scand*, 73(3), 255-260.

Simons, J.H. (1939). Statistical Analysis of 100 Abortions, *Am. Journal of Gynae and Obs*, 37, 840.

Singh, S. and Darroch, J.E. (2000). Adolescent Pregnancy and Childbearing: Levels and Trends in Developed Countries. *Fam. Plan. Perspect*, 32(1), 14-23.

Spitz, Fisher-Med. (1969). *Legal Investigation of Death*, 2nd ed., 79-84.

Stock, Bell and Boyer, Konel (1997). Adolescent Pregnancy and Sexual Risk-Taking Among Sexually Abused Girls, *Fam. Plann. Perspect.*, 29(5), 200-203, 227.

Tietze and Lewitt (1969). Abortion, *American Science*, 220, (21).

WHO (1978).*Techn. Rep.Ser.* No. 623.

WHO (1980). Adolescent Health, *The Work of WHO 1978-79*, 29-36.

WHO (1987) Maternal Mortality: Helping Women off the Road to Death, *WHO Chronicle,* 40 (5), 175-83.

Zimmerman, M. (1976). Law and Policy, *The George Washington University Population Report*, 3rd ed, 26-44.

10

Sexual Behaviour and Reproductive Health of Unmarried Munda Adolescent Girls of Ranchi District, Jharkhand

Dr. Ruby Alambusha & Prof. Sulabha Parasuraman

Summary

This paper addresses the sexual behaviour and related reproductive health awareness among tribal adolescent girls of Ranchi District, who are vulnerable to HIV/AIDS. The broad objective of the present study was to understand the reproductive health and sexual behaviour of Munda adolescent girls of Ranchi District, Jharkhand. In the tribal society, boys and girls have rights of mate selection within the community. Culturally premarital sexual relation and childbirth is acceptable in Munda community. This leniency is misused when tribal adolescent girls come in contact with sex hunters in guise of employers, co-workers and boyfriends. In tribal society, women are more laborious than men, so they are taking initiatives to come out and earn money for their family, while male members are staying back in their villages. Thus, there is more migration among adolescent girls and they become vulnerable. Tribal girls get employment as domestic servants, brick kiln workers, daily wage workers, etc. These girls neither receive full payment nor get physical security as they are subject to sexual exploitation and rape. Sometimes, they make sexual relations willingly and sometimes, it is forced. In both cases, they are highly susceptible towards pre-marital pregnancies, which lead to unsafe induced abortion. While pre-marital childbearing and pregnancies are acceptable in tribal society, still adolescents go for abortion to untrained tribal dais and vaidyas. These abortions adversely affect their reproductive health.

Introduction

The past decade has witnessed a growing concern about women's health in the developing countries evidenced by the safe-motherhood initiatives and by adoption of national strategies from women's health perspectives addressing child survival, family planning and women's needs in developmental issues. In general, women's health and women's reproductive health in particular, is currently receiving considerable attention in the political arena as well as in the programs of the funding agencies. While politicians and advocates of youth tend to refer to the term 'health', the scientists are more apt to focus on morbidity or the absence of health; unfortunately, the terms are often used interchangeably. The past decade also witnessed a considerable concern over the adolescent health and the adolescents' sexual behaviour. Therefore, before making plans for the adolescents, it is vital to be clear about who the adolescents are, what are their needs and why there is a need to pay special attention to them?

The concept of adolescent is fairly new and dates back only to a few decades, especially in the developing world.

The term adolescence originates from the Latin word 'Adolecere' which means 'to grow up' or 'to grow to maturity'.

Demographically, the WHO defines adolescents as individuals between 10 - 19 years of age (WHO Technical Series Report; 1999). For the first time, the International Conference on Population and Development (ICPD, 1994) at Cairo, internationally acknowledged that adolescent reproductive and sexual health involve a specific set of needs that are distinctly different from the adult needs in that area. Consequently, ICPD 1994 focused on adolescent population all over the world, and cared for their health needs through various specific plans of actions (ICPD, 1994, Population and Development, Vol-1). Sociologically, adolescents may be seen as young persons in transition period between childhoods to adulthood. Psychologically, adolescents may be viewed as a behavioral transition phase of a young person between a period of rapid development as an individual and a period in which the individual makes adjustment to the needs of self, others and community. Along with other psychological, social and physiological changes, a very remarkable and dramatic change that occurs during adolescence is the 'emergence of sex drive' (Davis and Blanke, 1956).

Adolescence is traditionally regarded as a period of no health problems. But according to many researches, it is a crucial period in which unseen malnutrition and infections can have a devastating effect both for the short and the long run. A number of factors prevalent in developing societies have contributed much to aggravate the reproduction related health risks for adolescents. Some of the factors are lowering of the age of menarche, an increase in the age of marriage, change in social values induced by increasing urbanization, exposure to foreign cultures through migration, tourism and the mass media and a disintegration of extended families. These factors increase the chances of unwanted adolescent pregnancies, abortions and unwanted child-birth. This change has brought a greater awareness to the adverse medical, psychological, educational and economic consequences to the adolescent mother and her early child, whether wanted or unwanted (Friedman and Edstrom, 1983).

Some decades ago, many societies of world did not consider sex related information (sex education) necessary to be imparted to adolescents prior to the marriage. The common belief of seniors from these societies was that the sexual activities occur and should occur only within wedlock. However, with modernization, industrial development, unitization of families and the increasing influence of electronic mass media, socio-cultural environment faced changes in the norms and values related to sex and sexual behaviour. With incorrect information about sex in one hand and sexual temptation on the other hand, majorities of adolescents from all over world are landing in unsafe and unprotected sexual activities (WHO, 1999). While outlining the needs of conducting research on adolescents, the WHO defines:

- In developing countries, maternal mortality is two to five times higher among girls below 18 years than women between 18-25 years.
- Adolescent abortions are estimated between 1 million to 4.4 million per year, while most of them are unsafe in nature because they are performed illegally and under hazardous conditions by unskilled practitioners.
- Each year more than one out of 20 adolescents contracts a curable STD, excluding viral infection.
- Globally, more than halves of all new HIV infected persons fall in the age group of 15-24 (WHO, 1999).

The above facts depict adolescents as a major risk group. This is mainly because of lack of factual information to adolescents on issues pertaining to sexuality and the consequences of unprotected sexual activities and their limited access to appropriate and affordable family planning and health facilities. The stakes are particularly high for adolescent girls who are more vulnerable both socially and biologically. In adolescent girls, pre-marital sexual activities appear to be about 10.0%, but evidence suggests that this might be increasing (Jejeebhoy, 1996). In absence of appropriate contraceptive methods, unmarried adolescent girls usually resort to unsafe abortions, often very late in pregnancy.

Importance of Tribal Adolescents

It is clear from above discussion that adolescent itself is a vulnerable group in any population. However, adolescent is not a homogenous group. The vulnerability among adolescent from tribal groups is much higher. In one hand, tribals are very permissive towards their culture but contact with outside their community make them more vulnerable. Earlier these tribal communities were not so exposed to the urban areas as they are now, i.e., all because of increased transportation facilities, and increasing level of education, exposure to mass media, industrialization, urbanization and over all modernization. In the same way, adolescent are particularly vulnerable because of lack of information and access to relevant services (Kumar, 2002).

Tribals are simple and innocent people having their own rich cultural heritage and well governed norms and practices, but after coming in contact with modern outer world, they got deprived of their facilities and their norms and practices got contaminated. Spread of education increased their needs and this made them come out of their native place in search of sustenance and livelihood. Ignorance of protection from malaise of modern world has made the tribal adolescents the most vulnerable group (Stephen and Julia, 1997).

Proportion of Adolescent Population

According to 2001 census, India had 22.50 million people falling in the age group of 10 to 19 years, among which 10.54 million were female. As phenomenal with developing countries, in India also the huge number of adolescent females is more vulnerable to various health risks. The National Population Policy (2000) talks about the needs of adolescents such as nutrition, contraceptive use, prevention from STDs and other population related issues. In the present study, an attempt has been made to focus on adolescent girls from an indigenous population of Jharkhand state, to understand their vulnerability.

Literature Review on Sexual Behaviour of Adolescent

There exists a wide body of literature on the reproductive health, sexuality and developmental aspects of different tribes of different states of India, but unfortunately not much information are available on tribes of Jharkhand state separately. Very few studies were carried out related to reproductive and sexual health of unmarried tribal youth girls in the districts of Jharkhand. Pre-marital sexual relations are freely tolerated, either in the dormitories wherever they exist, or in the homes of girls. Such relations are considered a manner of courting. However, if a girl becomes pregnant, these sex relations cease and she is married off (Stephen, 1974).

The Munda believe that sexual congress is a good thing; it does you good; it is healthy and beautiful; when performed by the right people, at the right time and in the right place, it is happiest and best thing in life (Fuchs, 1974). Looking at the gap in literature, for concrete evidence based policy that acts towards reduction of sexual risk among adolescent Munda girls, it is important to have a specific study with regard to the problem. This study has examined the variations in attitudes and practices towards premarital sex, contraceptive use and actual practices and their effect on health seeking behaviour of Munda adolescent girls. Premarital sexual activities are very common among tribal communities. So when they mix with non- tribal communities and get allured, then they show least resistance to premarital sex activities and this makes them a vulnerable group. Earlier these tribal communities were not so exposed to the urban areas as they are now. This is all because of increased transportation facilities, spread of education, exposure to mass media and migration in search of livelihood etc. In this process, adolescents are particularly more vulnerable because of their lack of information on sex and access to relevant services (ICPD 1994; Vol-1).

Reproductive Health (RH)/Sexual Health (SH) Problems

In a review of reproductive behaviour of adolescents in India, Jejeebhoy (1996) suggests that about 20.0-30.0% of all males and up to 10.0% of all females, mainly from urban areas are sexually active at adolescent age before marriage. Adolescent health care in rural India is very limited. Most public services target only on adult married women and are not having any facility for adolescent use, especially for unmarried ones. Unmarried adolescents do not seek safe abortions for a number of reasons including out of fear that services are not confidential, inability to pay the fees, the prerequisite of parental/partner approval in such cases, the stringent abortion laws and the apprehension that health workers will react negatively and will not be sensitive to their needs.

Given the above background, the necessity was felt to carry out a study to understand the reproductive health and sexual behaviour of Munda adolescent girls of Ranch District of Jharkhand state.

Hypotheses

1. There is a positive relation between the girls who had never been to school and/or who became school drop-out and their entry in work force.
2. Early entries in work force make them more vulnerable and they are become more likely to have sexual experience.
3. There is a positive relationship between seasonal and temporary migration and sexual experience.
4. Girls who have migrated are more vulnerable and are more exposed to sexual experience.

Method

Study Area and Group

The study was focused on 13-19 year adolescent unmarried girls from Munda community of Ranchi district.

According to census 2001 report, Jharkhand has a population of 26.90 million consisting of 13.86 million males and 13.04 million females. The district in which capital Ranchi is located populations of 2.78 million.

Since the Ranchi District was having 44.0% of tribal population, the study considered the district for data collection. This district consisted of 20 blocks. Out of these 20 blocks, 5 blocks were inhabited by Munda tribe (District Gazette of Jharkhand, 2002). Munda tribe is also known as Horo-hon or Mura, which means headman of the village. The Munda lives in the states of Bihar, West Bengal, Assam, Tripura, Madhya Pradesh and Orissa (Singh, 1997). The Indo-Aryan languages, Sadri and Hindi, are used by Munda for inter-group communication and their script is Devanagari.

Munda society is a patriarchal society but girls have more freedom regarding choice of life partner. Girls can come out of marriage, if they are not comfortable with their life partner. Contrary to the non-tribal community, parents of tribals girls' get bride price during marriage. Pre-marital child birth is accepted in Munda society and they are brought up either by girl's parents or by the girl herself, if agreed by the husband. Widow re-marriage is always permitted. There is no social restriction on going of girls outside for education and livelihood. By nature tribal girls are more laborious and hard working than tribal boys. Men are generally residing in their houses and women are commuting or migrating outside for employment. Tribal men are more prone to local rice beer (handia) and so they are lazy. The Munda are mainly nature worshipers. They also worship their ancestors. The Sing Bonga is their most important deity, who is the source of all power and energy.

Sampling Design and Technique

The present study aimed at examining the reproductive health and sexual behaviour among tribal adolescent girls. The study also focused at examining the tribal's norms, culture and practices related to sexual behaviour, reproductive health and the treatment seeking behaviour. In order to achieve the objective, Khunti - a block nearer to the district headquarter was selected while another block called 'Arki' which is far away from the district with more Munda population was selected.

Multi-stage sampling technique was used for selection of blocks and probability proportionate to size (PPS) was used for village selection. House listing was carried out for selection of household having adolescent girls aged between 13-19 years. From each blocks, five villages were selected on the basis of probability proportionate to size (PPS) where size of Munda tribal population was considered for selection. From each village, 35 Munda households with at least one unmarried adolescent Munda girl aged between 13-19 years was selected by Systematic Random Sampling technique after household listing in each village. In case of more than one unmarried adolescent girl in the household, the eldest girl of the household was selected as a respondent. The logic for the selection of the eldest one was that she would have longest exposure to sexual activity.

Tools for Data Collection

Both quantitative and qualitative data collection techniques were applied. Some case studies of highly vulnerable adolescent girls were carried out to understand their sexual behaviour and reproductive health problems. The study was carried out in three phases.

- In the first phase, qualitative techniques such as in-depth interviews (with traditional medical practioners, adolescent girls and elderly women of the villages), FGDs with adolescent girls were carried out. Altogether, 30 in-depth interviews and four FGDs were done.
- In the second phase, quantitative survey was carried out with 315 adolescent girls with the help of a Semi-structured Questionnaire.
- In the third phase again, case studies of 20 adolescent girls were done based on the informant's vulnerability to sexual activities and reproductive health problems

Results

About 55.0% of the adolescent girls belonged to the age group of 13-15 years and 45.0% were aged between 16-19 years. Majority of them came from the nuclear families and mostly belonged to Hindu and Christian religion groups.

About 82.0% of the adolescent girls were literate while 18.0% were illiterate. Among the literates, 34.0% of them were attending schools and rests of them were either school drop-out or had completed certain level of education.

Out of 315 respondents, 45.0% of them were working in different unorganized sectors as domestic assistant, daily wage earner, as brick kiln workers and/or as venders. Girls who were illiterate and those who had low level of education entered in work force at an early age. Poverty was mainly responsible for illiteracy and lack of education among Munda adolescent girls. Parents were not interested in higher education of their children and more number of children proved to be detrimental for the eldest one's higher education.

Respondents' parents were mainly illiterate and mainly engaged in agricultural activity. Almost all the adolescent girls were exposed to some form of mass media (radio, TV. newspaper, movie, and magazine). About 69.0% respondents are exposed to radio at daily basis and only 12.0% respondents are daily exposed to T.V.

Pubertal Changes and Reproductive Health Related Behaviour

The study revealed that Munda girls were having good hygienic practices. Majority of the girls used to change their pads or cloths two to three times a day. Though most of the girls used cotton cloths as pads, some girls had started using sanitary napkins also. For menstrual health problems, most of the girls did not seek any treatment. They used to treat it as a natural to their life.

All the 315 respondents started menstruation. The mean age at menarche among this group of girls was 13 years. Only 34.0% of the girls had prior knowledge about menstruation before it actually started. About 58.0% of the girls' aged between 13-15 years and 42.0% aged between 16-19 years had prior knowledge about menstruation. The level of knowledge about the issue among Munda adolescent girls with different educational background varied. The knowledge regarding pubertal changes and the myths and misconceptions that prevails in the mind of adolescent girls were assessed by both qualitative as well as quantitative data. The immediate reactions of the girls after getting their first menstruation cycle were fear, worry, confusion and feeling of disgust.

During the menstruating period, girls were not allowed to perform any puja and not allowed to do heavy work. Although there was no social restriction, but 33.0% of the parents insisted girls not to interact with the boys much.

About 93.0% of tribal adolescent girls reported regular menstrual cycle while 7.0% reported it to be irregular. The main problems faced during menstruation were lower abdominal pain, irritation, weakness, pains in limbs and backache. Almost all adolescent girls reported about abdominal pain and irritation during menstruation and 94.0% girls stated that they had a feeling of weakness. More than half of them reported having pains in limbs and backache during menstruation.

Very few girls sought treatment for menstrual problems. About one-fifth of the girls sought treatment for menstrual related problem. The rest four-fifth adolescent girls who did not seek treatment justified the reasons for not seeking treatment, which include ignorance of family members, it being natural phenomena, felt shy and/or poor financial condition. However, about 15.0% of the respondents went for traditional local herbs.

Sexual Behaviour and Reproductive Health

The broad objective of the study was better understanding of sexual behaviour of Munda adolescent girls. Since the school going girls and working girls were more exposed to education and outside world, they became more aware of abortions and contraceptive methods.

During qualitative survey, mothers of adolescent girls and adolescent girls stated that pre-marital sex and marriage is allowed only in their own clan. If inter clan relationship is traced then parents used to opt for forced marriage of girls on their own clan. Generally, they get involved in sexual activities during festivals and some special occasions. Like other non-tribal societies, arranged marriage was not a compulsion. For marriage of a girl, virginity was not an essential factor. Earlier there was a dormitory system prevailing in Munda tribe known as 'Dhumkhuria'. This is the place where the young boys and girls get chance to mingle with each other during late nights. But now-a-days, due to influence of NGO's and missionary schools the system of 'Dhumkhuria' is vanishing from these tribal societies. Now, the tribal boys and girls are studying in co-education schools where they get more and more chance to have interactions among themselves without any restriction (supervision of old men and women). Only after experiencing bad effects of increased education, migration and contact with non tribal communities (dhikus), some restriction were imposed on them like coming back home before sunset, going for marriage settled down by parents only etc. This all happened as the young tribal girls started coming in contact with non tribal groups (dhikus) and get attracted towards non tribal norms, culture, life style practices. Due to exposure to mass media and to non-tribal communities, now the young tribal girls do not stick to relations within their own community. Many adolescent girls who are studying and working outside get involved in a boy friend-girl friend relationship or affair within or outside the community. Due to increased mode of transportation, migration of tribal girls from their community has also increased. They come outside of their community for getting better jobs and in this process they get exploited by agents, contractors and sometimes by their masters also. Since sex is not a taboo for them, they become an easy prey to sex hunters and sometimes after finishing their jobs during daytime these adolescent girls are made to indulge in sexual activities in nights. To some of them, it becomes an easy money making method. Those girls who are working in the urban area try to adopt life style of non-tribal people. Sometimes, for getting good money from the employer, girls indulged themselves in sexual relation with the employer and did not disclose it in their own society. Sometimes, the adolescent tribal girls who come outside of their community to sell seasonal forest products get stuck at their work place by missing their last bus or jeep. In that situation, they often get trapped by sex hunters for sexual activities. Since they are far from their own houses they fall prey to the situation and get exploited. The high incidence of migration was because of the prevalence of mass poverty in the Munda community. The seasonal and short-term migration is a common feature. Adolescent girls of Munda community mostly work in agricultural sector as daily labourers, as rajas in brick kilns and construction projects and sometimes as domestic assistants.

One girl mentioned

> *"Sometime when she goes to urban area as daily vender of vegetables or wood and if she did not earn enough money from that selling, she stays back to that urban area and tries to get money by making sexual relation with anyone. Sometime she gets a rickshaw puller, truck driver and sometimes they were approached by small hotels even. Next day she comes back to her own village with hand full of money".*

Another girl mentioned

> *"She is hadia (rice beer) seller. She sits near roadside of local court and many men come to her for drinking hadia. Sometimes she comes across with some men (police man, clients of lawyers, auto drivers, khalasi etc.) who approach her for sexual relation and tell her that they will give her that*

> *much money which she will not earn after selling that hadia for the whole day. Getting more money fascinates her so many times she go to places where these men calls her. Generally these men belong to non tribal community".*

From the focus group discussion with adolescent girls, it was found that the girls who were more exposed to urban life became more aware of modern methods of contraceptives.

A 17 years old girl, who was working as domestic servant said:

> *"After finishing my daily household chores, usually I watch T.V. As where I am working both didi and jija ji are working in offices so they come back late night so I don't have any work before late evening. So I watch almost all T.V serials and good movies which come on different channels. Between these serials and movies lots of advertisement comes about contraceptives. So I come to know about them. But I don't know any of the traditional herbs which are used as contraceptives".*

In-depth interviews with traditional healers and dais disclosed that modern contraceptive methods are rarely used because they are not available in the rural areas. In case of unwanted pregnancy, the girls normally approach to the traditional healers and/or dais for abortion as stated. Regarding method of treatment for termination of unwanted pregnancies, the traditional healers were reluctant to disclose the method. However, after persuasion they disclosed the traditional method of treatment for abortion. The medical plants, which were mainly used by the tribes, include Karand, Karkati, Padal, Kena, Betel leaves, Betel nuts (kasaili), Awala, Baheda, Bhagrud. Traditional methods are very painful. Since modern contraceptive methods are not easily available in the interior rural areas people opt for traditional methods only.

Effect of Socio-economic Background on Sexual Behaviour of Adolescents:

Adolescent girls aged 13-15 years were less (16.0%) exposed to sexual encounter than adolescent girls of 16-19 years (70.0%). Similarly, 54.0% Christian girls were exposed to sexual encounter as compared to 33.0% Hindu girls. In general, girls from poor families and illiterate were most vulnerable to sexual encounter.

There was a difference in terms of working status of adolescent girls and sexual encounter. About 42.0% of the girls who were working as domestic assistants were exposed to sexual encounter while 91.0%, 83.0% and 53.0% of the girls working as brick kiln worker, daily vender, and daily wage workers exposed to sexual encounter respectively. Sexual partners of these girls were mainly boy friend (60.0%) and/or employers (40.0%).

Since their life style habits i.e. daily drinking of rice beer was very different from non-tribal communities, it had also an effect on the sexual behaviour of adolescent girls. About 44.0% of girls who were exposed to this life style had sexual encounter, as compared to 26.0% girls who were not used to drink country made liquor. Out of these sexually exposed adolescent girls 15.0% of them became pregnant and most of them underwent abortion.

Regarding feeling of sexual experience, 39.0% of the girls mentioned that they were confused, 32.0% felt guilty, 26.0% stated that they enjoyed while rest 2.0% felt ashamed.

Contraceptive Awareness

All the 315 respondents had knowledge of at least one family planning method. All girls knew about female sterilization. However, there was a large difference in the knowledge of spacing methods among 'sexually active' and 'sexually inactive' respondents. About 90.0% of the sexually active respondents knew about contraceptive pills as compared to 100% of the sexually inactive respondents.

Knowledge of condom and IUD was much higher among sexually inactive respondents as compared to sexually active respondents. On the contrary, less number of sexually inactive girls knew about male sterilization that that of sexually active girls.

Out of 128 sexually active girls, 28 girls (22.0%) stated that they either used condoms or traditional methods to avoid pregnancy.

Reproductive and Sexual Health Problem

Out of 315 respondents covered in the study, 40.0% (128) of were sexually active while the rest 60.0% (187) were sexually inactive.

About 96.0% of the sexually active girls were found to be suffering from white discharge, 43.0% from itching around vagina, 12.0% from frequent urination and 12.0% from urination with burning sensation while none of them reported about uncontrolled urination. Among sexually inactive respondents, 58.0% reported suffering from white discharge, 33.0% from itching around vagina, 3.0% from frequent urination, 3.0% from uncontrolled urination and 3.0% from urination with burning sensation.

Treatment Seeking Behaviour of Adolescent Girls with RTI/STI

During in-depth interviews with girls revealed that they do not prefer to go anywhere for treatment for fear of disclosure of identity and thereby social boycott. More than half of the sexually active adolescent girls did not seek treatment for their problem while 70.0% of the sexually inactive girls did so. However, the adolescent girls who sought treatment mostly preferred to visit traditional healers. Only

6.0% of the sexually inactive adolescent girls had sought treatment from government doctors while 3.0% of the sexually active girls sought treatment from their relatives or friends.

Knowledge about STDs and HIV/AIDS

On overwhelming number of the adolescent girls (88.0%) were aware of STDs while 93.0% of them had heard about HIV/AIDS. The knowledge level about STDs and HIV/AIDs was higher because of awareness programmes of local NGOs in the field.

Changes in Culture and Its Impact on Sexual Behaviour and Reproductive Health

During in-depth interviews with adolescent girls, it was found that the mobility of the tribal population has affected the life styles of tribal population negatively. Positive aspects of mobility are getting modern education, exposure to modern facilities, and exposures to mass media and exposure to modern life style.

During in-depth interviews with mothers of adolescent girls it was found that, in the missionary schools children are getting free mid day meal, school uniform, medical facilities. By getting impressed with these facilities tribals started sending their children in modern school instead of in Goitiar or Dhumkuria. Previously tribals had an institution called youth dormitory (Goitiara or Dhumkhuria) to impart the education and training to the youth. These institutions were both separate for boys and girls.

In-depth interviews further unearthed that majority of the girls involved in sex trade and prostitution was uneducated and poor. Sex trade was reported to be in a disguised form in the study areas. The tribal girls who worked as 'dai' were also involved in sex trade with their masters/ employers. Their customers were mainly contractors, bus drivers, truck drivers, police, and rickshaw pullers.

Previously tribal girls used to decorate their body by tattoos, flowers, seeds, feathers, garland or headgear to attract the customers. Over a period of time, the concept has changed. Now they prefer to use ornaments made up of gold, silver etc. Varieties of bangles and churi have reached among them.

Conclusion

School going tribal adolescent girls had more knowledge and awareness about sex and reproductive health. The girls who had never been to school and engaged in economic activities were more exposed to sexual encounter. Adolescent girls of joint families were less vulnerable to sexual encounter than that of girls of single families. However, girls working as domestic servant were less vulnerable to sexual encounter. Migrated girls were found to be more sexually active than that of their counterparts i.e., non-migrated girls. Girls migrated with any relatives, friends and/or alone were less sexually active than those who migrated with dalal and/or agent. Although, the study revealed that the sexually inactive girls were more aware of contraceptive methods than sexually active girls, although in reality the situation should be reverse. The sexually active girls pretended to remain as ignorant about family planning methods to give a feel to outsiders that they are sexually inactive. Most of the adolescent girls did not seek treatment for their reproductive and sexual health problems. Sexually active adolescent girls took treatment from government doctors as they don't have any fear about their identity. Awareness about STDs and HIV/AIDS among Munda adolescent girls was higher.

REFERENCES

Davis, K. and Blanke, J. (1956). '*Social Structure And Fertility: An Analytical Framework*', Economic Development and Cultural Change, 4.

Friedman, H. L. and Edstrom, K.G. (1983). *Adolescent Reproductive Health an Approach to Planning Health Services Research*. World Health Organization, Geneva, Switzerland Printers.

Jejeebhoy, Shrieen, J. (1996). '*Adolescent Sexual and Reproductive Behaviour: A Review of the Evidence from India*'.

ICPD (1994). *Population and Development, Vol-1*. United Nations Publications.

Kumar, A. (2002). *Tribal Development in India*. Sarup and Sons, New Delhi.

Stephen, J. A. and Julia, H. (1997). *Motherhood at Early Age. The Journal of Family Welfare, 43* (2), 8-14.

Stephen, Fuchs (1974). *The Aboriginal Tribes of India*, The Macmillan Co. of India, New Delhi.

WHO (1999). *Technical Report Series, Programming for Adolescent Health and Development*.

11

A Gynaecologist's Perspective of Adolescent Health

Dr. Rahul Sen

Summary

Adolescence is a highly stressful time of life. There are numerous very important physical and psychological changes that take place during this period. Moreover, during these very years a person becomes capable of procreation. This puts at risk the adolescents, specially the adolescent girls. Furthermore, as they are often still mentally juvenile, they become victims of deceitful individuals. Hence is the need for a general awareness about the risks of adolescence. The article has been divided into two parts - social health and reproductive health of adolescence. Both are very important and are complimentary to each other. Society surely will undergo drastic changes over the years, and nobody can stop the wheels of change. Hence we need to adapt to the changes and survive. And here comes the importance of adaptive awareness, and reinforcement of certain basic guidelines. Due to the uniqueness of a female body, a girl is more prone to contract serious and damaging infections than a boy. Hence special precautions are needed for her. We sincerely hope this book will help the concerned authority to device certain guidelines to safeguard the health of an adolescent girl.

Social Health

In May 2008, accidental discovery of a most grotesque incident in Amstetten, in Austria, shook the entire international community. Amstetten is a small town in Austria, and the citizens could not believe that such an incident could ever take place in their peaceful community.

In that town, a father had imprisoned his daughter for more than twenty years in the cellar of his house. He had repeatedly abused her sexually, fathering seven children from the incestuous relationship. When one of these children fell ill and had to be hospitalised, this bizarre incident came to light. The entire population of Austria was in shock, and the country's media urged the citizens to face the truth and seriously contemplate what went wrong. The girl had been held hostage since she was only eighteen years old. When finally rescued at the age of forty-two, she was a psychological wreck. The father was unrepentant and claimed he was not a monster.

Austria has had a few such other cases where adolescent girls were held hostage by older men, and were regularly abused and tormented. In Belgium, a most horrific case was reported where a man had constructed a prison in his cellar and held captive several teenage girls. One of these girls managed to escape, and her subsequent brave efforts helped unfurl the entire case and get the perpetrator arrested.

These cases, reported from the highly developed Western European nations makes one wonder if there are cases in India? In England, the author of this article encountered almost on an everyday basis, horrific cases of crimes being reported in the media. It often led a sense of self-gratification thinking that these would never occur in to the researcher's own country, India. However, it is interesting to note what a colleague of the present author, a doctor of Indian origin, who had migrated from Pune and had become a British citizen had to say:

> *'It also happens in India. But it's not reported like here.'*
>
> *Although his response was not pleasing, in all probability, he was correct.*
>
> *Now even the Indian media regularly reports the ghastly crimes taking place all across the country. But how does it affect the girl child?*

The girl child is the most vulnerable in the Indian society. Female foeticide is rampant in India. As an obstetrician, the present author frequently, meets couples who are only interested in a male offspring. Many of these couples come from very affluent backgrounds, and they have no scruples in spending hefty sums of money, or embrace illegal means to reach their goal. Some North Indian states are reeling under the skewed male-female ratio, which had led to several-fold increase in the crimes against women.

Women are often considered as commodities or sex objects. They are frequently looked down upon. Once, the Department of Applied Psychology, University of Calcutta, organised a series of lectures in different schools of Kolkata in connection with an intervention study on adolescent reproductive health, funded by the Indian Council of Medical Research, New Delhi with a view to impart correct knowledge on the issue among young students. The author of this article being one of the resource persons for ICMR study realised through interactions with the students that the abuse of the girl child was not at all uncommon in Indian society.

While conducting a programme in one of the well known schools in south Kolkata, the author of this paper encouraged the students to ask questions by writing their queries on a slip of paper keeping their names and identities secret if they wished so.

At the end of this particular session, the present author was confronted with a particularly disturbing query. One of the girl students had stated that she was being regularly sexually abused by her father. Even the teachers, sitting at the back, were taken aback by the revelation. This girl was in desperate need for help. Although the teachers were urged to find her out and kindly do whatever they could, it is seriously doubted whether the girl would ever come forward in the open. She would thus continually suffer, and would be psychologically scarred forever.

The present author was told another instance by the victim that a friend of her dad also abused her. When she had reported the incident to her mother, all she got was a slap on her face. The mother of the unfortunate girl did not have the courage to stand up to the situation, and had anxiously tried to bury the incident by punishing the victim rather than the perpetrator. In the film 'Monsoon Wedding', by Mira Nair, a similar problem had been deftly dealt with, and it could be a lesson for those who are afraid to raise their voice against these kinds of misdeeds.

Before the tour of lectures, organised by the ICMR Task force Research Team of the Department of Applied Psychology, University of Calcutta had been held, the author was invited to give a lecture on adolescence, in one of the most famous schools of Kolkata. It was a coeducation school and the pupils came from the most affluent part of the society. The then principal of the institution, a very progressive and charming lady, was the main force behind organising such a session, which was probably one of the first of its kind in the Kolkata city.

Classes were taken, separately with boys and girls, and then together. It was a very stimulating exercise. Though initially there were giggles and nudges, soon the bright, young pupils started actively interacting with the team. Their questions were on a variety of related topics – even abortions and many arose from a very mature state of mind.

The school-counsellor reportedly was extremely worried about the plight of the girls. Many of the female students in the school regularly received nasty phone calls from the boys and were quite helpless in this regard. These pupils were brought up amidst vulgar affluence, and very few seemed to have the opportunity to spend some quality time with their parents. They were mostly looked after by an army of servants and chauffeurs. The abuse the girls were facing from their class mates never came up directly in the sessions. Probably the girls were afraid to come out with it in an open discussion and thus get marked and face more abuse. The school atmosphere is often nothing but a jungle, with several sets of tooth and claw out in the open. Bullying, verbal insults, and physical abuses are common in schools all over the world. We thought the Columbian massacre would never happen in India. But the culture of fatal shootings in school had come to India. Even parents are instigating and teaching their child to go the violent way in the school to take revenge. We have indeed reached a very dangerous crossroad.

The school environment can thus be very stressful. Changing of schools can be more so. It can lead to devastating consequences. In another case, when a girl child was brought from a small town to Kolkata School, and was admitted to a renowned institution, she could not cope with the stress of adjustment. She had desperately asked her relatives to let her remain in her former school. But the ambitious parents had other plans. The depressed girl committed suicide within a very short span of joining the new school. New peers can be ruthless, to say the least. If the scenario at home is not a happy one, and the school is competitive and ruthless, a sensitive and delicate young adolescent can go nowhere to find respite. She is bound to develop acute anxiety and go into severe depression. Adolescence in itself is a very stressful time of human life, when one is neither a child nor an adult; if one is burdened with abnormal stresses, one is sure to crack.

The teachers have a supreme role in this regard. Students look up to the teacher with great respect, and if they find a real friend in him/her, then they can draw the necessary strength to survive in the unkind, materialistic world of expectations and competition. I cannot help but cite another example from Bollywood. A teacher, as shown in 'Taare Zameen Par', can save several disasters in this world.

Recently the present author had come across another case of exploitation and abuse. A teenage schoolgirl was brought to the author with a unique obsessive disorder. Physically more developed than normal for her age, she had a hankering for physical relationships. A classmate of hers had rejected her advances. Thereafter, she developed friendship with an elderly man whom she met at a bus stop. Finding her an easy victim, the man took her to several places and had sex with her. The young girl, obsessed with her desires, had taken to several habit disorders like masturbation. She was marked in the school as a 'bad girl' and was rapidly going downhill socially. Fortunately, she came across a kind lady, who counselled her and took her to trained psychologists for therapies. It was a most sad case, where the society had paid no attention to a soul, who desperately needed professional help. If she is not helped and looked after, she will again fall prey to unscrupulous men. They would surely destroy her completely, both psychologically and physically.

Reproductive Health

As has been stated earlier, adolescent itself is a highly stressful time of human life. This is the period of transition, when a carefree child is gradually transformed into a responsible adult. For a lad of the Massai tribe in Africa, killing a lion with his own hands earns him a membership in the adult club. In India, the stresses of adolescence are basically two-folds. One is to succeed in the gruelling, career-building examinations, and the other is to attain a place of respect among the peers and more importantly, the opposite sex.

During the several lectures offered by the present author in schools, the school, intriguingly, a set of similar questions kept reappearing in the unnamed slips sent by the students. The girls were worried about the dimensions of a certain body part, whereas, the boys were anxious about their heights. These, to these young adults, are very important corporal indices determining their attractiveness to the other sex.

As women have the privilege of bearing a child, their development during the adolescence is much more fine and intricate. They go through well-defined stages, though the final development is not completed till the first pregnancy. These stages of development vary greatly among individuals, and often follow a typical familial pattern. If a girl attains puberty (when the girl is physically capable of procreation) before ten years of age, we refer to it as 'precocious puberty'. The world record still lies with Lina Medina from Peru, who became pregnant at the tender age of five. The final phase of puberty ends in 'menarche' - the beginning of the menstruation. Over the last hundred years, the age of menarche has decreased considerably. Nowadays the girls are reaching puberty earlier, thanks to the general improvement of health and good nutrition. If a girl does not have spontaneous menstrual period by the age of eighteen, she should be taken to a gynaecologist for further investigation.

The problem with precocious puberty is just the opposite. The girl quickly reaches the final stage of reproductive maturity, but mentally she still remains a child. Hence she becomes very vulnerable to sexual abuses and their consequences. She must therefore be carefully protected.

The period or menstruation is associated with lot of misconceptions. When the adolescent girls of a well-known, posh school were asked if they were allowed in the sacred places, or even in the kitchen, while they were bleeding, none answered in the affirmative. Menstrual period is nothing but the shedding of the extra lining of the non-pregnant womb, and yet it is almost universally regarded as an inauspicious and filthy thing. But this is a very wrong and unscientific attitude to a physiological happening. This outlook often further aggravates the discomforts associated with a period. The girls who live in households, which have more scientific attitude towards the menstrual cycle and regard it as nothing but a natural phenomenon to cope better with the associated discomforts of these few days. Hence an awareness drive is required in this direction.

Another burning problem we are seeing nowadays is delayed cycles. Adolescent girls are missing periods for more than a month or even for months. This is often due to a condition known as "Polycystic Ovarian Syndrome", or PCOS. The incidence of PCOS is increasing globally, and there is a plethora of scientific papers on it. The condition basically arises due to the resistance of the body to the internally secreted insulin hormone. This leads to a cascade of hormonal disturbances. The effects are delayed menstrual cycles, obesity, acne, and abnormal growth of hair on the face and other parts of the body. Obesity is both the cause and effect of the condition. The unhealthy lifestyle, especially of the urban adolescent girls, has led to an epidemic of PCOS. High-calorie junk food, and lack of exercise, are leading to obesity, and this in turn is aggravating PCOS. The human body is programmed for daily hard work. We had been hunter-gatherers for thousands of years, and were exposed to extreme physical hardship. For the last hundred years or so, our body has suddenly become confined in tiny residential apartments. Genes did not have enough time to adapt to this abrupt change, and hence the body has started to malfunction.

Young adolescents of the city are over-burdened by their curriculum, and as soon as they finish school they rush to designated tutorials. They do not have time for physically challenging games or exercises. Their only recreation is watching the television. This is causing havoc to their bodies. As they develop PCOS, they become more prone to obesity, have reproductive problems, and become susceptible to diabetes mellitus in the later stages of their lives. Awareness in this respect is urgently to improve the health of our teenage girls. Healthy lifestyle and regular doses of exercise are very important; otherwise there would be a deluge of sub-fertile and diabetic ladies in this country in near future.

The reproductive tract of a female is open to the exterior by nature. Hence infections can travel through this canal to inside of their abdomen. They have a natural defence line, but this is weakened considerably just before and after a menstrual period. Silent, ascending infections can damage their reproductive capability permanently.

By the same pathways, Sexually Transmitted Diseases (STD) can have devastating effects on adolescent girls. Syphilis and Gonorrhoea are easily treatable in modern times, but their places have been taken over by Chlamydia, Genital herpes, HPV, and above all, HIV/AIDS.

Chlamydia is now one of the most common infections. Even the next-door teenager may be suffering from this. Though this infection is no way life threatening, it can seriously damage the fallopian tubes, leading to permanent sterility in future.

Genital herpes has now become the most common sexually transmitted infection in USA. Every year, 90000 new cases are diagnosed. Even in India, gynaecologist reports a rising incidence. Though again not life threatening, it cannot be completely cured and tends to recur regularly throughout one's lifetime. It can seriously damage a baby during childbirth. Moreover, using a condom during sexual intercourse cannot prevent its spread.

HPV is also sexually transmitted. And it is a virus, which can lead to the development of cervical cancer in an infected lady.

It is not necessary here to go into the details about HIV/AIDS. The bad news is that there is still no cure for the disease. However, the good news is with the modern anti-retroviral medicine it can be converted into a chronic ailment, thus removing the danger of immediate death. If a patient takes the medicine regularly, he can live up to around ten years. But women are more prone to this infection than men. As after sexual intercourse the infected sperm stays put inside the female body for hours, the exposure to the virus is much prolonged.

But the common factor is that all these infections are sexually transmitted. And that has to be seen in the context of the present social behaviour of the adolescents. Promiscuity is on the rise and the young adolescents are given more and more freedom. Peer pressure, constant provocation from the media, regular night-outs in the ever mushrooming night clubs, easy availability and increasing acceptance of alcohol, are all contributing to the adoption of a more Western type of lifestyle by our young adults. These are bound to have inevitable consequences.

Nowadays, gynaecologist comes across several unwanted pregnancies in unmarried, young girls. However, it is good that most of them are accompanied by their boyfriends, who are responsible enough to bring them to a reputed clinic. Pregnancy termination by a specialist in a reputed hospital or nursing home hardly leads to any complication. Nowadays, there are also licensed drugs, which can successfully terminate an early pregnancy. The treatment can be taken at home and surgical interference can be thus avoided.

An unwanted pregnancy has a huge social and domestic significance. The girl is often afraid to disclose it to her parents, and this makes her more vulnerable. In England, if there is a referral for termination of pregnancy in a young girl, it follows certain specific guidelines. The referral comes from the General Physician (GP), who, in UK, acts as the guardian for the family. The GPs in developed countries act as the main pillar for rendering health care services to the general populace. They are responsible for physical and social health of each and every member of the families registered under them. In case of an unwanted pregnancy of a young girl, the GP writes two referrals - one to a consultant gynaecologist in the hospital for taking care of the termination of the pregnancy, and the other to the social service counsellor to look into the situation of the hapless girl. The counsellor immediately contacts the girl, takes into stock the domestic situation to see whether she will receive adequate support from the home front. If not, the social service provider will take care of that. After this, the counsellor will write a separate letter to the consultant in the hospital, describing the social situation in detail. Then only the hospital will go ahead with the procedure after replying back both to the concerned GP and the counsellor.

Teenage pregnancies in UK are fairly common. If the girl wishes to continue the pregnancy, ample support is available from the state social organisations. The present author has even come across a mother aged only eleven, father thirteen, both adequately supported by the parents and the social networks. Such systems make all the difference between a developed and a developing country.

But there are unscrupulous people out there, who never think twice to exploit these naïve couples in danger. In one instance, the present author received a desperate phone call from a schoolgirl who reported had several unprotected intercourses while she was away from home on a school excursion, and was very worried about the prospect of becoming pregnant. She had had consulted other professionals, and were confused by their advices. It is clear that the helpless girl was being exploited by several dishonest individuals.

Once a girl catches an STD through unprotected sex, the scenario becomes gloomier. It can cause lifelong damage to her reproductive machinery, or can even lead to death in the long run. Moreover, if somebody acquires HIV infection, she surely would become ostracised by the society.

In another instance, the present author received a frantic call from one of his patients - a young and unmarried who reportedly had repeated unprotected sex with a man from another city, being fully aware that the same gentleman has the habit of sleeping around with other women as well and was not worried about the risk of her picking up HIV infection. If the man had indeed been HIV positive it might have been too late to do anything. But as the man was reasonably healthy and fit, the risk was low. Nevertheless, it was a pretty foolish thing to do.

As Indians are mimicking the Western lifestyle, the Westerners on the other hand are preaching abstinence, celibacy, and fidelity to lead a long and healthy life. The awareness of these risks should begin from as early as adolescence. The youth should understand that the more they expose themselves to a variety of partners the greater is the chance of picking up a serious STD.

Recommendations for Social Health

1. The parents should prepare themselves and have some training before bringing up a family. Interestingly,

certain urban centres in India have begun training classes for parents. A loving, caring, and supportive home can be the best stress-buster for an adolescent. The parent must also be aware and vigilant.

2. The teachers in the school have a very important role to play. They must interact as a friend with each and every pupil in the class, and quickly pick up any distress signal. They must help develop the special talents in the students, plus encourage them to develop compassion and camaraderie towards friends. I have often found that distress signals are first picked up by a close friend, and if any such is reported, the teacher should not hesitate to take prompt action. The teachers should look out for aggressive bullying in school and punish the perpetrators with iron fist, and protect the victim from any sort of backlash.

3. Anybody who has a proven history of child abuse in any form should be barred from any employment where he/she may come in contact with growing children.

4. There should be a Social Welfare Service, particularly for the troubled adolescents. It should have a strong liaison with Department of Child Psychology of a reputed institution. In all the developed countries there are such services, which are brilliant and most effective. They work in close conjunction with the General Physicians and have all the power to come to the rescue of any troubled adolescent. They can even separate an adolescent or a child from the parents if there is any suspicion of child abuse at home.

5. There should be a well-developed Department of Child Psychology, having special proficiency in dealing with young adults. There should be provisions for free sessions of psychotherapies for depressed and helpless adolescents.

6. There should be extensive awareness programmes about high-risk sexual behaviours. This should specially target the adolescent population.

Recommendations for Reproductive Health

1. The parents should be aware of the hormonal turbulence of adolescence, and treat their children with compassion and understanding. They should remain ever vigilant. In the face of an unwanted incident, they should come out of their moral rigidity and be on the side of their child. Otherwise, the child would look for a solution secretly and can land up in serious trouble. Anyone, especially a kid, can make a mistake.
2. If there is a family physician, he should be actively involved in the decision- making. He should help the family to choose a right specialist for the case.
3. Ideally, the government should develop a social service network to provide the necessary psychological and logistical support to the family.
4. The social service provider should have a liaison with a reputed health centre. The centre should have a panel of specialists who can efficiently deal with the problem. Ideally there should be a 24-hour helpline, and the number should be regularly put up in the major dailies. The confidentiality of the caller should be protected at all cost.
5. Awareness drives should be started at the schools from as early as class five. The children of today are very bright and they can assimilate lot of information, if it is provided the right way.
6. There should be general awareness programmes about menstruation and hygiene, specially targeting the girls, once they reach the age of menarche.

7. The STD clinics in the state hospitals are often very insensitive in handling the patients. There should be clinics where secrecy and confidentiality are given the utmost priority. The patients should be dealt with sensitively and with compassion. The doctor should not be judgemental; rather, he/she should highlight the risks and give the best possible advices. The health service providers should not take the role of social reformers, which, it appears is a different discipline altogether.

8. The general populace should be aware of the use emergency contraception pills. Vending machines selling condoms is a good idea, because the pharmacist's attitude in a medicine shop may drive away a young, potential buyer.

12

Strategies for Improving Adolescent Health for Strengthening RCH Programme in India

Dr. (Ms.) Ranjana Kar

Summary

Adolescents constitute a major part of our population. Their development and empowerment is realized as a key strategy for successful implementation of the health and population policy. Their development and empowerment can be possible only when they have a right to health information and services. This article addresses strategies for improving adolescent health for strengthening RCH Programme in India. Taking in to account global reviews and guidelines on adolescent health operational strategies and policy implications for adolescents have been delineated

Introduction

Adolescents generally mean the age group of 10 to 19 years. This period is characterized by physical, mental and emotional changes to prepare for adult role in almost all aspects of life, including marriage, motherhood and earning. But young women and men face many health risks as they receive inadequate information, guidance and services to help them negotiate the difficult passage to adulthood. The growth and development in the human life cycle does not follow a uniform pattern and occurs in two major spurts, one in infancy and other during adolescence.

About 245 million i.e. 21.5% of the total population of India are adolescents at present in India 17.0% of total fertility is attributed to women in the 15-18 years age group. In India, according to NFHS-3, 2006 between the age group 15-19 years, young girls of India get married, which leads to teenage pregnancy and motherhood. Young women, who become pregnant and give births, experience a number of health related, social, economic, and emotional problems. In addition to the relatively high level of pregnancy complications among young mothers because of physiological immaturity, inexperience associated with child care practices also influences maternal and infant health. Moreover, an early start to child bearing greatly reduces the educational and employment opportunities of women and is associated with higher levels of fertility.

Accordingly to NFHS-3 (2005-06), in India about 12.0% of women aged 15-19 years have become mothers and 4.0% of women in the age group 15-19 years are currently pregnant with their first child. This means that one in six women in the age group15-19 years have begun child bearing. The percentage of women in India who have begun child bearing increase sharply with age, from 3.0% at age 15 years to 36.0% at age 19 years.

The proportion of women in the age group between15-19 years that have begun child bearing is more than twice as high in rural areas (19.0%) as in urban areas (9.0%). The level of teenage pregnancy and motherhood is 9 times higher among women with no education than among women with 12 or more years of education. More than one-quarter of women, in the age group 15-19 years, with no education, have become mothers and almost one-third of them have begun child-bearing.

Only a few never married women aged 15-19 years (less than 0.05%) reported a pregnancy or childbirth. However, 58.0% of married women aged 15-19 years have experienced motherhood or a current pregnancy. Almost one-third of women between the age group 15-19 years, who are widowed, divorced, separated, or deserted have had a live birth. By religion, the level of teenage motherhood and pregnancy is higher for Hindu and Muslim women aged 15-19 (16.0-17.0%) than for Jains (13.0%). Buddhists/ Neo-Buddhists (11.0%), Christians (8.0%), and Sikhs (6.0%). The proportion of women aged 15-19 that have begun childbearing is higher among women from scheduled castes (20.0%) and scheduled tribes (21.0%) than women from other backward classes (16.0%) and women who do not belong to any of these communities (12.0%). The level of teenage pregnancy and motherhood is five times as high for women in households with the lowest wealth index than for women in households with the highest wealth index.

The proportion of women in the age group 15-19 years, who have had a live birth or who are currently pregnant with their first child by state. The proportion of women aged 15-19 years, who have begun childbearing is highest in Jharkhand (28.0%), West Bengal (25.0%) and Bihar (25.0%), all in the East Region. The level of teenage childbearing is lowest (less than 5 percent) in Himachal Pradesh, Goa and Jammu and Kashmir.

In NFHS-3 (2005-06), 80.0% children in the age group 6-14 years are attending schools. The attendance rate drops off sharply at age 15-17 years, where it is 41.0% for the age group 6-17 years, the attendance rate is 75.0% for males, 66.0% females and 71.0% for the population of both sexes. Atter dance rates are higher in urban areas than in rural areas. In urban areas, attendance rates are almost the same for males and females except for the age group 15-17 years, although males have a slight higher percentage. According to this survey, the common reason for drop out is 'not interested in studies' followed by costs too much and then required for 'outside work for payment in cash or kind'. About 6.0% of the girls in rural areas and 2.0% of girls in the urban areas drop out of school due to their marriage.

In many countries, the topic of adolescent sexuality and reproductive health is still politically sensitive and reproductive health information and services simply do not reach most adolescents. Recently about 55 countries have taken policy and programme measures to address the health needs of adolescents including reproductive health. For the need of the youth, the youth centers have been established in urban areas offering re productive health services and peer based education.

Global Experience in the Field of Adolescent Health

Worldwide experience has shown that programmes for adolescents should:

- Recognize and address the fact that the programme needs of young adults differ according to their sexual experience and other key characteristics.
- Start with what young adults want and with what they are doing already to obtain reproductive health information and services.
- Include building skills (both generic and specific to reproductive health) as core interventions.
- Engage adults in creating a safer and more supportive

environment in which young adults can develop and learn to manage their lives, including their reproductive health.

- Use a greater variety of settings and provide private and public, clinical and non-clinical programs for sexual and reproductive health information and services.
- Make the most of what exists. Building upon and linking existing programmes and services in new and flexible ways so that they reach many more young adult.

Discussion

Adult constitute a subculture of their own, with their own points of views, values and even vocabulary. We should know what they want to know? And how do they want to learn it? And what guidance and services are thy need and want? Whom will they trust? Obviously, they are an important starting point of the programme. There should not be a gap between what the adults want and what health programme offer to them? And what they have been informed about the health services. Different sections of the adult population want different services and for that they want specific health information. We should test the field before implementing plans and products and messages for information should be suitable to solve the problem. For an example adult enjoy music, videos, films, drams and other entertainment media and these can be good formats for messages about reproductive health. Mass media is a good source of information about 'Family Life'. There what they see and hear may be incorrect, incomplete, misleading or misguiding and depicts irresponsible behavior as exciting and even rewarding. It is most important that the adolescence education should not only be for the students but also for the parents, teachers and even for the officials. Proper attention should be given to the reproductive and maternal health, gender equality and psychological development of the youngsters. It is also necessary to integrate the adolescence education and strategies into the school curriculum. Family life education should begin early, even before adolescence, to help young adults through the years when they are reaching puberty, learning about their sexuality and beginning to be interested in sexual matters. Women marry at much younger ages than men, and both men and women marry at younger ages in rural areas than in urban areas. Half of the adolescents are either sexually active or married. These adolescents face all the problems of early motherhood, specially the risk of death and disability for both the mother and her newborn child. They also suffer from sexually transmitted diseases and half of them suffer from nutritional anemia.

Adolescent period is the more crucial period for a girl. At the age of 12-18 years girl grows quickly. We should give her more body building food during this period. During this period monthly menstrual starts for which, they require more care, nutrition, iron and iodine supplemented food.

As regard the psychological development, at the adolescent stage there should be equal care and affection for the boy as well as girl within the family, in the school and in the society. Girls should not be treated as others' property and that is why they are neglected. The girls require recreation by playing and reading like boys. The age at marriage of girls should be at least 18 years and she should be pregnant after 21 years (National Health Policy, 2000).

Unprotected sexual relations place adolescent pregnancy and both girls and boys at risk for STDs, including HIV/AIDS. They need not only preventive services, but also youth friendly health services including diagnosis, treatment, information and counseling. The existence of sexual problems among adolescents are social, psychological, medical and behavioral consequences. So it is important to introduce transparency in communication on these subjects especially between young children and the parents.

NGOs have been particularly active in testing new approaches to reaching adolescents, such as peer education, skill building, counseling and other services. Actions to foster understanding and support among adults in the family and in the community are now also recognized as a key investment; women's empowerment activities, supports sexual and reproductive health education in youth centers about teenage pregnancy, STDs and HIV/AIDS, substance abuse and nutrition. The programme also meets the contraceptive needs of adolescents.

A sizeable number of abortion seekers are adolescent girls and many such abortions are conducted illegally causing complications, due to lack of awareness and social stigma.

The needs of adolescents, including protection from unwanted pregnancies and sexually transmitted diseases (STD), have not been specifically addressed in the past. Programmes should encourage delayed marriage and child bearing, and education of adolescents about the risks of unprotected sex. Reproductive health services for adolescent girls are specifically significant in rural Orissa, where adolescent marriage and pregnancy are widely prevalent. Their special requirements comprise information, counseling, population, education and making contraceptive services accessible and affordable, providing food supplements and nutritional services through the ICDS, and enforcing the child marriage Restraint Act, 1976.

In Reproductive Child Health Care, Government of India has emphasized to follow the following guidelines for strengthening the Adolescent Health Care.

- Adolescent's Education.

- Adolescent's Employment.
- Right age at marriage of adolescents i.e. not below 18 years but should be after 21 years.
- Knowledge of adolescent about family life and reproductive health.
- Knowledge of adolescent about hygiene and sex life.

Policy Implication for Adolescents

Adolescents represent about a fifth of India's population. The basic need of the Adolescents is (i) protection from unwanted pregnancies and (ii) protection from sexually transmitted diseases (STD).

These two problems have not been addressed in the past. The programmes need to encourage (i) delayed marriage and child bearing and education of adolescents about the risks of unprotected sex. Reproductive health services for adolescent girls and boys are especially significant in rural area, where adolescent marriage and pregnancy is widely prevalent. Special requirements of the adolescents are (a) information, counseling, population education, (b) making contraceptive services accessible and affordable (c) providing good supplements and nutrition services through the ICDS and (d) enforcing the Child Marriage Restraint Act 1976.

Operational Strategies

The operational strategies are described in the following Action Plans:

(1) Ensuring for adolescents access to information, counseling and services including reproductive health services that are affordable and accessible. Strengthen primary health centers and sub-centers to provide counseling both to adolescents and also to newly weds (who may also be adolescents). Emphasize proper spacing of children.

(2) To provide the adolescents the package of nutritional services available under the ICDS programme. Improvement in health status of the adolescent girls has an inter-generational impact. Nutritional supplements for adolescents will reduce the risk of low birth weight and minimizes neo-natal (death below 228 days of the baby) mortality malnutrition is a problem that seriously impairs the health of adolescents and adult women and has its roots in early childhood. It has been extensively studied and the causal linkages between anemia and low birth weight, prematurely, perinatal mortality and maternal mortality has been established.

(3) The incidence of teenage pregnancies has been reduced by enforcing the Child Marriage Restraint Act, 1976. It is a matter of national concern that to prevent the marriage of girls below the legally permissible age of 18 years and better after age 20 years. With the increase in the age of marriage the proportion of retention of girls at schools also increases and is also likely to encourage participation in the paid work force.

(4) To provide integrated intervention in pockets with unmet needs for the Adolescents in the urban slums, remote rural areas, border districts and among tribal populations.

(5) **Adolescent Centric Programme**: Adolescents are characterized by their individuality and nonconformity. They constitute a subculture of their own, with their own points of view, values and even vocabulary. Programs can be developed as per adult's response as follows. (i) What do they want to know? (ii) How do they want to learn it? (iii) What guidance and services do they need and want? (iv) Whom will they trust?

These important standing points of the programme can be identified and the gap between what adolescent want and what programmes offer can be accessed. For an example, in different countries at different areas different Programmes are run. In Kenya recently adolescents wanted to learn about the safe period and prognancy prevention which has been introduced in the programme.

(6) **Field Test Plans and Products:** Initial research with the clients is not enough but repeated investigation with the client, can be done. Specific plans, services and messages should be tested.

REFERENCES

Report of National Family Health Survey (NFHS-3) 3.

13

Efficacy of Intervention Programme in Imparting Reproductive and Sexual Health Education among Adolescents

Dr. Sibnath Deb

Summary

Adolescents are becoming more prone to risk behaviour both in the developed and the developing countries owing to a number of factors. The broad objective of the present study was to understand the efficacy of intervention programme for imparting reproductive and sexual health education among adolescents with a view to reducing risk-taking behaviour among adolescents. In order to achieve the objective of the study first a baseline study was conducted in the four selected schools in and around Kolkata covering a group of 864 adolescents from class IX and XI and data were collected using a structured questionnaire. Afterwards inputs were given to adolescent boys and girls following classroom lecture approach by subject specific experts on the basis of the six modules developed for this study covering six broad aspects of adolescent reproductive and sexual health.

The classroom lectures were followed by question-answer sessions. In addition, brief educational materials were distributed among the adolescents. Other approaches adopted for clarification of queries of adolescents included workshops, teen-clubs, question box and exhibition. After two rounds of the intervention, i.e., after one year of baseline study, end-line data were collected from a group of 777 available adolescents using the same questionnaire. Findings clearly indicated that the intervention programme was effective in disseminating complete and correct information about the various aspects of reproductive and sexual health among adolescents, except nutritional issue, which needs attention in future intervention programme. At the end, some measures have been suggested for effective implementation of future intervention programme in the same area.

Introduction

Incidents of risk-taking behaviour among adolescent boys and girls have increased over a period of time across the world because of a number of factors like immaturity, curiosity about sexuality, psychological and physiological changes, a desire for experimentation, peer influence, influence of media, lack of proper knowledge about various aspects of reproductive health, communication gap between parent-child relationships, cultural inhibition for clarification of queries of adolescents about sexuality and other related issues in the educational institution and at home, lack of parental supervision and so on (Chakraborty, 2008; Deb, 2006; Deb 2005).

A number of studies were carried out across the globe on adolescent risk behaviour and most of the studies reported that either adolescents have lack of knowledge about various aspects of reproductive and sexual health and/or they are involved in some form of risk behaviour. Nowadays more adolescents begin to participate in sexual activity at an earlier age than they did before (O'Reilly and Aral, 1985). On an average, first sexual intercourse occurs at age 16 and begins as early as age 12 in some urban settings (Rodrigues et al., 1998). Obviously, education aimed at modifying behaviour needs to begin before sexual activity normally begins, and needs to be repeated or revised at regular intervals (Vanichseni and Choopunya, 1990). It is, therefore, much easier to teach them positive behaviour at an earlier age than to try to change negative behaviour later. In an impact evaluation study on HIV/STD educational programme for middle school students, it has been observed that it significantly increased students' knowledge about STDs and condom use, and increased their communication with parents. The impact on knowledge was statistically significant for both boys and girls (Middlestadt et al., 1998). In another study conducted in rural Uganda on promotion on open discussions of sexuality to enable behaviour change among the youth revealed that youth have shown positive responses to receiving sex education (Kharim et al., 1998). Bury (1991) stated that it is essential to encourage adolescents to learn how they might be at risk and how this risk can be avoided. Information needs to be presented in a personally relevant way so that adolescents can clarify their own values and attitudes and can start understanding how the information is essential to them as individuals.

McIntosh (2005) examined the experiences of a sample of 43 pre-teenage drug users. The main reasons, which they gave for using drugs, were enjoyment and boredom. Huang et al., (2005) found that Chinese students had a lot of misconceptions about HIV transmission. Further study indicated that 14.0% of Chinese university students were sexually active and risk behaviors tended to increase with age. Refaat (2004) disclosed that about 30.0% of Egyptian university students lack adequate knowledge on AIDS. Most of those who had sexual relationships did not use contraceptives or any method of protection from sexually transmitted infection.

In India, few studies have been carried out on adolescents with regard to patterns and determinants of sexual behaviour and their vulnerability to HIV infection. In a study, the authors found that adolescents' vulnerability to HIV is determined by societal factors. The controlling family structures and values, while seeking to protect adolescents, may paradoxically increase their vulnerability (Sodh, 1998). Sharma et al., (1997) suggested that the school is an ideal setting for educating students regarding HIV/AIDS transmission and safer sex education. In an experimental study it shows that students have good power to participate in the prevention and control of HIV/AIDS. If properly guided and trained they could be the most potent force to fight the disease within their area of residence (Angeles, 1998). Deb (2006) carried out a study covering 141 adolescents in Kolkata with a view to understanding the knowledge, attitude and perception of adolescent boys and girls of Kolkata about different aspects of reproductive health. Although most of the students were aware of HIV/AIDS (97.2%) and family planning methods (82.3%), a large number of them had some misconceptions and incomplete knowledge about the said issues. Findings of another study carried out by Deb (2005) in Orissa revealed certain knowledge gaps and misconceptions among adolescents about various aspects of reproductive health. Deb further stated that the knowledge gap of adolescents regarding the reproductive organs and their functions clearly indicates defective teaching methodology. In another study, it was found that most of the heads of educational institutions in Bhubaneswar, Orissa were in favour of implementation of reproductive health education despite cultural barriers (Deb, 2000). Findings of a recently conducted study in Kolkata show that about one-fifth to one-third of the adolescents are involved in risk behaviour. Incidences of engagement in premarital sexual relation was found more among boys (30.4%) than girls (21.7 %) (Chakraborty, 2008).

The Universe is having more than one billion adolescent population. If they are guided properly, this huge human potential could make a prosperous society. On the other hand, research indicates that the tendency of taking risk behaviour is increasing among adolescents. Therefore, the global health-policy makers have become concerned about the reproductive health issue of the adolescents and intend to empower them though sharing of correct and complete information about the issue. Given this background, the necessity was felt to carry out an intervention study in imparting reproductive and sexual health education among adolescents for reducing risk-taking behaviour among adolescents through empowerment.

Method

Sample: For the purpose of the present study, adolescents of class IX and XI were covered from four schools located in and around Kolkata.

Study Tool: One structured questionnaire was developed for collection of data from the adolescent boys and girls and it was developed by a group of experts of ICMR Task Force Study. The questionnaire comprised of the following eight sections:

- Identification Information
- Background Information
- Adolescents' Needs and Practices
- Knowledge and Practices
- Sexuality
- Interpersonal Relationship

- Understanding RTIs, STIs and HIV/AIDS
- Life Skill Development, Risk Taking Behavior and Substance Abuse.

The questionnaire was then translated into local language for collection of data from the Bengali medium school. Prior to the collection of baseline data, a pro tooting of the questionnaires was done on a sample of 50 adolescents. On the basis of pre-testing results, minor modifications were made in the locally translated questionnaire and it was finalized. It is relevant to mention here that at the time of endline data collection a few more items were incorporated in the original questionnaire for understanding the adolescents' perception about the intervention programme and its efficacy.

Collection of Baseline (BL) Data: Baseline data were collected using a structured questionnaire from a group of 864 adolescents, 480 covered from class IX and 384 from class XI; and they were selected purposively from four selected schools in and around Kolkata

Intervention Phase

(i) *Development of Intervention Modules:* For providing correct and complete information to adolescent boys and girls during the intervention phase, six educational modules were developed, which are as follows:

- *Module I:* Growing Up Concerns and Nutrition
- *Module II:* Reproductive and Sexual Health and Hygiene
- *Module III:* Body Image, Sexuality and Risk Taking Behaviour
- *Module IV:* Interpersonal and Gender Relationships
- *Module V:* Understanding RTIS/ STIS and HIV/AIDS

- *Module VI*: Life Skill Development and Scholastic Achievement

(ii) *Development of Leaflet*: Based on the modules, six leaflets were developed and the same were shared with teachers, adolescent students and parents.

(iii) *Other Activities during the Intervention Phase*:

First, teacher parent sensitization programme was organised in all the four selected schools on the day of parent-teacher meeting with a view to providing them information about the objectives of the study and to ensure their cooperation and support. In fact, teacher parent sensitization programme was very much beneficial to make them understand about the utility of the study and also it helped to clarify the confusions of some of the parents as well as teachers.

Second, a tentative time schedule was developed for the two-stage intervention programme in consultation with the school authorities and the teacher-coordinator. After a gap of six months, the second intervention was given. Classroom lectures were arranged in all the four schools. Information about reproductive and sexual health was provided by the subject specific experts on the basis of the six modules. The classroom lectures were followed by question-answer sessions. In addition, brief educational materials were distributed among the adolescent boys and girls on the basis of the six modules. Other approaches adopted for clarification of queries of adolescents included workshops, teen-clubs, question box and exhibition. Question Box approach was adopted to encourage adolescent boys and girls to come out with their queries, which they could not raise openly out of feeling of embarrassment. This approach encouraged a good number of adolescents to write their queries in a slip without disclosing their identity. Further all the questions were collected and clarified by the subject specific experts during the lecture session.

Collection of Endline (EL) Data: After two rounds of the intervention i.e., after one year of baseline study, end-line data were collected from a group of 777 adolescents who participated in the baseline study and also attended the intervention programme. Out of 777 adolescents, 401 were from class IX students and 376 from class IX students. End-line data were collected using the same Structured Questionnaire, which was used during baseline study. A few additional questions were added to the Structured Questionnaire for collection of some additional information during the end-line study in order to understand the views of the students about the method of implementation of the intervention programme, utility of educational materials and its efficacy.

Ethical Issues: For consideration of ethical issues the following steps were adapted:

- First, all the school authorities were informed about the objectives of the study and their permission obtained.
- Secondly, during the parent-teacher sensitization programme again all of them were briefed about the objectives and utility of the study and their queries were clarified. All the teachers and the parents agreed to extend their cooperation for the success of the study.
- Third, prior to data collection, informed consent was obtained from the study subjects in writing and confidentiality of information was ensured.

Results

Most of the adolescents were Bengali-speaking while rest spoke Hindi. The data reveals that the students who were studying in class IX mostly belonged to the age group of 13 – 15 years while those studying in class XI belonged to age group 16 –18 years, irrespective of gender. The average number of the family members ranged from 4.90 to 5.18. So far as the number of sibling is concerned, the data clearly revealed a picture of nuclear family.

Adolescent Needs and Practices

Findings reveal that the adolescents, irrespective of the gender and classes, had a curiosity about the various aspects of reproductive health. However, the major areas were puberty, pregnancy, family planning abortion, sexual activities, career, gender relations, friendship with the opposite sex, etc.

So far as the adolescent practices are concerned for proper growth and development, data indicate that more than 50.0% of the adolescents, irrespective of gender and class, go for outings and participate in various recreational activities like games and sports, and also do exercise. Findings also revealed that 40.0 – 50.0% of the cases, adolescents had inhibition in free communication with teachers, parents/guardians about the various sensitive issues. Strangely, very few of them discussed or shared information about reproductive health issues and also indulged themselves in sexual activities at this age.

Knowledge and Practices

Adolescents were aware as to what food items should be included in their balanced diet but were not quite sure as to what nutrients are found in various food items. Intervention programme did help them to enhance their knowledge in this regard, but more efforts in this direction are needed.

During adolescence a lot of bodily changes occur. Findings revealed that a majority of them observed rapid gain in height and weight. So far as the reaction of the adolescents after noticing the bodily changes is concerned, data indicates that 10.0 –18.0% of them became worried, 1.0 –13.0% felt embarrassed, 7.0 –12.0% of them thought it is natural, 2.0 – 6.0% became anxious, while the rest felt happy and matured. Interestingly, after the intervention the feelings of anxiety decreased significantly in case of the class IX students.

Health and Hygiene

Regarding health and hygiene, especially for cleaning the different parts of the body like face, hands, hair etc, adolescent boys and girls mostly use water followed by soap or shampoo. Usage of water and shampoo has increased significantly after the intervention among all categories of respondents (Table 1).

Table 1
What do Adolescents Use to Clean Their Body Parts?

Materials Used For Cleaning	*Class IX*				*Class XI*			
	Boys		*Girls*		*Boys*		*Girls*	
	BL	*EL*	*BL*	*EL*	*BL*	*EL*	*BL*	*EL*
1	*2*	*3*	*4*	*5*	*6*	*7*	*8*	*9*
Significance Level: 95%	a	b	c	d	e	f	g	h
Significance Level: 99%	A	B	C	D	E	F	G	H
Base: All	300	238	180	163	174	195	210	181
1. Water	65.0	90.0 A	66.0	80.0 C	72.0	90.0 E	73.0	97.0 G
2. Soap/ Shampoo	11.0	90.0 A	10.0	98.0 C	80.0	98.0 E	81.0	98.0 G
3. Natural material	1.0	6.0 A	1.0	4.0	9.0	8.0	19.0	17.0
4. Don't feel the necessity to wash	-	*	-	-	1.0	1.0	*	-
77.Others	-	1.0	1.0	2.0	-	1.0	1.0	-
No response	30.0 B	3.0	31.0 D	1.0	5.0 f	1.0	9.0 H	1.0

Note: (i) Decimal places rounded to nearest whole number;
(ii) Columns Tested for Significance Test: A:B, C:D, E:F, G:H;
*(iii) * Symbol in place of percentage indicates the value is below 0.5%*

For cleaning genital or sexual parts the adolescent boys and girls mostly use water followed by soap or shampoo. In this regard, the intervention program was found to have a significant impact (Table 2).

Table 2
What do Adolescents Use to Clean The Genital/ Sexual Parts of the Body?

Materials Used For Cleaning The Genital/ Sexual Parts of Body	*Class IX*				*Class XI*			
	Boys		*Girls*		*Boys*		*Girls*	
	BL	*EL*	*BL*	*EL*	*BL*	*EL*	*BL*	*EL*
Significance Level: 95%	A	b	c	d	e	f	g	h
Significance Level: 99%	A	B	C	D	E	F	G	H
Base: All	300	238	180	163	174	195	210	181
1. Water	72.0	85.0 A	71.0	76.0	72.0	88.0 E	74.0	98.0 G
2. Soap/ Shampoo	8.0	73.0 A	7.0	61.0 C	66.0	90.0 E	51.0	94.0 G
3. Natural material	*	2.0	-	1.0	5.0	13.0 E	6.0 H	-
4. Don't feel the necessity to wash	*	*	-	-	2.0	1.0	1.0	-
77. Others	-	*	1.0	7.0 C	2.0	-	-	-
No response	25.0 B	3.0	27.0 D	10.0	3.0	3.0	11.0 H	1.0

Note: (i) Decimal places rounded to nearest whole number;
(ii) Columns Tested for Significance Test: A:B, C:D, E:F, G:H;
*(iii) * Symbol in place of percentage indicates the value is below 0.5%*

Knowledge about Reproductive Organs and Pregnancy

The knowledge of the adolescents, irrespective of gender, was comparatively better about the male and female reproductive organs than about the functions of the same. The intervention had a significant impact in increasing the knowledge level of adolescents about the male and female reproductive organs and their functions.

Regarding pregnancy i.e., how a woman conceives a child, findings reveal that a large number of adolescents had misconceptions. However, majority of the respondents ranging from one-third to two-thirds of the adolescents had correct knowledge about the issue i.e., a woman conceives a child when the sperm of man and the egg of woman fuse together inside the woman's body. After the intervention, knowledge level had increased significantly among adolescent girls only.

Regarding the prevention of pregnancy, almost equal number of adolescent boys and girls with minor variations replied that abstinence and the use of family planning methods are the best options for the prevention of pregnancy. In this regard, a significant difference has been observed between the baseline and endline data i.e., there is a gain in knowledge after the intervention (Table 3).

Table 3

How Pregnancy can be Avoided?

Method For Avoiding Pregnancy	*Class IX*				*Class XI*			
	Boys		*Girls*		*Boys*		*Girls*	
	BL	*EL*	*BL*	*EL*	*BL*	*EL*	*BL*	*EL*
Significance Level: 95%	a	B	c	D	e	f	g	h
Significance Level: 99%	A	B	C	D	E	F	G	H
Base : All	300	238	180	163	174	195	210	181
1.Use of family planning methods	31.0	58.0	24.0 A	39.0	47.0 C	69.0	35.0 E	87.0 G
2.Absti-nence/ Not having	33.0	35.0	33.0 D	16.0	29.0	50.0 E	33.0	77.0 G

(Contd...)

1	*2*	*3*	*4*	*5*	*6*	*7*	*8*	*9*
sex								
99.Don't know	31.0 B	10.0	41.0	34.0	26.0 F	6.0	21.0 H	4
77.Others	7.0	6.0	3.0 C	13.0 f	9.0	3.0 H	4.0	-
No response	5.0 A	10.0	4.0	6.0	3.0 e	9.0 H	15.0	3.0

Note: (i) Decimal places rounded to nearest whole number;
(ii) Columns Tested for Significance Test: A:B, C:D, E:F, G:H;

A large number of adolescent boys and girls had a wrong perception about gender determination of child. However, after the intervention, a significantly higher number of them reported that the father is responsible for determining the gender of the child (Table 4).

Table 4
Knowledge of Adolescents about Gender (Sex) Determination of the Child

Determining The Gender (Sex) of The Child	*Class IX*				*Class XI*			
	Boys		*Girls*		*Boys*		*Girls*	
	BL	*EL*	*BL*	*EL*	*BL*	*EL*	*BL*	*EL*
Significance Level: 95%	a	b	c	d	e	f	g	h
Significance Level: 99%	A	B	C	D	E	F	G	H
Base: All	300	238	180	163	174	195	210	181
1.Mother	11.0 B	1.0	7.0 D	1.0	5.0	7.0	2.0	27.0 G
2.Father	16.0	25.0 a	22.0	48.0 C	26.0	59.0 E	50.0	45.0
3.Both	37.0	33.0	20.0	20.0	36.0 F	19.0	19.0	14.0
99.Don't know	32.0	38.0	48.0 D	26.0	30.0 F	13.0	16.0 H	7.0
No response	4.0	3.0	3.0	5.0	3.0	2.0	13.0 h	7.0

Note: (i) Decimal places rounded to nearest whole number;
(ii) Columns Tested for Significance Test: A:B, C:D, E:F, G:H;
*(iii) * Symbol in place of percentage indicates the value below 0.5%*

Data from the above table indicates that adolescents, irrespective of gender or class, prefer to discuss issues like friendship with opposite sex, marriage, adult movies etc, mainly with friends, followed by classmates and cousins.

The meaning of the term 'sex' is different among adolescents. Majority of the adolescents, irrespective of gender and class, stated that it means distinction between male and female gender, followed by other understanding like intercourse, reproduction, hugging or kissing the opposite sex, boy or girl, man or woman, love between opposite sex and something pleasurable.

Regarding the prevention of pregnancy, almost equal number of adolescent boys and girls, with minor variations, replied that abstinence and the use of family planning methods are the best options for the prevention of pregnancy. In this regard also a significant difference is observed between the baseline and endline data. After the intervention the number increased significantly.

Knowledge about Family Planning Methods

The knowledge of adolescent boys and girls about both male and female family planning methods was poor except one male family welfare method i.e., condom. In this regard, intervention had a positive impact on adolescents in increasing their knowledge about the issue (Table 5).

Adolescents are curious to know as to who may use the family planning methods, why and how to use the same, their costs, source of availability and whether there are any side effects of the family planning methods. For effective communication of information about the family planning methods and other reproductive health issues, adolescents were of the view that lecture is the best approach, followed by booklet, TV, internet, documentary films, radio and posters. Regarding social agents for dissemination of information about reproductive and sexual health, doctor was the first choice, followed by counselor, teachers, peers and parents.

Table 5
Identification of Family Welfare Methods by Adolescents for Male

Family Welfare Method For Male	*Class IX*				*Class XI*			
	Boys		*Girls*		*Boys*		*Girls*	
	BL	*EL*	*BL*	*EL*	*BL*	*EL*	*BL*	*EL*
Significance Level: 95%	a	b	c	d	e	f	g	h
Significance Level: 99%	A	B	C	D	E	F	G	H
Base: All	300	238	180	163	174	195	210	181
Condom	67.0	80.0 A	51.0	66.0 C	84.0	85.0	69.0	97.0 G
Vasectomy	18.0	24.0	15.0	30.0 C	26.0	43.0 E	22.0	73.0 G
Coitus interruptus/ withdrawal before ejaculation	28.0	37.0 a	16.0	44.0 C	32.0	69.0 E	19.0	68.0 G
Abstinence/ natural family planning method	27.0	61.0 A	16.0.	45.0 C	43.0	52.0	17.0	77.0 G
Others	4.0	5.0	1.0	3.0	1.0	1.0	1.0	6.0 G
No response	28.0 B	5.0	43.0 d	33.0	12.0 F	3.0	28.0 H	3.0

Note: (i) Decimal places rounded to nearest whole number;
(ii) Columns Tested for Significance Test: A:B, C:D, E:F, G:H;

Although more than 65.0% of the adolescents, irrespective of gender and class, stated that they are aware of the meaning of abortion, a large number of them openly admitted that they are not aware of the meaning of the same. However, after the intervention programme, knowledge level among class XI girls has increased significantly. More than 65.0% adolescents, irrespective of gender and class, felt that abortion should be performed by a qualified and/or authorized doctor and in this regard the knowledge level among class IX boys and girls has increased significantly after the intervention programme. A good number of adolescents across the board had misconception about the issue.

Data in Table 6 indicates that majority of the adolescents had correct knowledge about the safe period for abortion i.e., it should be performed during early pregnancy (up to 12 weeks). Although a large number of them either had no knowledge or had misconceptions about the issue, intervention improved the knowledge of the adolescent boys and girls significantly, except for adolescent girls of class IX.

Further, those who stated that they are aware of the safe period for abortion were asked what problems an unsafe abortion could cause. Majority of the adolescents stated that fatal incidents i.e., death could occur in case of unsafe abortion, followed by bleeding/hemorrhage, perforation of uterus and sepsis. After the intervention, significant changes in knowledge concerning two major problems had been observed in case of adolescent girls of class XI.

The knowledge of more than 85.0% of the girls was correct about the meaning of menstruation, though they were not sure of the cause of it. The intervention program also failed in this aspect probably because girls believed in what their mothers had told them and were not ready to accept the knowledge provided to them easily. Majority of the adolescent girls either had misconception or no knowledge about the issue as to whether a woman can become pregnant if she has intercourse during menstruation. However, knowledge level had increased significantly among the girls after the intervention programme. More than half of the girls, irrespective of class, faced problems during menstruation

Table 6
Knowledge of Adolescents about Safe Period of Abortion

Knowledge About Safe Period For Abortion	*Class IX*				*Class XI*			
	Boys		*Girls*		*Boys*		*Girls*	
	BL	*EL*	*BL*	*EL*	*BL*	*EL*	*BL*	*EL*
Significance Level: 95%	a	b	C	d	e	f	g	h
Significance Level: 99%	A	B	C	D	E	F	G	H
Base: Those who know about abortion (Q53)	199	153	121	98	119	144	139	140
1.During early pregnancy (up to 12 weeks)	61.0	72.0 a	45.0	38.0	50.0	76.0 E	48.0	84.0 G
2.Late pregnancy (after 12 weeks)	15.0	10.0	11.0	9.0	4.0	28.0 E	6.0	12.0
3.Any time	7.0	3.0	4.0	17.0 C	6.0	8.0	1.0	12.0 G
4.Don't know	25.0	16.0	41.0	31.0	37.0 F	11.0	46.0 H	2.0
No response	1.0	2.0	2.0	7.0 c	3.0	2.0	1.0	3.0

Note: (i) Decimal places rounded to nearest whole number;
(ii) Columns Tested for Significance Test: A:B, C:D, E:F, G:H;

which included headache, mostly reported by class XI girls during endline study, followed by stomachache/cramps, as reported by 2.0–6.0% girls of class IX only, and some other problems like body ache, tiredness/weakness, laziness pain in breast and in legs, as reported by 1.0 – 3.0% girls. So far as gynaecological problems are concerned, 2.0 – 8.0% girls reported thin watery discharge while only 3.0% girls of class IX during baseline study reported having problems like discharge with foul smell. So far as psychological problems are concerned, mostly they reported irritation, with minor variations among class IX and XI adolescent girls, followed by weakness, bad mood, fear, anxiety, depression, messiness, embarrassment and so on.

Regarding perception of adolescent boys about semen discharge, mixed responses was found. The most common responses included semen discharge is a sign of adulthood/ masculinity, natural process, effect of hormones, containing sperms which cause pregnancy, and weakness. So far as perception of adolescent boys about masturbation is concerned, about one-forth to half of them had correct perception about the issue i.e., it is a natural practice during adolescence period. However, a large number of the adolescent boys had a lot of misconceptions about masturbation i.e., it reduces interest/attention in studies, it weakens body, it is a dirty/messy act, it leads to impotency, it can cause dysfunction and/or deformity in sexual organs, it makes one sexually inactive and it is an immoral act/a sin.

Regarding wet dream, mixed response was found. Majority of them stated that wet dream means loss of semen during sleep, followed by a natural process, watery discharge during sleep, a pleasurable dream, unhealthy and safe. More than one-third of the adolescent boys, irrespective of class, stated that they had nocturnal emission/wet dream, which was more among boys of class XI. About 17.0 – 39.0% of the adolescent boys stated otherwise. About half and above number of adolescents stated they had discussed about nocturnal emission/wet dream mostly with friends or peers, followed by brother, mother, father, relatives, doctor and teacher.

Sexuality

Sexuality is another very sensitive issue, which is never discussed openly in the Indian society. Most of the adolescents, irrespective of gender and class, stated that they want to be friendly and make friendship with opposite gender and meet them whom they like or love most.

Replies were sought to a question regarding what the activities adolescent boys and girls would like to do with their dream girl/boy. Findings revealed a range of activities they would like to do with their dream girls/ boys. Maintaining healthy friendship was the response received from most of the adolescent boys and girls, followed by holding hands, which was equally prevalent among boys and girls, seeing a movie and going for a picnic and restaurant. A large number of them, especially boys, expressed some sexual desires like hugging, kissing and spending a night together. On the other hand, a good number of them shared opposite views i.e., asking the partner to wait for marriage or till he/she completes studies/ becomes independent.

Regarding legal age of marriage for boys, more than 60.0% boys and girls (ranging from 61.0% to 94.0%) were of the opinion that boys should marry after 21 years of age. The knowledge level has increased significantly among both boys and girls after the intervention programme. Regarding legal age of marriage for girls, similar picture was found. Vast majority felt that a girl should marry after 18 years of age.

Majority of them, irrespective of gender and class, felt that sexual act should happen only after marriage. On the contrary, a large number of boys and girls were of the opinion that it should take place only when consented mutually, only when matured enough and when involved in a love affair. Regarding pre-marital sex, most of the adolescent boys and girls (ranging from 31.0 to 66.0%) stated that it is risky while the second highest category with minor variations stated that it is bad or immoral while a good number of them, especially boys, stated that it is moral.

About 1.0 – 9.0% of the adolescent boys and girls reported having intimate relationship/sexual intercourse mostly during 13 – 16 years of age. Prevalence of sexual abuse and/or harassment among adolescent boys and girls was ranging from 1.0 – 11.0%. The perpetrators included unknown person, own relative/intimate relatives, friend, a person whom they liked and others. Mostly opposite gender forced sexually in case of girls while in case of boys, persons of same sex mostly forced sexually.

Interpersonal Relationship

Interpersonal relationship of the adolescents with the parents was friendly and it improved significantly in the case of class XI adolescents after the intervention programme. However, the interpersonal relationships of the adolescents were also found to be indifferent in the case of a good number of them.

Mother was the nearest person for sharing of feelings. However, during the endline study the adolescents stated that friends of the same gender and opposite gender were the first choice for sharing of personal feelings followed by mother, father, teachers, siblings and relatives. So far as the future aspirations of the adolescents are concerned, data indicates that a good number of them want to be teachers / doctors/engineers/executives. In addition a large number of them expressed the desire to be involved in business. But a large number of them, irrespective of gender and class, have given a very realistic answer i.e., the situation in future will determine their occupation.

Adolescents are also affected by stress. Studies and load of studies is the prime cause for the stress for more than one-third of the adolescent, irrespective of gender and class, followed by poor academic performance, loneliness, strained relationship, physiological changes, reproductive and sexual health, etc. However, the stress reduced significantly after the intervention programme.

Knowledge about STDs including HIV/AIDS

Regarding knowledge of adolescents about sexually transmitted diseases, data indicates that more than 65.0% of them were aware of the diseases and awareness level did increase significantly after the intervention among all the categories of study subjects, except of girls of class IX (Table7).

Table 7
Awareness of Sexually Transmitted Diseases (STDs) among Adolescents

Awareness about STDs	*Class IX*				*Class XI*			
	Boys		*Girls*		*Boys*		*Girls*	
	BL	*EL*	*BL*	*EL*	*BL*	*EL*	*BL*	*EL*
Significance Level: 95%	a	b	c	d	e	f	g	h
Significance Level: 99%	A	B	C	D	E	F	G	H
Base: All	300	238	180	163	174	195	210	181
1. Yes	66.0	89.0 A	67.0	70.0	68.0	94.0 E	75.0	98.0 G
2. No	29.0 B	4.0	29.0	21.0	25.0 F	3.0	18.0 H	-
No response	5.0	8.0	4.0	9.0 c	7.0 f	3.0	8.0 H	2.0

Note: (i) Decimal places rounded to nearest whole number,
(ii) Columns Tested for Significance Test: A:B, C:D, E:F, G:H;

As far as the symptoms of STDs are concerned, findings reveal that about one-fourth to one-third of them, irrespective of gender and class, were aware of the symptoms. In this regard, the intervention had a positive impact for increasing the knowledge about the symptoms and related issue (Table 8).

Table 8
Awareness about the Symptoms of STDs

Awareness about Symptoms of STDs	*Class IX*				*Class XI*			
	Boys		*Girls*		*Boys*		*Girls*	
	BL	*EL*	*BL*	*EL*	*BL*	*EL*	*BL*	*EL*
Significance Level: 95%	a	b	c	d	e	f	g	h
Significance Level: 99%	A	B	C	D	E	F	G	H
Base: Those who heard about STDs	198	211	120	114	118	184	157	178
1. Yes	31.0	50.0 A	34.0	64.0 C	28.0	72.0 E	26.0	82.0 G
2. No	63.0 B	37.0	58.0 D	32.0	61.0 F	20.0	66.0 H	8.0
No response	6.0	13.0 a	8.0	4.0	11.0	9.0	8.0	10.0

Note: (i) Decimal places rounded to nearest whole number;
(ii) Columns Tested for Significance Test: A:B, C:D, E:F, G:H;

The primary source of information about the disease was newspaper, followed by friends, teachers and doctors. Majority of the respondents were aware of the mode of transmission of HIV/AIDS. So far as the mode of transmission is concerned, the majority was aware of the four established modes of transmission. At the same time, a good number of them had a lot of misconceptions and wrong understanding about the mode of transmission and its prognosis but it decreased significantly after the intervention.

Life Skill Development, Risk Taking Behaviour and Substance Abuse

Around 15.0 to 21.0% of the adolescent boys of class IX and XI smoke cigarette, perhaps occasionally or for fun, while in case of girls the percentage of smoking behaviour varies from 2.0 to 3.0%. About 3.0 - 50% of the adolescents of class IX and XI did try the narcotic drugs, while in case of girls it was one percent. Replying to a question whether adolescents are dependent on any drug or alcohol, about 1.0% boys, irrespective of class, and 1.0% girls of class IX during baseline study reported that they were dependent on either alcohol or drug. However, a good number of respondents did not respond to this question and their number varies from 2.0 to 34.0%.

One-fourth to two-fifth of the adolescent boys and girls came across serious crisis in life. Failure in academic performance was the most common crisis faced by the adolescents, irrespective of gender, followed by death of close family members, love affairs, accident/injuries, financial crisis in the family, domestic violence, prolonged diseases, sexual and reproductive health and some other problems. The above problems common among the adolescent boys and girls of class IX and XI with some variations. The two most common coping strategies adopted by the adolescents, irrespective of gender and class, were discussion of the issue with someone close to them and counselling. Other coping strategies included counselling by teachers, meditation, exercise, and reading some literature/spiritual books. A few of them became dependent on alcohol or drug for which they felt scared and/ or ashamed afterwards.

Adolescents' Perception about the Intervention Programme

Overall perception of the adolescents about the

intervention programme was very positive and beneficial. An overwhelming number of the respondents stated that all the topics covered in the intervention programme were informative and useful. A vast majority of the adolescents stated that the activities which were undertaken during the intervention phase, including classroom lectures/ presentation, question and answer sessions, exhibition, teen club, question box and distribution of educational materials benefited them immensely. More than 80.0% of the adolescents stated that appropriate time was given to each topic in the intervention programme except girls of class IX. Vast majority of the respondents stated that their doubts were clarified clearly during the intervention and they participated in the programme actively. More than 55.0% of the adolescent boys and girls did put up questions in the question box, which was more among adolescent boys of class IX.

Finally, two more questions were asked to the adolescents to know whether there was any change in their knowledge and behaviour after the intervention programme with respect to the various aspects of reproductive health. So far as enhancement of knowledge about different aspects of reproductive and sexual health is concerned, data clearly indicates that it has increased among adolescents, irrespective of gender and class.

Discussion

Physiological and psychological changes during the transition phase make adolescents curious to explore and experiment various aspects in life, especially sexuality and substance. Some of them also feel tempted to make friendship with opposite gender. Making friendship with the opposite gender is a source of fun for some of them (Deb et al., 2001). Peer pressure triggers their desire to explore and experiment and in the process some of them get involved in high-risk behaviour unconsciously. Findings of previous studies reveal that adolescents lack knowledge about different aspects of reproductive health (Deb 2005, 2006). It happens mainly because of social and cultural barriers within their family and in their educational institutions to discuss about these issues, especially about the physiological changes. In fact, there is no scope for them to share their personal problems, especially those regarding some of the sensitive issues of reproductive health like physiological changes, sexuality etc., which becomes a cause of anxiety and stress. And in turn it affects their interpersonal relationships and/or academic career. Feeling of guilt and embarrassment are common among adolescents due to onset of physiological and/or pubertal changes.

Research shows that adolescents are being involved in various types of high-risk behaviours, which is a prime cause of early pregnancy and/or getting the HIV/AIDS infection (O'Reilly and Aral, 1985; Rodrigues et al., 1998). Rate of unwanted pregnancy among the late teenagers is also on the rise in the city of Kolkata (*Times of India*, May 26, 2000). The nature of high-risk behavior among the adolescents has been thoroughly investigated by experts in different parts of the world. Comparatively less number of studies was conducted in developing countries like India on the issue of adolescent reproductive and sexual health.

This issue of adolescent reproductive health has come into the limelight after the international conference on Population and Development held in Cairo (1994) where the international health policy makers unanimously felt the need to bring all the health related programmes under one umbrella called Reproductive and Child Health (RCH). The Government of India has adopted the same under the ninth Five-Year Plan and integrated the related programs of the eighth plan. The concept of RCH is to provide the beneficiaries need-based, client centered, demand driven, high quality integrated services. The components, which were covered under the RCH, included prenatal care, antenatal care, adolescence care, respiratory tract infection, immunization, and awareness of HIV/ AIDS etc.

After the advancement of the HIV/AIDS, the issue of adolescent reproductive and sexual health has become the primary concern for the researchers and the academicians, and they started exploring the current level of knowledge, awareness and behaviour of the adolescents about reproductive health.

Given this background, the present study made an effort to empower adolescent boys and girls about reproductive and sexual health, providing them complete and correct information about the issue on the basis of six modules developed for the programme.

Overall analysis of baseline and endline data indicates that there is a positive change in the knowledge and behaviour of the adolescent about most of the aspects of reproductive and sexual health addressed in the study, except nutrition, which needs further investigation. Findings of some of the previous studies corroborate with the findings of present study (Middlestadt et al., 1998; Kharim et al., 1998). Regarding nutrition, it may be stated that reinforcement of information about nutrition is needed. Although statistically significant differences were found in most of the aspects of reproductive and sexual health, a good number of adolescents have some misconceptions, which need to be presented in a personally relevant way so that adolescents can clarify their own values and attitudes and can start understanding how the information is essential to them as individuals (Bury, 1991). Positive aspect of the programme is an active participation and cooperation from the adolescent boys and girls. To most of the adolescents, this was an opportunity to clarify their queries and confusion about reproductive and sexual health. A sense of relief from tension and anxieties on account of suppressed queries has been observed in a large number of adolescents.

Conclusion and Recommendations

In fine, it may be stated that the intervention programme was effective in disseminating complete and correct information about various aspects of reproductive and sexual health and the modules were well accepted by the adolescent boys and girls. Interventions provided a platform for interaction of the school adolescents with an outside resource person. It provided the ice-breaking tool for the school adolescents. In fact, adolescents felt that they need to gain more knowledge about various aspects of reproductive and sexual health. However, in a few areas significant changes were not observed, which needs attention of future researchers.

While implementing an intervention programme on a sensitive issue like reproductive and sexual health, researches should first brief the objective of the programme to the science teachers, especially the biology teacher, and through them researchers have to take the authority of different institutions in confidence. Academic session of the school is an important issue. This type of programme should start at the beginning of academic session when academic pressure is less.

Parents' participation in the programme should be mandatory for improving their knowledge about the issue and enhancing their skills in dealing with curiosities of adolescents and in developing healthy parent-child relationship. During the intervention much emphasis should be given on the nutrition issue followed by sexuality and HIV/AIDS, and educational materials should be developed in precise form using simple language.

REFERENCES

Angeles, R. E. (1998). The Development of Students as HIV/AIDS Educators Reaching Out to their Peers in School, Members of Their Family, Relatives, Friends and Neighbours. Paper Presented In The *12th World AIDS Conference* Held in Jeneva, 295.

Bury, K. J. (1991). Teenage Sexual Behaviour and the Impact of AIDS. *Health Education Journal*, 50, 43-48.

Chakraborty, Tanusree (2008). Probing into the Nature of Risk Behaviour and Psychological Stress among Adolescents and Its Impact on their Mental Health. *An Unpublished Doctoral Dissertation,* Calcutta University, Kolkata.

Deb, Sibnath (2005). Knowledge, Attitude and Perception of Adolescents about Different Aspects of Reproductive Health: A Cross-Sectional Study, *Social Science International*, 21, 1, 70-92.

Deb, Sibnath (2006). Adolescents' Perceived Reproductive Health: A Cross-sectional Study in Kolkata, *Social Science International,* 22, 1, 38-58.

Deb, Sibnath, Mitra, Kathakali and Mukherjee, Indrani (2001). A Study on Adolescents' Perceived Social Norms and Values: A Calcutta-based Study. *Journal of the Indian Academy of Applied Psychology,* 27, 1-2,13-21.

Deb, Sibnath (2000). Attitude and Perception of Heads of Educational and Industrial Institutions towards Introduction of Reproductive Health Education. *Indian Journal of Psychological Issues,* 8(2), 37-47.

Huang, J, Bova, C, Fennie, K.P., Rogers, A., and Williams, A.B. (2005). Knowledge, Attitudes, Behaviors, and Perceptions of Risk Related to HIV/AIDS among Chinese University Students in Hunan, China. *AIDS Patient Care STDS.* 19(11), 769-77.

Kharim, H., Asuzi, S., Tani, S., Waka, P., Idoro, J.W. and Homsy, J. (1998). Promoting Open Discussions about Sexuality to Enable Behaviour Change among the Youth In Rural Uganda. Paper Presented in The *12th World AIDS Conference* Held in Geneva, 245.

McIntosh, J. (2005). Pre-Teenage Children's Experiences of Drug Use.16.1, 37-45.

Middlestadt, S.E., Kaiser, J., Hirsch, L., Simkin, L., Radosh, A., Santelli, J., Banspach, S., and Collins, J. (1998). Impact of an HIV/STD Prevention Intervention on Urban Middle School Students. Paper presented in the *12th World AIDS Conference* Held in Jeneva, 239.

O'Reilly, K.R. and Aral, S.O. (1985). Adolescence and Sexual Behaviour: Trends and Implication for STD. *Journal of Adolescent Health Care*, 6, 298-310.

Refaat, A. (2004). 'Practice and Awareness of Health Risk Behaviour among Egyptian University Students.' *East Mediterr Health J.*, 10(1-2), 72-81.

Reproductive and Child Health Programme: Schemes for Implementation, Department of Family Welfare, Ministry of Health and Family Welfare, Government of India, Oct.1997.

Rodrigues, A., Kerr-Pontes, L., and Mota, R.M. (1998). Sexual Behavior and AIDS Transmission among High School Students in a Megacity from The North-Eastern of Brazil. Paper Presented in *The 12th World AIDS Conference* Held in Geneva, 244.

Sodh, G., Zoysa, De I., Sen A., and Varma, M. (1998). Patterns and Determinants of Sexual Behaviour of Adolescents in a Slum of New Delhi, India. Paper presented in the *12th World AIDS Conference* Held in Geneva, 246.

Sharma, A.K., Sehgal, V.N., Kant, S., Choubey, D., and Bharadwaj, A. (1997). Knowledge, Attitude, Belief and Practice Study on AIDS among Senior Secondary Students. *Indian Journal of Community Medicine*, XXII, 4, 168-171.

Vanichseni, S. and Choopunya, K. (1990). AIDS KAP Survey among Secondary School Boys. *Thai AIDS Journal*, 2, 76-80.

Acknowledgements: The author wishes to extend his gratitude to Indian Council of Medical Research (ICMR), New Delhi for sponsoring this study. Significant contributions of Dr. R.N. Gupta and Dr. A.S. Kundu from ICMR deserve special appreciation. All the Principal Investigators of different centres viz., Prof. M.K.C. Nayar, Prof. R.S. Goyal, Dr. Shashi Prateek, Dr. Seema Sahay, and Dr. Pandy made a significant contribution in developing the educational materials and questionnaires. I duly acknowledge my gratitude to all of them. Finally, thank is due to all the research team members of Calcutta University Centre, all the school authorities and the study subjects for their cooperation for the success of the study.

III. HIV/AIDS

14

Reproduction in Women with HIV / AIDS

Prof. Bibhuti Saha & Dr. Ayesha Chowdhury

Summary

The HIV pandemic has played a major role in shaping the current understanding of human sexuality and reproduction. The health issues involve improving women's sexual and reproductive health, treating HIV infection and preventing mother-to-child transmission. Family planning counseling should be comprehensive and address HIV prevention. The consistent use of condoms is advocated to protect them from acquiring and transmitting HIV and other STIs. Contraceptive measures are highly individualized as it is based on the stage of disease, life-style and personal desires. Skilled care is needed during pregnancy, childbirth and postpartum. Although pregnancy does not have a major effect on the progression of the HIV diseases, women living with HIV/AIDS have greater risk of adverse pregnancy outcomes, such as intrauterine growth restriction and preterm delivery. Pregnant women living with HIV have an increased risk of developing malaria and require additional precautions. The benefit of elective caesarean section in reducing HIV transmission needs to be balanced against the risk of surgical procedure. They also have increased risk of post-operative morbidity especially infective complications. Post-partum follow-up and care may extend beyond six weeks postpartum period of the infant. Infant feeding depends on the women's choice and her social standing. Immunization of the infant should be also included in the counseling during the postpartum period. Providing anti-retroviral therapy (ART) for women living with HIV/AIDS is essential in reducing maternal mortality, effectively preventing mother-to-child transmission and improving the survival of children born to women living with AIDS. All efforts must be made to ensure that all women have access to ART.

Introduction

AIDS is the most devastating new disease to have emerged in recent history. According to the latest (2007) WHO and UNAIDS global AIDS estimates, worldwide, approximately as many women as men are living with HIV, and in sub-Saharan Africa, women constitute 61.0% of the people living with HIV. Gender inequalities as well as biological factors make women and girls especially vulnerable to HIV and to the impact of AIDS.

Pregnancy in HIV infected women is an important event having bearings on the health of the women. Specific guidelines are available to provide them optimum care. HIV infected mothers can transmit the infection to offspring's in utero, during child birth as well as through breast milk. Out of the total of 2.5 million [1.8–4.1 million] people newly infected with HIV in 2007, children under 15 years were 4,20,000 [3,50,000–5,40,000]–mostly as a result of transmission of infection from mother. Recommendations for prevention of peri-natal transmission of HIV in various health care settings are available. HIV exposed babies are specially vulnerable to various childhood illnesses apart from the HIV associated infections. Health care workers should be familiar with protocols for care of such children.

Problems Faced by Women with HIV

Most women living with HIV/AIDS suffer or fear stigmatization (WHO, 2003). Forms of stigma and discrimination include: perceptions that women living with HIV/AIDS are promiscuous; blame for bringing HIV into a relationship or family; being deemed irresponsible if they desire to have children; and being considered as vectors of HIV transmission to their children. Some health care workers may be hesitant to provide care for women living with HIV/AIDS because of fears of HIV transmission. Moreover, health workers may have negative attitudes or biases towards women living with HIV/AIDS, particularly regarding their sexual and reproductive health practices. Sex workers and injecting drug users living with HIV/AIDS may face additional stigma.

Diagnosing HIV Infection in Women

Knowledge of HIV status plays an essential role in efforts to prevent and treat HIV. Although HIV testing and counseling is considered part of essential care during pregnancy, many women deliver without being offered testing and counselling.

Offering HIV testing and counseling around the time of labour or shortly thereafter has been shown to be feasible for the women who have not accessed HIV testing during pregnancy (Bulterys et al., 2004; Chersich et al., 2004). However, given the benefits of knowing one's HIV status, HIV testing and counseling should be made available to women attending all reproductive health services (UNPFIPPF, 2004). Further, confining HIV testing and counseling to antenatal care and childbirth settings reinforces the perception that the primary objective of identifying HIV infection in women is to prevent transmission to infants rather than to benefit of the women themselves.

Counseling is an opportunity to identify barriers to disclosure of HIV status and support women in assessing the safety and feasibility of disclosing it to their partners. Further, all women who undergo HIV testing should be offered counseling and support for negotiation of safe and consensual sex, including dual protection options and access to male and/or female condoms. Women who have experienced gender-based violence have low self-esteem or thoughts of suicide and require additional counseling and support. Referral to health workers with specific training in these areas may be necessary.

Reproductive Health Issues in HIV

Improving women's sexual and reproductive health, treating HIV infections and preventing new ones are important factors in promoting the social and economic development of communities and countries and thereby reducing poverty. Sexual and reproductive health services are uniquely positioned to address each of these factors.

All women have the same rights concerning their reproduction and sexuality, but women living with HIV/AIDS require additional care and counseling during their reproductive life.

HIV testing and counseling is the entry point to HIV-related care and support, including antiretroviral therapy. Knowledge of HIV status is essential for tailoring reproductive health care and counseling according to the HIV status of women and to assist women in making decisions on such issues as the number, spacing and timing of pregnancies, use of contraceptive methods and infant-feeding practices. Further, information and counseling are critical components of all sexual and reproductive health services and support women in making these decisions and carrying them out safely and voluntarily.

Family planning services have great potential in promoting sexual health and in efforts to prevent and treat HIV/AIDS. Further, helping women living with HIV/AIDS avoid unintended pregnancies is an important component of programmes to prevent HIV among infants. Transmission of HIV and other sexually transmitted infections (STIs) warrants special consideration during family planning counseling. The consistent and correct use of condoms continues to be the most effective contraceptive method that protects against acquiring and transmitting HIV and other STIs. Family planning services must be comprehensive and address HIV prevention including, where appropriate, the benefits of abstinence, the risk associated with unprotected sex with multiple partners as well as the promotion and provision of dual protection. In addition to the medical eligibility criteria, the social, cultural and behavioural context must be considered and specific recommendations are to be made about contraceptive methods individualized for each woman based on her stage of disease and treatment as well as lifestyle and personal desires. Women living with HIV/AIDS can safely and effectively use most contraceptive methods. However, several antiretroviral drugs have the potential to either decrease or increase the bioavailability of steroid hormones in hormonal contraceptives.

The control of STIs has received renewed attention because of the strong correlation between the spread of STIs and HIV transmission. Systematic screening for STIs, consisting of history-taking, clinical examination and laboratory screening for syphilis, is part of the initial clinical evaluation of a woman with HIV. Appropriate and prompt case management of STIs reduces the risk of transmitting HIV to sexual partners and the reproductive-tract and obstetric complications associated with STIs. Although the presentation and response to treatment of some STIs – in particular genital herpes and chancroid – may be altered in women living with HIV/AIDS, standard treatment protocols are effective. In many countries, cervical cancer is the most common malignancy among women and the leading cause of women's deaths from cancer. Screening programmes can significantly reduce the number of new cases of cervical cancer and the mortality rates of cervical cancer.

Contraception

Women using no form of contraception do not necessarily intend to become pregnant but may lack significant power in their sexual relationship, be under pressure from the partner or the family to have children, may not have disclosed their HIV status to their partner, be unaware of their options concerning contraception or believe they cannot become pregnant, have a disorganized lifestyle that precludes consistent use of contraception, or simply have decided to take their chances.

Hormonal methods of contraception, particularly combined oestrogen-progestin oral contraceptives (OCs), can have significant drug interactions, resulting in either decreased contraceptive effectiveness or increased or decreased concentrations of the co-administered drug. Alternative methods of contraception should be considered; if OCs are used, lowest effective doses of affected hormonal components should be prescribed and an additional method is to be recommended.

Concerns have been raised about possible increased risk of HIV transmission or acquisition in hormonal contraceptive users. At present, given their effectiveness, overall safety, and ease of use, hormonal methods of contraception remain an appropriate option for HIV-infected or at-risk women. These women should be advised that these contraceptives do not protect against HIV transmission and consistent condom use should be emphasized.

Use of the intrauterine device (IUD) has been accompanied by concerns about a potential increased risk for HIV susceptibility. However, a recent large prospective cohort study of almost 2500 HIV-uninfected women found no association between IUD use and HIV transmission; there was also no increased risk associated with increasing duration of use (Kapiga et al., 1998). Furthermore, another study from Kenya found no increase in overall complications or infection-related complications in HIV-positive IUD users as compared to HIV-negative IUD users and complications did not differ by CD4 count (Morrison et al., 2001). However, risk of pelvic inflammatory disease is increased in IUD users who are at an increased risk of acquiring other sexually transmitted infections (STIs), and a recent study found an association between IUD use and bacterial vaginosis, also a risk factor for PID. Furthermore, copper IUDs are associated with increased menstrual flow and duration, possibly contributing to transmission risk and anaemia in HIV-positive women. The IUD should be used cautiously in the setting of HIV infection.

Spermicidals have in vitro activity against HIV; however, standard spermicidal doses of nonoxynol-9 (N-9) have been associated with an increase in irritation, colposcopic and histologic evidence of inflammation, and decreased numbers of vaginal lactobacilli in N-9 users, compared to placebo recipients (Stafford et al., 1998). In a randomized placebo-controlled clinical trial of N-9 conducted among commercial sex workers with high rates of sexual activity, N-9 did not protect against HIV infection, resulted in increased vaginal lesions, and possibly caused increased transmission (Richardson, 2002). Although these adverse effects might not occur with less frequent use, given current evidence, spermicidals containing N-9 should not be recommended as an effective means of HIV prevention.

Condoms - used consistently- reduce HIV transmission risk by 80.0% and provide the best known protection against sexual transmission of HIV. They should be emphasized for all HIV-infected and at-risk women to decrease the risk of HIV transmission/acquisition and transmission/acquisition of other STIs. Other barrier contraceptive methods provide limited STI protection and have not been shown to offer significant protection against HIV transmission.

Because male and female condoms are used for both prevention of infection and prevention of pregnancy, these two separate issues should be distinguished when counseling patients. There is some evidence that condom use is less likely in HIV-infected women using other methods of contraception. Condom use should be reinforced for HIV-positive or at-risk women even when prevention of pregnancy is not a concern: for postmenopausal women, during pregnancy, despite infertility, and with the use of other methods of contraception. As with the use of contraception in general, use of condoms for HIV prevention is related to education, relationship to sexual partner, and chaos in life. There is some indication that use of HAART and decrease in viral load may lead to drop-off in condom use.

HIV and Fertility

Recent studies in Africa, as well as in the developed countries, have suggested that HIV may have an adverse effect on fertility in both symptomatic and asymptomatic women. A cross-sectional study from Uganda found that the likelihood of pregnancy is lower in HIV-positive women as compared with HIV-negative women and is the lowest in women who were symptomatic from HIV or were co-infected with syphilis.

Effect of Pregnancy on HIV Infection

In both HIV-positive and HIV-negative women the

response of CD4 cell counts to pregnancy is variable. Many studies have suggested that there is a decline in absolute CD4 cell counts in pregnancy, which return to the baseline level at the end of pregnancy or during the postpartum period. The decline in CD4 count is thought secondary to hemodilution; on the other hand, percentage of CD4 cells remains relatively stable. Therefore, percentage, rather than absolute number, may be a more accurate measure of immune function for HIV-infected pregnant women (European Collaborative Study Report, 1997). HIV RNA levels (viral load) remain relatively stable throughout pregnancy in the absence of treatment (Burns et al., 1998). However, recent data suggest that the HIV-RNA levels increase during the postpartum period regardless of ARV treatment (although use of HAART appears to blunt the effect), possibly due to immune activation associated with hormonal changes or due to the unmasking of a pregnancy-related viral load suppression. The increase in viral load postpartum does not appear to reflect a long-lasting effect of pregnancy on viral load (Minkoff et al., 2003).

Clinical Course of HIV in Pregnancy

Most studies till date examining the impact of pregnancy on HIV related disease have been small but have not shown significant differences in HIV progression or survival between pregnant women and non pregnant women with HIV infection. A recent meta-analysis of seven prospective cohort studies found no overall significant differences in death, HIV disease progression, progression to an AIDS-defining illness, or fall in CD4 count to below 200/mm3 between cases and controls (French and Brocklehurst, 1998). In addition, a long-term observational study showed no difference in viral load, CD4, or clinical disease progression in women with repeat pregnancy, compared to those with only one pregnancy (Minkoff et al., 2003).

Effect of HIV on Pregnancy Course and Outcome

Adverse pregnancy outcomes may occur secondary to underlying disease processes (or their treatment), as well as for unknown reasons. Data have accumulated that HIV, especially when more advanced, may result in increases in certain pregnancy complications. However, results of studies are conflicting. Some studies suggest that HIV-infected women have an increase in other risk factors for adverse pregnancy outcome (such as smoking, drug use, poor prenatal care) and if these risk factors are controlled for, there is no independent effect of HIV on adverse outcomes (Lambert et al., 2000). Furthermore, concerns have been raised that antiretroviral treatment itself may increase some adverse outcomes in pregnancy. A recent study of 497 HIV-infected pregnant women enrolled in a perinatal clinical trial found that risk factors for adverse pregnancy outcomes (preterm birth, low birth weight, and intrauterine growth retardation) in antiretroviral-treated women are similar to those reported for uninfected women (Lambert et al., 2000).

Adverse Pregnancy Outcomes and Their Relationship to Untreated HIV Infection

There is increased risk of spontaneous abortions and stillbirth in the developing countries. Intrauterine growth restrictions, preeclampsia are recorded in the intrapartum period. There are evidences of low birth rate and pretem delivery. Peri-natal and infant mortality are increased in the developing countries. However, there are no data relating to gestational diabetes, placental abruption and placenta previa. Chorioamnionitis have been found in the post partum period. No evidence of increased risk of foetal malformation.

Both HIV and pregnancy may affect the natural history, presentation, treatment, or significance of certain infections, and these, in turn, may be associated with pregnancy complications or peri-natal infection. During pregnancy, vulvo-vaginal candidiasis tends to proliferate. It can be treated with topical azoles for 7 days. Bacterial vaginosis is to be treated by metronidazole 250 mg po tid x 7 days or clindamycin 300 mg po bid x 7 days for HSV. Because most neonatal infection occur during vaginal delivery, if genital lesions or prodromal symptoms are present at the time of labour or membrane rupture, caesarean section should be performed. Caesarean section is not indicated for recurrent HSV distant from the genital tract (e.g., thigh, buttocks) (ACOG Practice Bulletin, 1999). Treatment of symptomatic HSV infections and suppressive therapy fcr frequent recurrences should be offered during pregnancy to HIV-infected women (USPHA/ISDA, 2001). The risk for herpes is high in infants of women who acquire genital HSV in late pregnancy and such women should be managed in consultation with an expert. Acyclovir is the drug of choice for HSV therapy during pregnancy and there is no current evidence for increased risk for major birth defects or other adverse pregnancy outcomes. In women with large volume or bulk of genital warts treatment in late pregnancy with laser, excision, or cavitronic ultrasonic aspiration may be considered. Caesarean section is not currently recommended to prevent neonatal exposure to HPV; although in rare instances caesarean section may be indicated when extensive lesions obstruct the vagina. Pregnant women with abnormal Pap smears should undergo colposcopy and cervical biopsy, if indicated; increased bleeding may occur with biopsy during pregnancy. Endocervical currettage should not be performed during pregnancy. Pap smear should be repeated with or without colposcopy at 34–36 weeks of gestation in women with initial abnormal Pap smear, to rule out progression of dysplasia. Women with preinvasive cervical lesions can deliver vaginally, if otherwise appropriate; women with suspected invasive cervical cancer should be referred to a gynaecologic oncologist. Congenital syphilis can generally be prevented by identification and appropriate treatment of syphilis during pregnancy. All pregnant women should have serologic testing for syphilis at the beginning of prenatal care and testing should be repeated at the 28th week of gestation and at delivery, particularly in women who remain at risk for infection. Any woman with stillbirth after 20 weeks of gestation should be tested for syphilis.

Perinatal Transmission

Most children living with HIV acquire the infection through mother-to-child transmission (MTCT), which can occur during pregnancy, labour and delivery or during breastfeeding. In the absence of any intervention, the risk of such transmission is 15.0% – 30.0% in the non-breastfeeding populations. Breastfeeding by an infected mother increases the risk by 5.0% – 20.0% to a total of 20.0% – 45.0% (De Cock *et al.*, 2000).

The risk of MTCT can be reduced to under 2.0% by interventions that include antiretroviral (ARV) prophylaxis given to women during pregnancy and labour and to the infant in the first weeks of life, obstetrical interventions including elective caesarean delivery (prior to the onset of labour and rupture of membranes), and complete avoidance of breastfeeding (Read et al., 2005). With these interventions, new HIV infections in children are becoming increasingly rare in many parts of the world, particularly in high-income countries.

In many resource-constrained settings, elective caesarean delivery is seldom feasible (Stanton and Holtz, 2006) and it is often neither acceptable nor safe for mothers to refrain from breastfeeding. In these settings, the efforts to prevent HIV infection in infants initially focused on reducing MTCT around the time of labour and delivery, which accounts for one to two-thirds of overall transmission, depending on whether the mother breastfeeds.

Recently, to increase the effectiveness of PMTCT (prevention of mother-to-child transmission) programmes, many countries with a heavy burden of HIV have adopted more effective ARV regimens, beginning in the third trimester of pregnancy, which can reduce the risk of transmission during pregnancy and childbirth to 2.0–4.0% (Shapiro et al., 2006). Even when these regimens are used, however, infants remain at substantial risk of acquiring infection during breastfeeding. Research is ongoing to evaluate several new approaches to preventing HIV transmission during breastfeeding (Gaillard et al., 2004).

If the goal of eliminating HIV infection in infants and young children is to be achieved, all pregnant women eligible for ART must have access to it, and countries must adopt more efficacious ARV regimens for preventing MTCT among pregnant women who do not yet require ART.

Current recommendations take into account situations where women present later in pregnancy or around childbirth, including those women who deliver at home. The criteria for initiating ART for pregnant women are the same as for non-pregnant women; with the exception that initiation of such therapy is recommended for those pregnant women who have clinical stage 3 diseases and a CD4 cell count below 350 cells/mm3.

ART for Pregnant Women is therefore Recommended for:

- All women in clinical stage 4, irrespective of the CD4 cell count;
- Women in clinical stage 3, with the CD4 <350 cells/mm3 count, if available; if the CD4 cell count is not available, all women in stage III should be treated; and
- Women in clinical stage I and 2 with a cell count of CD4 <200 cells/mm3.

In pregnancy, haemodynamic changes occur in all women, whether or not they are living with HIV. Women have lower CD4 cell counts during pregnancy as compared to the postpartum period, partly due to pregnancy-related haemodilution. Thus, CD4 levels will rise after the end of pregnancy. The impact of this on using the CD4 350 cells/ mm3 threshold (determined during pregnancy) is not known. Further data are needed as to whether particular corrections need to be made.

Pregnancy During ART

When a pregnancy is recognized during the first trimester, the potential benefits and risks of ART for the health of the woman and the foetus (the risk of MTCT and in utero exposure to ARV drugs) should be considered. The risk of birth defects induced by ARV drugs has been assessed through the Antiretroviral Pregnancy Registry. Among prospectively followed pregnancies, the prevalence of birth defects in infants who were exposed to ARV drugs during the mother's pregnancy did not differ significantly from rates in the general population (APRSC, 2005). Concerns remain about Efavirenz (EFV)-induced foetal effects. For women receiving EFV who become pregnant and this is recognized during the first trimester, it is recommended that NVP be substituted for EFV, or alternatively a triple nucleoside reverse transcriptase inhibitor (NRTI)-or a protease inhibitor (PI)-based regimen can be given. Pharmacokinetic data indicate that when NVP is substituted for EFV, women should immediately commence NVP at 200 mg twice a day, as an escalation in the dose of NVP is associated with sub-therapeutic NVP levels in these individuals.

Most women will not realize they are pregnant during this early period and if the patient is already in the second or third trimester when her pregnancy is recognized, EFV could be continued, given that the high-risk exposure has already occurred. Based on current evidence of the extent of risk of

EFV-induced fetal effects, exposure to EFV during pregnancy should not be viewed as an indication for abortion. It is important to note that an exaggerated perception of foetal risk can result in a woman terminating an otherwise wanted pregnancy (Koren and Pastuszak, 1998).

Although women who become pregnant while receiving EFV may consider temporarily suspending treatment, this is not recommended. Discontinuing treatment during pregnancy has been associated with viral rebound and renewed CD4 cell decline (Bucceri et al., 2003), possibly compromising a woman's health and increasing the risk of MTCT. Further, data indicate that an interruption in treatment among adults receiving ART for their own health, who have a good immune response to ART, increases their risk for HIV-related disease. There are concerns about a potential association between exposure to Tenofovir (TDF) in utero and abnormal foetal bone development. However, for women receiving TDF who become pregnant, the benefits of continuing treatment are likely to exceed the theoretical risks of toxicity for the infant. Further safety data are awaited. Pregnancy-associated nausea and vomiting may affect a woman's ability to adhere to ART and occasionally require that treatment be temporarily suspended. If nausea and vomiting are significant problems and not amenable to medication, a temporary suspension of treatment may be necessary until the symptoms are controlled. The ARV dose for women during labour is likely to be especially important for reducing MTCT at this time. During labour, therefore, women receiving ART should continue to adhere to their ART regimen, whenever possible.

The WHO recommended regimen consists of: antepartum – azidothymidine (AZT) from the 28 week of the pregnancy (or as soon as possible thereafter); intrapartum – AZT and lamivudine (3TC) plus a single dose of nevirapine (Sd-NVP); and postpartum – AZT and 3TC for seven days for women and Sd-NVP and AZT for one week for infants. Widespread implementation of this regimen will dramatically reduce the number of new HIV infections in infants and young children and result in low levels of HIV viral resistance.

Research in high-income countries has focused on more complex regimens and has shown that triple-ARV combinations given to women during pregnancy and labour can reduce the risk of transmission to under 2.0% (Cooper et al., 2002). These regimens are discontinued after childbirth for women without indications for ART. In lower-income countries, the choice of drugs for such women is more problematic, as PI drugs are reserved for second-line therapy. Countries with a high burden of HIV initially focused their efforts to prevent HIV infection in infants on reducing MTCT around the time of labour and delivery. Prophylactic regimens in the third trimester of pregnancy which, together with intrapartum and postpartum prophylaxis, can reduce the risk of transmission during pregnancy and childbirth to 2.0–4.0% (Shapiro *et al.*, 2006).

Concerns remain that the development of viral resistance with increased use of partly suppressive ARV prophylaxis – especially regimens containing Sd-NVP – may have a negative impact on future ART options for women and infants who become infected. Accruing data suggest that the incidence of resistance may be decreased by giving dual NRTI drugs intrapartum and for a short period postpartum following Sd-NVP (McIntyre, 2006). As NVP has a long half-life, with drug levels persisting for up to three weeks after women receive Sd-NVP, giving dual NRTI drugs for a period after exposure to Sd-NVP is expected to suppress viral replication and decrease the risk of developing resistance.

Among breastfeeding women, the long-term efficacy of ARV prophylactic regimens is diminished due to the risk of postpartum transmission throughout the breastfeeding period. Long-term efficacy in breastfeeding women, as determined by the child's infection status at 18–24 months of age (which accounts for the continued risk of acquiring HIV infection during the breastfeeding period) has been confirmed, although it is reduced for short-course AZT, single-dose NVP for mothers and infants, and for a combination of AZT and 3TC from the 36 week of the pregnancy.

Omission of the NVP dose for the mother may be considered if she has received AZT for at least four weeks during her pregnancy. If the NVP dose is not given to the mother, or delivery occurs less than two hours after she is given the labour dose, the infant must receive Sd-NVP immediately after birth and be given AZT for four weeks instead of one week (Mirochnick et al., 2003). If the NVP dose is not given to the mother, she must be given AZT intrapartum but she will not require 3TC intrapartum or the AZT and 3TC regimen postpartum. Thus, avoiding the NVP dose for the mother removes the risk of her becoming resistant to NVP but increases the overall complexity of the prophylactic regimen, which needs to be considered when programme decisions are made.

In settings without adequate capacity to deliver the recommended regimen, it may be necessary to use other regimens. Programme managers may opt to administer a regimen of AZT from 28 weeks of pregnancy and intrapartum, and for seven days to the infant plus Sd-NVP, without the seven-day tail of AZT/3TC. However, while this regimen is still as effective as the combination of AZT and Sd-NVP plus the seven-day tail of 3TC, it is associated with a higher risk of resistance to NVP. In circumstances where the infrastructure does not allow for longer antepartum regimens to be implemented, Sd-NVP can be given to prevent MTCT. Sd-NVP is an effective regimen, reducing transmission by over 40.0% (Guay et al., 1999), but it is less effective than the recommended regimen. If Sd-NVP is used, it is better if possible to include AZT and 3TC given intrapartum and for seven days to the woman because this reduces resistance. AZT and 3TC are available in a fixed-dose combination, simplifying administration even in sites with limited infrastructure. If the infrastructure does not permit the AZT and 3TC component to be given to the mother, Sd-NVP alone should be administered.

If a woman is given AZT and Sd-NVP but receives less than four weeks of AZT during pregnancy, the AZT prophylactic regimen for the infant should be increased from one to four weeks. This is based on a trial in Thailand in which women received AZT from the 35 week of the pregnancy and the risk of HIV infection was lower in infants given AZT for six weeks than in infants given it for three days (Lallemant et al., 2000).

The recommended regimen for women living with HIV who are in labour and who have not yet received ARV drugs is:

- *Intrapartum – Sd-NVP + AZT and 3TC; postpartum – AZT and 3TC is to be given to the woman for seven days, plus for the infant, Sd-NVP should be given immediately after delivery and AZT for four weeks.*
- *If delivery is expected imminently, the NVP dose for the mother should be omitted, and the same recommendations and considerations apply as for infants born to women living with HIV who do not receive antenatal or intrapartum ARV prophylaxis.*
- *When delivery occurs within two hours of the woman taking NVP, the infant should receive Sd-NVP immediately after delivery and AZT for four weeks.*

Infants born to women living with HIV, who have not received ARV drugs during pregnancy or labour:

- Sd-NVP immediately after delivery and AZT for four weeks are recommended for infants born to women living with HIV who do not receive any ARV prophylaxis, because this regimen results in a greater reduction in transmission than does administering only Sd-NVP to the infant.
- ARV prophylaxis for infants born to women living with HIV who had not received antenatal or intrapartum ARV prophylaxis; this should begin immediately after delivery or within 12 hours after delivery, if possible.

Women with indications for ART who have *severe anaemia* (Hb <7g/dl) should be started on a non-AZT-containing regimen and receive treatment for anaemia. The alternatives to AZT are d4T or ABC. For pregnant women living with HIV without indications for ART, the priority is to treat the severe anaemia. AZT-containing prophylactic regimens should only be initiated after severe anaemia has been corrected (Hb >7g/dl). Alternatively, the antenatal component of prophylaxis could be avoided and women may receive only ARV prophylaxis, beginning in labour. This will not, however, be as efficacious for preventing MTCT.

Infant Feeding

Breast-feeding provides the infant with all the required nutrients and immunological factors that help to protect it against common infections. This protection is reduced when the child is given water or any other substance during exclusive breast-feeding. Mixed feeding, i.e., breast milk and formula feeds combined, is the most hazardous form of infant feeding. Exclusive replacement feeding is the ideal option but it may not be affordable and feasible where safe drinking water, fuel or clean utensils are scarce. In such a scenario, HIV - infected women should be counseled during the antenatal period about infant feeding choices and should be advised to make an informed decision. Where exclusive replacement feeding is AFASS - acceptable, feasible, affordable, sustainable and safe, avoidance of all breast-feeding is recommended. The mother who has chosen not to breast-feed must be able to prepare feeds hygienically and should be advised to use cup feeding and not bottle-feeding. In case replacement feeding is not possible, exclusive breast-feeding for the first six months of life with early cessation is recommended. The risks of HIV transmission, especially if combined with ART, may be less than 0.5%, if exclusive breast-feeding is done. If family support is not present, exclusive breast-feeding may be difficult and the parent/s may need consistent psychosocial support. When the child reaches the age of six months or earlier, breast-feeding should be stopped within two weeks while ensuring the comfort level of both the mother and the infant. At the same time, good quality complimentary foods should be introduced, ensuring adequate amounts of energy proteins and micronutrients.

HIV-exposed children should be *immunized* according to the routine national immunization schedule with the following notes:

- BCG should not be given in symptomatic HIV-infected children.
- HiB vaccine should be given to all who are confirmed HIV-infected on the basis of 2 positive DNA PCR tests done at 6 weeks of age.
- Additional vaccines such as Pneumcoccal, Varicella, Hepatitis A, Influenza Virus etc. may be given as necessary.
- Vitamin A supplementation should be as per the UIP schedule.

Cotrimoxazole prophylaxis protects the infant from PCP, toxoplasmosis and other bacterial diseases. It is the standard component of HIV care to reduce the morbidity and mortality of children less than five years of age. All HIV-exposed infants should get CTX prophylaxis from age of 4–6 weeks. The recommended dose is 5 mg/kg/day as a single daily dose.

Conception in HIV Infected People

Seroconcordant couples should be counseled to use condoms to prevent reinfection with another strain of the virus. When planning a pregnancy, they should be advised to attempt conception at fertile times of the menstrual cycle to limit exposure.

Serodiscordant couples in which a sexually active woman living with HIV/AIDS has an HIV-negative male partner must engage in protected sex using a condom to ensure that the male partner remains uninfected. For those desiring children, various options should be discussed, including the possibility of adoption. Guidelines from the Office of the United Nations High Commissioner on Human Rights and UNAIDS state that 'The HIV status of a parent or child should not be treated any differently from any other analogous medical condition in making decisions regarding custody, fostering or adoption' (UNAIDS Guidelines for HIV/AIDS and Human Rights, 1998). Artificial reproduction techniques can significantly influence the prevention of HIV transmission among discordant couples.

Preventing male-to-female transmission is more complex since there is no risk-free method to ensure safe conception. Ways to help reduce risk of transmission include:

- Lowering the seminal plasma viral load to undetectable levels with antiretroviral therapy;
- Timing conception at the fertile time of the menstrual cycle to limit exposure;
- Using postexposure prophylaxis for the woman. (Lyerly and Anderson, 2001).

Experience with these techniques in resource-constrained settings is inadequate for making recommendations.

Abortion

Both surgical and medical (using pharmaceuticals) methods of abortion are safe and, if they are provided according to international standards, complications are very rare (WHO Guidelines for Safe Abortion, 2003). Nevertheless, since women living with HIV/AIDS are more likely to have anaemia, making them less able to resist infections or to survive haemorrhage, particular care must be exercised to eliminate any potential complications with surgical abortion. For this reason, in pregnancies up to 12 weeks of gestation, vacuum aspiration should be used in preference to dilatation and curettage since it is safer and less painful and does not require general anaesthesia (WHO Guidelines for Safe Abortion, 2003). From 12 completed weeks of pregnancy, dilatation and evacuation is the safest and most effective surgical technique if skilled and experienced providers are available (WHO Guidelines for Safe Abortion, 2003). Antibiotics at the time of surgical abortion reduce the post-procedural risk of infection, and they should be provided.

Medical Termination - Up to nine weeks of pregnancy, a combination of mifepristone administered orally and misoprostol administered vaginally (medical method of abortion) is safe and effective. After 12 weeks of pregnancy, a combination of oral mifepristone followed by repeated doses of misoprostol or gemeprost is considered safe and highly effective (WHO Guidelines for Safe Abortion, 2003). However, no data currently exist on the effectiveness, acceptability and possible side effects and complications of medical abortion among women living with HIV/AIDS versus HIV-negative women nor on the interactions between drugs for medical abortion and antiretroviral medication.

Conclusion

- Comprehensive AIDS education and prevention programmes can help women and girls protect themselves from HIV.
- HIV testing and counseling should be made available to women attending all reproductive health services.
- Scaling up HIV testing needs to be accompanied by access to integrated treatment, care and prevention services as well as improved protection from stigma and discrimination.
- Providing antiretroviral therapy and HIV-related care for women living with HIV/AIDS is essential for reducing maternal mortality, effectively preventing HIV infection among infants and improving the survival of children born to women living with HIV/AIDS.
- All efforts should be made to ensure that all women who require antiretroviral therapy have access to it.

HIV/AIDS programmes that invest in the specific needs of women and girls and promote gender equality can not only reduce their vulnerabilities to HIV, but also contribute to their overall well being. Hence, investing in women and girls will contribute to the MDG goal of combating HIV/AIDS, TB and Malaria, as well as the MDG goal of promoting gender equality and women's empowerment.

REFERENCE

ACOG. Management of Herpes in Pregnancy. *ACOG Practice Bulletin 8*, October 1999.

Antiretroviral Pregnancy Registry Steering Committee. *Antiretroviral Pregnancy Registry international interim report for 1 January 1989 – 31 July 2005*. Wilmington, NC, USA, Registry Coordinating Center, 2005 (http://www.APRegistry.com).

Burns, D.N., Landesman, S., Minkoff, H. et al., (1998). The Influence of Pregnancy on Human Immunodeficiency Virus Type-1 Infection: Antepartum and Postpartum Changes in Human Immunodeficiency Virus Type-1 Viral Load. *Am J Obstet Gynecol*, 178, 355–359.

Bulterys, M., et al., (2004). Rapid HIV-1 Testing During Labor: A Multicenter Study. *JAMA,* 292, 219–223.

Bucceri, A.M. et al., (2003). Discontinuing Combination Antiretroviral Therapy During the First Trimester of Pregnancy: Insights From Plasma Human Immunodefi Ciency Virus-1 RNA Viral Load and CD4 Cell Count. *American Journal of Obstetric Gynecology,* 189(2), 545–551.

Cooper, E.R. et al., (2002). Combination Antiretroviral Strategies for the Treatment of Pregnant HIV-1-Infected Women and Prevention of Perinatal HIV-1 Transmission. *Journal of Acquired Immune Deficiency Syndromes*, 29(5), 484–494.

Chersich, M.F. et al., (2002). Initiating Early Postpartum Voluntary Counselling and Testing in a Resource-Constrained Setting. 14th International Conference on AIDS, 7–12 July 2002, Barcelona, Spain (abstract TuPeF5398; http://www.aegis.com/ conferences/iac/2002/TuPeF5398.html).

De Cock, K.M. et al., (2000). Prevention of Mother-to-Child HIV Transmission in Resource-Poor Countries: Translating Research into Policy and Practice. *Journal of the American Medical Association,* 283(9), 1175–1182.

European Collaborative Study and the Swiss HIV Pregnancy Cohort. Immunological Markers in HIV-Infected Pregnant Women. (1997). *AIDS*, 11, 1859–1865.

French, R., and Brocklehurst, P. (1998). The Effect of Pregnancy on Survival in Women Infected with HIV: A Systematic Review of the Literature and Meta-Analysis. *Br. J. Obstet Gynaecol,* 105, 827–835.

Gaillard, P. et al., (2004) Use of Antiretroviral Drugs to Prevent HIV-1 Transmission Through Breast-Feeding: From Animal Studies to Randomized Clinical Trials. *Journal of Acquired Immune Defi ciency Syndromes*, 35(2), 178–187.

Guay, L.A. et al., (1999). Intrapartum and Neonatal Single-Dose Nevirapine Compared With Zidovudine for Prevention of Mother-to-Child Transmission of HIV-1 In Kampala, Uganda: HIVNET 012 Randomised Trial. *Lancet*, 354 (9181), 795–802.

HIV-infected Women and Their Families: Psychosocial Support and Related Issues. A Literature Review. Geneva, World Health Organization, 2003 (http://www.who. int/reproductive-health/publications/rhr_03_07/index.html).

HIV/AIDS and Human Rights, International Guidelines. Second International Consultation On HIV/AIDS and Human Rights, Geneva, 23–25 September 1996. Geneva, Office of the United Nations High Commissioner on Human Rights and UNAIDS, 1998 (http://www.ohchr. org/english/issues/hiv/guidelines.htm).

Integrating HIV Voluntary Counseling and Testing Services Into Reproductive Health Settings. Stepwise Guidelines for Programme Planners, Managers and Service Providers. New York, United Nations Population Fund and International Planned Parenthood Federation, 2004 (Http://Www.Unfpa.Org/Publications/ Detail.Cfm.).

Kapiga, S.H., Lyamuya, E.F., Lwihula, G.K., and Hunter, D.J. (1998). The Incidence of HIV Infection Among Women Using Family Planning Methods in Dar es Salaam, Tanzania. *AIDS*, 12,75–84.

Koren, G., Pastuszak, A., and Ito, S. (1998). Drugs in Pregnancy. *New England Journal of Medicine*, 338(16), 1128–1137.

Lallemant, M. et al., (2000). A Trial of Shortened Zidovudine Regimens to Prevent Mother-to-Child Transmission of Human Immunodefi Ciency Virus Type-1. *New England Journal of Medicine,* 343(14), 982–991.

Lambert, J.S., Watts, D.H., Mofenson, L.M. et al., (2000). Risk Factors for Preterm Birth, Low Birth Weight, And Intrauterine Growth Retardation In Infants Born To HIV-Infected Pregnant Women Receiving Zidovudine. *AIDS*,14,1389–1399.

Lyerly, A.D., and Anderson, J. (2001). Human Immunodeficiency Virus and Assisted Reproduction: Reconsidering Evidence, Reframing Ethics. Fertility and Sterility, 75, 843–858.

McIntyre, J.A. (2006). Controversies in The Use of Nevirapine For Prevention of Mother-To-Childtransmission of HIV. *Expert Opinion on Pharmacotherapy*, 7(6), 677–685.

Mirochnick, M. et al., (2003). Predose Infant Nevirapine Concentration With The Two-Dose Intrapartum Neonatal

Nevirapine Regimen: Association With Timing of Maternal Intrapartum Nevirapine Dose. *Journal of Acquired Immune Defi ciency Syndromes* , 33, 153–156.

Morrison, C.S., Sekaddo-Kigondu, C., Sinei, S.K., Weiner, D.H., Kwok, C., and Kokonya, D. (2001). Is The Intrauterine Device Appropriate Contraception for HIV-1-Infected Women? *BJOG*, 108, 784–790.

Minkoff, H., Hershow, R., Watts, D.H. et al., (2003). The Relationship of Pregnancy to Human Immunodeficiency Virus Disease Progression. *Am J Obstet Gynecol*, 189, 552–559.

Read, J. et al., (2005). *A Prospective Cohort Study of HIV-1-Infected Pregnant Women and Their Infants in Latin America and the Caribbean: The NICHD International Site Development Initiative Perinatal Study*. 12th Conference on Retroviruses and Opportunistic Infections. Boston, MA, USA. 22–25 February 2005 (Abstract 790).

Richardson, B.A. (2002). Nonoxynol-9 as a Vaginal Microbicide For Prevention Of Sexually Transmitted Infections: It's Time To Move on. *JAMA*, 287, 1171–1172.

Safe Abortion: Technical and Policy Guidance For Health Systems. Geneva, World Health Organization, 2003 (http://www.who.int/reproductivehealth/publications/safe_abortion/safe_ abortion.html).

Shapiro, R. et al., (2006). Maternal Single-Dose Nevirapine Vs. Placebo as Part of an Antiretroviral Strategy to Prevent Mother-to-Child HIV Transmission In Botswana. *AIDS*, 20 (9), 281-8.

Stanton, C.K., and Holtz, S.A. (2006). Levels and Trends in Cesarean Birth in the Developing World. *Studies in Family Planning*, 37(1), 41–48.

Stafford, M.K., Ward, H., Flanagan, A. et al., (1998). Safety Study of Nonoxynol-9 as a Vaginal Microbicide: Evidence Of Adverse Effects. *J Acquir Immune Defic Syndr Hum Retrovirol*, 17, 327–331.

15

Empowering Women through Advances in HIV Prevention: The Role of Microbicides

Dr. Seema Sahay

Summary

In the era of the AIDS epidemic, the stark reality of woman's vulnerability is even more pronounced. Women's biological risk of HIV acquisition twice that of men, combined with their existing socio-cultural lacunae underscores the need to empower them. This chapter sheds light on the factors leading to woman's vulnerability, quest for woman-initiated option called microbicides and the challenges that research faces in the development of such a product. The product development does not remain a manufacturing process in the laboratories and industries; rather, it encompasses the individual woman, her sexual partner and the community. Coupled with the preclinical testing and human clinical trials of microbicide research, acceptability research needs to be conducted to inform the researchers and the pharmaceutical companies that would eventually develop the product. An integrated multidisciplinary approach together with civil society and community advocates is recommended for conducting microbicide trials in India. Education, delay in age at marriage, reducing age mixing and supporting women with technology can empower them to protect themselves.

Woman in the Era of AIDS

Biologically, women are twice more likely to become infected with HIV through unprotected heterosexual intercourse than men (Downs et al., 1996; Auvert et al., 2001). Women are at greater risk because of the greater area of their mucous membrane exposed during sex; the greater quantity of fluids transferred from men to women; the higher viral content in male sexual fluids; and the micro-abrasions that can occur in vaginal (or rectal) tissue from sexual penetration. Some studies have suggested that 85.0% of women in India were infected through heterosexual sex, and around 90.0% said that they had had only one sexual partner, usually their spouse (Gangakhedkar et al., 1997; Solomon et al., 2005). The socio-cultural milieu highlights important gender issues. Women's vulnerability to HIV infection in India has been attributed to their low socioeconomic status. Women are also less likely to be able to negotiate condom use and are more likely to be subjected to non-consensual sex. Together, these issues increase a woman's risk of being infected with HIV through heterosexual transmission. At the end of 2007, the Joint United Nations Programme on HIV/AIDS (UNAIDS, 2007) estimated that out of the 30.8 million adults worldwide living with HIV, around half were women. Ninety eight percent of these women live in developing countries.

Vulnerability

Vulnerabilities associated with women and resulting compromising situations place them at higher risk of contracting HIV. The ensuing discussions will present some of these vulnerabilities, various mechanisms to overcome those vulnerabilities, women and HIV and meeting the challenge of woman's vulnerability by moving the microbicide research forward. These vulnerabilities may be the product of the existing social and economic environment such as traditional norms that lead to gender inequality in foods security, education, and sexual relationships.

Traditional Vulnerability

In all societies, gender norms, which are reinforced by social sanctions, have defined acceptable behaviour for men that put both women and men at risk. In some societies, women have few rights within sexual relationships and the family. Often men make the majority of decisions, such as whom they will marry and whether the man will have more than one sexual partner. The power imbalance between men and women makes it more difficult for women to protect themselves from HIV. For example, a woman may not be able to insist on the use of a condom if her husband is the one who makes the decisions.

Patterns of sexual mixing may also account for differences in HIV/STI infection levels between men and women. Some of the discrepancy could be explained by a small number of highly sexually active HIV-infected men infecting a large number of women in their age group. This pattern could not be confirmed in studies that collected detailed sexual behaviour data (Buve et al., 2001). Age mixing has been shown to contribute to HIV risk among younger women (Helleringer and Kohler, 2007). Therefore, a more likely explanation is the frequent sexual relationships between younger women and older men, increasing the likelihood that a young woman will encounter an already HIV-infected partner, and become infected herself (Laga et al., 2001). In the context of our country also, marriage does not always protect a woman from contracting HIV because it may lead to young women marrying older men. In India, social norms make it desirable for girls to get married at 'right' age. The obvious age difference between the partners is overlooked since males most always hold financial power. In the recent NFHS-III survey (2007), in India, almost half (46.0%) of women aged between 18-29 years were married before the legal minimum age of 18; median age of women for marriage is 17.2 years. Many new infections occur within marriage or long-term relationships outside marriage.

Additionally, women who are victims of sexual violence are at higher risk of being exposed to HIV. The lack of condom use and the forced nature of sex (rape) mean that women are immediately more vulnerable to HIV infection. One study of 1,366 South African women concluded that those women who were beaten or dominated by their partners were much more likely to become infected with HIV than women who were not (Dunkle et al., 2004). Based on the NFHS-III survey in India, Silverman et al., (2008) estimated that among the sub sample of 28,139 married Indian women experiencing both physical and sexual violence from husbands have greater HIV infection prevalence as compared to those not experiencing intimate partner violence (IPV). Thus, given the choice between the immediate threat of violence and the relatively hypothetical subsequent threat of HIV, women often resign themselves to sexual demands and indiscretions that may increase their risk of HIV acquisition (Go et al., 2003).

Education, Status and Role

AIDS is a disease of crises. The first crisis AIDS-affected children are abandoning education. Girls are more likely than boys to leave school to care for ill family members or to support siblings when parents die of AIDS (Global Coalition on women and AIDS, 2004). There are currently an estimated 15 million AIDS orphans around the world, and the number is expected to reach 25 million by 2010. Most of them will be unlikely to have the resources to pay school fees and when extended family members step in to help, once again they often choose to pay for boys (UNICEF/UNAIDS, 2003). According to the Global Campaign for Education, '*research shows that a primary education is the minimum threshold needed to benefit from [health information] programs. Not only is a basic education essential to be able to process and evaluate information, it also gives the most marginalized groups in society—notably young women—the status and confidence needed to act on information and refuse unsafe sex (Global campaign for education, 2004).*' The 2008 UNAIDS report cites a study in rural South Africa which found that each additional year of educational attainment reduced the risk of HIV infection by 7.0% (UNAIDS, 2008). In a study conducted with HIV infected Voluntary Counseling and Testing (VCT) facility attendees in India, adult women with higher level of education have more anxiety when seeking an HIV test (Sahay et al., 2007). This comes as a surprise because education should have helped them to be aware and perhaps at ease. However, higher level of anxiety prior to HIV test is perhaps a surrogate indicator of a woman's status in the society and her anxiety to be socially desirable.

Right to Property, Food Insecurity and Risk

The denial of a woman's inheritance and property rights can increase her vulnerability to HIV. Not being able to own property means that women have limited economic stability. This can lead to an increased risk of sexual exploitation and violence, as women may have to endure abusive relationships or resort to informal sex work for economic survival. The abuses of human rights that women deal with on a daily basis can become nearly insurmountable obstacles when HIV/

AIDS is involved. One of the most serious economic effects of HIV for women has been the loss of property. A study in Uganda of HIV-positive widows revealed that 90.0% of the women interviewed had difficulties with their in-laws over property and 88.0% of those in rural areas were unable to meet their household needs (Global Coalition on Women, 2004). Also in Uganda, another study found that 37.0% of widows compared to 17.0% of widowers had migrated from their original homes because they were generally not entitled to inherit their husband's property (Ntozi, 1997).

Laws are not enough to change these conditions. India, for example, has a law dating back to 1956 that allows some women to inherit property from their fathers. Despite the law, women rarely inherit, are often unaware of their rights or are exploited emotionally by the men in the paternal home. Thus, India, although, a signatory to numerous international agreements on the rights of the women yet it has failed to protect the human rights of women satisfactorily, particularly those of sex workers (Mawar et al., 2005). Some of the Human Rights Accords and Commitments for women directly influence their situation in the context of sexually transmitted diseases. In the International Conference on Population and Development (ICPD, 1994), Article C, Chapter 7 addresses sexually transmitted diseases and the prevention of HIV from the perspective of women's vulnerability to the epidemic, setting out key recommendations for addressing HIV through reproductive health services. The 4th World Conference on Women (Beijing), Declaration and Platform for Action had a strategic Objective C.3, which is to undertake gender-sensitive initiatives that address sexually transmitted diseases, HIV/AIDS and sexual and reproductive health issues. The Millennium Development and Declaration in 2004 cites goal# 3, which calls upon the nations to promote gender equality and empower women and goal# 6 to Combat HIV/AIDS,

Malaria and other diseases. The article 14 of the declaration of UN General Assembly Special Session (UNGASS) on HIV/ AIDS (2002) stresses that gender equality and the empowerment of women is the fundamental element in the reduction of the vulnerability of women and girls to HIV/ AIDS.

Sexually Transmitted Disease (STD) and HIV

Genital ulcer diseases like chancroid, genital herpes and syphilis are known risk factors for HIV acquisition (Gadkari et al., 1988; Holmberg et al., 1988; Plummer et al., 1991; Castro et al., 1988; Reynolds et al., 2003). The discharge syndromes like gonorrhea; chlamydial infections and trichomonas interact with HIV infection in a unidirectional manner by promoting HIV transmission without a synergistic increase in their own incidence or prevalence. Way back in 1992, Wasserheit recommended diagnosis and treatment of both symptomatic and asymptomatic discharge STD syndromes. Human Papilloma Virus (HPV) infection is the third category of STD-HIV interaction with HPV appearing as traditional opportunistic infection, the expression and progression of which is augmented by HIV infection. Herpes Simplex Virus-2 (HSV-2) is the fourth category of STD-HIV interaction. There has been indirect evidence that HSV-2 infection increases infectiousness of HIV in co-infected individuals is provided by studies of genital HIV shedding (Reynolds et al., 2003; Celum, 2004). In a meta-analysis of the effect of HSV-2 infection on HIV acquisition, prevalent HSV-2 infection was associated with a three-fold greater risk of heterosexually acquired HIV infection in the general population (Freeman et al., 2006).

Global HIV Scenario

In the 1990s, the WHO had predicted that by 2010, 90.0% of HIV infections would result from heterosexual contact, and more women than men would be infected (Merson, 1992). Today, an estimated 33.2 million (30.6 – 36.1 million) individuals are living with HIV globally. Of these 30.8 million are adults, 15.4 million are women and 2.5 million are children under 15 years of age (UNAIDS, 2008). Around half of these infected adults worldwide are women, 98.0% of whom live in developing countries (UNAIDS/ UNFPA/ UNIFEM, 2004). The estimated number of adults living with HIV/AIDS in India is 2.47 million (equivalent to 0.36% of the adult population) (NACO, 2007). Most countries in the Asian region are in the so-called 'concentrated' epidemic phase, where greater than 5.0% of high-risk subgroups (e.g. commercial sex workers, men having sex with men, injecting drug users, etc.) are HIV-sero-positive, yet HIV-sero-prevalence is less than 1.0% in the general population. This epidemiological status is particularly important from an intervention point of view given the high population density and the high prevalence of background risk behaviours in Asia. It is important to study the efficacy of interventions where they are to be applied, to understand impact of the unique regional, social, behavioural, economic and cultural determinants of the epidemic.

Trend of HIV among Women in India

In India, the National AIDS Control Organization (NACO) carries out the country's National AIDS Programme, which includes formulation of policy and implementation of prevention and control programmes. It was established in 1993 and is now running the third phase of the National AIDS Control Project (NACP-III). According to the National AIDS Control Organisation, women account for 39.3% of estimated adult infections (NACO, 2007). The presence of a large sex industry and a high HIV prevalence among female sex workers (FSWs) in India has led to the introduction of targeted interventions focused on creating awareness in this community and social marketing of condoms by governmental agencies like the NACO and state public health departments as well as various non-governmental organizations. The prevalence of HIV infections among high-risk populations of FSWs and STD clinic attendees reported in our studies range between 47.0% and 49.0%, with an incidence of 10.2% per year; much higher in women than in men (Mehendale et al., 1996). Very low prevalence of HIV was reported among low-risk pregnant women in remote rural areas of Maharashtra (Arole et al., 2005). Brahme et al., (2006) assessed the impact of awareness regarding safe sex in a cohort of FSWs by studying trends in HIV prevalence, sexually transmitted diseases (STDs), and risk behaviors. This study, conducted from 1993 to 2002 in Pune, India suggests that safe sex interventions have had a positive impact on FSWs in Pune, India. Another study has demonstrated a decline in HIV prevalence rates among young men and women in southern India (Kumar et al., 2006), suggesting for the first time that community-based HIV prevention efforts may be decreasing the risk of HIV infection in some regions of India. The lower HIV transmission rate among discordant couples in a study conducted by Mehendale et al., (2006) may also reflect the positive impact of intensive risk reduction counseling, receiving repetitive counseling and information technically termed as cohort effect as well as effective STI diagnosis and treatment and typical risk only due to the spouse (Rao et al., 2004; Mehta et al., 2006).

HIV Prevention in Context of Woman's Vulnerability

Since the early 1980s, evidence of the effectiveness of male condom approach in preventing HIV has accumulated (Conant et al., 1986; van de Perre et al., 1987, Carey et al., 1992; Weller et al., 2002; Holmes et al., 2004). Current prevention interventions have been associated with a decline in HIV prevalence in some settings, at least in the short term.

Examples include programs to delay the age of onset of sexual activity, decrease the number of sexual partners, and increasing the frequency of condom use properly, all of which are effectively captured in the 'ABC' (Abstinence, Behaviour change, and Correct and Consistent use of Condoms) strategy for HIV prevention. However, the effectiveness of male condoms can be as high as 95.0% when used 'consistently' (Pinkerton et al., 1997). Moreover, the use of male condom is user dependent; several other methods have been developed to protect women like the female condom, cervical caps, diaphragm and microbicides. Another promising HIV prevention option is the male circumcision. Results of three separate randomised trials showed the uniform and unequivocal protective effect of male circumcision in reduction of HIV acquisition (Auvert et al., 2005; Bailey et al., 2007; Gray et al., 2007; UNAIDS, 2007). Various other behavioural interventions have also been reported to be effective but, in general, they have not been shown to have a sustainable impact beyond 6-12 months.

Proving the efficacy of HIV prevention interventions thus requires novel ideas and concepts, and their evaluation in clinical trials (Hallet et al., 2007). As discussed extensively already, women are more vulnerable to HIV than men in many developing country settings, and gender and its implicit power issues are some of the main reasons for their increased vulnerability. Condom use among married couples is universally perceived as next to impossible, because married partners do not want to admit having other partners. Increasingly, women as young as 30 or even 25 are seeking sterilization or relying on non-barrier methods of contraception in order to avoid pregnancy and women are sexually active after they have completed child-bearing.

Feminization of the HIV epidemic globally (UNAIDS, 2004) has emphasized the need for female-controlled methods for HIV/STI prevention (Stein, 1990). While feminists have long observed diminished autonomy for women in many cultures and contexts, as well as difference in gender norms with regard to how women experience and value autonomy (Nedelsky, 1989), HIV prevention research lays open a plethora of additional questions about woman's vulnerability and autonomy. Socio-cultural, economic, and gender differentials contribute to the high incidence of HIV infection among women by restricting their ability to negotiate the use of male condoms (Heise and Elias, 1995; de cruz-Grote; 1996; Abdool, 2001). The Indian epidemic is predominantly heterosexual; considering women's status, their needs for protection may be culturally different (Morrow et al., 2003; Severy et al., 2005). The condom use practices in men attending STD clinics demonstrated that the condoms were being used preferentially with sex workers, but majority of these men (>70.0%) continued to have sex with their spouses without condoms even in the presence of active STDs (Bentley et al., 1998). Married women do not have adequate understanding or perception of risk of STD/HIV from their spouses (Mawar et al., 1997). In a study among women attending STD clinics in Pune from 1993 to 1996, prevalence of HIV infection was observed to be 49.9% in FSWs and 13.6% in those who were not sex workers with majority reporting single sexual partner. This was the first evidence of a high HIV prevalence in married monogamous women in India with a strong suggestion of risk from their husbands (Gangakhedkar et al., 1997). Subsequently, several other studies confirmed the risk of HIV acquisition among monogamous women (Newmann et al., 2000; Panda et al., 2000; NACO, 2007). Unlike commercial sex workers and patients attending sexually transmitted infection (STI) clinics, married couples are not typically targeted for HIV risk reduction programs in India. Thus, married partners of HIV-infected individuals are at particularly high risk for HIV infection. Recently in a trend analysis of STD clinic attendees followed for 10 years, Mehendale et al., (2007) reported the first direct evidence for a decline in HIV incidence rates in FSWs and male patients with STIs over time. They also reported a lack of change in HIV infection risk among non-sex worker women, which highlights the need for additional targeted HIV prevention interventions. The stark urgency of providing women with the means of protecting themselves in the face of limited autonomy is evident. She has to depend on 'men for the use of male condoms which is the only reliable option available for preventing HIV/ STIs. As Godbole and Mehendale (2005) have cautioned, there is no justification for complacency and the focus of HIV prevention in India should be on evidence-based interventions among vulnerable communities. There appears to be a need for an integrated and all-inclusive approach as opposed to a compartmental, prevention-centered approach.

There is a profound need for new and effective prevention methods that women can use with or without cooperation from their male partners, and even perhaps without their knowledge. The Programme of Action for the International Conference on Population and Development (1994), now known as the *Cairo Agenda*, includes as one of its objectives the prevention of 'sexually transmitted diseases, including HIV/AIDS . . . with special attention to girls and women.' The following year at the 4th World Conference, the Beijing Platform for Action adopted on Women highlighted that women and, particularly, adolescent girls and young women often do not have the power to insist on safe and responsible sex practices and have little access to information and services for the prevention and called on Governments to:

> *"Support and expedite action-oriented research on affordable methods, controlled by women, to prevent HIV and other sexually transmitted diseases, on*

> *strategies empowering women to protect themselves, from sexually transmitted diseases."*
>
> *and*
>
> *"Provide financial and institutional support for research on ... methods to protect against HIV/ AIDS and the other sexually transmitted diseases ..."*

Between 70.0 and 90.0% of all HIV infections in women are acquired during heterosexual intercourse. Prevention efforts have not resolved the gender issues related to HIV/ AIDS. Even in the three countries in the developing world where prevention efforts are succeeding to some extent, namely Thailand, Senegal and Uganda, men are still experiencing lower infection rates than women. Similarly, in developed countries, it is men in the gay community who have succeeded better than men and women in heterosexual relationships in reducing sexual transmission of HIV. As stated in the WHO/UNAIDS Information Pack, 1997:

> *"The public health rationale for introducing a method that provides protection against pregnancy and STI/HIV is clear. Globally, health and human rights advocates have been demanding that scientists develop fertility regulation methods that are safe and reversible, under the control of the user, not systemic in action, which protect the user against STIs and HIV, and do not need to be provided by a health service. The female condom comes closer to these requirements than any other family planning methods."*
>
> *"Twenty-third special session of the UN General Assembly entitled "Women 2000: gender equality, development and peace for the twenty-first century", called for the "development of safe, affordable,*

effective and easily accessible female-controlled methods including methods such as microbicides and female condoms . . ." as a matter of priority.

In the face of these staggering statistics and recommendations, research has begun to focus on women-initiated options. The female condom, a barrier method that can be used by women came into advent. The effects of the female condom on semen exposure and sexually transmitted infection rates have been assessed in several clinical trials; however, the ability of the female condom to prevent HIV infection has not been directly assessed (Fontanet et al., 1998; Feldblum et al., 2001; French et al., 2003; Galvao et al., 2005). Safety and acceptability of Reality and Reddy female condoms have been assessed in India also (Table-1).

The cervical caps and diaphragms, although developed initially as contraceptive devices, might be protective against HIV acquisition (Howell et al., 1997; Zhang et al., 1999; Pudney et al., 2005). Up till now, effect of a cervical barrier in prevention of HIV transmission has been examined in only one trial, the MIRA (Methods for Improving Reproductive Health in Africa) trial where the researchers found no additional protective effect of latex diaphragm, lubricant gel, and condoms compared with condoms alone (Padian et al., 2007).

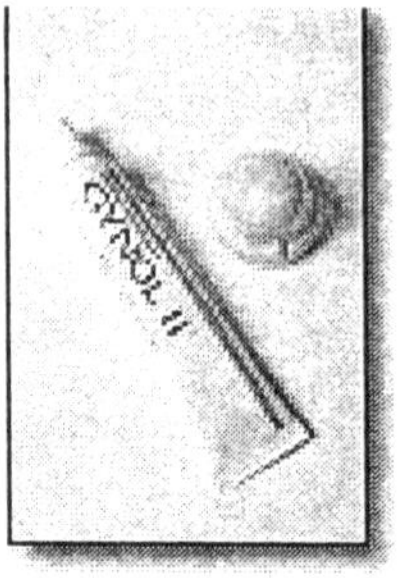

a: Cervical cap-thumb

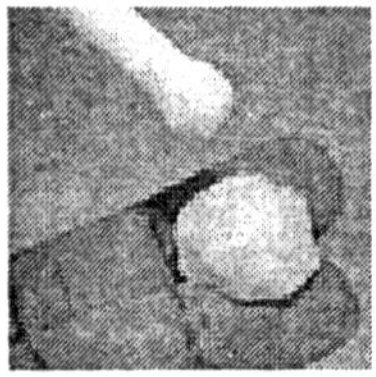

b. Microbicide in gel form with applicator

c. Diaphragm

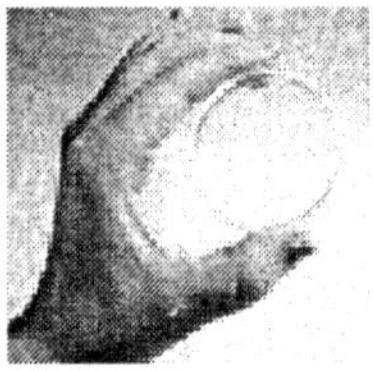

d Ring

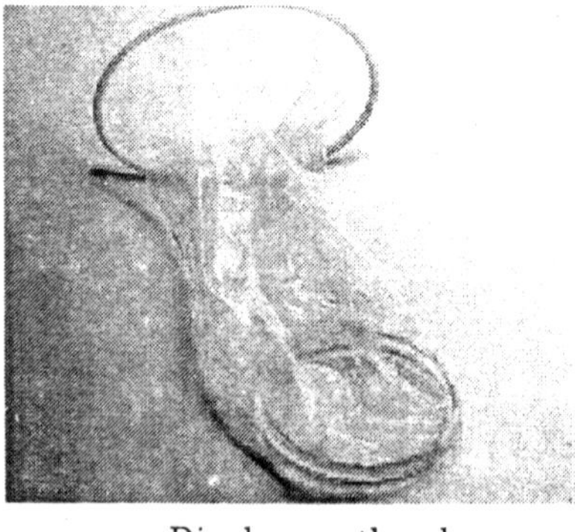

e. Diaphragm-thumb

Figure 1(a-e): *Several types of women initiated options under research*

Microbicides

Microbicides are the group of prevention products being developed to prevent the sexual transmission of HIV when applied topically on the inside of the vagina or rectum. Topical microbicides are products for vaginal administration that women can use themselves independent of their male partners (Elias, 1996). Functionally, a microbicide is any substance that can substantially reduce the transmission of STIs when applied in the vagina or rectum. The ideal topical microbicide would be safe, effective, and acceptable to many potential users, perhaps spermicidal and inexpensive. Microbicides potentially can be produced in many forms like gel, cream, film, suppository, or sponge (Fig1. a-b). By using a product that can be applied overtly or covertly (i.e., with or without a partner's knowledge, awareness, or consent), individuals can control their own protection against HIV and perhaps other STDs. However, at present, no antimicrobial products have been proven to protect against vaginal or rectal HIV acquisition (Padian et al., 2008). Today the research for microbicide has become three-pronged viz. 1) Testing compounds like anti-retrovirals to inhibit HIV replication 2) Product formulation of long acting dispersal methods and delivery mechanisms that are not coitally dependent e.g. vaginal ring for sustained release of microbicide for prolonged action (Fig. e) as product delivery system 3) Combination of products with varying mechanisms of action.

Vaginal Microbicide Trials Conducted in India

In January 2007, two Phase III clinical trials of a candidate microbicide, Usher cell, a gel containing cellulose sulfate (CS), among women at high risk of HIV in India, South Africa, Benin, Uganda, and Nigeria were halted (Horwood, 2007). Safety of this product was already established (Doncel, 2007) but the trial was stopped based on preliminary analysis by the Independent Data Monitoring

Committee that indicated that the product was associated with an increased risk of acquiring HIV (Krishnan, 2007; Van Damne et al., 2008). Up until now, several products that meet these criteria have been tested in phase III trials but were ineffective or even harmful (Feldlum et al., 2008; Van Damme et al., 2002; Van Damme et al., 2007; Pop council, 2008; Halpern et al., 2007; Kreiss et al., 2002; Peterson et al., 2007). The Alliance for Microbicide Development maintains a detailed database of ongoing clinical trials of microbicides globally that can be accessed at *www.microbicide.org*. Still, the quest for the ideal microbicide search should not stop here. Recently, at Microbicide 2008 conference, held at New Delhi, Honorable Health Minister of India, Sri Anbumani Ramadoss announced ... "*women need a product that they can control and even use without their partners' consent or knowledge." Effective microbicides would offer an alternative method of protection for women* (Kaiser Daily HIV/ AIDS Report, 2008).

Figure 2: National AIDS Research Institute, Pune, India affiliated with Indian Council of Medical Research, Department of Health Research, Government of India.

Table 1
An Overview of Majority of the Vaginal Microbicide Trials and Studies on Female Condoms Conducted in India

Trial product		*Trial phase*	*Participants*	*Study aim*	*Reference*
Nonoxynol-9 Vaginal Pessary [Today ™]	Detergent, kills the sexually transmitted pathogens including HIV in the in vitro studies	Phase-I	Low-risk women	Safety & acceptability	*Joshi et al, 2003*
Buffer Gel: Topical Microbicide	Strengthening the normal physiological acidity in the vagina, since HIV and most STI organisms are sensitive to acidic pH	Phase-1	Low-risk women	Safety & acceptability	*Van de Wilgert et al., 2001* *Bentley et al., 2004*
0.5% PRO 2000:	Inhibits initial	Phase-1	HIV uninfected	Safety &	*Joshi et al., 2006*

(Contd...)

Trial product		*Trial phase*	*Participants*	*Study aim*	*Reference*
Vaginal Gel	binding of the virus to the susceptible cells		women	acceptability	*Joglekar et al., 2007*
Praneem: Poly Herbal Vaginal Tablet	Mechanism of action uncharacterized	Phase-1	HIV uninfected women	Safety & acceptability	*Joshi et al, 2005* *Joglekar et al., 2006*
Praneem: Poly Herbal Vaginal Tablet	Mechanism of action uncharacterized	Phase-1	HIV uninfected female sex workers	Safety & acceptability	*NARI website*
Praneem: Poly Herbal Vaginal Tablet	Mechanism of action uncharacterized	Phase-II	HIV uninfected women	Expanded safety study	*Joshi et al, 2008*
Cellulose Sulphate	Entry inhibitor	Phase-III	High risk women	HIV incidence	*Van Damme et al, 2008*
1% Tenofovir Gel	Anti retro viral	Phase-II	HIV uninfected women	Safety, acceptability & adherence	*NARI website: Epidemiology Division*
Female Condom Reddy Reality*	Mechanical barriers	Comparative study	Low risk couples	Acceptability	*Joshi et al, 2005*
Reddy Condom	Mechanical barriers	Comparative study	Low risk HIV uninfected couples	Two shaft length acceptability	*NARI website: Epidemiology Division*

In India, majority of the vaginal microbicide trials and female controlled options have been taken up by National AIDS Research Institute (NARI), Pune (Fig. 2), an institute that specializes in conducting clinical, basic science, socio-behavioral, epidemiological research under the aegis of Indian Council of Medical Research (ICMR), New Delhi. NARI has been conducting HIV prevention and therapeutic trials in the country. In India, several Phase I and phase II B trials of vaginal microbicides and comparative studies of female condoms have been conducted (Table -1).

Challenges in Conducting Vaginal Microbicide Trials

Development of new products like vaginal microbicide requires conducting clinical trials with women. The contradictions and dilemmas for the clinical trials researchers are many. Vaginal microbicide are the products that are expected to be utilized by women in the absence of relative autonomy that they have with their sexual partners. However, bioethics mandate for clinical trial is 'the autonomous decision making' by the woman participant. But the western concept of autonomy does not translate it across various cultures (Hyun, 2002). Woodsong et al. (2006) provide an expanded model of informed consent (Fig. 3) which indicates that by working at the community, couple and individual levels; researchers may be able to facilitate greater autonomy among women to make independent decision to participate in vaginal microbicide trials.

Effectiveness of Microbicide: A Function of Acceptability and Use

There can be several specifications for the product based on the type of microbicide (spermicidal and/or microbicidal), coital dependant, formulation type-like tablet, gel, duration of action and activity against a range of microbes. The socio-behavioral aspect comes into picture when we start visualizing the use of an efficacious product by the population. The proven

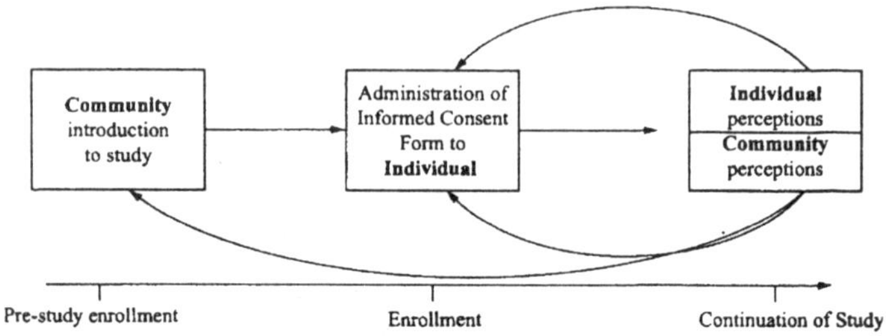

Figure 3: Expanded informed consent process
Adapted from Woodsong et al., 2006

efficacy of a technology does not necessarily guarantee effectiveness. Effectiveness depends on whether the product is used consistently and correctly. Consistent and correct use depends on acceptability and use. This issue becomes clear with the following example of percent efficacy versus correct use. A 30.0% of efficacious vaginal microbicide, if used 60.0% of the times would provide more protection than a method that is 90.0% of efficacious but used only 20.0% of the time (Watts et al., 1998). Therefore, it is also necessary to take several of the following parameters into account: 1) Product disposability, 2) Affordability 3) Smell, 4) Taste), 5) Product viscosity, 6) Shelf life & storage conditions, 7) Stability at room temperature 8) Ease of insertion 9) Packaging 10) Cultural and social context. Hence, studying microbicide acceptability even in the clinical trial stage becomes important because acceptability has its implications for product use by the masses later. According to Morrow and Ruiz (2007), greater emphasis on studying behavioral and social factors associated with microbicide use and non-use in non-clinical and clinical contexts may lead to more effective uptake post licensure.

Concept of acceptability is complex as the term is not only utilization of the product but it is a dynamic interaction of product, product characteristic, environment, sex partner, economic status, living conditions, social and cultural norms. Foremost, a woman who will be the potential user should:

- Know the risk of STIs and HIV/AIDS in her own context
- Understand how to use the product correctly
- Understand level of efficacy and how to balance protection against her risk
- Know about other prevention options

Product development must follow the path of preclinical testing and human trials before reaching the user. A product will have to undergo 1-2 years of phase-I human trial and, if promising, it will undergo phase-II human trials and like wise phase-III trial that may take as long as 2-3 years and 4-5 years respectively. All these phases of human trials include low-risk as well as high-risk women. The next step is manufacturing and distribution, education, access and use. One must remember that at any of these stages of trials, a product may fail. Hence researchers should avoid raising the hope of the community, disseminate results both good and bad and start afresh for the next promising product when it becomes available.

It is important to study acceptability outcome in all categories of women, which includes low risk as well as high-risk women. Many clinical trials do not have provision of conducting acceptability research, yet Microbicide Development Strategy (MDS Working Groups, 2006) does reccommend incorporating behavioral and social research into the microbicide development process. Acceptability research can reveal what formulations or what type of device may be acceptable to users and this can be done at the earliest stages of product development. The aim is to formulate a product that is user friendly at its earliest stage of development. This may save resources that go into developing a product that ultimately may not be acceptable to the population. One example of such resource management is that of a product named COL-1492. Ramjee and Colleagues (1999) conducted acceptability research with participants to address concerns related to the formulation of COL-1492 and implications for dry sex. These data were used to ascertain whether the product was initially acceptable and whether it compromised traditional sexual practices of the cohort being considered for large-scale efficacy trials. Obviously, acceptability research of all new microbicide products is not only recommended but it needs to be studied especially in the context of culture and social norms existent in the country where it might be used.

Acceptability Research: Where are We?

The goal of acceptability research is to determine the factors that would influence the decision and practice to use a certain product. The decision-making factors for the product uses may depend on the individual, couple, family and community (Table-2).

Globally, a number of acceptability studies have been conducted in conjunction with the clinical trials of different products. In the acceptability studies of microbicides like acidiform gel with a diaphragm, Carragard, 6.0% Cellulose Sulphate, Pro 2000 and Buffer gel, acceptability was measured mostly in the women and not their partners (Ramjee et al., 2007; El Sadr et al., 2006; Bentley et al., 2000; Kilmarx et al., 2006). In these studies, a mixed method approach was used to obtain information on acceptability. Women rated the study product on: 'Safety and Ease of use'. Sexual pleasure was among the most important characteristics of acceptable microbicides (Morrow et al., 2003) both in context of wet and dry sex. Participating in research was reported as an empowering experience by the women. Women said that as a result of participating in research, they developed good negotiation skills. Therefore more partner involvement was reported in this case. Wetness was one nuisance factor; however, Bentley (2000) had aptly remarked that this could be over come by potential use of microbicide in HIV prevention. Only one study on applicators has been published where concerns over the ease of insertion, reusability, and the need for softer material were raised (Coetzee et al., 2001). Another acceptability factor was that the product should lubricate the vagina (Carballo-Dieguez et al., 2007, Braunstein and van de Wijgertl, 2005, Joglekar et al., 2007, Orner et al., 2007,). Men felt that acceptability may increase if promoted as genital hygiene product/product for enhancement for sexual pleasure also.

Table 2
The Factors that may Influence an Individual's Decision to Use a Microbicide: The Decision Encompasses Several Area of Product Characteristic

Influencing Factors	*Level*	*Area of influence*	*Possible Solution*
Needs	Individual/ community	Safety	Clinical trials and message clarity about safety
Experience	Individual/ couple	Pleasure	Acceptability by both men & women
		Skills needed for use	Training, ease of instructions
Product	Individual	Design	Aesthetics
	Individual/ family	Packaging	Not noisy, ease of unpacking
Living conditions	Individual/ family	Privacy requirements	Storage, Hygiene, Disposability, Insertion, coitally independent
Cultural context	Family/ Community	Social and community norms	Understanding of woman's status, role and socially desirable expectations

In India, acceptability studies have been performed in conjunction with clinical trials of several candidate microbicides viz. Nonoxynol 9, Buffer Gel, Praneem, 0.5% PRO 2000 and 1.0% Tenofovir gel. Sixty one percent of the participating Indian women showed willingness to use the product in future; while discharge or product remnants were the problems, many reported an increase in sexual pleasure [53.0% - 95.0%] (Joshi et al., 2003, Bentley et al., 2004, Joglekar et al., 2006). A range between preferences for no odor in the microbicide by the abstinent cohort to preference for fragrant product in couple setting has been reported in India setting (Bentley et al., 2004; Joglekar et al, 2006). A mixed method approach utilized in studying the acceptability of 0.5% PRO 2000 in India revealed the decision-making process that may go into product use among Indian women. Covert use was never supported because of male dominated culture.

> *"They said that they (men) should be informed about microbicide use by the women in order to avoid suspicion. Men perceived themselves as primary decision makers in the family".*
>
> *"Participants [women] preferred a fragrant product".*
>
> *"Packaging specification was required as women reported that package made small noises while tearing and therefore it was difficult to be used at night"* (Personal communication with Neelam Joglekar, Behavioral Scientist conducting the study at NARI).

All these findings indicate the use of research conducted outside the structure of clinical trials, where social science research can be used to define the special needs of populations who are not involved in clinical trials but who may represent potential users of topical microbicides. For example, men, despite them not being direct users, have their own views like:

> *"We [Men] would be willing to allow use of the product if we had reason to be worried about HIV/AIDS. We would allow its use on the condition that our female partners managed to use the product independently".*

The acceptability of the microbicide would depend not only on women's choices but also her partner, family and to a certain extent the prevalent social and cultural norm. However, the challenge that will remain is that of 'correct, consistent use and sustained practice'. Hence, acceptability research for each product seems to be imperative. It is also imperative that acceptability be understood in the cultural context, social environment and living conditions of the potential users.

Conclusion

To protect themselves, women need empowerment with education and autonomy. Increasing women's autonomy may be a multi-step process that will require targeting the gender norm; enhancing women's reproductive uptake of health services; and providing women with tools that they can use themselves to make autonomous decisions about their health, including pregnancy and protection from STI and HIV. Governments must make a strong political commitment to developing the vaginal microbicide, a tool that may have profound implications for human rights and health.

Conducting microbicide trials in India would require active acceptability research to satisfy individual needs in the right socio-cultural context, active involvement of civil society organizations to safeguard participants' rights and attention to communication and dissemination of research. A network of epidemiologists, demographers, social and behavioral scientists, community advocates, media, ethicists and civil society will be critical to ensure adequate protection of the participating women, obtain reliable and valid data driven by its applicability to the existing social and cultural environment.

Recommendations

(i) Using Education to Prevent HIV

Schools can be a primary source of information about prevention methods in the fight against HIV. Even though women everywhere continue to be constrained by unequal power relations, evidence from across the world shows that increased education empowers women to secure greater decision-making power in the family and the wider community.

(ii) Age at Marriage Should Be Delayed

In India, most of the women attain sexual debut at marriage, which is at around 17 years of age (NFHS-III). Delay in age at marriage gives young girl opportunities that may get lost once she is married. In Bangladesh and Ethiopia, increasing education has played a vital role in reducing child marriage, in part by ensuring that girls have access to the information and social networks that can protect them (Global Campaign for Education, 2004).

(iii) Avoiding Large Age Mixing

Age difference between man and women has shown to be risk for younger women. In India, due to social and family pressures girls agree to early and 'timely' marriages, because delayed wedding among girls carries social stigma. In several places in the world young girls married to older men have shown to be at higher risk for HIV and STI acquisition. Thus, studies need to be conducted to tailor structural interventions and messages pertaining to large age mixing in the country.

(v) Sexual Education

Sexual education, which must begin before young people start having sex, helps them to postpone unwanted sex and to protect themselves better when they do begin to have sex. Therefore, sex education at school is an important initiative to be taken up in India.

(vi) Women-oriented Information and Education about Vaccines and Microbicides

As women have lower rates of literacy than men, their right to information must be protected by providing them with information about trials. Moreover, information on the use of microbicides and vaccines must be made easily understandable.

(vii) Post-trial Access

Once developed and approved, microbicides and vaccines (as well as male and female condoms) should be easily accessible everywhere. In addition to funding product development, donors must ensure that resources are sufficient to ensure broad accessibility of all products once they have been approved. Governments, too, must work to promote the widespread use of microbicides.

(viii) Multi-pronged HIV Prevention Strategy

None of the uni-dimensional strategies would work in the case of HIV prevention. Hence, both program officials and researchers should work towards a 'combination prevention package' to control HIV among both men and women.

(ix) Advocacy and Community Involvement

Community involvement should be an ongoing, transparent, two-way communication between research teams and community members (Van de Wijgert and Jones,

2006). The researchers should take care, however, not to raise community members' expectations about the imminent availability of a successful product.

Acknowledgements

I would like to thank Ms. Amruta Kashikar, Senior investigator at NARI for providing extensive support in literature search for this write-up. I acknowledge the support that I received from my institute without which this work would not have been complete. I sincerely acknowledge the support of my daughter, Prachi and son, Shishir, whose precious family time was spent on completing this work. I would like to thank Dr. Aparna Shrotri, Retired Professor, Obstetrics and Gynaecology, B.J. Medical College, for scientific review of the manuscript. I would like to thank Mr. Govind Rangrass, Fulbright Fellow at NARI for performing critical review and editing the writeup.

REFERENCES

Abdool, K. (2001). Barriers To Preventing Human Immunodeficiency Virus In Women: Experiences From Kwazulu-Natal, South Africa. *J Am Med Womens Assoc.*, 56, 193–96.

Arole, S., Premkumar, R., Arole, R., Mehendale, S., Risbud, A., and Paranjape, R. (2005). Prevalence of HIV Infection In Pregnant Women in Remote Rural Areas of Maharashtra State, *India. Trop Doct,* 35, 111, 2.

Auvert, B., Ballard, R., Campbell, C. et al., (2001). High Prevalence of HIV Infection Among Youth in a South African Mining Town Is Associated With HSV-2 Seropositivity and Sexual Behaviour. *AIDS,* 15, 885 –898.

Auvert, B., Taljaard, D., Lagarde, E., Sobngwi-Tambekou, J., Sitta, R., and Puren, A. (2005). Randomized, Controlled Intervention Trial Of Male Circumcision For Reduction Of HIV Infection Risk: The ANRS 1265 Trial. *PLoS Med,* 2, e298.

Bailey, R.C., Moses, S., Parker, C.B., et al., (2007) Male Circumcision For HIV Prevention In Young Men In Kisumu, Kenya: A Randomized Controlled Trial. *Lancet,* 369, 643–56.

Bentley, M.F., Spratt, K., Shepherd, M.E., Gangakhedkar, R.R., Thilakavathi, S., Bollinger, R.C. and Mehendale, S.M. (1998). HIV Testing and Counseling among Men Attending STD Clinics in Pune, India: Changes in Condom Use and Sexual Behaviour Over Time. *AIDS,* 12, 1869-77.

Bentley, M. E., Morrow, K., Fullem, A., Chesney, M. A., Horton, S. D., Rosenberg, Z., et al., (2000). Acceptability of a Novel Vaginal Microbicide During a Safety Trial Among Low-Risk Women. *Family Planning Perspectives*, 32(4), 184–188.

Bentley, M.E., Fullem, A.M., Tolley, E.E., Kelly, C.W., Jogelkar, N., Srirak, N., Mwafulirwa, L., Gertrude, R.N., Sakutukwa, K., and Celentano, D. (2004). Acceptability of a Microbicide Among Women and Their Partners in a 4-Country Phase I Trial. *Am Pub Health,* 94 (7), 1159-1164.

Brahme, R., Sahay, S., Joglekar, N., Ghate, M., Joshi, S., Gangakhedkar, R., Risbud, A., Bollinger, R., and Mehendale, S. (2006). Correlates and Trend of HIV Prevalence among Female Sex Workers Attending Sexually Transmitted Disease Clinics in Pune, India (1993:2002). *J. Acquir. Immune Defic. Syndr.,* 41 (1).

Braunstein, S., Van de Wijgert, J. (2005). Preferences and Practices Related to Vaginal Lubrication: Implications For Microbicide Acceptability and Clinical Testing. *Journal of Women's Health,* 14(5), 424–433.

Carballo-Dieguez, A., Balan, I. C., Morrow, K., Rosen, R., Mantell, J.E., Gai, F., and Hoffman, S. (2007). Acceptability of Tenofovir Gel As a Vaginal Microbicide By US Male Participants in a Phase I Clinical Trial (HPTN 050). *AIDS Care,* 19(8),1026-31.

Carey, R.F., Herman, W.A., Retta, S. M., Rinaldi, J.E., Herman, B.A., and Athey, T.W. (1992). Effectiveness of Latex Condoms as a Barrier to Human Immunodeficiency Virus-Sized Particles Under Conditions of Simulated Use. *Sex Transm Dis,* 19: 230–34.

Castro, K.G., Lieb, S., Jaffe, H.W., Narkunas, J.P., Caisher, C.H., Bush, T.J., Witte, J.J., and Belle, Glade (1988). Field Study Group. Transmission of HIV In Belle Glade, Florida: Lessons for The Other Communities in The United States. Science, 239, 193-197.

Celum, C.L. (2004). The Interaction Between Herpes Simplex Virus And Human Immunodeficiency Virus. *Herpes,* 11 (Suppl 1), 36A–45A.

Coetzee, N., Blanchard, K., Ellertson, C., Hoosen, A.A., and Friedland, B. (2001). Acceptability and Feasibility of Micralax Applicators and of Methylcellulose Gel Placebo for Large-Scale Clinical Trials of Vaginal Microbicides. *AIDS,* 15, 1837–1842.

Conant, M., Hardy, D., Sernatinger, J., Spicer, D., and Levy, J.A. (1986). Condoms Prevent Transmission of AIDS-Associated Retrovirus. *JAMA,* 255, 1706.

Correlates of Anxiety and Depression among HIV Test-Seekers at a Voluntary Counseling and Testing Facility in Pune, India. Qual Life Res. 2007 Feb;16(1):41-52.

D'Cruz-Grote, D. (1996). Prevention of HIV Infection In Developing Countries. *Lancet,* 348, 1071–74.

Doncel, G. (2007). Update on Current Microbicide Trials: Update on The CONRAD Cellulose Sulfate Trial, Preclinical Evaluation of Cellulose Sulfate. Presentation at the Fourteenth Conference on Retroviruses and Opportunistic Infections; 2007 Feb 25-28; Los Angeles. Available from: http://www.retroconference.org/2007/data/files/webpage_for_CROI.htm accessed on 21 September, 2008.

Downs, A.M., and de Vincenzi, I. (1996). Probability of Heterosexual Transmission Of HIV: Relationship to The Number of Unprotected Sexual Contacts. *J Acquir Immune Defic Syndr Hum Retrovirol,* 11, 388 -395.

Dunkle, K.L., Jewkes, R.K., Brown, H.C., Gray, G.E., McIntryre, J.A., and Harlow, S.D. (2004).'Gender-Based Violence, Relationship Power, and Risk of HIV Infection in Women Attending Antenatal Clinics in South Africa'. *Lancet,* 363 (9419), 1415-21.

El-Sadr, W. M., Mayer, K. H., Maslankowski, L., Hoesley, C., Justman, J., Gai, F., Mauck, C., Absalon, J., Carballo-Dieguez, A., Morrow, K., Ma^sse., B, Soto-Torres, L. and Kwiecien, A (2006). For the HIV Prevention Trials Network (HPTN) 049 Protocol Team. Safety and Acceptability of Cellulose Sulfate as a Vaginal Microbicide in HIV-infected Women. *AIDS,* 20(8), 1109–1116.

Feldblum, P.J., Kuyoh, M.A., Bwayo, J.J., et al., (2001). Female Condom Introduction And Sexually Transmitted Infection

Prevalence: Results of a Community Intervention Trial in Kenya. *AIDS*, 15, 1037–44.

Feldblum, P., Adeiga, A., Bakare, R., et al., (2008). SAVVY Vaginal Gel (C31G) For Prevention of HIV Infection: A Randomized Controlled Trial in Nigeria PLoS ONE 2008; 3: e1474.

Fontanet, A.L., Saba, J., Chandelying, V., et al., (1998). Protection Against Sexually Transmitted Diseases by Granting Sex Workers in Thailand the Choice of Using the Male or Female Condom: Results From a Randomized Controlled Trial. *AIDS*,12, 1851–59.

Freeman, E.E., Weiss, H.A., Glynn, J.R., Cross, P.L., Whitworth, J.A., and Hayes, R.J. (2006). Herpes Simplex Virus 2 Infection Increases HIV Acquisition in Men and Women: Systematic Review And Meta-Analysis of Longitudinal Studies. *AIDS*, 20, 73–83.

French, P.P., Latka, M., Gollub, E.L., Rogers, C., Hoover, D.R., and Stein, ZA. (2003). Use-EffEctiveness of The Female Versus Male Condom in Preventing Sexually Transmitted Disease in Women. *Sex Transm Dis.*, 30, 433–39.

Gadkari, D.A., Quinn, T.C., Gangakhedkar, R.R., Mehendale, S.M., Divekar, A.D., Risbud, A.R., Chan-Tack, K., Shepherd, M., Gaydos, C. and Bollinger, R.C. (1998). HIV-1 DNA Shedding in Genital Ulcers and its Associated Risk Factors in Pune, India. *J AIDS Hum Retroviruses,* 18, 277-81.

Galvao, L.W., Oliveira, L.C., Diaz, J., et al., (2005). Effectiveness of Female and Male Condoms in Preventing Exposure to Semen During Vaginal Intercourse: A Randomized Trial. *Contraception*, 71,130–36.

Gangakhedkar, R.R., Bentley, M.E., Divekar, A.D., Gadkari, D.A., Mehendale, S.M., Shepherd, M.E., Bollinger, R.C. and Quinn, T.C. (1997). Rapid Spread of HIV Infection Among Married Monogamous Women Attending STD Clinics in India. *JAMA*, 278:2090.

Global Campaign for Education (2004). Learning to Survive: How Education for All Would Save Millions Of Young People From HIV/AIDS. p. 2.Available at http://www.unfpa.org/hiv/women/report/endnotes.htm#c5h1, accessed on 20 September 2008.

Global Coalition on Women and AIDS (2004). 'Media Backgrounder: AIDS and Female Property/Inheritance Rights.' www.unaids.org/en/events/coalition_women_and_aids.asp

Global Coalition on Women and AIDS (2004). 'Media Backgrounder: AIDS and Girls' Education.' www.unaids.org/en/ events/ coalition_women_and_aids.asp.

Go, V.F., Sethulakshmi, C.J., Bentley, M.E., Sivaram, S., Srikrishnan, A.K., Solomon, S., et al., (2003). When HIV-Prevention Messages and Gender Norms Clash: The Impact of Domestic Violence on Women's HIV Risk in Slums of Chennai, India. *AIDS Behav,* 7, 263-72.

Godbole, S., and Mehendale, S.M. (2005). HIV/AIDS Epidemic in India: Risk Factors, Risk Behaviour and Strategies for Prevention and Control. *Indian J Med Res.*, 121, 356-368.

Gray, R.H., Kigozi, G., Serwadda, D., et al., (2007). Male Circumcision For HIV Prevention in Men in Rakai, Uganda: A Randomised Trial. *Lancet,* 369, 657–66.

Guest, G., Johnson, L., Burke, H., Rain-Taljaard, R., Severy, L., von Mollendorf. C., and Van Damme, L.. (2007). Changes In Sexual Behavior During a Safety And Feasibility Trial of a Microbicide/Diaphragm Combination: An Integrated Qualitative and Quantitative Analysis. *AIDS Educ Prev.*,19(4),310-20.

Gupta, A., Mehta, S., Godbole, S., Sahay, S., Walshe, L., Reynolds, R., Ghate, M., Gangakhedkar, R., Risbud, A., and Mehendale S. (2006). Same-Sex Behavior and High Rates of HIV among Men Attending Sexually Transmitted Infection Clinics in Pune, India (1993:2002). *J Acquir Immune Defic Syndr*, 43 (4).

Hallett, T.B. et al., (2007). Appropriate Evaluation Of HIV Prevention Interventions: From Experiment to Full-Scale Implementation. *Sex Transm Infect.*, 83 Suppl 1: i55-60.

Halpern, V., Wang, L.,, Obune, O., Ogunsola, F., Mehta, N., Onyejepu, N., Oduyebo, O., Taylor, D., Otusanya, S., Umo-Otong, J., McNeil, L., Bragg, V., and Cates W. (2007). Effectiveness of Cellulose Sulfate Gel for Prevention Of HIV: Results of The Phase III Trial in Nigeria. 4th *IAS Conference on HIV Pathogenesis, Treatment and Prevention* 2007.

4thIAS Conference on HIV Pathogenesis, Treatment and Prevention; Sydney, Australia; July 22–25, 2007.

Heise, L.L., and Elias, C. (1995). Transforming AIDS Prevention To Meet Women's Needs: A Focus On Developing Countries. *Soc Sci Med.*, 40: 931–43.

Helleringer, S., and Kohler, H. (2007). Sexual Network Structure and The Spread of HIV in Africa: Evidence from Likoma Island, Malawi. *AIDS*, 21,2323–2332.

Holmberg, S.T., Stewart, J.A., Gerber, A.R., Byers, R.H., Lee, F.k., O'Melley, P.M., and Nahmias, A.J. (1988). Prior Herpes Simplex Virus Type 2 Infection as a Risk Factor for HIV Infection. *JAMA*, 259, 1048-1050.

Holmes, K.K., Levine, R., and Weaver, M. (2004). Effectiveness of Condoms in Preventing Sexually Transmitted Infections. *Bull World Health Organ*, 82, 454–61.

Horwood, J. (1999). Cellulose Sulphate Microbicide Trial Halted. *The Lancet Infectious Diseases*, 7(3),183 – 183.

Howell, A.L., Edkins, R.D., Rier, S.E., et al., (1997). Human Immunodeficiency Virus Type 1 Infection of Cells and Tissues from the Upper and Lower Human Female Reproductive Tract. *J Virol*, 71, 3498–506.

Joglekar, N., Joshi, S., Kakde, M., Fang, M., Cianciola, M., Reynolds, S., and Mehendale, S. (2000). The HIV Prevention Trial Network (HPTN) 047 Protocol Team. Acceptability of PRO2000 Vaginal Gel among HIV Un-infected Women in Pune, India. *AIDS Care*, 19: 817-821.

Johnson, A.M., and Laga, M. (1988). Heterosexual Transmission of HIV. *AIDS*. 2 Suppl 1,S49-56.

Joshi, S., Joglekar, N., Ghate, M., Unni, J., Risbud, A., Bentley, M., Shepherd, M., Bollinger, R., Mehendale, S. (2003). Phase I Safety and Preliminary Acceptability of Nonoxynol-9 Vaginal Pessary as a Vaginal Microbicide in Low Risk Women in Pune, India. *Indian J Med Res.*, 117,152-57.

Joshi, S., Joglekar, N., Rochelle, D., Kumar, B., Callahan, M., Solomon, S., and Mehendale, S. (2005). Comparative Acceptability Study of the Reality® Female Condom and The Version 4 of Modified Reddy Female Condom in India. *Contraception*, 72 (5),366 371.

Joshi, S., Dutta, S., Bell, B., Profy, A., Kuruc, J., Gai, F., Cianciola, M., Soto-Torres, L., Panchanadikar, A., Risbud, A., Mehendale, S., and Reynolds, S.J. (2006). Phase I Safety Study Of 0.5% PRO 2000 Vaginal Gel among HIV Un-Infected Women in Pune, India. *AIDS Res Ther.*, 3,4.

Joshi, S., Katti, U., Godbole, S., Bharucha, K., Kumar, K., Kulkarni, S., Risbud, R., and Mehendale, S. (2005). Phase I

Safety Study of Praneem Polyherbal Vaginal Tablet Use among HIV-Uninfected Women in Pune, India. *Transaction of Royal Soc of Tropical Medicine and Hygiene,* 99,769-74.

Joshi, S., Dutta, S., Kumar, B.K., Katti, U., Kulkarni, S., Risbud, A., and Mehendale, S. (2008). Expanded Safety Study of Praneem Polyherbal Vaginal Tablet among HIV Un-Infected Women in Pune, India: A Phase II Clinical Trial Report, *Sex trans Inf available online.*

Kaiser, Daily HIV/AIDS Report (2008). Science and Medicine, Feb 26, 2008. Available on http://www.kaisernetwork.org/Daily_reports/rep_index.cfm?DR_ID=50597, accessed on 21 September 2008.

Kilmarx, P.H., van de Wijgert, J.H., Chaikummao, S., Jones, H.E., Limpakarnjanarat, K., Friedland, B.A., Karon, J.M., Manopaiboon, C., rojana, Nucharee, U., Srivirojana, N., Yanpaisarn, S., Supawitkul, S., Young, N.L., Mock, P.A., U-Blanchard, K., Timothy, D., and Mastro, T.D. (2006). Safety and Acceptability of The Candidate Microbicide Carraguard in Thai Women: Findings From a Phase II Clinical Trial. *J Acquir Immune Defic Syndr,* 43(3),327-34.

Kreiss, J., Ngugi, E., Holmes, K., et al., (1992). Efficacy of Nonoxynol-9 Contraceptive Sponge Use in Preventing Heterosexual Acquisition of HIV in Nairobi Prostitutes. *JAMA,*268, 77–82.

Krishnan, S. (2007). Lessons from the Recently Halted Microbicide Trial in India. *IJME,* 4(3).

Laga, M., Schwartlander, B., Pisani, E., Sow, P.S., and Carael, M. (2001). To Stem HIV in Africa, Prevent Transmission to Young Women. *AIDS,* 15,931-934.

Mawar, N., Mehendale, S., Thilakavathi, S., Shepherd, M., Rodrigues, J., Bollinger, R. and Bentley, M. (1997). Awareness and Knowledge of AIDS and HIV Risk among Women Attending STD Clinics in Pune, India. Ind. *J Med. Res.,* 106,212-22.

Mawar, N., Sahay, S., Pandit, A., and Mahajan, U. (2005). The Third Phase of HIV Pandemic: Social Consequences of HIV: AIDS Stigma and Discrimination and Future Needs. *Indian J Med Res.,* 122, 471-484.

MDS Working Groups.The Microbicide Development Strategy. Silver Spring, MD: Alliance for Microbicide Development (2006).

Mehendale, S.M., Ghate, M., Kumar, K., Sahay, S., Gamble, T., Godbole, S., Thakar, M., Kulkarni, S., Gupta, A., Gangakhedkar, R., Divekar, A., Risbud, A., and Paranjape, R. (2006). Low HIV-1 Incidence among Married Serodiscordant Couples in Pune, India. *J Acquir Immune Defic Syndr.*, 41,1Y3.

Mehendale, S.M., Gupte, N., Paranjape, R.S., Brahme, R., Kohli, R., Joglekar, N., Godbole, S., Joshi, S., Ghate, M., Sahay, S., Kumar, K., Gangakhedkar, R.R., and Risbud A.R. (2007). Declining HIV Incidence among Patients Attending Sexually Transmitted Infection Clinics in Pune, India. *J Acquir Immune Defic Syndr.*,45,564-569.

Mehendale, S.M., Rodrigues, J.J., Brookmeyer, R.S., Gangakhedkar. R.R., Divekar. A.D., Gokhale, M.R., Risbud, A.R., Paranjape, R.S., Shepherd, M.E., Rompalo, A., Sule, R.R., Tolat, S.N., Jadhav, V.D., Quinn, T.C. and Bollinger, R.C. (1995). HIV-1 Incidence and Predictors of Seroconversion in Patients Attending Sexually Transmitted Diseases Clinics in India. *J Inf. Dis.,* 172,1486-1491.

Mehendale, S., Shepherd, M., Divekar, A., Gangakhedkar, R., Kamble, S., Menon, P., Yadav, R., Risbud, A., Paranjape, R., Gadkari, D., Quinn, T., Bollinger, R. and Rodrigues, J. (1996). Evidence for High Prevalence and Rapid Transmission of HIV among Individuals Attending STD Clinics in Pune, India. *Indian Journal of Medical Research.*104,327-35.

Mehta, S., Gupta, A., Sahay, S., Godbole, S., Joshi, S., Celentano, D., Risbud, R., Mehandale, S., and Bollinger, R. (2006). High HIV Prevalence among a High-Risk Subgroup of Women Attending Sexually Transmitted Infection Clinics in Pune, India. *J Acquir Immune Defic Syndr.*, 41(1).

Merson, M. (1992). Epidemiological Trends In The Epidemic [Plenary Address]. VIII Internation Conference on AIDS/ III STD World Congress, 1992.

Morrow, K.M., and Ruiz, M.S. (2008). Assessing Microbicide Acceptability: A Comprehensive and Integrated Approach. *AIDS Behav.*, 12(2), 272-83.

Morrow, K., Rosen, R., Richter, L., Emans, A., Forbes, A., Day, J., et al., (2003). The Acceptability of An Investigational Vaginal Microbicide, PRO 2000 Gel, Among Women in a Phase I Clinical Trial. *Journal of Women's Health*, 12(7), 655–666.

NARI Website. A Phase-II Study to Assess Safety, Acceptability and Adherence of a Candidate Microbicide 1% Tenofovir Gel. Available At Research Activity Report, Division of Epidemiology, Www.Nari-Icmr.Res.In Accessed on 22 September 2008.

NACO (2007) 'HIV Sentinel Surveillance and HIV Estimation, 2006'.

NFHS-III: National Family Health Survey (NFHS-3), 2005-06, India: Key Findings. International Institute for Population Sciences (IIPS) and Macro International. 2007. Mumbai: IIPS.

Ntozi, James P. M. (1997). 'Widowhood, Remarriage And Migration During The HIV/AIDS Epidemic in Uganda.' *Health Transition Review*, 7 (Suppl.), 125-144.

Orner, P., Harries, J., Cooper, D., Moodley, J., Hoffman, M., Becker, J., McGrory, E., Dabash, R., and Bracken, H. (2006). Challenges to Microbicide Introduction in South Africa. *Soc Sci Med.*, 63(4),968-78.

Padian, N.S., Buvé, A., Balkus, J., Serwadda, D., and Cates, Jr. W. (2008). Biomedical Interventions to Prevent HIV Infection: Evidence, Challenges, and Way Forward. *Lancet.com,* 372, 2008, 585-599.

Padian, N.S., van der Straten, A., Ramjee, G., et al., (2007). Diaphragm and Lubricant Gel For Prevention of HIV Acquisition in Southern African Women: A Randomised Controlled Trial. *Lancet*, 370, 251–61.

Peterson, L., Nanda, K., Opoku, B., et al., (2007). SAVVY (C31G) Gel For Prevention of HIV Infection in Women: A Phase 3, Double-Blind, Randomized, Placebo-Controlled Trial in Ghana. PLoS ONE 2007; 2: e1312.

Pinkerton, S.D., and Abramson, P.R. (1997). Effectiveness of Condoms in Preventing HIV Transmission. *Soc Sci Med.,* 44, 1303–12.

Plummer, F.A., Simonsen, J.N., Cameron, D.W., Ndinya-Achola, J.O., Kreiss, J.K., Gakinya, M.N., Waoiyaki, P., Cheang, M., Piot, P., Ronald, A.R., and Ngugi, E.N. (1991). Cofactors in Male Female Sexual Transmission of Human Immunodeficiency Virus Type 1. *J inf Dis.*,163, 233-239.

Population Council. Trial Shows Anti-HIV Microbicide is Safe, But Does Not Prove It Eff Ective: Research Advances HIV

Prevention Field. http://www.popcouncil.org/pdfs/Media%20Center/News_CarrResults_letter.pdf (accessed Feb 18, 2008).

Program for Action. International Conference on Population and Development (1994). Cairo, Egypt Available at http://www.un.org/ecosocdev/geninfo/populatin/icpd.htm. accessed on 22 September 08.

Pudney, J., Quayle, A.J., and Anderson, D.J. (2005). Immunological Microenvironments In The Human Vagina And Cervix: Mediators Of Cellular Immunity Are Concentrated In The Cervical Transformation Zone. *Biol Reprod.*, 73,1253–63.

Ramjee, G., Govinden, R., Morar, N.S., and Mbewu, A. (2007). South Africa's Experience of The Closure of the Cellulose Sulphate Microbicide Trial. *PLoS Med.*, 4(7), e235.

Reynolds, S.J., Risbud, A.R., Shepherd, M.E., Zenilman, J.M., Brookmeyer, R.S., Paranjape, R.S., Divekar, A.D., Gangakhedkar, R.R., Ghate, M.V., Bollinger, R.C., and Mehendale, S.M. (2003). Recent Herpes Simplex Virus Type 2 Infections and the Risk of Human Immunodeficiency Virus Type 1 Acquisition in India. *JID*,187, 1513-21.

'Silverman, J.G., Decker, M.R., Saggurti, N., Donta, B., and Raj, A. (2008). Intimate Partner Violence and HIV Infection Among Married Indian Women. *JAMA,* 300(6),703-710.

Solomon, S. et al., (2005). 'A Guide to The Clinical Care Of Women With HIV', Chapter XV1: International Issues. Ed. Anderson, J.R. Health Resources and Services Administration (HRSA).

UNICEF/UNAIDS (2003). "UNICEF, UNAIDS Applaud Milestone in Coordinated Global Response to Children Orphaned Due to AIDS." Joint Press Release. Geneva. 21 October. Www.Unicef.Org/Media/ Media_15081.Html.

UNAIDS *Report on Global AIDS Epidemic*, 4th Global Report, UNAIDS 2004.

UNAIDS (2007). Male Circumcision: Global Trends And Determinants of Prevalence, Safety and Acceptability. Geneva: Joint United Nations Programme on HIV/AIDS.

UNAIDS (2008). 'Report on the Global AIDS Epidemic'.

UNAIDS/UNFPA/UNIFEM (2004). 'Women and HIV/AIDS: Confronting the Crisis'. .

UNGASS. The UNGASS, Gender and Women's Vulnerability to HIV/AIDS in Latin America and the Caribbean. December 2002. http://www.paho.org/English/ad/ge/GenderandHIV-revised0904.pdf, acessed on 24September, 2008.

Van Damme, L., Govinden, R., Mirembe, F., et al., (2007). Phase III Trial of 6% Cellulose Sulfate (CS) Gel For The Prevention of HIV Transmission. *4th IAS Conference on HIV Pathogenesis, Treatment and Prevention; Sydney, Australia;* July 22–25, 2007.

Van Damme, L., Ramjee, G., Alary, M., et al., (2002). Effectiveness of COL-1492, a Nonoxynol-9 Vaginal Gel, On HIV-1 Transmission in Female Sex Workers: A Randomised Controlled Trial. *Lancet,* 360, 971–77.

Van Damme, L., Govinden, R., Mirembe, F.M., Guédou, F., Solomon, S., Becker, M.L., Pradeep, B.S., Krishnan, A.K., Alary, M., Pande, B., Ramjee, G., Deese, J., Crucitti, T., and Taylor, D. (2008). Lack of Effectiveness of Cellulose Sulfate Gel for the Prevention of Vaginal HIV Transmission. *NEJM,* 359, 463-472.

Van de Wilgert, J., Fullem, F.A., Kelly, C., Mehendale, S., Rugpao, S., Kumwenda, N., Chirenje, Z., Joshi, S., Taha, T., Padian, N., Bollinger, R. and Nelson, K. (2001). Phase 1 Trial of Tropical Microbicide Buffer Gel Safety Results From Four International Sites. *JAIDS,* 26, 21-7.

Van de Perre, P., Jacobs, D., and Sprecher-Goldberger, S. (2001). The Latex Condom, An Efficient Barrier Against Sexual Transmission of AIDS-Related Viruses. *AIDS,* 1, 49–52.

Van de Wilgert, J., and Jones, H. (2006). Challenges in Microbicide Trial Design and Implementation. *Studies in Fam Plan.* 37 (2).

Wasserheit, J.N. (1992). Epidemiology Synergy: Interrealtionships Between Human Immunodeficiency Virus Infection and Other Sexually Transmitted Diseases. *Sexually Transmitted Diseases,* 19, 61-77.

Weller, S., and Davis, K. (2002). Condom Effectiveness in Reducing Heterosexual HIV Transmission. *Cochrane Database Syst Rev.,* 1: CD003255.

Watts, C.H., Thompsom, W.A., and Heise, L.L. (1998). The Effectiveness of Microbicides for HIV Prevention. Abstract

Number 33161, Abstract Book, p 624. *12th World AIDS Conference*, Geneva, Switzerland, June 28-July 3, 1998.

Women and HIV/ AIDS: Confronting the Crisis. A Joint Report UNAIDS/ UNFPA/ UNIFEM: http://www.unfpa.org/hiv/women/report/chapter7.html

Woodsong, C., MacQueen, K., Namey, E., Sahay, S., Morar, N., Milingo, M., and Mehendale, S.M. (2006). Womens Autonomy and Informed Consents in Clinical Trials. *Journal of Empirical Research in Human Research Ethics*, 1,3,11–26.

Zhang, Z., Schuler, T., Zupancic, M, et al., (1999). Sexual Transmission and Propagation of SIV and HIV in Resting and Activated CD4+ T Cells, *Science*, 286, 1353–57.

16

Counseling for Reproductive Health and HIV / AIDS

Dr. Sushma Mehrotra

Summary

In India, counselling services have expanded vastly in number, without having adequate knowledge of concepts and understanding of the process. This lack of sensitivity as well as lack of knowledge among the counsellors is mainly because of inadequate and/or improper training. There are a large number of HIV/AIDS patients who suffer emotionally without their needs being addressed. Moreover, some milestones of professional development have taken place recently like training of reproductive health counsellors, developing a counselling manual and even to develop the curriculum and manual for nation-wide HIV/AIDS counselling. Present requirements dictate that mental health professionals fill the gap in knowledge by extending their services to the community and organise training programmes where require. HIV/AIDS counselling services are available usually in health set-ups, family planning set-ups, as stand alone clinics and even in STI clinics, TB set-ups and ART centres. A re-evaluation of our current system of education is necessary with respect to its relevance to society. A proactive approach is needed to place the adequately trained personnel in the relevant areas. Students have to be given proper training to fulfil the lack and to bring reforms at the grass-root level.

Where are We?

Over the last 15-20 years there has been a spurt of counseling services in the area of public health. Counseling services have vastly expanded without adequate know- how and understanding regarding the subject matter. The experts in public health are confused between health education, health information and counseling. The training of counselors and the service delivery is usually managed by Non-Governmental Organizations (NGOs) where the focus is on the field realities. Academicians are still engaged in teaching from textbooks about the theories and practices of psychotherapies in a classroom and to the limited areas of applications.

Counseling has become a misleading term in the area of HIV/AIDS. Presently, counseling is conceptualized as the provision of advice and education for personal care while completely ignoring the concomitants of psychological counterparts. A number of NGOs have mushroomed with quick courses of 2-3 week durations covering basic elements of counseling skills excluding all the technical and methodological components required to understand the complexities of human behaviour. The areas of counseling are pre test, post-test, HIV risk reduction, treatment adherence, mother to child transmission, confidentiality and the concern of further spread to partners. The important issue here is towards those that fall in the highest risk for infection category. Sensitivity is of utmost importance with respect to these marginalized groups, particularly sex workers, men who have sex with men (MSM) and intravenous drug users.

Contraception, safe abortions, sexual health, birth spacing, STI and RTI are the reproductive health categories of focus.

Who Cares About Mental Health?

Counseling in the health sector focuses only on relationship issues, making people feel comfortable with effective communication skills and centers around the concerns related to the outside world with a public health mind set. The observation of some of the counseling sessions highlighted the fact that the counsellor speaks 80.0 - 90.0% of the time, giving the opportunity to the clients only to nod or speak a few words, answering questions raised by the counsellors. If one asks the counsellor about the symptoms of any mental illness, they would be at a complete loss. This lack of knowledge is due to the counselling service provider's failure to connect with psychiatrists. Though there is data available of a number of people infected with HIV and a number of people being tested for HIV, there is no data regarding the stress and emotional trauma faced by these individuals. There is no record on mental health issues. One comes to know through the media about people committing suicide due to the public knowledge of their HIV status. There are large numbers of HIV infected or affected people who suffer emotionally but their needs are not addressed through counseling.

The scenario is not any different in the field of reproductive health. While conducting a training session for reproductive health counsellors and interacting during the demonstration sessions it was seen that counsellors are mostly engaged in information provisioning. The counsellors mentioned that generally, clients expect advice and health education and they are not used to listening to the personal concerns of the clients.

Some Milestones for Professional Development

Recently a large organization engaged in the reproductive health field in South Asia has come up to train the reproductive health counsellors and to develop a counseling manual for dealing with trauma, guilt and self esteem issues of the attendees at the family planning centre. This approach was a complete departure from the usual counseling practices. While developing the manual for the counsellors, care was taken to introduce client centered, behavioural and cognitive approaches and family counseling without mentioning the theoretical rhetoric.

Similarly efforts were made to develop the curriculum and manual for the National AIDS Control Organization by involving 235 faculty members of 111 academic institutes across 30 states of the country and the manual is widely used by HIV counsellors working in the Government sector. The reverse needs to happen, which is, our academic institutes need to introduce the relevant curriculum during formal training so that our young professionals can be qualified after their academic years.

Who are the Counsellors?

The counsellors come from various backgrounds such as commerce and art faculties and at times undergraduates from any social sciences. Government positions have guidelines to select counsellors from the psychology, social work and human development faculties. However, it is difficult to fill remote, non-urban locations. There are several set-ups for the reproductive health sector where counseling is provided by nurses or similar health workers. Most of the South East Asian countries including Maldives, Sri Lanka, Nepal, Burma, Thailand, Cambodia, Vietnam, Indonesia, Laos and Timor Leste recognise nurses and midwives to take over the duties as counsellors as some of them do not have sufficient manpower or they do not want to increase the burden on the health care system with additional positions. India and Pakistan usually have sufficient qualified manpower in the counselling sector; however, the quality of service delivery is not any different.

In a given scenario, we as mental health professionals must fill the knowledge gap by moving towards the community and participating in training programs for these unsung barefoot counsellors.

Scope of HIV /AIDS Counseling Services

Counseling services are usually located in health setups and at times away from urban dwellings. Interestingly they are not even connected with the departments of Psychiatry wherever possible. The services are delivered in the following methods:

- Voluntary Counseling and Testing Centers (VCTC) which are usually located in the department of microbiology or pathology
- Prevention from Mother to Child Transmission Centers (PMTCT) which are located in the Ante Natal Clinics or departments of Obstetrics and Gynaecology
- Integrated Counseling and Testing Centers (ICTC) which caters to all the population supposed to be tested for HIV
- Stand-alone centers
- Family planning set ups

Occasionally, services are available in Sexually Transmitted Infection (STI) Clinics and also in TB set ups. HIV counseling is also made available at Anti Retroviral Treatment (ART) centers where clients receive long term treatment and care. There are Government supported community based centers where HIV infected individuals receive care and support.

Besides the above mentioned services which are meant for people from the general population, the counseling services are provided in Drug De-Addiction centers. These centers are more concentrated in the North East States because of the close proximity to and availability of drugs and its high usage. The prevalence of HIV is high in Manipur and Nagaland which is closely associated with intravenous drug users (IDU). There are drop-in centers which cater to the needs of the IDUs in the community set ups. Similarly there are setups for the other high risk populations such as sex workers. It is difficult to provide the numbers of these set ups but they are many.

The Following Questions should be posed by Mental Health Professionals:

- How many of us are catering to this population?
- Have we trained our students to take up jobs here?
- Have we designed our curriculum at the university level to include the issues related to the populations mentioned above?

We are still placing our students at Child Guidance Clinics, mental health set ups, rehabilitation clinics for substance users, schools, shelter homes, psychiatric set ups and industries.

Our curriculum is heavily loaded with theories and our counselors are talking about CBT, RET, Rogerian and similar other phenomenons while practicing. Will they work in these set ups or will the health care system accept psychotherapy in pure form? Do we have enough trained counsellors/ psychologists who are confident to practice once they graduate from university?

These questions raise doubt in our current education system and its relevance to society. We as mental health professionals must give serious thought to the relevance of our teaching and its applicability in the society. Psychology being the applied field is lost in the textbook and the knowledge component is not supporting the needs of the people working in the field. We as psychologists feel hurt when our jobs are done by others who are less academically qualified or have completely different educational backgrounds from unrelated fields.

The Way Ahead

It is time that we take a proactive approach and become a practical scientist. We have to take stock of the ground realities and conduct a situational analysis. Currently the psychology interns are placed in pure mental health sites where hardly 10.0 - 15.0% of them get employment and the remaining must fend for themselves. Some of them even take jobs for event management, call centres, receptionist work, travel agencies and list is endless. The fact is that the skills learned over the years are not used for professional development in the pure form. However, if we look around, there is scope for our professional growth and we can venture into diversified fields. The health sector is currently undergoing reforms where multi skills are being utilized to treat the patients beyond medicines and physical treatment. We have to groom our students and expose them to the outside world. For us there is tremendous scope as manuals and workbooks are being developed for counseling specific areas, populations, issues and situations. With some creativity we can prepare curriculums and apply our skills and knowledge for the specific needs. One may criticise this as dilution of core subjects but another perspective will take us beyond the ivory towers to the ground level grassroots work.

IV. Family Planning Methods

17

Family Planning in India: Changing Perspectives

Prof. A. K. Sharma

Summary

Commenting on the history of family planning policy in post-independence India, this paper argues that the complexity of population processes in India has led to shifting paradigms in policy. This reflects the changes in global social policy rather than the accumulated knowledge of population processes at the community level. The new policy framework focuses on education, gender equality, reproductive rights and reproductive health facilities. This is in sharp contrast to the older focus on 'advising women' caused by perceived, alarming consequences of rapid population growth, resulting in target oriented approach and coercion to adopt terminal methods. The paper suggests that in the new age greater demographic contributions are needed from micro and participatory studies, linking the global problem of imbalance between population and resources with the local solutions acceptable to people in different social milieus. People should decide what is best for them and how should they evolve sustainable model of development in the value framework of their culture, keeping in view their limited resources. It warrants that the social scientists act as facilitators, rather than experts and be receptive to idea of multiplicity of perspectives.

Introduction

India was the first country to launch the family planning programme immediately after independence. Thus, today the country has more than fifty-five year of experience in running family planning programme. Enormous literature has been produced during this time on various aspects of population dynamics and population policy. This includes theoretical, analytical as well as empirical material on population composition and trends. However, the problem of population growth is still unsolved and ill understood. One of the reasons is that the population processes have been of highly dynamic in nature; no theory could explain all that has happened in the last fifty-five years. The complexity of population processes has, however, led to shifting paradigms in policy, reflecting more the global social policy rather than the accumulated knowledge of population processes at the community level. The new policy framework focuses on education, gender equality, reproductive rights, and reproductive health facilities; replacing the old focus on targets and terminal methods which was based on alarm about consequences of rapid population growth. In this context, this paper presents the background of National Population Policy 2000 and Tenth Five Year Plan approach to population policy. It is suggested that the new policy not only addresses the problem of excessive population growth, but it also focuses on empowerment and community participation.

Time Line of Population and Development Debate

Family planning programme has an intricate link with discourses on population and development. At the outset, it is important to take note of the milestones in population policy in India, and how the perceptions of population planners have changed over time. To decide, what is required and what can work in the future, it is of utmost importance to know what was done in the past and what results followed. Table 1 attempts to draw the time line of the family planning discourse in India. It exhibits what kind of changes have been occurring in factual and normative orders with regard to population variables, i.e., how the planners and policy makers in India were responding to population reality in the light of changes in socio-political situation in the country.

The time line shows that India was the first country to launch a state sponsored family planning programme as early as 1952. At that time, the political elite and planners had felt a need to control population, but as in their perception political climate was not ready to implement stringent measures in family planning they decided to go for a more acceptable Gandhian approach. This, of course, aimed at drawing people's attention to necessity of population control but openly advocated only natural methods of family planning e.g., abstinence and rhythm methods. Today, it may look quite absurd to believe that natural methods could have solved the population problem of India but those were the days of idealism. Moreover, in Europe, natural methods had played the most important role in reducing family size in the initial period. Gradually, with greater involvement of modernist lobby and greater access to hard facts several experiments have been made in the area of population control: clinical approach emphasizing opening of family planning clinics in different parts of the country; extension approach aiming at providing information at door step through a mix of interpersonal communication and mass media; camp approach attracting groups of men to sterilization camps through incentives in cash and kind; cafeteria approach stressing more on choice than on a fixed method with strong target orientation; target free approach; and finally the rights based approach.

The above changes reflect the changing perceptions of the international community, experts and donors on the matter of population control as well. Influence of ideas prevailing in the developed countries on national debate is not a new thing. To quote from the First Five Year Plan:

> *If a doctor feels that a woman patient cannot undergo again the strain of pregnancy and parturition without danger to health, it is obviously the duty of the doctor to give such advice as is necessary to enable the person to prevent conception. In these circumstances, the doctor would be justified in suggesting any chemical, mechanical or biological methods of contraception or sterilization as may be indicated for the individual case. The giving of advice on birth control has been a procedure allowed by the Ministry of Health in U.K. in medical centres maintained by the local authorities.*

In the second half of the last century, the dominant thinking among the demographers and planners was that excessive growth of population is detrimental to development and there was an urgent need for implementing family planning programme. The reasons for this were: (a) other factors remaining same, rapid growth of population increases demand for consumption and investment in human capital; (b) it also reduces per capita improvement in income; and (c) high fertility is commonly associated with rigidity of social stratification, high infant and maternal mortality, and high income inequality. Contrary to this view, the Tenth Five Year Plan identified that the pace of demographic transition is heavily dependent on development. According to the Tenth Plan Five Year Plan Draft, the three major causes of excessive population growth in India are unmet needs, high wanted fertility due to high child mortality, and proportionately large population in reproductive age groups. Their respective contribution to population growth is 20.0, 20.0 and 60.0% respectively. Thus, the major factors in fertility decline are knowledge and availability of family planning methods, reduction in infant and child mortality, and effective health delivery services. Age distribution of population cannot be modified in the short run.

Table 1
The Time Line of Family Planning Policy in India

Before Independence	*General support for population control among elite classes*
	• Lack of awareness among common people • Arguments in favour of population policy among the political and intellectual elites • Isolated efforts to establish clinics and inform people • Strong support for population control by Gandhi and Nehru despite difference in understanding of population dynamics and approaches to means of birth control
1952	**Family planning starts with Gandhian approach**
	• State sponsored family planning programme started • Gandhian approach with abstinence and rhythm as the main methods
1950-60	**Clinical approach**
	• Economic models suggesting a negative relationship between population growth and development • Estimation of demographic rates and ratios

(Contd...)

Before Independence	*General support for population control among elite classes*
	• Knowledge, attitude and practice (KAP) studies • Research in reproduction • Clinical approach
1960-70	**Extension approach and experimentations** • Extension programme • IUCD programme • Target orientation (Third Five Year Plan) • Organizational changes
1970-80	**Camp approach** • The concept of sustainable development • Mass vasectomy camps • National level studies in family planning • First population policy statement announced • Policy under Janata Govt. asserting voluntarism
1980-90	**Cafeteria approach** • Cafeteria approach and emphasis on limitation of family size rather than on contraception • Planning in terms of NRR (with the goal of achieving NRR of unity by 1996)
1990-2000	**Target free approach** • Collection of detailed national and regional level data on population, development and well-being • Abolition of targets • Shift from national to area specific approach

(Contd...)

Before Independence	*General support for population control among elite classes*
2000-	**National Population Policy 2000** • National Population Policy • Unmet needs concept • A rights based approach • HIV/AIDS • Participatory approach

Lessons of Five Decades of Research

Population dynamics has been the most studied area in social sciences in India after independence. No other area of social sciences has been explored as much as population. The question is: what do the studies show? Fifty years of research in population processes have produced many significant findings. Some major findings of population research in India, on which there is enough agreement, may be summarised as follows:

1. India is a developing country with diverse patterns of socio-economic development.
2. Lessons learnt from one setting cannot be used in other settings. After success of population control programme in Kerala many demographers and planners started talking about Kerala model in 1990s, but it has now become clear that since the socio-economic, infrastructural, and geographical conditions of high fertility states (UP, Bihar, Rajasthan and Madhya Pradesh) are markedly different from those of Kerala, the Kerala model cannot be applied there mechanically. All regions with their specificities will help to develop their own models of action.
3. The whole world is moving from one type of

demographic regime to another (Premi, 1991). In the past, children were of great importance to family and society and high fertility had its own instrumental rationality. In the modern world, children are the source of several types of anxieties and have lost their economic and other significance. Women are no more interested in mother's role (United Nations, 2000). India is not an exception to this. During the transitional phase, demographic factors interact with socio-economic, psychological and environmental factors but completion of demographic transition puts an end to all major differentials. In the new demographic regime, as in Europe, children do not have as significant a place in couples' life as they had in traditional society. This is a general problem and no social class seems to differ appreciably from the general pattern.

4. The demographic situation in India is highly fragmented. Population problems as well as the status of health in India have religious, regional, ethnic, social class and urban-rural dimensions. National Family Health Survey-III (Das et al., 2001), NSSO's survey on morbidity, health care and the condition of the aged (NSSO, 2006), and smaller surveys have established the nature of variation in population and health parameters according to socio-economic and cultural characteristics of people.

5. Seemingly opposite factors such as affluence and poverty may produce the same result in the form of fertility transition, affluence through rational choice model, and poverty through Malthusian pressure.

6. Demographic change has both positive and negative implications for human resource development.

7. Ignoring the concept of sustainable development, i.e.

the neglect of demography of environment will be perilous to society.

8. Human behaviour is determined primarily by matrix of personal projections, and appeals in the name of society are not very helpful. Moral appeals have not been found to be effective in any other area, be it politics or corruption.

Studies have consistently shown that the relationships between socio-economic factors and demographic factors do not have a fixed pattern. Yet, an overwhelming majority of people in both urban and rural areas want a small family. However, some of them have access to acceptable contraception and some do not. As said earlier, in India the unmet need for contraception (i.e., percentage of couples who do not want more children but are not practicing family planning) is about 20.0%. Some people want a large family (Mukherjee, 1983) but their number is very small. Most of them want large family because of high infant and child mortality. Some people do not want a child at all. With time as mortality declines their number will increase further. All developed countries are facing the problem of couples not having enough motivation to produce a baby. This is a very dangerous situation and in the future, this may happen in India also.

A large number of couples in different parts of the country do not want a girl child. Social structure and difficulties associated with raising a girl child, protecting her honour, and arranging for her marriage are discouraging parents from producing a female child (Desai, 1994). Moreover, affordable means to detect the sex of the baby during pregnancy and technical facilities to abort it are now easily available. Ironically, some of the regions where sex selective abortions are more prevalent are socio-economically the most developed regions of the country. The combination of sex preference, medical technology and economic development poses a very serious threat to social development and an effective strategy has to be developed to counter this pattern.

The Major Concerns of the New Millennium

All ideas belong to an age. Historical developments lead to new concerns among intellectuals and planners. Academic concerns are intertwined with social structure and, therefore, change with time. It is also true that at any point of time in history different people will perceive things differently. From both rights and efficiency perspectives the differences have to be respected. Yet there are some dominant social representations: no society ever functions without some minimum consensus on matters of common interests. Some new concerns of the new millennium in India may be stated as follows:

- Recognition of 'differences';
- Linking local with global;
- Learning from local communities;
- Need to combine demographic values with survival or progress;
- A strong commitment for empowerment and emancipation; and
- Combining personal rationality with ethical and moral concerns.

As the socioeconomic and cultural systems in India are highly diversified, it is natural that the demographic conditions too are diversified (Bose, 1991). Studies have also shown that the perceptions of effects of population growth on people are as much linked with culture as with natural resources. They have also shown that experts and lay persons do not share the same value systems or ideas about good life. Population control is an important issue for experts but it may be a non-issue for people in the high fertility context. There are people in the country for which survival is the highest value: even housing or shelter is of secondary importance to them. Among them the goal of intervention cannot be the reduction in family size. It has to be survival, or to put it differently, the empowerment. Globalization and the resulting marginalization of many classes, castes, tribes, and communities interact with demographic trends. There may be a need to encourage certain peoples to produce a female baby or even to produce a baby at least for eugenics or structural reasons.

The most crucial problem of population policy in India at the moment is the problem of lack of understanding of reproductive decision-making process. Reproductive rationality is a rather unexplored area. Linking personal choices with social ethics is one of the greatest challenges of our times. Traditional societies do not have this problem because individuals are closely tied to traditions and ego is only weakly developed. Modern societies too do not have this problem because they have developed institutionalized ways of handling problems arising out of individuation and alienation, though even modern societies have not so far been successful in changing attitudes of people in the interest of society if the micro level calculations are against the change. Otherwise, they would not be facing the problems of fertility declining to below replacement level and the subsequent problem of ageing. Social scientists must address this problem.

A consensus seems to be emerging that population planning issues should form a part of empowerment and emancipation. The National Population Policy 2000 rightly gives importance to education, immunization, lowering infant mortality rate, raising marriage age, increasing institutional deliveries, information/counselling, containing spread of HIV/AIDS, promotion of Indian Systems of Medicine, and related social sectors programmes. Some of these issues were included in the earlier policies statements too but the shift of emphasis from national level to community level is the biggest achievement of the new policy. It is this framework of empowerment that should guide studies on and approaches to population policy and reproductive decision rationality. The issue is: how does one decide about family size or contraceptive uses so that the community supported ideas of well-being are locally actualized? It is not an easy question to answer.

International Conference on Population and Development (ICPD) 1994

ICPD 1994, held at Cairo, maintained that size, growth, age structure and rural-urban distribution of a country have critical impact on development prospects and it called on countries to 'fully integrate population concerns into development strategies, planning, decision-making and resource allocation at all levels.' The conference recognized that investing in people to broaden their potential as human beings is the key to sustained economic growth and sustainable development. The ICPD Programme of Action fixed the following 'mutually supportive' goals:

- Gender equality in education;
- Reduction in infant, child and maternal mortality (infant and child mortality to 35 and 45 and maternal mortality to below 60);
- Reproductive health services;
- Improvement in education so that at least 90.0% of all children are in schools by 2010;
- Provision of wide range of reproductive health services (including family planning services, essential obstetric care, and prevention and management of reproductive tract infections in all health care facilities by 2015);

- Ensuring that by 2015, 90 percent of all births are assisted by skilled attendants;
- Meeting unmet need for family planning; and
- Providing access to HIV/AIDS prevention methods, and voluntary testing, counselling and follow up services.

In the following year 4th conference on women was held in Beijing and it lent further support to the above goals.

Millennium Development Goals

ICPD 1994 goals further reverberate in the United Nations Millennium Development Goals (MDGs) 2000 (Box 1). MDGs too focus on social development, removing gender disparity in development and provision of services.

Box 1: MDGs

1. Eradicate extreme poverty and hunger
2. Achieve universal primary education
3. Promote gender equality and empower women
4. Reduce child mortality
5. Improve maternal health
6. Combat HIV/AIDS, malaria and other diseases
7. Ensure environmental sustainability
8. Develop a global partnership for development

For all the MDGs, targets are fixed for all the countries, which should be achieved by 2015. All countries are required to report to the United Nations General Assembly on progress towards the MDGs, through National Millennium Development Goals Reports.

National Population Policy, 2000

Reflecting the ICPD goals and MDGs, in India the National Population Policy 2000 has called for a more human approach to population planning and for paying greater attention to social development with particular emphasis on improving education, reproductive health and unmet needs of slums and other special categories of population. To quote:

> *The National Population Policy, 2000 (NPP 2000) affirms the commitment of government towards voluntary and informed choice and consent of citizens while availing of reproductive health care services, and continuation of the target free approach in administering family planning services. The NPP 2000 provides a policy framework for advancing goals and prioritizing strategies during the next decade, to meet the reproductive and child health needs of the people of India, and to achieve net replacement levels (TFR) by 2010. It is based upon the need to simultaneously address issues of child survival, maternal health, and contraception, while increasing outreach and coverage of a comprehensive package of reproductive and child health services by government, industry and the voluntary non-government sector, working in partnership.*

One major factor of new thinking is the stress on three points: (a) importance of area specific approach about which some academicians were arguing for a long time (Misra, 1992); (b) a need to recognize the importance of reciprocal relationship between population and development; and (c) acceptance of the fact that there could be multiple perspectives on social and organizational issues (Riley and McCarthy, 2003). The goals of NPP 2000 are further operationalized in terms of facilities for people. For example, the goal of reducing maternal mortality ratio has been translated into increasing institutional deliveries under National Rural Health Mission (NHRM) involving ASHAs.

Box 2 shows the paradigm shift that began in the Ninth Five Year Plan of Government of India and became fully operationalized in the Tenth Five Year Plan.

Box 2: Paradigm Shift in Population Policy in the Tenth Plan

- Demographic targets to focusing on enabling couples to achieve their reproductive goals;
- Method-specific contraceptive targets to meeting all the unmet needs for contraception to reduce unwanted pregnancies;
- Numerous vertical programmes for family planning and maternal and child health to integrated health care for women and children;
- Centrally defined targets to community need assessment and decentralized area specific micro-planning and implementation of programme for health care for women and children, to reduce infant mortality and reduce high desired fertility;
- Quantitative coverage to emphasis on quality and content of care;
- Predominantly women centred programmes to meeting the health care needs of the family with emphasis on involvement of men in planned parenthood;
- Supply driven service delivery to need and demand driven service; improved logistics for ensuring adequate and timely supplies to meet the needs;
- Service provision based on providers' perception to addressing choices and conveniences of the couples.

A significant change in the National Population Policy 2000 has been the introduction of HIV/AIDS. Linking population dynamics to HIV/AIDS has generated whole lot of new issues in the area of reproductive health, sexuality, sexual networking, male involvement in reproductive health, mapping of high risk groups, awareness of risks, authority of woman in decision making at family level, and role of community support. It may be stressed that all these issues have led to disenchantment with positivism and scientism, and established importance of social constructivism, yielding self-reports, qualitative studies, and discourse analysis as methodological tools. Situation analysis and mapping, with involvement of community members rather than trained researchers, have become the most important tools with donors and policy makers.

Need For a New Approach

It is not possible to address the new issues caused by shifting paradigm in the conservative framework of research. The paradigm shift needs a change in orientation and a change in research methodology. Table 2 presents the key aspects of the old approach and some suggestions for the future. It is proposed that what the population planning needs today is a participatory approach with the aim of empowering the community. The conservative approach was based on the neo-Malthusian theory that population growth has adverse effects on development and that it is of utmost importance to reach replacement level fertility as soon as possible. This was a wrong assumption. The relationship between population and development is dynamic, situational and symmetrical. Subjective understanding of population depends heavily on the history, culture, awareness, social structure and resource map of the people (Chambers, 1980; Chambers, 1997). An effective population policy must address the issue of population in a holistic manner and community rather than regional and national level planning would offer the best solutions. Solutions should emerge from participatory exercises (Kumar, 2002) and not from the tool kits of experts.

Table 2
Approaches to Population Studies: Old and New: Experts Driven to Participatory

Old	*Approach*	*New Approach*	
1.	Major assumptions	Population growth has adverse effect on development	The relationship between population and development is dynamic, situational and symmetric
2.	Social theory	Positivism	Social constructivism
3.	Approaches to reality	Analytical	Holistic
4.	Methodology	Survey, fieldwork	Situation analysis and mapping (by the community members rather than trained researchers)
5.	Level of analysis	National and l regiona	District and community (with special emphasis on SC/ST, OBC, and urban slums)
6.	Concepts	Scientific, objective	Subjective and relative
7.	Emphasis	National and regional plans	Community interventions
8.	Major actors	Government (with or without involvement of NGOs)	Research groups and NGOs/CBOs
9.	Goal of research	Objective knowledge	Enabling the community to analyse their problems and empowering people
10.	Resources	Hard facts	Conceptual maps, social representations and networks
11.	Goals of policy	Population stabilization through education and services	Participatory development involving community resources, public-private partnership

There is a caveat here. Participation is often a misunderstood term. There is a need to define the term in the present framework. In some or other form the notion of participation has always been that there in a population policy. In the past also population policy suggested making family planning a people's movement but it was just pretence to impose the elite perspective of population on people. Participation of people was seen either as *consultative participation*, in which people were supposed to come to clinics and get counselling and services, or *functional* in which participation was seen as a means to achieve the project goals. There is a need to go for *interactive participation* in which people participate in joint analysis, development of action plans, group decision making, and move towards self-mobilization (Jennings, 2004). This also entails understanding of social representations of family and health at the community level.

Under the aegis of participatory model, social scientists must try to unearth the meanings and social representations of life and social processes and the role of family size (number of children) in this. Health psychologists have already done pioneering work in the field of social representations of health and social scientists working on population and development issues may benefit immensely from the works of such health psychologists (Murray et al., 2003; Herzlich, 1973; Herzlich and Pierret, 1987; Moscovici, 2000). These studies show that social representations of reproductive health are fluid and are intertwined with social arrangements in society. For example, Bhatia and Cleland (2008) found that anxiety, stress and overwork might be associated with reported gynaecological morbidity among pocr urban women. According to NSSO data (NSSO, 2006) as many as 50.0% spells of ailments in urban areas remained untreated because they were not considered to be serious. Modernization and post-modernization have posed challenges to traditional culture and demographers need to understand its full implications for finding ways of development of various communities and classes.

Conclusion

To conclude, in the new age greater demographic contributions are needed from micro and participatory studies, linking the global problem of imbalance between population and resources with the local solutions acceptable to people in different social milieus. Let the people decide what is best for them and how should they evolve sustainable model of development in the value framework of their culture, keeping in view their limited resources. Let the social scientists act as facilitators, helpful to them in arriving at their own solutions. Econometric and statistical models have certainly played a role in the past in estimating the unknowns and in suggesting macro level solutions but when it comes to developing effective intervention strategies they have proved to be limited by the very nature of social abstraction. Voluntary action groups, research NGOs, and those receptive to idea of multiplicity of perspectives are the most suited people to evolve the workable development plans in the fragmented society of India in our times. Time has come to learn about and empower community with involvement of the community members.

REFERENCES

Bose, Ashish (1991). *Demographic Diversity of India: 1991 Census*, B. R. Publishing Corporation, Delhi.

Bhatia, J. C., and John, C. Cleland (2008). "Perceived Gynaecological Morbidity: Health Seeking Behaviour and Expenditure in Karnataka", In Koenig, M. A., Shireen Jejebhoy, John C. Cleland, and Bela Ganatra (eds.), *Reproductive Health in India: New Evidence*, Rawat Publications, Jaipur, 266-282.

Chambers, Robert (1980). *Rural Development: Putting the Last First*, Longman, Harlow.

Chambers, Robert (1997). *Whose Reality Counts? Putting the First Last*, Intermediate Technology Publications, London.

Das, N. P., Misra, Vinod K. and Saha, P.K. (May, 2001). "Does Community Access Affect the Use of Health and Family Welfare Services in Rural India?", *National Family Health Survey Subject Reports*, No. 18, International Institute for Population Sciences, Mumbai and East-West Centre, Population and Health Studies, Hawaii.

Desai, Sonalde (1994). *Gender Inequalities and Demographic Behaviour*, The Population Council, New York.

Herzlich, C. and Pierret, J. (1987). *Illness and Self in Society*, John Hopkins University Press, Baltimore.

Herzlich, C. (1973). *Health and Illness: A Social Psychological Analysis*, Academic Press, London.

Kumar, Somesh (2002). *Methods for Community Participation: A Complete Guide for Practitioners*, Vistaar Publications, New Delhi.

Misra, B. D. (1992). *Area - specific Approach in Health and Family Welfare - Uttar Pradesh*, State Institute of Health and Family Welfare U.P.

Moscovici, S. (2000). *Social Representations: Explorations in Social Psychology*, Polity Press, Cambridge.

Mukherjee, Ramakrishna (1983). 'Population and Social System', In Narain, Vatsala, and C.P. Prakasham (eds.), *Population Policy Perspectives in Developing Countries*, Himalaya Publishing Company, Bombay, 18- 33.

Murray, Michael, Daryl Pullman and Theresa Heath Rodgers (2003). 'Social Representations of Health and Illness among 'Baby-boomers' in Eastern Canada', *Journal of Health Psychology*, 8, 5, 485- 499.

National Sample Survey Organisation, *Morbidity, Health Care and the Condition of the Aged*, NSS 60th round, January – June 2004, National Sample Survey Organisation, Ministry of Statistics and Programme Implementation, Government of India, 2006.

Premi, M. K. (1991). India's Population: Heading Towards A Billion, B. R. Publishing Corporation, New Delhi.

Riley, Nancy E. and McCarthy, James (2003). *Demography in the Age of the Postmodern*, Cambridge University Press, Cambridge.

United Nations (1999). "Below Replacement Fertility", *Population Bulletin of the United Nations*, Special Issue Nos. 40/41.

United Nations Population Fund (UNFPA), *State of World Population 2004: The Cairo Consensus at Ten: Population, Reproductive Health and the Global Effort to End Poverty*, UNFPA, 2004, 2-12.

Visaria, Leela, and Pravin Visaria (1998). "India's Population in Transition", In Singh, J. P. (ed.), *Studies in Social Demography*, M. D. Publications Pvt. Ltd., New Delhi, pp. 1-66.

Internet Sites

Ray Jennings, Ray (2004). "Participatory Development as New Paradigm: The Transition of Development Professionalism". Found at http://www.usaid.gov/hum_response/oti/pubs/pbdv1000.pdf, April 2004.

National Commission on Population, Found at http://www.populationcommission.nic.in/npp_obj.htm, 19 March 2004.

18

Family Planning Methods and Programmes in India

Dr. Suresh Sharma

Summary

The Family Welfare Programme in India has experienced significant growth and adaptation over the past half century since its inception in 1951. The direction, emphasis and strategies of the Family Welfare Programme have changed over time. Over the decades, there has been a substantial increase in contraceptive use in India. The contraceptive needs of considerable proportions of women and men and improving the quality of family planning services continue to be a challenge. The 1990s witnessed a growing recognition of this, and several innovative policy and programme initiatives have been launched to address these issues. The objectives of this article was to trace the roots of this change in orientation, document the programme's achievements till date and examine the challenges that remained at the policy level and at the implementation level and also review evidence from surveys and studies conducted in the 1990s. Declining fertility in large part was due to women's increased usage of contraception. For the first time ever, more than half of currently married women in India were using contraception, and their usages of modern contraceptive methods increased from 43.0% to 49.0% between NFHS-2 and NFHS-3. This raises the question of whether the focus, priorities and responsibility of the family planning programme should remain the same in the future. The paper made some suggestions for areas that need further improvement and research attention.

Introduction

In 1952, India became the first developing country to establish a national family planning programme to address the issues of high fertility and rapid population growth. In more than four decades of its existence, the Indian family planning programme has been both highly visible and the subject of intensive international interest and analysis. A primary explanation for this interest lies in India's global demographic significance. With more than 1.12 billion population India is going to surpass China in the next few years. Over the past four decades, significant growth and expansion of the Indian family planning programme have been evident. Starting from virtually no infrastructure, the Indian programme has grown to encompass over 150,000 primary health centres (PHCs) and sub-centres, employing more than 300,000 family planning personnel. This network of services now extends to almost the entirety of India's people, three-fourths of who continue to reside in 600,000, often small and isolated, communities. As evidenced by the most recent National Family Health Survey in India, knowledge of family planning among reproductive-aged women is by now almost universal, and by the early 1990s, 41.0% of couples were currently using a method of contraception (IIPS, 1995). Largely as a result, total fertility rates in India have declined significantly over the last several decades, from 6.0 births in the 1950s to 3.4 births by the early 1990s. In addition, the programme has gradually expanded the range of services it offers to include immunization, antenatal and delivery care, preventive and curative health care, and, most recently, reproductive health care. These achievements notwithstanding, it is difficult to escape the conclusion that the Indian family planning programme remains characterized by considerable unfilled potential and promise. Its modest progress stands in marked contrast to the progress of a number of neighboring family planning programmes in Asia - most notably Bangladesh, Indonesia, and Thailand, which despite having launched their programmes much later, have achieved considerable success in raising levels of contraceptive use. Nowhere is this disparity more apparent than in the large and populous northern states, which are home to more than 400 million people, more than 40.0% of India's total population. The reasons for the limited success of the Indian programme extend far beyond the service delivery program itself. They encompass a host of other social, cultural, and economic factors - including low levels of female and overall educational attainment, continuing high mortality, low status of women, and extreme poverty - which influence the demand for fertility limitation (Cassen 1978; Satia and Jejeebhoy 1991). In recent years, however, there has been a growing consensus among policymakers, researchers, and informed observers that the program itself - as reflected in its priorities, emphasis, and the implementation of services - must be accorded primary responsibility for the limited success of family planning in much of India. The objectives of this article are to trace the roots of this change in orientation, document the program's achievements till date and examine the challenges that remain at the policy level and at the implementation level and also to review evidence from surveys and studies conducted in the 1990s and thereafter on contraceptive use dynamics for contraception in India. This raises the question of whether the focus, priorities and responsibility of the family planning programme should remain the same in the future.

Programme Implications

The studies included in this paper collectively provide the most comprehensive and up-to-date picture of the Indian family planning programme in terms of actual implementation at the field level. In a study of this nature, some degree of repetition and duplication in findings is perhaps inevitable. While many of the findings reported are by no means novel, collectively they provide a compelling and disturbing picture of the realities of family planning service delivery within India's public sector. The general view that emerges is of a programme that has, over time, seriously strayed from its initial mandate to improve the health and wellbeing of Indian women and their families. India's Family Welfare Programme remains characterized by an overriding concern for numbers—as measured by the recruitment of sterilization acceptors—frequently at the expense of higher-quality, client-centered service. While such gaps are perhaps most acute in the large, populous North Indian states, many of the same quality of care concerns are also evident within the Central and South Indian states, the latter now widely recognized as emerging demographic success stories.

Moreover, family planning programmes function not in isolation but within the broader context of social relations in a particular setting. Within India, these relations are determined largely on the basis of caste, social class, and gender. Within such systems, the poor, especially the poor women, have traditionally been accorded few rights - including the right to receive sympathetic and respectful treatment. The fact that a majority of women in Central and South India have adopted contraception (overwhelmingly female sterilization) may indicate that, under conditions of strong motivation for small families and autonomy among women to make fertility choices, small families may be achieved despite the barriers to fertility regulation presented by poor quality of care. The findings nevertheless leave the reader with the unequivocal impression that an absence of attention and priority to client needs and poor overall quality of care have played important roles in the disappointing performance of the Indian Family Welfare Programme to date. In early 1996, the government abolished the nationwide system of contraceptive method targets, which has dominated the family planning programme for much of its existence. In late 1997, the government launched the new Reproductive and Child Health Programme to replace the much narrower programmes on MCH and family planning, with the objective of more effectively addressing the broader reproductive health needs of the family. Given the fact that these policy changes were made only recently, their implementation remains uneven and incomplete, and it is too early to assess their impact at the field level. Progress is likely to be measured more in decades than in years. A clear understanding and recognition of the nature of the problems confronting the Indian Family Welfare Programme represent important first steps toward effectively addressing them.

Knowledge and Trends in Contraceptive Methods

Women are most likely to know about pills and least likely to know about IUDs. Men are also least likely to know about IUDs, but their knowledge of condoms is very high (more than 90.0%). Women are more likely than men to know about pills and IUDs, but less likely to know about condoms (see Fig-1). Because contraceptive knowledge is quite high among adolescents, the differentials by background characteristics are not large. Women and men aged 20-24 are slightly more knowledgeable about contraceptive methods than those aged 15-19. Adolescent women and men from urban areas and those who are currently married are more likely to know about contraceptive methods than other women and men.

Fig 1.Knowledge of Pills, Condoms, and IUDs among Youth

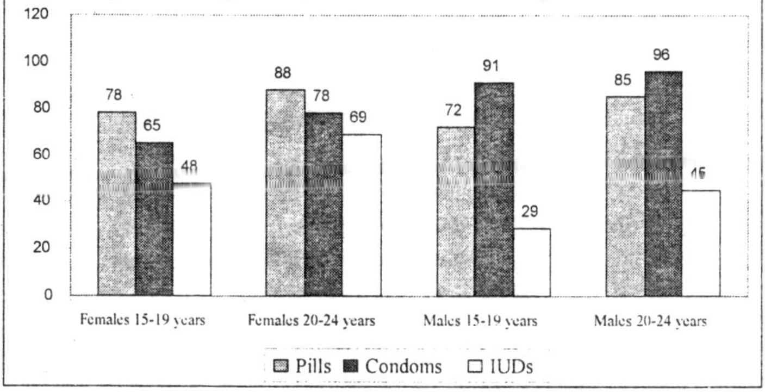

Current Use of Contraception Methods

The current level of contraceptive use, i.e., the contraceptive prevalence rate (CPR), defined as percentage of currently married women aged 15-49 years who are currently using a contraceptive method or whose husbands are using a contraceptive method, is one of the principal determinants of fertility. It is also an indicator of the success of family planning programmes. Current use of different methods of family planning among currently married women and sexually active unmarried women is shown by age group and residence in Fig-2. The contraceptive prevalence rate in India is 56.0%. As shown earlier, the extent of ever use of contraception is 66.0%, which implies that 85.0% of ever users are currently using a contraceptive method. Eighty-six percent of current users are using modern methods and the remaining 14 percent are using traditional methods. Female sterilization accounts for two-thirds of total contraceptive use and 77 percent of modern method use. Among the spacing methods, the most widely used methods are condoms and rhythm (each used by 5.0% of currently married women each). The use of the family planning programme's three modern spacing methods together accounts for 18 percent of the CPR. Similar to the age pattern of ever use, current use also increases with age, peaks at 73.0% in the age group 35-39, and decreases thereafter. The highest use of modern spacing methods (14.0%) is by women aged 25-29 years. The contraceptive prevalence rate is 11 percentage points higher in urban areas than in rural areas. However, the prevalence of female sterilization, male sterilization, and traditional methods is almost the same among urban and rural women. The use of modern spacing methods (pill, IUD, and condom) is considerably higher in urban areas than in rural areas. Condom use is three times as high in urban areas as in rural areas.

Fig 2: Couple using Family Planning Methods (%), NFHS III-2005-06

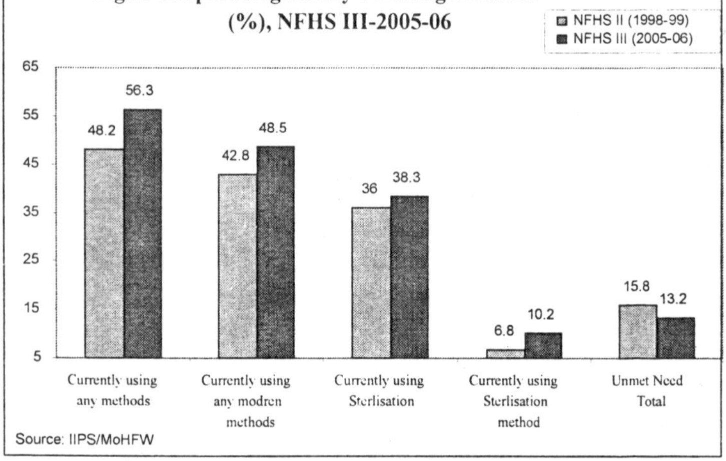

The comparison of the use of different contraceptive methods in India from NFHS-1, NFHS-2, and NFHS-3 are shown in below figure. Over the past 13 years there has been a steady increase in the CPR from 41.0% in NFHS-1 (1992-93) to 48.0% in NFHS-2 (1998-99) and further to 56.0% in NFHS-3 (Figure 3). The use of contraception has increased steadily in both urban and rural areas, but the pace of change has been somewhat faster in rural areas. Since NFHS-1, the use of each modern and traditional method, except male sterilization and the IUD has increased. The share of female sterilization in the CPR decreased slightly from 67.0% in NFHS-1 to 66.0% in NFHS-3. In the same period, the share of the three officially sponsored spacing methods increased from 14.0 to 18.0%. Between NFHS-1 and NFHS-3, the CPR increased more in rural areas (16 percentage points) than in urban areas (13 percentage points).

Fig 3. Trends in Current Contraception Use by Residence

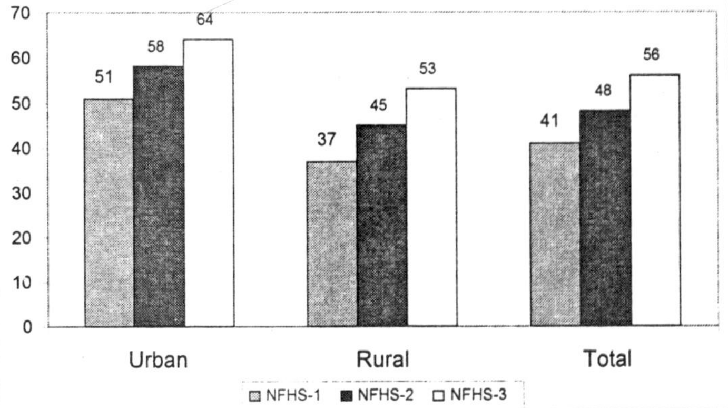

Source of Family Planning Methods

Family planning services and supplies in India are provided primarily through a network of government hospitals and urban family welfare centres in urban areas and Primary Health Centres (PHC) and sub-centres in rural areas. Family planning services are also provided by private hospitals and clinics and nongovernmental organizations (NGO). From time to time, sterilization camps are organized to provide sterilization services. Pills and condoms are also available in pharmacies, and condoms are also available in shops. Information on sources of modern contraceptives can help family planning managers evaluate their programmes. Women currently using a modern method of contraception were asked where they obtained the method most recently.

Table 1
Source of Modern Contraceptive Methods

Methods	*Public Medical Sector*	*NGO or Trust Hospital / Clinic*	*Private Medical Sector*	*Other Source*
Female sterilization	83.6	0.9	15.5	0.1
Male Sterilization	85.3	0.3	10.0	0.0
Pill	15.3	0.0	63.7	20.2
IUD	45.6	1.1	51.8	0.2
Injectables	11.2	0.0	82.7	4.7
Condom/Nirodh	13.3	0.2	45.8	40.4
All Modern Method	70.6	0.8	22.8	5.5

Source: NFHS-3, 2005-06

The source of the current contraceptive method is shown by residence in Table-1. The public medical sector is the source of modern methods for 71.0% of current users. Almost one-quarter of users obtained their method through private medical sources, and 6 percent received their method through other sources. Less than 1.0% of users obtained their method through an NGO or trust hospital/clinic. The public sector is by far the most commonly used source for both female and male sterilizations (84.0-85.0%). About 51.0% of female sterilizations and 46.0% of male sterilizations were done in government/municipal hospitals. Eighteen percent of female sterilizations were done in community health centres, rural hospitals, or Primary Health Centres, and 12.0% were done in camps. The private medical sector is the most common source for all spacing methods. The majority of IUD users 51.0% and users of injectables 69.0% obtained their method from a private hospital or a private doctor/clinic. About 51.0% of pill users and 39.0% of condom users obtained their contraception from a pharmacy. In general, the primary source of contraceptive methods is the same in urban and rural areas, but a higher proportion of users in rural areas than in urban areas have availed of public sector sources for each of the contraceptive methods.

Exposure to Family Planning Messages

An instrument that has become increasingly important these days is the use of mass media in promotion of small family norm and providing information on reproductive and child health services. The rapidly increasing exposure to electronic media has made this an important channel of behavioural change communication. The analyses of NFHS data have shown that the exposure to mass media and family planning messages through these sources have strong independent effects on the current use of contraception, and future intention to use among non-users. It used to be contended that interpersonal communication is a more effective agent of behavioural change than the mass media. But recent research shows that messages though media stimulate discussion between husband and wife, among friends and neighbours and with health workers. Thus mass media and interpersonal channels should be seen as complementary rather than substitutes in the process of developmental communication. Research shows that exposure to mass media has a strong independent effect on the use of family planning methods. Mass media has a wide reach, and would help to raise curiosity and create grounds for interpersonal communication to occur. The communications media have played an important role in promoting the family welfare programme in India. In 1968-69, the Mass Education Media (MEM) division was created in the Department of Family Welfare. Channels of communication such as the Television, Radio, Song and Drama Division, Directorate of Field Publicity, and the print media promote reproductive health and population issues. Exposure to family planning messages is seen as widening the horizon of understanding on issues related to contraceptive use and helping to achieve desired family size. Measuring the extent of exposure to such information helps programme managers and planners to effectively target population subgroups for information, education, and communication (IEC) activities.

Table 2
Exposure to Family Planning Messages

Sources	*Women*	*Men*
Radio	32.8	52.9
Television	49.5	64.1
Newspaper or Magazine	22.2	50.1
Wall painting or Hoarding	26.7	55.9
None of these four media sources	38.7	8.1

Source: NFHS-3, 2005-06

In NFHS-3, both women and men were asked if they had heard or seen any message about family planning on the radio or television, in a newspaper or magazine, or on a wall painting or hoarding in the few months prior to the survey. Table-2 provides information on women's exposure to family planning messages. Slightly more than three in five women reported that they heard or saw a family planning message in the past few months. Nearly half of women saw a family planning message on television; one-third heard a family planning message on the radio; about one-quarter saw a family planning message on a wall painting or hoarding; and 22.0% saw a family planning message in a newspaper or magazine.

However, surveys show that in EAG states, regular exposure to mass media has not yet reached desirable levels to have a wider impact. It is therefore required to raise exposure to mass media in EAG states by providing DVD/CD player and Television set to PHCs, FRUs and Mahila Mandals. As a part of this scheme, imaginatively produced DVD/CDs on reproductive and child health, including information on various methods of contraception, could be distributed. Facility surveys show that less than 20.0% of the PHCs have telephone connections. For efficient referral services and monitoring of the programmes, telephone connections are essential. It is therefore important to provide telephone connections to every PHCs, FRUs and CHCs. PHCs and FRUs receiving at least 10 outpatients/maternity cases in a day in EAG states could be identified for the supply of DVD/CD Players and TV sets. For moving the TV set between OPD and inpatient ward, a trolley could also be provided. During fixed hours in a day, DVD/CDs on RCH and family planning could be played for viewing by the outpatients/women coming for delivery. DVD/CD players and TVs could also be supplied to Mahila Mandals on the condition that they would arrange DVD/CD viewing sessions (along with TV shows) at fixed hours in a day. ANMs during their field visits should check whether these are effectively used. The production of DVD/CDs could be out-sourced. Telephone connections should be supplied to all PHC/FRU/CHCs.

Strengthening Family Welfare Infrastructure

The sub-centre, manned by an auxiliary nurse midwife (ANM), is the most peripheral health institution available to the rural population. As per the norms established under the Basic Minimum Services programme in 1997, there should be one sub-centre for every 5,000 population in plain areas, and for every 3,000 population in hilly/tribal areas. In 2002, there were 1,37,271 sub-centres, or one subcentre for 4,579 rural population. The primary health centre (PHC) is a first referral unit for six sub-centres. In 2002, there were 22,975 PHCs, one for every 27,364 rural populations. PHCs provide outpatient services and have 4-6 inpatient beds. According to the norm they should have one medical officer and 14 paramedical and other supporting staff. But in many remote areas there are no functional PHCs. Community Heath Centres (CHC) is planned as first referral units (FRUs) for four PHCs for offering specialized care. According to the norm, they should have at least 30 beds, one operation theatre, X-ray machine, labour room and laboratory facilities. The staff should consist of at least four specialists, a surgeon, a physician, a gynaecologist and a paediatrician who should be supported by 21 paramedical and other staff. Currently there are 2,935 community health centres, or one for every 2,14,000 people. But majority of the CHCs do not function as FRUs as they either do not have the required number of specialists or the facilities. The facility survey undertaken as a part of RCH project has brought out the serious shortfalls in physical infrastructure, staff and supplies at pubic health institutions. The survey considered a heath institution as adequately equipped if it had 60.0% of the critical inputs. According to this criterion, at the all India level, only 36.0% of the PHCs had adequate physical infrastructure such as building, water and electricity supply, laboratory and labour room, vehicle etc., 38.0% had adequate staff in position, 31.0% had adequate supplies of kits, drugs, vaccines and contraceptives, and 56.0% had the adequate equipments in function, such as weighing machine, vaccine carrier, BP instruments, autoclave, etc. The position of the CHCs, FRUs, and district hospitals were somewhat better, but they too had severe shortage of supplies. Only 10.0-15.0% of them had adequate supplies. The staff in position in the CHCs (25.0%) and the FRUs (46.0%) was also far from adequate. In the EAG states, the position of the PHCs was far worse than the all India average. Only15.0-20.0% of them had adequate infrastructure, staff and supplies. It was also observed that only 12.0% of medical and paramedical staff (only 4.0% in EAG states) had received adequate in-service training. The FRUs/CHC and district hospitals attended only about 10 referred cases of delivery in a month.

Involvement of Local Self-Governments

The 73rd and 74th Constitutional Amendments made health and family welfare a responsibility of local bodies. Being closer to the people, a decentralized institution is expected to meet their needs and preferences. The whole idea of decentralized governance is based on some key factors like people's participation, accountability, transparency and fiscal transfers. How far decentralization of services helps in improving the quality and coverage of healthcare delivery? Experiences from across the country indicate that a precondition for enhancing the effectiveness in delivery of public health services is community participation in decision-making and programme implementation. This can be facilitated through the intervention of the PRIs by making health services responsive to local needs, more accountable to the local population, focusing on local problems, prioritizing the requirements, generating public demand for the services, and making efficient use of the available resources. The National Population Policy (NPP-2000) reiterates the crucial role of panchayats in planning and implementation of health and family welfare programmes. Decentralization is expected to bridge the existing gap between the service providers and the clients to a great extent. However, for the PRIs to be effective in health service delivery, more responsibilities need to be given in the sector-specific budget allocations, revenue-raising powers and training. In reality, the functions and powers devolved to the Panchayats vary considerably across the states. Since one-third of elected members at the local bodies are women, this is a good opportunity to promote a gender sensitive, multi-sectoral agenda for population stabilization with the help of village level health committees. Under the National Rural Health Mission (NRHM), ASHAs would be selected by and be accountable to the village panchayats (the coverage under NRHM for various health facilities/functionaries).

Family Welfare Programme: Achievements and Limitations

In India, as in many other developing countries, the family planning programme is the most direct public policy measure initiated to reduce the population growth rate. Since the formal beginning of the programme in the early 1950s, it has gone through many structural, administrative and implementation strategy changes. All those changes will not be described here; instead focus will be on only critical areas of programme activity and their impact on achievements and their limitations. There is no doubt that the facilities and services made available for family planning have increased substantially over time. In the rural areas, at the beginning of April 1991, there were 130,978 sub-centres, 22,059 primary health centres, and 1,923 community health centres (Department of Family Welfare, 1990/91:257-263). The above statistics are just one of the indicators which show that the programme has certainly succeeded in establishing a very good infrastructure through which family planning facilities and services have increased over time. However, there are some doubts about the full utilization of these services and the quality of service standards being provided by these centres (Singh, 1989:39).

Table 3
Number of Couples Effectively Protected By Various Family Planning Methods, Selected Years From 1970 to 2005

Period	*Eligible Couples (thousand)*	*Sterilization*	*IUD*	*Other*	*All methods*
1970-71	94,489	7,584 (8.0)	1,288 (1.4)	1,963 (2.1)	9,853 (10.4)
1980-81	116,033	23,321 (20.1)	1,173 (1.1)	3,809 (3.3)	26,444 (22.8)
1990-91	145,140	43,497 (30.3)	9,664 (6.7)	17,814 (12.3)	64,071 (44.1)
2000-01	173,835	50,168 (28.9)	12,442 (7.2)	25,844 (14.9)	79,352 (45.6)
2004-05	185,177	52,252 (28.2)	12,559 (6.8)	33,483 (18.1)	86,324 (46.6)

Source: Ministry of Health and Family Welfare, 'Family welfare Statistics in India-2006, Govt. of India, (New Delhi)

Table 4
Demographic Characteristics if Acceptors of Vasectomy, Tubectomy and IUD, From 1980-2004

Years	*Vasectomy*		*Tubectomy*		*I.U.D*	
	Mean Age of Wife	*Average No.of Living Children*	*Mean Age of Wife*	*Average No. of Living Children*	*Mean Age of Wife*	*Average No. of Living Children*
1980-81	31.6	3.5	30.5	3.7	28.0	2.6
1998-99	28.7	2.5	28.3	2.9	27.3	2.2
2003-04	30.4	2.7	29.0	2.9	27.6	2.1

Source: Ministry of Health and Family Welfare,"Family Welfare Statistics in India-2006, Govt. of India, (New Delhi)

The programme has contributed to large-scale awareness about family planning, contraceptives and available facilities (Mahadevan et al., 1989). There are reports of an increasing number of sterilization operations, IUD insertions and use of other contraceptive methods (Raina, 1994:172), all of which have increased the couple protection rate. According to the Department of Family Planning Statistics, the percentage of couples effectively protected increased from 10.4% in 1971 to 46.6% in 2005 in the Tables- 3, (Department of Family Welfare, 2006). Since the goal of the family planning programme has always been established in terms of demographic targets, it is logical that its performance would have to be evaluated in terms of its impact on the reduction of the birth rate. The various fertility indicators certainly do show some trends towards declining fertility in India. The crude birth rate seems to have declined from about 45.0% thousand in the 1950s to 28.5% thousand in 1993. The total fertility rate has also declined from about 5.2 children per woman (1970-72) to 3.7 (1990-92). This amounts to a nearly 28.0% decline in fertility during the period 1970-1990. A number of other demographers (Visaria and Visaria, 1994) also reported a reduction in fertility during the last few decades.

Questions have been raised whether the decline has been sufficiently large to merit applause for the efforts of the family planning programme. It is our view that birth rates and total fertility rates are still too high. Also, the pace of the fertility decline is slowing; it almost came to halt in the 1980s (Jain, 1989:2729; Raina, 1994:197).

Another aspect of the programme, which needs to be evaluated, concerns the number of acceptors of family planning and their demographic characteristics. Even though the couple protection rate has increased from 10.4% in 1971 to 46.6% in 2005, most of this increase has been achieved through sterilization alone. In 1991 nearly 69.0% of the total couple protection rate was accounted for by sterilization. Also, there has been some inconsistency between the couple protection rates and total fertility rates observed among various states. This raises a question concerning the accuracy of reporting the non-reversible methods used and the efficiency with which they have been used. The demographic characteristics of the couples concerned also are not very conducive to a steep decline in fertility. The mean age of acceptors is above 30 years. These couples on average have at least 3.1 living children in the Table-4. This profile has hardly changed over the years. This means that the programme has not been very successful in recruiting younger couples with lower parity. It also has not been able to popularize the use of reversible methods.

One can safely say that, although some progress has been made, it has not been enough. This raises the question of whether family planning has affected human reproductive behaviour to the extent of being able to promote the ideal of a small family size. In light of this we need to look at certain aspects of the programme, both in terms of its philosophy and implementation strategies of the past.

It is also appropriate to look at the recently proposed changes to India's population policy. The proposed population policy (draft document, as it is called) emphasizes that the policy needs to be tailored to suit the particular socio-cultural and socio-economic factors prevailing in each area of the country. Such a shift in approach is fundamental to achieving a population policy driven by people perceived needs. It proposes that the current target-oriented approach of a centrally sponsored/vertical programme be replaced by a people-oriented, decentralized approach. The principle of integration and decentralization in this proposed policy document also calls for a restructuring of the Ministry of Health and Family Welfare (Expert Group on Population Policy, 1994:27). The proposed policy argues that there is a need for a structure, which has the requisite authority, autonomy and accountability to make this happen. Under the new structure, the establishment of a Population and Social Development Commission is proposed. The commission's responsibilities would include formulation and implementation of population policies and strategies. It is argued in the proposed policy document that the setting up of such a commission supported by a 'population and development fund' would enable the governmental and non-governmental organizations concerned to have the means, flexibility, will and enthusiasm to achieve national goals. Based on this, it is necessary to address those issues, which will increase the effectiveness of the programme in the future.

Decentralization

The family planning programme has been accepted since its beginning as an integral part of the planning process in India. The pattern of funding and the working strategy adopted under the programme has resulted in centralized planning and centralized decision-making. The family planning programme had traditionally delivered the "same packages" to all areas of the country. A major shortcoming of this approach was its failure to recognize that, in a diverse and pluralistic society such as India, it is seldom possible to build consensus quickly and to organize effective support for implementing nationwide programmes. Among the developing countries, India presents a unique case in terms of the sheer number of people involved and the extreme heterogeneity of its cultures, languages and socio-economic conditions. An important lesson to be learned from past failures is that the family planning programme in India must be planned in the context of the country's diversity. Hence, there is a need to achieve greater decentralization, both in planning and implementation. To improve the effectiveness of the family planning programme, it must be decentralized to reach the grass roots level (Gandhi, 1989). The Eighth Plan envisages the need for people's participation and a community-based system. The Expert Group on National Population Policy in its draft policy states: 'policies and programmes will have to be tailored to suit the particular socio-cultural and socio-economic factors prevailing in each area. The year 1994 provides an excellent opportunity for promoting the concept of unity in national population goal but diversity in implementation strategies. With the Panchayat Raj Act coming into force in all States and Union Territories, there is a real opportunity for planning at the grassroots level'. (1994:3)

Based on the national population policy framework, each *panchayat* (village council, or local administrative unit) or similar local government body can be encouraged to prepare a socio-demographic profile and develop a plan of action for achieving population stabilization. The benefit of such an approach is that programme decision-making would be brought into direct contact with those whose needs are ultimately to be served or whose preferences in matters of reproduction it is hoped to influence. This should help the family planning programme to become 'internalized'. In the past, the family planning programme failed to pay adequate attention to the users' perspectives. This resulted too often in a failure to achieve high rates of contraceptive acceptance and prevalence (Zeidenstein, 1989). Recently, the central Government came to the realization that the success of the programme demands as much in terms of the initiative and cooperation of the people as it does with regard to its status as an official programme. Hopefully this realization will soon be translated into action through the process of decentralization.

The Family Planning Programmes (FP)

As to demographic policies, women aged 15 to 49 are the specific target of Family Planning programmes (FP). Even if the main objective of FP programmes is demographic, indirect effects on women's economic conditions through maternal and child health improvements are surely to be expected. The FP Programme in India has undergone important changes in recent years and particularly during the 1990s. At the beginning in 1952, it was primarily a clinic-based family planning programme monitoring the family on the basis of family planning targets to achieve a couple participation rates to the health system of 60.0%. After the adoption of the 'extension approach' in 1963 and subsequent integrations with the maternal and child health programme, the activities of the programme broadened significantly. In addition to family planning, the programme provided a variety of services to mothers and children, including antenatal, delivery, and postnatal care, immunization of children against various vaccine-preventable diseases, and counseling on maternal and child health problems and nutrition. In the 70s and the 80s, the FP programme has been accused of using unacceptable methods to induce people to be sterilized and to fulfill administrative targets even after the so called 'emergency period' imposed by the Prime Minister Indira Gandhi in 1976-77 (Saavala, 1999). The central administration gave local health workers targets for the number of women they were to sterilize each month. The actual name is 'Family Welfare Programme'. We rename it FP for expositional purposes, in order to make a clear distinction between demographic and economic welfare policies. During the years, the emphasis on achieving method-specific targets, particularly sterilization targets, has created a situation in which targets for numbers of acceptors gained precedence over everything else and the programme was not driven by demand.

The International Conference of Population and Development in 1994 in Cairo marked the abolition of the target-oriented approach. The programme was gradually reoriented towards the Reproductive and Child Health Programme that includes components relating to sexually transmitted diseases and reproductive tract infections. After some initial experiments in a few selected districts, in 1996 the 'target-free' approach was implemented throughout the country and was renamed the Community Needs Assessment. This approach modified the system of monitoring the programme and made it a demand-driven system in which a worker would assess the needs of the community at the beginning of each year. From then on, FP workers are sent in rural areas to assess the needs of the village communities on the basis of consultations with families, and give advice on a series of problems, not only concerning health (Ministry of Health and Family Welfare, 1998b). The NFHS includes several questions on the quality of care of health and family welfare services provided by the public sector and the private sector. The success of FP programmes in our period of analysis is particularly evident in States with demographic and social indicators below the Indian average. Taking as an example one of the most underdeveloped States, Uttar Pradesh, in 2005, 53.0% of women aged 20-24 were married by age 18, an indicator that was equal to 64.0% in 1999. In the same period, the total fertility rate has dropped from 4.06 to 3.82 and the median age at first birth has increased from 18.8 to 19.4 years. The percentage of married women with two living children and wanting no more children has risen from 45 to 64. As far as maternal and reproductive health is concerned, antenatal care has increased from 35.0 to 67.0% of births in the preceding three years, 29 to 64 in rural areas. This fact, together with the increase in institutional deliveries, has led to a decrease in infant mortality from 89 to 73 per 1000 births in the past five years.

The FP programme in India is still being reformed. The recent National Population Policy, released in February 2000, stresses the commitment to reproductive and child health with the statement that 'the overriding objective of economic and social development is to improve the quality of lives that people lead, to enhance their well-being, and to provide them with opportunities and choices to become productive assets in society' (Ministry of Health and Family Welfare, 2000).

A New Approach

Soon after the Cairo Conference, the Ministry of Health and Family Welfare proposed that one or two districts with well-performing programmes from each of India's major states begin using a target-free approach to family planning on an experimental basis. The announcement of the new approach, however, was made suddenly and without adequate preparation. A year later, in April 1996, the government of India took an even bolder step: it announced that the national family planning programme would become target-free. This decision also was made without adequate discussion about what would replace the old system and without assessing the experience of several districts that had become target-free in 1995. The target-free approach of 1996 meant that centrally determined targets would no longer 'be the driving force behind the programme.' Instead, the community's service needs would determine the programme's priorities. With the new approach, planning was to be decentralized and responsibilities were to reside at the level of the primary health centers: Targets would be set by local health workers, 'in consultation with the community at the grassroots level.' At the policy level, the central government's shift to a target-free family planning approach was a necessary first step toward enhancing the quality of services nationwide. At the state and district levels, however, where the new programme was to be implemented, programme staff was offered little guidance other than receipt of the program's target-free manual to orient them to decentralized planning. An examination of data on annual acceptors of various methods of family planning, however, indicates that contraceptive prevalence has not declined since the programme's inception: After experiencing some decrease in the absolute number of acceptors during 1996-1997, the acceptance of all methods improved during 1997– 1998.

In October 1997, the government launched the Reproductive and Child Health (RCH) Programme. The RCH programme entails a change not only in programme policy but in management and implementation as well. The goals of the RCH program include: removing all targets; phasing out incentive payments to both providers and acceptors of family planning methods; increasing utilization of existing facilities rather than creating new structures; and using the voluntary and private sectors to increase access to services and fill gaps left by public-sector providers. The RCH program utilizes district-level planning and monitoring to make it more responsive to local needs, and it focuses on improving the quality of care by emphasizing the needs of the client, involving the community, improving the client-referral system and providing local oversight for female health workers. The programme strives to revitalize the existing network of rural health facilities by improving supplies of drugs and equipment and enhancing training so that workers can provide better information and counseling to clients and communities.

Under the RCH program, the government is implementing national initiatives for information, education and communication activities, for training and for programme monitoring while also introducing reproductive and child health interventions in selected districts. This approach allows districts to gain experience in limited areas, track the programme's progress and identify problems prior to larger scale expansion. In addition, 24 districts or cities with weak social indicators are implementing focused interventions to increase access to health care for particularly disadvantaged groups, such as scheduled castes and tribes and the urban poor. Besides addressing quality of care and informed choice, the RCH programme also promotes the creation of a forum for policy dialogue and for periodic programme reviews. The programme also stresses that states should have flexibility when implementing recommendations emanating from evaluations and reviews. While the details of the RCH program can be debated and discussed, it does attempt to address several issues that have thus far been neglected in India's Family Welfare Program.

Conclusion and Recommendations:

In the 1990s, the Government of India has taken several bold steps towards a more comprehensive, woman-sensitive health programme. Method-specific family planning targets have been removed, a new reproductive and child health program has been initiated and there is a greater openness to working with, and learning from, nongovernmental organisations. What is important now is that the momentum not be lost and that the shift in orientation be reflected at the implementation level and in the mind-set of service providers, programme implementers and policymakers on the one hand, and among clients on the other hand?

The review indicates that the vast majority of unmarried, sexually active adolescents are engaging in unprotected sex, and whenever they use a method, pregnancy prevention seems to be the overriding concern rather than preventing both pregnancy and sexually transmitted infections. This indicates the need for educational and counselling efforts emphasising the dual protection properties of condoms. There is evidence that trained traditional medical practitioners could be effectively engaged to increase contraceptive knowledge about reversible and non-reversible methods among rural women (Kambo et al., 1994). The involvement of the community in planning and monitoring remains minimal, and concerted efforts to promote community participation are needed. Research is also required to determine men's needs for services and information in specific communities. Operations research is required to assess how educational campaigns could effectively promote shared responsibilities. As methods of fertility regulation available to men are limited, priority should be given to developing male methods of family planning. Available evidence suggests that an increasing proportion of unmarried adolescents are sexually active. However, data on their contraceptive behaviours are grossly inadequate. Additional research is required to understand why women discontinue use, and whether efforts to provide detailed information under the new programmes have improved contraceptive continuation rates. Similarly, explorations into whether the new rhetoric on quality of care has been translated into reality and impacted contraceptive use dynamics are critically needed. Apart from data from the Reproductive and Child Health Survey–2 currently under way and a few small-scale studies, in-depth insights into the impact of new initiatives are scarce.

Declining fertility is in large part due to women's increased use of contraception. For the first time ever, more than half of the currently married women in India are using contraception, and their use of modern contraceptive methods increased from 43.0% to 49.0% between NFHS-2 and NFHS-3. A rise in the average age at marriage is also contributing to the drop in fertility. Forty-seven percent of women aged 20-24 were married before the legal age of marriage of 18 years, compared with 50.0% seven years earlier. This shift in age at marriage also influences the median age at first birth, which increased by six months to 19.8 years for women age 25-49. Knowledge of contraception is nearly universal: 98.0% of women and 99 percent of men age 15-49 know one or more methods of contraception. Over 94.0% of women and men know about female sterilization. More than four in five women and men know about contraceptive pills. Knowledge of contraception is widespread even among adolescents: 96.0% of young women and 97.0% of young men have heard of a modern method of contraception. Two-thirds of currently married women have used a family planning method at some time in their lives. Since NFHS-2, ever use of any method among currently married women has increased by 11 percentage points. The increase is greatest for spacing methods; ever use of condoms and the rhythm method has increased by 6 percentage points each. Slightly more than three in five women heard or saw a family planning message in the few months before the NFHS-3 survey, most often on television or radio. By contrast, over 90.0% of men have been exposed to family planning messages in the past few months.

In this article, we have outlined the process through which India has shifted its priorities from a narrow family planning focus to a broader reproductive health orientation in which quality and informed choice are prominent features, and we have identified the tasks that lie ahead in making this shift a reality. Altering the perspective of stakeholders to accept more fully the new approach, though, remains an overarching challenge that cannot be underestimated. It is somewhat naive to expect that well-entrenched practices and messages established over 25 years will change on their own, without resistance, simply because of a centrally sponsored policy change. Indeed, service providers, programme implementers and policymakers at all levels need to grasp, and be convinced of, the rationale underlying the shift in priorities and delivery strategies. Clients, equally, need to grasp that health services are their due and to demand accountability from the health system. It is critical that changes in priorities and programmes be translated and communicated effectively and convincingly.

REFERENCES

Cassen, R.H. (1978). *India: Population, Economy, Society.* New York: Holmes and Meier Publishers.

Gandhi, R. (1989). Gandhi Addresses The World on Family Planning, *International Family Planning Perspectives,* 15(3), 106-107.

International Institute for Population Sciences (IIPS) (1995). *National Family Health Survey (MCHand Family Planning), India 1992–93.* Mumbai: IIPS.

International Institute for Population Sciences (IIPS) and ORC Macro. (2000). *National Family Health Survey 2–India.* Mumbai: IIPS.

International Institute for Population Sciences (IIPS) and ORC Macro. (2005-06). *National Family Health Survey 3–India.* Mumbai: IIPS.

Kambo, I.P., Gupta, R.N., Kundu, A.S. et al., (1994). Use of Traditional Medical Practitioners to Deliver Family Planning Services in Uttar Pradesh, *Studies in Family Planning* 25(1), 32–40.

Mahadevan, K., Sivaraju, S., Reddy, P.J. and Sumangala, M. (1989). Development of Population Policies in India, In: K. Mahadevan (ed.) *Fertility Policies of Asian Countries* (New Delhi: Sage Publications), 187-213.

Ministry of Health and Family Welfare (MOHFW) (1997). *Reproductive and Child HealthProgramme: Schemes for Implementation.* New Delhi: MOHFW, Government of India.

——. (2000). *National Population Policy 2000.* New Delhi: MOHFW, Government of India. Department of Family Welfare, MOHFW, Government of India. Available online at: http://www.health.nic.in

Raina, B. L. (1994). *The Population Challenge,* B.R. Publishing Corp., Delhi.

Saavala, M., (1999). Understanding the Prevalence of Female Sterilization in Rural India, Studies in Family Planning, 30(4), 288-301.

Satia, J. K. and Giridhar, G. (1991). Supply Aspects Of Meeting Demand For Family Planning, in Satia, J.K. and Jejeebhoy, S.J., eds., *The Demographic Challenges: A Study of Four Large Indian States,* Bombay: Oxford University Press, 114–148.

Singh, H. (1989). Eighth Plan: Strategies And Approaches To Health And Family Welfare Programme in India, In N. Sawhaney and Others (eds.) *Present FW Programme Strategy: Some Alternatives* (Lucknow: Army Printing Press).

Visaria, L. and Visaria, P. (1998). Family Welfare Program in India After ICPD: A Case Study, Prepared For Cairo In Action: Review of Case Study Findings, Rockefeller Foundation, New York, Aug. 24–26.

World Bank, *India: Reproductive and Child Health Project,* Project Appraisal Document, Report No. 16393-IN, Washington DC: World Bank, 1997, p. 7.

Zeidenstein, G. (1989). Population Control: Strategies and Experiences, In: G.P. Talwar (ed.) *Contraception Research for Today and the Nineties: Progress in Birth Control Vaccines* (New York: Springer-Verlag).

19

Enhancing Family Planning Services among Couples in Urban Slums of Mumbai: Findings From An Intervention Study

Dr. Balaiah Donta, Dr. Dattaram, D. Naik, Dr. Saritha Nair, Dr. Umesh Iddya & Dr. Anil Bandivadekar

Summary

The Millennium Development Goals (MDGs) aim to promote human development by ensuring improvement in a range of areas including poverty alleviation, education, health and environment. To alleviate poverty and attain sustainable development, it is essential for couples to plan smaller families. For attaining this, in addition to creating awareness among men and women, it is important to provide quality family planning services. To provide better services, it is imperative to understand the family planning needs of the couples. This study tried to understand the various issues related to the dynamics of contraceptive use in the urban slums of Mumbai, the involvement of men, the challenges faced by the health care providers to meet the family planning needs of the urban slum dwellers and the impact of intervention. Baseline information were collected from three similar study areas and appropriate interventions were carried out by addressing men in experimental area one, addressing couples in experimental area two and continuing ongoing health programmes as before in the control area. After the intervention, data were collected to evaluate the impact of intervention in the contraceptive knowledge, practice and behaviour. Both pre and post intervention data were used to illustrate the various issues related to contraceptive use. Compared to the baseline, the majority of men (78.0% from experimental area-1 and 73.0% from experimental area-2) reported being more aware than before regarding the various contraceptives. Women's data also depicts similar results. The proportion tested for contraceptive use at the baseline and the post intervention survey among men, revealed a significant increase in condom use in both the experimental areas.

Introduction

The Millennium Development Goals (MDGs) aim to provide a new international framework for measuring progress towards sustaining development and eliminating poverty. Nonetheless, to eliminate poverty and realize sustainable development, it is imperative to attain reproductive health for all.

To attain reproductive health for all, in addition to creating awareness among men and women on various issues of reproductive health ranging from human sexuality to family planning, gender bias, high risk sexual behavior and STIs including HIV/AIDS, it is important to provide better reproductive health care services. Reproductive health of couples is influenced by a blend of biological, cultural, and psychosocial factors. Hence, attainment of reproductive health requires a multi-faceted intervention. Providing reproductive health service is an inevitable intervention to address the various reproductive health problems faced by men and women.

Reproductive health services include family planning to help men and women to avoid high-risk pregnancies and increase the time between births, thereby preventing maternal deaths and improving the quality of life. Also, these services help reduce the various reproductive illnesses by providing access to better information and services to couples. Health care providers, especially reproductive health care providers, can play a major role in addressing the various reproductive health issues, by providing integrated services. Nonetheless, to provide better services, it is imperative to understand the needs and reproductive health problems of the couples.

Family planning has not been explicitly cited among the Millennium Development Goals, but is one of the important means towards attaining the goals mentioned. As more people adopt family planning, fertility rates drop and population growth slows down. This is a major boon in protecting the environment, as slower population growth conserves resources, preserves clean air and water, improves health, eases pressure on cities, and helps avoid conflict. Slower population growth aids development. It buys time and, with more of the population in their productive years, provides a demographic bonus that can be invested in education, job creation, health care and other efforts to raise living standards (Ray, 1995). The sooner fertility falls to low levels, the better most countries will be able to achieve sustainable development. This would be one of the means towards reducing poverty, reducing maternal mortality, infant and child mortality and also attaining gender equality (Potts and Fotso, 2007).

There has been a general agreement among the countries in the world, particularly after the International Conference on Population and Development (ICPD), held at Cairo in 1994, that there is a need for ensuring participation of men in family planning and reproductive health with a view to promote gender equality, share reproductive responsibilities and also to meet the men's own reproductive health needs. At the 1994 International Conference on Population and Development (ICPD), held in Cairo, representatives from more than 180 countries formally recognized the importance of men in improving women's reproductive health and also recognized the importance of men's own reproductive health (Basu, 1994). The movement to involve men in reproductive health has many names, that is, men vis–a-vis participation, responsibility, motivation, as partners and reproductive health (Helzner, 1996). Whatever the term used, the purpose is to describe a complex process of social and behavioural change that is needed for men to play more responsible roles in reproductive health. Men's participation can be seen as a means to an end, rather than as a goal in itself. The goal is good reproductive health for all, and men can help in many different ways to make that a reality. The changes needed in men's sexual and reproductive behaviour suggest that programmes should focus on communicating with men and couples (Green and Danforth, 1996). When more men know the basic facts about and the benefits of condoms and vasectomy, more will prefer and use these (AVSC International, 1997).

In many countries, family planning clinics are already encouraging men's participation. Since 1990, the number of reproductive health activities that include men has increased sharply (Danforth and Green, 1997; Green, 1997). Experience in Brazil, Colombia, and Uganda suggests that men accept information and services from either male or female counsellors or providers so long as the providers are knowledgeable and respectful. Providers can advice and suggest well by being aware of men's concerns. When men visit clinics, at first they may want to talk about something other than the real reason for the visit.

In India, according to a study conducted in Agra (Khan and Patel, 1997), 85.0% men approved of family planning after two children, 65.0% believed that men should initiate discussion on reproduction and about a quarter (29.0%) indicated an unmet need for family planning. But most of them did not want to undergo vasectomy, as they believed it would cause weakness and its failure could cause social disaster. Nor did men like to use condoms because of their poor quality and non-availability when required. Studies conducted in Mumbai and Thane districts of Maharashtra have also revealed a similar trend: FP acceptance was very low among 3072 married men in one Primary Health Centre (PHC) area consisting of 86 villages (4.5%) and 550 married men in village Juchandra (3.0%) (Balaiah et al., 1999 and 2001). Even urban data reveal no different picture (Balaiah et al., 1997 and 2001).

A few intervention studies made an attempt and succeeded up to some extent to enhance the participation of men in the welfare of their families. A study conducted in the central part of Mumbai, India, demonstrated that involving male service providers i.e., male social workers and male clinicians in the programme and expanding educational efforts at the community and the clinic levels, one can promote the small family norm, reduce prevalence for male children preference, increase the knowledge of correct use of various contraceptive methods, improve inter-spouse communication regarding family planning issues, reduce vasectomy-related misconceptions and increase overall contraceptive use (Balaiah et al., 2005). Another study conducted in the Iloilo province of Philippines revealed that the contraceptive prevalence rate significantly increased in intervention areas as compared to the control area due to the mobilization, training and involvement of volunteer health workers and male peer counsellors (Teresita Adle-Chuva et al., 2005). A study conducted in Jordan through the 'Together for a Happy

Family' campaign contributed to a marked improvement in the knowledge and attitudes of Jordanian men and women regarding specific modern family planning methods. Royal endorsement, religious leaders' involvement and support, private sector leverage and strategic planning helped to create positive social norms (Soliman and Amjad, 2005).

Gender roles and norms are culturally specific and thus vary tremendously around the world. Almost everywhere, however, men and women differ substantially from each other in power, status, and freedom. In virtually all societies men have more power than women have (Berer, 1996). Generally, young women who marry much older men have less power than women who marry someone closer in age to them. Research over more than 40 years consistently demonstrates that men and women who discuss family planning are more likely to use contraception, to use it effectively, and to have fewer children (De Silva, 1994). Spousal communication is an important way of including men. 'Since men, as well as women, play key roles in reproductive health, communication is necessary for making responsible, healthy decisions' (Drenen, 1998). In particular, better-educated women can communicate more easily with their husbands. A woman who has some economic power also may be more likely to discuss family planning with her husband. In Togo, women who worked for cash and invested some of it in credit or savings plans reported the highest levels of communication with their husbands about family planning. The level was substantially higher than among women who worked for cash but did not invest or who did not work for cash at all (Gage, 1995).

Most of the research has been either male-oriented or female-oriented, and has indicated the need to understand both the husband's and the wife's perspective of contraceptive knowledge and usage. Increasingly, health care providers and researchers are realizing that the most appropriate client for reproductive health information and services may be the couple rather than the individual (Becker, 1996; Becker and Robinson, 1998). Thus, understanding the perspectives of the couples would help design appropriate interventions for effective utilization of family planning services. In addition to the IEC messages and community-based campaigns, it is essential to orient the providers regarding the clients' demands, needs and expectations. Also the challenges faced by the provider in providing these services need to be understood in order to enhance the overall acceptance and knowledge of contraception.

Objectives

This study made an attempt to understand the various issues related to dynamics of contraceptive usages in the urban slums, the involvement of men, the challenges faced by the health care providers to meet the family planning needs of the urban slum dwellers and the impact of the intervention.

Method

The study draws data from a larger study on 'Interventions in urban slums for enhancing participation of men in reproductive health' funded by the Ministry of Health and Family Welfare, Government of India, in collaboration with the Municipal Corporation of Greater Mumbai.

Study Design: This intervention study was carried out in three similar urban slums of L ward, Kurla and Ghatkopar area of the Municipal Corporation of Greater Mumbai (MCGM). One is experimental area-1 (Mohili village) where intervention was addressed to husbands only, second is experimental area-2 (Bail Bazar) where intervention was addressed to couples and third was the control area (Asalfa village) where there was no intervention. The motto of the intervention was to enhance knowledge about reproductive health issues among men and take appropriate actions to motivate couples to seek and avail reproductive health services. The ongoing government reproductive health and family planning programmes continued in all the three selected areas.

Being an intervention study, assuming 50.0% (P1=0.50) of contraceptive (male and female methods) use among couples in baseline and an expected increase of 10.0% at least (P2=0.10) after intervention with 95.0% confidence limits (a=0.05; two tailed) and 90.0% power of the test (b=0.10), the required sample size was estimated as 518 subjects for each group. Thus around 550 couples were selected from each group. Systematic random sampling method was adopted to select married couples. In total, information regarding family planning issues was collected through structured interviews from 1755 couples during the baseline study and 1728 couples were interviewed during post intervention survey.

Baseline data has been obtained from a random sample of 1755 eligible couples through semi-structured interview schedule from the above-mentioned three slum areas of the city of Mumbai during 2005. Collecting information from both husband and wife provides opportunity to understand their reproductive health and also offers necessary information for health care providers so that appropriate measures can be taken. Data include socio-economic and demographic information about the couples and their reproductive health perceptions and practices including family planning, maternal health and STIs/RTIs including HIV/AIDS and health-seeking behaviour. In order to avoid contamination of information, male and female investigators collected information separately from the husband and the wife on the same day. Informed consent was obtained from both the husband and the wife before the respective interviews. Privacy of the respondent and confidentiality of the information was taken care of by the interviewers. Focus group discussions among men and women were conducted to elicit information on family planning. This information has been used to substantiate the survey data. After the intervention period, to assess the effectiveness of the intervention, post intervention survey was conducted during July – December 2007 in the same community and the same parameters measured during the time of baseline were reassessed. For the current paper, data pertaining to family planning issues have been analyzed. Also, specific information with regard to family planning intervention has been provided. Information from both the husband and the wife has been analyzed and presented in the paper.

This paper starts by describing the health care scenario of the study areas and the community settings, and then proceeds to describe the observations from the baseline data on family planning matters. Following this are illustrated the interventions carried out in the community in order to bring about a change with regard to family welfare, and the findings from the post-intervention survey are presented. Information pertaining to both men and women has been used for the purpose of analysis. The paper concludes by providing the discussion and recommendations for future research and programmes.

The Health Care Scenario

There are nine health posts, and a major municipal hospital named K. B. Bhabha Hospital, located in L-Ward area. There are 18 private nursing homes and around 150 healthcare providers practicing Allopathic, Ayurveda, Homoepathy, Unani, Siddhi as well as other medicinal practices not related to these. Men and women of this area refer to these service providers for their immediate concerns.

Study Setting

Around 1,00,000 people lives in each of the three areas selected for study. The population belongs to low socio-economic status with majority of the men working as unskilled labourers. There are many political and cultural groups, anganwadi/balawadi, sports clubs/mandals and non-governmental organizations, like World Vision working on community development and Lok Seva Sangam providing services for leprosy and tuberculosis to the population in the community. Even women's groups are present in the area.

Profile of the Respondents

Majority (70.0%) of the couples were Hindus, followed

by Muslims (20.3%) and Buddist (5.8%). About 72.0% of the respondents belonged to nuclear families. The mean age of the husbands was 37.18 (S.D. ± 7.93), the ages ranging from 19 to 60 years. Majority (45.2%) of them had secondary school education. The occupational status of the men indicated that 39.0% were unskilled. Forty one percent of the wives were between 17 and 29 years of age (SD. ± 6.8). Majority (49.2%) of the women had education up to level upper primary with the mean being 6.97 (S. D. ± 4.40) years of the women education. Majority were (91.4%) housewives and 8.6% were working (paid work). Income status of couples indicated that 42.2% of the couple had income up to Rs. 3000/- per month. About 41.0% of the couples had three or more living children. The average interval between two births as reported by men and women was 39 months. An almost similar profile is obtained for the respondents of the post-intervention survey.

Pre-Intervention Results

To assess the awareness, knowledge and practice of contraceptives, specific responses pertaining to these were elicited from the couples. In addition, information on decision to use the contraceptives, inter-spousal communication and health-seeking behaviour was also collected. Following is the description of the information collected on each of the parameters:

Correct Knowledge of Contraceptive Methods

About 72.0% of the husbands and 34.8% of the wives had correct knowledge about condom; 56.3% of husbands and 33.1% of the wives had knowledge of oral pills; 51.2% of the husbands and 33.8% of the wives had knowledge of IUD; 74.3% of the husbands and 53.3% of the wives had knowledge of tubectomy; 54.1% of the husbands and 15.6% of the wives had correct knowledge of vasectomy, one % of the husbands and 0.4% of the wives heard of non-scalpel vasectomy; 8.3% of the husbands and 2.4% of the wives had correct knowledge of injectables, 0.4% of the husbands and 0.1% of the wives had correct knowledge of emergency contraception, similarly

0.8% of the husbands and 0.4% of the wives had correct knowledge of female condoms (Table 1).

Regarding the natural method, about 49.0% of the husbands and 17.6% of the wives had correct knowledge of withdrawal; 11.5% of the husbands and 10.6% of the wives had correct knowledge about rhythm; and 32.1% of the husbands and 9.9% of the wives had knowledge of abstinence. Significant differences were observed between the husband's and the wive's knowledge regarding male condom, oral pills, IUD, tubectomy, vasectomy, non-scalpel vasectomy, injectables, withdrawal, rhythm and abstinence, while no differences observed with respect to female condom and emergency contraception.

Table 1
Correct Knowledge about Contraceptive Methods (Pre and Post Intervention)

Contraceptive Methods	*Husband*		*Wife*	
	Pre-intervention (N=1755)	*Post-intervention (N=1728)*	*Pre-intervention (N=1755)*	*Post-intervention (N=1728)*
Male Condom	72.3	91.7	34.8	75.5
Oral Pills	56.3	66.8	33.1	68.6
IUD	51.2	67.4	33.8	61.6
Tubectomy	74.3	78.6	53.3	82.0
Vasectomy (Traditional)	54.1	59.5	15.6	62.8
Non-Scalpel Vasectomy	1.0	49.8	0.4	27.1
Injectables	8.3	66.6	2.4	21.1
Emergency Contraception	0.4	14.2	0.1	7.0
Female Condom	0.8	5.3	0.4	1.7
Withdrawal	48.8	77.8	17.6	24.0
Rhythm	11.5	72.5	10.6	25.0
Abstinence	32.1	78.4	9.9	24.5

In order to understand more about vasectomy so as to promote male involvement not only in encouraging the use of methods by women but also use by men - reasons for not adopting vasectomy were elicited. Both the men and the women groups felt that men do not accept contraception because of lack of correct knowledge about contraceptive methods and poor motivation. The focus group discussions among men and women reveal that both men and women felt that men would become physically weak after adopting vasectomy and as men are the chief earners for the family they should not go for vasectomy. Also they felt that failure of vasectomy may cause social problems, such as the consequence of women becoming pregnant despite their husband having undergone vasectomy. The woman would then be ostracized by the society as she would be suspected of having illicit relationship. Both the men and the women said that the health care provider also advised women to undergo tubectomy rather than advising the men to undergo vasectomy. Most of the men and the majority of the women said that the women were being forced to go for tubectomy by their husbands. Even for spacing methods, the burden of using methods is more on women as reported by both men and women. About 70 % of the husbands and 42.7% of the wives reported that they discussed about using the spacing methods with their spouses. There are significant differences among study areas with respect to husbands, wives and also between the husbands and the wives reporting of having discussions with each other on use of contraceptives. Almost similar percentage was reported with regard to the use of permanent method(s).

Most of the husbands (99.0%) and wives (96.5%) reported television to be a source of information, followed by hospitals (94.5% husbands and 88.6% wives). With respect to IEC material, 58.1% of the husbands and 41.8% of the wives received information from displayed IEC material (Table 2).

Even regarding the source of information, significant differences are observed between husbands, and wives' reporting of source of contraceptive information - hospitals, newspapers, displayed IEC material or various awareness programmes. This clearly calls for different strategies of reaching husbands and wives for dissemination of information.

Questions were asked regarding the need for interval between two births so as to understand the couples' desire to use family planning methods to space the birth of kids. Almost all of husbands and wives felt that there should be interval between the births of children. Majority of the men and women reported that 2 to 3 years interval is the ideal interval. Significant difference was observed between the husbands' and the wives' reporting need for interval between two births.

On the timing of use of contraception, majority of the men and their wives were of the opinion that a couple should start using contraceptives after the birth of the first child. Regarding decisions on the contraceptives to choose and use, both (husband and wife) said that usually joint decisions were being taken regarding the use of contraceptive methods. The type of method to be used is usually suggested by the health care provider. Both the husband and the wife feel that communication between husband and wife regarding the use of spacing method is low and they mainly discussed the adoption of permanent method after completing the desired family size.

About 66.0% of the couples reported that they were using one or another method of contraception (Table 3). A little more than two-fifths of the husbands (43.4%) reported that their wives had undergone tubectomy and 10.1% of the husbands reported that they are using condom as a contraceptive method. Only one person had undergone vasectomy. Regarding future intentions to use contraceptives, 30.0% of the husbands reported that they would not like to use contraceptive method in the future. Of these, majority of the husbands (36.7%) reported that adoption of FP was against their religion. About one third (32.0%) of the men reported that they used condom in the past. Analysis of the wives' data depicts similar results.

The observations indicate the need for intervention on a range of issues, starting from decision making to usage of family planning methods, specifically the methods used by men. The data also throw light on the major role health care providers could take in promoting any family planning method as they have been reported as one of the sources of information on family planning. Also, since men and women visit the health care providers for issues ranging from minor illness to serious matters, this provides opportunity for the health care providers to discuss family planning issues with the couples.

Interventions

Various interventions programmes have been carried out for only married men in intervention area-1 and for couples in intervention area-2 during the period April 2006 to March 2007. The intervention programmes have been through Information, Education and Counseling (IEC). The clinical and other services provided at the MCGM health posts are supported by the staff from the institute. Several issues concerning both genders were addressed through the various programmes. The current paper provides information only on the programmes related to family planning, though it may be noted that a holistic approach of providing information on all aspects of reproductive health was followed. The following paragraph provides a brief description of the programmes, which tried addressing the various issues related to family planning among couples in the urban slum community.

(i) Street Plays

Street plays were organized in both areas on issues

concerning, family planning and contraception. Five street plays were organized in each of the experimental areas (i.e., experimental area-1 and experimental area-2) on family planning and contraception; 2475 persons from experimental area-1 and 2025 persons from experimental area-2 attended.

(ii) Smaller Group Meetings

Information on family planning and contraception was provided in smaller group meetings. In the area -1, 292 group meetings were organized for husbands, in which 2089 husbands took part. In the area-2, 126, 128 and 41 meetings were organized for husbands, wives and couples respectively, in which 866 husbands, 1002 wives and 170 couples participated respectively.

(iii) Inter-personal Communication (IPC)

Men from area-1, as well as men, women and couples from area-2 were contacted personally and information on issues concerning family planning and contraception was provided to 2683 husbands from Mohili Village and 1006 husbands, 1260 wives and 1247 couples from Bail Bazar. Information on the correct use of condoms was provided to 2799 husbands from Mohili Village and 1090 husbands, 1359 wives and 1454 couples from Bail Bazar. Information on non-scalpel vasectomy (NSV) was provided to 1598 husbands from Mohili Village, and 934 husbands, 1210 wives and 1164 couples from Bail Bazar.

(iva) IEC Material (Self Learning Material)

Pamphlets containing information with messages for men on safe motherhood and family planning were prepared and distributed to 4500 men in experimental area-1 and 4500 couples in experimental area-2.

(ivb) Educational Programmes On Reproductive Health Issues

Twenty-nine audio-visual programmes were organized

for providing information on family planning in Mohili village, in which 908 husbands attended. In Bail Bazar, 23 programmes were organized, 123 wives and 140 couples attended the same programmes.

(v) Orientation Programmes to Staff Involved in Health Centres and Community Programmes

Two orientation programmes on family planning, contraception and reproductive health were organized in each experimental area for Integrated Child Development Scheme (ICDS) project staff (i.e., anganwadi teachers and workers) and peer volunteers from both the experimental areas (i.e. experimental area-1 and experimental area-2). Fifteen ICDS project staff and 10 peer volunteers from Mohili Village and sixteen ICDS project staff and 10 peer volunteers from Bail Bazar attended these programmes.

(vi) Contact Visits

Project teams along with Community Health Volunteers (CHVs) made 102, 13 and 95, visits respectively to general physicians, local mandal/NGOs and Volunteers in experimental area-1 (Mohili Village). The corresponding figures for experimental area-2 (Bail Bazar) are 109, 12 and 93 visits respectively. The purpose of the visit was to solicit the cooperation of General Physicians, Local mandal/NGOs and volunteers co-operation in achieving the goal of the study.

(vii) Counselling Clinic

As a part of the intervention, counselling services were provided since September 2005 in area-1 at the municipal health post Mohili Village and in area-2, at Bail Bazar municipal health post. Counselling and information on family planning issues such as spacing contraceptive methods and Non Scalpel Vasectomy (NSV) were provided in these clinics once in a week on Monday in area-1 and on Tuesday in area-

2 health post. In experimental area-1, 389 husbands, 14 wives and 117 couples attended to this clinic whereas, in experimental area-2, 86 husbands, 490 wives and 87 couples attended this counselling clinic.

(viii) Services for Addressing Reproductive Health Concerns

As a part of interventions, a clinic for Reproductive Health Services, 'Clinic for Men', was initiated at the Mohili Village Municipal health post, and a 'Clinic for Couples' was initiated at Bail Bazar Municipal health post for couples in the month of June 2006. Both the clinics functioned on Sunday between 10.00 am to 1.00 pm. These activities continued during the year 2007-2008. Apart from providing services on family planning issues, other reproductive health problems (white discharge, primary and secondary infertility, sexual problems, sexually transmitted infections, gynecological problems, burning micturition), information on ANC/PNC, counselling for HIV positive and suspected cases, motivation for condom use and information on reproductive health issues were provided in these clinics by medical and para-medical staff.

In the experimental area-1, 126 husbands, 45 wives and 177 couples attended the clinic for men whereas, in experimental area-2, 73 husbands, 447 wives and 333 couples attended the clinic for couples. In the experimental area-1, 23 husbands, 47 wives and 147 couples attended the clinic for men for follow-up services whereas, in experimental area-2, 58 husbands, 596 wives and 205 couples attended the clinic for couples for follow-up services.

Post-intervention Results

The intervention was followed by the post-intervention survey, which was started in July 2007 and was completed in December 2007. During this period, 555 couples were interviewed from experimental area–2, 598 from experimental area–1 and 575 from the control area (Asalfa Village).

The same questionnaire was used to collect information on different issues of reproductive health. Table 1 illustrates the increase in contraceptive knowledge among both husbands and wives at the post intervention compared to pre-intervention. Regarding the knowledge of contraceptives, compared to the control area, both the experimental areas had better knowledge, clearly depicting the influence of the interventions carried out by the study. In experimental area-1 and 2, almost all the men (98.7%) had correct knowledge about condom. However, in the case of control area, a little more than three-fourth of the (77.4%) men had the correct knowledge. The women's data also depicts a similar picture. Majority of the women in the experimental area-1 (85.8%) and area-2 (96.9%), compared to only 44.0% women of the control area, had the correct knowledge regarding condom. Similar results are observed with regard to oral pills, IUD and tubectomy. Knowledge regarding injectables has increased considerably among the men in the experimental areas. Similar trend is observed in the case of the women's data. However, the increase has been minimal. Among all the methods, the increase in knowledge regarding emergency contraception has been the least. Knowledge regarding traditional vasectomy had increased both among men and women in the experimental areas. Comparatively, knowledge regarding non-scalpel vasectomy is less, though at post-intervention study the results have showed an upward trend.

Among the sources of information regarding contraceptives, in addition to television, hospital, radio, newspaper, IEC material and private clinics have been also been able to provide information on contraceptives among husbands and wives during the post-intervention survey as illustrated by Table 2. Area-wise analysis shows that almost all the men (94.5%) in experimental area-1 and 87.4% of the men in experimental area-2 reported having received information from the private clinics. In the case of women, though the figures are relatively less, more women (35.6% in experimental area-1 and 25.6% in experimental area-2) compared to both baseline and control areas have reported that they received information from the private clinics. This could be attributed to the intervention programmes in the community.

Table 2
Source of Contraceptive Information
(Pre-and Post-intervention)

Source of Contraceptive Information	*Husband*		*Wife*	
	Pre-intervention (N=1755)	*Post-intervention (N=1728)*	*Pre-intervention (N=1755)*	*Post-intervention (N=1728)*
Television	98.7	99.4	96.5	98.9
Hospital	95.4	92.7	88.6	93.3
Radio	72.7	89.1	73.5	91.2
Newspaper	69.9	87.4	34.8	36.6
Displayed IEC material	58.1	75.1	41.8	55.6
Printed IEC material	16.6	68.8	4.2	59.6
Private clinic	11.6	83.4	2.2	31.3
Awareness Program	3.5	54.7	39.5	16.4

On the current contraceptive usage, majority of the men (34.6% in experimental area-1 and 33.5% in experimental area-2) reported tubectomy as the method of contraception used. This is followed by usage of condom. One-fifth of the men in both experimental areas reported using condom (Table 3). Comparison of data with pre-intervention data, using proportion test, illustrates significant improvement in the usage of condom in both the experimental areas. A major achievement, though small in number, has been the number of men who have reported having undergone vasectomy. Three men have reported having undergone vasectomy.

Discussion and Conclusion

Apart from the educational messages and interpersonal communication to address the reproductive health issues, results depict the need for dedicated health services. Though the reproductive health programme was launched in the state in 1997, it has not been able to satisfactorily address the various issues surrounding reproductive health. The success of the reproductive health services provided by the project calls for the following strategies to be incorporated in the health system, so as to provide efficient services with respect to reproductive health.

Repeated contact visits to the health posts and advocacy work on client satisfaction and motivation among health post staff (including Community Health Volunteers) has been able to make a difference. The increased use of contraceptives for spacing as well as limiting pregnancies could be attributed to this. Regarding health care facilities, availability time of health care services was an important issue; both men and women prefer the health post service to be available on all days, including Sundays and holidays, so that both husband and the wife can go together. Currently the health post is open during the time when men go out for work. This causes inhibition in men as well as women, as going to the health post would mean losing a day's income, or men not being able to accompany women or not being able to consult the physician for his own reproductive health problems.

Thus combined effort of approaching the community with the IEC messages (both printed messages and street plays) and services providing at convenient time for couples has enhanced the knowledge of the clients, thus empowering them

Table 3
Current Contraceptive Use by Area
(Pre and Post Intervention)

Current contraceptive use	*Pre-Intervention*				*Post-intervention*			
	Exp –1 (N=606)	*Exp –2 (N=561)*	*Control (N=588)*	*Total (N=1755)*	*Exp –1 (N=598)*	*Exp –2 (N=555)*	*Control (N=575)*	*Total (N=1728)*
Male Methods								
Condom	64 (10.6)	44 (7.8)	70 (11.9)	178 (10.1)	127 (21.2)	114 (20.5)	75 (13.0)	316 (18.3)
Withdrawal	30 (5.0)	31 (5.5)	46 (7.8)	107 (6.1)	38 (6.4)	7 (1.3)	18 (3.1)	63 (28.6)
Vasectomy	0 (0.0)	1 (0.2)	0 (0.0)	1 (0.1)	0 (0.0)	1 (0.2)	0 (0.0)	1 (0.1)
Non Scalpel Vasectomy	-	-	-	-	2 (0.3)	0 (0.0)	0 (0.0)	2 (0.1)
Female Methods								
Oral pills	39 (6.4)	30 (5.3)	31 (5.4)	100 (5.7)	28 (4.7)	24 (4.3)	40 (7.0)	92 (5.3)
IUD	25 (4.1)	27 (4.8)	45 (7.7)	97 (5.5)	40 (6.7)	27 (4.9)	43 (7.5)	110 (6.4)
Abstinence	6 (1.0)	8 (1.4)	9 (1.5)	23 (1.3)	12 (2.0)	10 (1.8)	1 (0.2)	23 (1.3)
Rhythm	22 (3.6)	9 (1.6)	29 (4.9)	60 (3.4)	16 (2.7)	15 (2.7)	12 (2.1)	43 (2.5)
Injectables	1 (0.2)	1 (0.2)	0 (0.0)	2 (0.1)	2 (0.3)	0 (0.0)	0 (0.0)	2 (0.1)
Tubectomy	277 (45.7)	246 (43.9)	238 (40.5)	761 (43.4)	207 (34.6)	186 (33.5)	226 (33.5)	619 (35.8)
No Method								
No method	142 (23.4)	164 (29.2)	120 (20.4)	426 (24.3)	126 (21.1)	171 (30.8)	160 (27.8)	457 (26.4)

$\chi^2 = 42.399$ D.F. = 18 p-value = 0.001 $\chi^2 = 74.657$ D.F. = 20 p-value < 0.001

to make a choice regarding the method. The increased condom use can also be applauded for two reasons: i) for men being supportive in the use of contraceptives, thus spacing births; ii) for condom being used to protect couples from getting any sexually transmitted infections.

Acknowledgements

We are grateful to Dr. C. P. Puri, former Director, National Institute for Research in Reproductive Health for his continuous support and encouragement in successfully completing the study. We sincerely thank the Executive Health Officer (EHO), Municipal Corporation of Greater Mumbai, and the staff of Mohili village, Bail Bazar and Asalfa village health post, who helped in contacting men in the respective areas. We express our appreciation to the Ministry of Health and Family Welfare (MOHFW), Government of India, for providing financial assistance for conducting this study.

REFERENCES

AVSC International. Profamilia's Clinic For Men: A Case Study: New York, AVSC International, 1997,41p.

Balaiah, D., Ghule, M., Naik, D.D., Parida, R.C. and Hazari, K.T. (1997). Fertility Attitudes of Men in an Urban Setting - A Cross Sectional Survey Analysis. *Advances in Contraceptive Delivery Systems* 13 (1,2),1-11.

Balaiah, D., Naik, D.D., Parida, R.C., Ghule, M. and Hazari, K.T. (1999). Contraceptive Knowledge, Attitude and Practices of Men in Rural Maharashtra. *Advances in Contraception* 15, 217-234.

Balaiah, D., Ghule, M., Naik, D.D., Tapase, P., Iddya U., Parida R.C., Hazari K.T. and Kanbur A. (2001). Son Preference and Family Planning Practices among Married Men in Mumbai, India" *Reproduction and Contraception* 12 (4), 226-239.

Balaiah, D., Ghule, M., Naik, D.D., Parida, R.C. and Hazari, K.T. (2001). Fertility Attitudes and Family Planning Practices of Men in a Rural Community of Maharashtra. *The Journal of Family Welfare* 47 (1), 56-67.

Balaiah, D. et al., (2005). Participation of Men in Family Welfare: Learning From an Intervention Study in Mumbai, India. In: *Enhancing Male Partnership in Sexual And Reproductive Health.* Eds. Balaiah Donta, Kirsten M Vogelsong, Paul FA Van Look and Chander P Puri. Sha and Shaz Enterprises, Mumbai, 451-470.

Basu, A.M. (1994). The International Conference on Population and Development. Cairo. 1994. Is its Plan of Action Important, Desirable and Feasible? *Health Transition Review* 6(2), 225-229. Oct. 1996.

Becker, S. (1996). Couples and Reproductive Health: A Review of Couples Studies in Family Planning, 276(6): 291-306.. Nov/ Dec 1996.

Becker, S. and Robinson, J, C. (1998). Reproductive Health Care: Services Oriented to Couples. *International Journal of Gynaecology and Obstetrics.* 61(3): 275-281.

Berer, M. (1996). Men Reproductive Health Matters (7): 7-11.

Best, K. (1998). Men's Reproductive Health Risks. Network 18 (3): 7-10. Research Triangle Park, Family Health International. Spring, 1998.

Danforth, N. and Green, C.P. (i997). Involving Men in Reproductive Health: A Review of USAID-Funded Activities. Arlington, Virginia, Population Technical Assistance Project. 66.

De Silva, W. I. (1994). Husband-wife Communication and Contraceptive Behaviour in Sri Lanka, *Journal of Family Welfare,* 40 (2).

Drennan, M. (1998). Reproductive Health: New Perspectives on Men's Participation. Population Reports, Series J, No.46. Baltimore, Johns Hopkins University School of Public Health, Population Information Program.

Gage, A. J. (1995). Women's Socioeconomic Position, Contraceptive Use and Fertility Preference in Togo. *Studies in Family Planning* 26(5): 264-77.

Green, C.P. (1977). Male Reproductive Health Services: A Review of The Literature. New York. AVSC International, 76.

Green, C.P and Danforth, N. (1996). Involving Men in Reproductive Health: Policy Implications for Developing Countries. Presented at the Annual Meeting of the American Public Health Association, New York, 8.

Helzner, J.F. (1996). Men's Involvement in Family Planning. *Reproductive Health Matters* (7): 146-154.

Khan, M.E. and Patel, B.C. (1997). Male Involvement in Family Planning: A KABP Study of Agra District, India. Final Report. New Delhi: Population Council, Asia and Near East Operations Research and Technical Assistance Project, 27.

Potts, Malcolm and Jean-Christophe, Fosto (2007). Population Growth and the Millennium Development Goals, February, 369, 9559, 354-355.

Ray, M. (1995). Economics of Population and Development. *Economic and Political Weekly* Sept 9: 30 (6), 2263-2268.

Soliman, Farah and Amjad, Nawwas (2005). Reaching Men Through Entertainment Education. In: *Enhancing Male Partnership in Sexual and Reproductive Health.* Eds. Balaiah Donta, Kirsten M. Vogelsong, Paul, F.A. Van, Look and Chander. P., Puri. Sha and Shaz, Enterprises, Mumbai, 491-503.

Teresita, Adle-Chuva, Fely P David and Naida G Pasion (2005). An Evaluation of a Family Planning Intervention: Male Peer Counselors Versus Volunteer Health Workers as Educators and Motivators. In: *Enhancing Male Partnership in Sexual and Reproductive Health.* Eds. Balaiah, Donta, Kirsten, M. Vogelsong, Paul, F.A. Van, Look and Chander, P., Puri, Sha and Shaz, Enterprises, Mumbai. Pg 433-450.

United Nations International Conference on Population and Development 'Programme of Action of a Conference' Cairo, September 1994.

20

Family Welfare Programme in West Bengal as Reflected in the NFHS Results

Dr. J. N. Pandit

Summary

The Governmer of West Bengal implemented the National Family Welfare Programme in 1951, along with other parts of India, with the objective of reducing the birth rate to the extent necessary to stabilize the population at a level consistent with the requirement of the national economy. The programme evolved through the different Five Year Plans like fourth Five Year Plan (1969-74): The programme was clinically oriented. High priority was accorded to reduce the birth rate from 35 to 32. The objective of the Fifth Five-Year Plan (1974-79) was to reducing the birth rate to 30. There was phenomenal increase in sterilization. However rigidity in enforcement brought about a setback. Family Planning Programme was renamed 'Family Welfare Programme' (FWP). The change was not merely in nomenclature but essentially in the content of its objectives. The objective of the Sixth Five-Year Plan (1980-85) was to reduce the average size of the family from 4.4 children to 2.3 children; reduce birth rate to 21, and increase couple protection rate from 22.0% to 60.0%. The objective of the Seventh Five-Year Plan (1985 to 1990) was to decentralize the services through extension of facilities. The objectives of the Eighth Five-Year Plan (1992-97) were to impart impetus to the FWP new area projects such as IPP IV, IPP VIII (for urban areas), Universal Immunization Programme and Child Survival and Safe Motherhood Programme. The objective of the Tenth Five Year Plan (1997-2002) was to meet all felt-needs for contraception, reduce maternal and infant mortality, assess reproductive needs and undertake area-specific micro planning and to provide need-based, demand driven, high quality, integrated reproductive and child health care. For limitation of the family, temporary and permanent family planning methods were introduced, which were being implemented through the public and private sector, including NGOs. With a view to assess independently the achievement of the Family Welfare Programme, the Government of India carried out three National Family Health Surveys during 1992-93, 1998-99 and 2005-06. The surveys dealt with the use of modern methods, female sterilization, male sterilization, IUD, oral pills, condom, unmet need for family planning, unmet need for spacing and unmet need for limiting methods. The surveys revealed over the years as to how the programme has progressed. They revealed the status of utilization amongst the rural, urban and Kolkata population, acceptance amongst the non-literates and the different categories of literates. The analysis assisted the planners and implementers in adopting modified strategies or mid-course corrective measures.

Introduction

The Government of West Bengal implemented the National Family Welfare Programme in 1951, along with other parts of India, with the objective of 'reducing the birth rate to the extent necessary to stabilize the population at a level consistent with the requirement of the national economy'.

The Family Welfare Programme is recognized as a priority area, and is being implemented as a 100% centrally sponsored programme. As per the Constitution of India, Family Planning is in the concurrent list. The approach under the programme during the First and Second Five Year Plans was mainly 'Clinical', under which facilities for provision of services were created. However, on the basis of data brought out by the 1961 census, the clinical approach adopted in the first two plans was replaced by 'Extension and Education Approach' which envisaged expansion of services facilities along with spread of the message of small family norm.

Evolution of Family Welfare Program

Fourth Five-Year Plan: In the Fourth Plan (1969-74), high priority was accorded to the programme and it was proposed to reduce birth rate from 35 per thousand to 32 per thousand by the end of the plan period.

Fifth Five-Year Plan: The objective of the Fifth Plan (1974-79) was to bring down the birth rate to 30 per thousand by the end of 1978-79. The programme was included as a priority sector programme during the Fifth Plan with increasing integration of family planning services with those of Health, Maternal and Child Health (MCH) and nutrition, so that the programme became more readily acceptable. The years 1975-76 and 1976-77 recorded a phenomenal increase in performance of sterilization. However, in view of the rigidity in enforcement of targets by field functionaries and an element of coercion in the implementation of the programme in 1976-77 in some areas, the programme received a setback during 1977-78. As a result, the Government made it clear that there was no place for force or coercion or compulsion or pressure of any sort under the programme and the programme had to be implemented as an integral part of

'Family Welfare', relying solely on mass education and motivation. The name of the programme was changed to Family Welfare from Family Planning. The change was not merely in nomenclature but essentially in the content of its objectives.

Sixth Five-Year Plan: In the Sixth Plan (1980-85), certain long-term demographic goals of reaching net reproduction rate of unity were envisaged. The implications of this were to achieve the following by the year 2000 AD.

- Reduction of average size of family from 4.4 children in 1975 to 2.3 children.
- Reduction of birth rate to 21 from the level of 33 in 1978, death rate from 14 to 9 and infant mortality rate from 127 to below 60.
- Increasing the couple protection level from 22.0% to 60.0% with the assumption that reaching this level would stabilize the population to the desired level.

Seventh Five-Year Plan: The Family Welfare Programme during Seventh Five Year Plan (1985-90) was continued on a purely voluntary basis with emphasis on promoting spacing methods, securing maximum community participation and promoting maternal and child health care. In order to provide facilities/services nearer to the doorsteps of population, the following steps/initiatives were taken during the Seventh Plan period.

- It was envisaged to have one sub-centre for every 5000 people in plain areas and for every 3000 people in hilly and tribal areas. At the end of the Seventh Plan i.e.31.3.1990, more than 8000 sub centres were established in the state.
- The Post Partum programme was progressively extended to sub-district level hospitals.

- The Universal Immunization Programme started in phases and in 1985-86 was extended to cover all the districts by the end of the Seventh Plan. The achievements of the Family Welfare Programme at the end of the Seventh Plan were:

(i) Reduction in the crude birth rate to 28.2 in West Bengal as against 30.2 of India (SRS: 1990).

(ii) Reduction in the total fertility rate from 3.3 in West Bengal in 1991 as estimated by the state against 3.8 in India (SRS: 1990).

(iii) Reduction in infant mortality rate to 63 in West Bengal as against 80 in India (SRS: 1990).

(iv) Increase in the Couple Protection Rate to 35.6 as estimated by the state in 1990-91 against 43.3% (31.3.1990) in India.

(v) Setting up of a large network of service delivery infrastructure, which was virtually non-existent at the inception of the programme.

The approach adopted during the Seventh Five Year Plan was continued during the 1990-92 period. A major new initiative undertaken during 1991-92 was the Child Survival and Safe Motherhood Project, an integration of the Universal Immunization Programme with expanded/intensified MCH activities.

Eighth Five-Year Plan: To impart new dynamism to the Family Welfare Programme, several new initiatives were introduced and ongoing schemes were revamped in the Eighth Plan (1992-97), which included:

World Bank assisted Area Projects, which seek to upgrade infrastructure, and development of trained manpower have been continued during the Eighth Five Year Plan. Two new Area Projects namely India Population Project (IPP)-VIII and IX have been initiated during the Eighth Plan. The IPP-

VIII project aims at improving health and family welfare services in the urban slums in the cities of Delhi, Kolkata, Hyderabad and Bangalore. IPP-IX will operate in the states of Rajasthan, Assam and Karnataka.

Realizing that Government efforts alone in propagating and motivating the people for adaptation of small family norm would not be sufficient, greater stress has been laid on the involvement of NGOs to supplement and complement the government efforts.

The Universal Immunization Programme (UIP) was launched in 1985 to provide universal coverage of infants and pregnant women with immunization against identified diseases that are preventable with vaccines. From the year 1992-93, the UIP has been strengthened and expanded into the Child Survival and Safe Motherhood (CSSM) Project. It involves sustaining the high immunization coverage level under UIP, and augmenting activities under the Oral Rehydration Therapy, prophylaxis for control of blindness in children and control of acute respiratory infections. Under the Safe Motherhood component, training of traditional birth attendants, provision of aseptic delivery kits and strengthening of first referral units to deal with high risk and obstetric emergencies are being taken up.

Ninth Five-Year Plan (1997-2002): Reduction in the population growth rate has been recognized as one of the priority objectives during the Ninth Plan period. The objectives during the Ninth Plan are:

- To meet all the felt-needs for contraception
- To reduce the infant and maternal morbidity and mortality so that there is a reduction in the desired level of fertility.

The strategies during the Ninth Plan were:

- To assess the needs for reproductive and child health

at PHC level and undertake area-specific micro planning.

- To provide need-based, demand-driven, high quality, integrated reproductive and child health care.

Contraceptives

Condoms/Copper-T/Oral Contraceptive Pills

The National Family Welfare Programme provides the following contraceptive services for spacing births: a) Condoms; b) Oral Contraceptive Pill, and c) Intra Uterine Devices (IUD).

Whereas condoms and oral contraceptive pills are being provided through the free distribution scheme and the social marketing scheme, IUD is being provided only under the free distribution scheme. Under the Social Marketing Programme, contraceptives - both condoms and oral pills - are sold at subsidized rates. In addition, contraceptives are commercially sold by the manufacturing companies under their brand names. The Government of India does not provide any subsidy for the commercial sale.

(i) **Condoms:** Condoms are made available to the potential users by the Government of India through the following schemes:

- Free Distribution Scheme
- Social Marketing Scheme

Free Distribution Scheme: Free disbursement of condoms was started with the objective of making them available to those who cannot afford to pay for it. Under this scheme, the Department of Family Welfare procures condoms with the brand name NIRODH from various Indian Manufacturers and supply them to all the states/UTs for distribution to the users free of cost through dispensaries, hospitals, PHCs, Sub-centres etc.

Social Marketing Scheme: The Social Marketing Programme of condom was launched by the Government of India in 1968 with the objective of making condoms available to those who can afford to pay nominally for it. Under this scheme, three different varieties namely (i) New Lubricated Nirodh, (ii) 'Deluxe Nirodh' and (iii) 'Super Deluxe Nirodh" are procured from the indigenous condom manufacturers and supplied to marketing companies/NGOs (called Social Marketing Organizations) at subsidized rates for sale in the open market. In addition, distributing companies, i.e., SMOs are permitted to market condoms under their own brand name. A promotional incentive of 10 paisa per condom sold for Deluxe and Super Deluxe varieties and 3 paisa per condom sold for the New Lubricated variety is also being provided to the SMOs. Deluxe Nirodh is also sold by State AIDS Control Societies through their NGOs network.

(ii) *Oral Contraceptive Pills:* Oral Contraceptive Pills are also made available to the potential users through the following schemes:

- Free Distribution Scheme
- Social Marketing Scheme

Free Distribution Scheme: Under the free distribution scheme Oral Contraceptive Pills with brand name Mala N are procured and distributed to the acceptors free of cost in the same manner as is done with condoms.

Social Marketing Scheme: On the pattern of Social Marketing scheme of condoms, Social Marketing Scheme of Oral Pills was launched by the Government of India in 1987. Under this scheme, Government procures Mala D from the indigenous manufacturers and supplies them to marketing companies/NGOs (called Social Marketing Organizations) at subsidized rates. Distributing companies, i.e., SMOs are also permitted to market oral pills under their brand name. A promotional incentive of Re. 0.25 per cycle of oral pills sold is also being provided to the SMOs.

(iii) **Copper-T:** Cu-T is one of the important spacing methods offered under the Family Welfare Programme. Cu-T is supplied free of cost for insertion at the PHCs, sub-centres and hospitals by trained medical practitioners/trained health workers. The earlier version of Cu-T 200 'B' (IUDs) has been replaced by Cu-T 380-A from 2002-03 onwards, which provides protection for a longer period (about 10 years) as against Cu-T 200 'B' which provided protection for about 3 years only.

Permanent Methods of Male and Female Operation: Male and female operations are carried out by Tubal Ligation, by Minilap /Laparoscopic tubal ligation, Vasectomy and No Scalpel Vasectomy at the different tiers of public facilities.

Laparoscopes/Tubal Rings: Laparoscopes/Laparocators are essentially required for undertaking Laparoscopic sterilization - that is a relatively quicker method of female sterilization. 25 Central Laparoscopic Training Centres have been identified for the purpose of training medical and paramedical personnel in this technique. The training is imparted to a team consisting of gynaecologist /obst./surgeons with minimum three years experience in the field, operation theatre nurse and operation theatre attendant. At present, Laparoscopes are supplied at the rate of 1.5 Laparoscope per trained team. To meet this requirement, the Laparoscopes are procured centrally and distributed among the states/UTs. Tubal Rings for this purpose are also procured centrally and distributed to the states/UTs as per their demand.

Growth of Population in West Bengal

The population rose from 169.4 lakhs in 1901 to 801.8 lakhs in 2001. The rise in population was gradual from 1901 to 1951. Since then the growth in population has shown steep rise. The bar diagram below reflects the same.

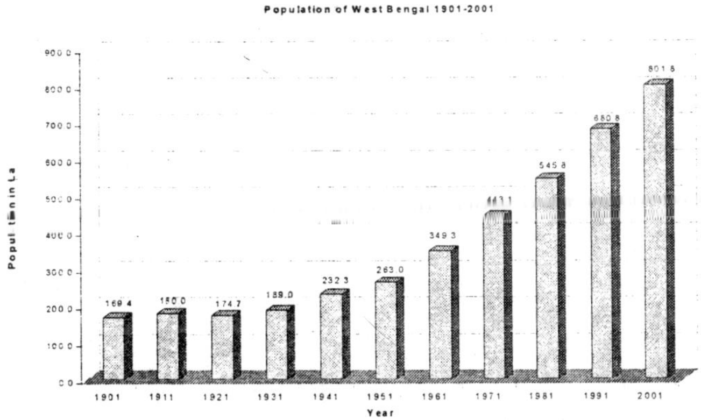

The growth of population in West Bengal is also reflected in the growth in the density of population as reflected in the graph below. As per the 1991 census, West Bengal has the highest density amongst the major states (767/sq k.m.)

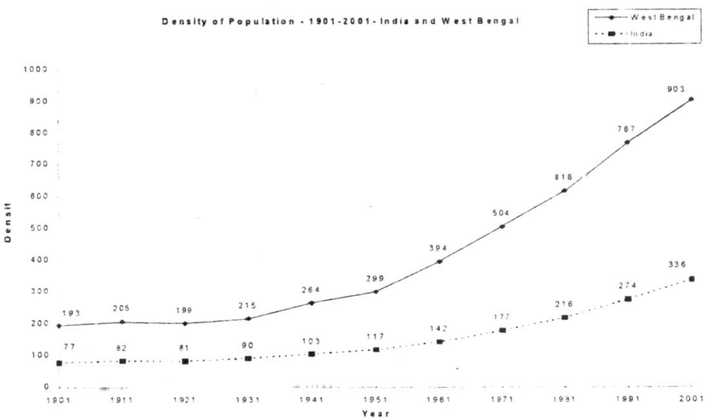

Key Indicators As Per The Three National Family Health Surveys:

Three National Family Health Surveys were conducted in the years as follows:

- NFHS-1 during 1992-93
- NFHS 2 during 1998-1999 and
- NFHS 3 during 2005-06

The result of the surveys is discussed below:

Family Welfare Methods: Acceptance: Any method

- There has been gradual improvement in the acceptance - 57.7% in NFHS 1, 66.6 in NFHS 2 and 71.2 in NFHS 3.
- Acceptance in the urban areas - 75.5% (77.0% in Kolkata) is higher than that in rural areas - 69.5% during the NFHS 3.

Educational status has very little influence on the acceptance, which is reflected as follows:

- No education - 70.2%
- Less than 8 years of education completed - 71.8%
- 8-9 years of education - 71.7% and
- 10 years of study or above - 72.0%

Any modern method: The trend is increasing from NFHS 1 through NFHS 3. The acceptance was as follows:

- NFHS- 1: 37.6%
- NFHS- 2: 47.3 % and
- NFHS- 3: 49.9

There is no difference in the level of acceptance as far as rural and urban areas are concerned. It is 49.9% in both the areas. In fact the % of acceptance in Kolkata is 45.6%, which is lower than both the rural and urban areas. It is difficult to explain this as the service network is favourable in Kolkata as compared to other urban areas and definitely better than that in the rural areas. Acceptance of modern methods and educational status:

- It is surprising to note that the acceptance is inversely proportional to the educational status which is reflected as follows:
- Acceptance amongst the illiterate is the highest at 54.4%
- Acceptance amongst those who completed 10 years of study or more is the least, 38.7
- Thus modern methods of family planning are to be popularized amongst the literate.

Female Sterilization: The acceptance has increased during the NFHS 2 (32.0%) as compared to NFHS 1 (26.5%). However it is surprising to note that over almost 9-10 years the NFHS-2 to NFHS-3 acceptance of method has remained the same around 32%. May be the restriction posed by the Supreme Court to avoid mishaps has resulted in the stagnancy.

Male Sterilization: The acceptance is the lowest amongst all the methods and has dwindled over the years as reflected below:

- NFHS-1: 4.3%
- NFHS- 2: 1.8%
- NFHS- 3: 0.7%

It is more popular in rural areas (0.8%) as compared to urban areas (0.5%) and even lower in Kolkata (0.2%) and the acceptance is more by the less the educated (1.0% amongst the illiterate) as compared to better educated (0.4% amongst those who have studied for 10 years or more).

IUD: The acceptance of IUD has dwindled over the years, as shown below:

- NFHS-1: 1.3%
- NFHS- 2: 1.4% (marginal improvement)
- NFHS- 3: 0.6% (gross fall)

The acceptance in urban areas (0.9%) is higher as compared to rural areas (0.5%). The acceptance in the Kolkata is the highest (1.4%) amongst all the three. This is because the method is more popular amongst the more educated (1.5% amongst those who completed 10 years or more of study) as compared to (0.5%) amongst the illiterates.

Oral Pill: This is one method, which has shown remarkable improvement over the years, as reflected below:

- NFHS- 1: 3.6%
- NFHS- 2: 9.2%
- NFHS- 3: 11.7%

The method is more popular in rural areas as compared to urban areas, as reflected below:

- Rural: 12.1%
- Urban: 10.7%
- Kolkata: 9.2%

It is more popular amongst those who are moderately educated as compared to the illiterate and those who have studied for 10 years or more, as reflected below:

- Less than 8 years of study: 14.1%
- Those studied for 8-9 years: 16.2%
- No education: 8.8%
- 10 years or more: 10.2%

Condom: Over the years the acceptance of condom has increased, as reflected below:

- NFHS-1: 1.9%
- NFHS- 2: 2.9%
- NFHS 3: 4.4%. There is a leap in the performance during NFHS-3 as compared to NFHS-2.

Acceptance of condoms in urban areas is much higher (8.9%). In Kolkata, it is 9.9% as compared to 2.7% in rural areas. The method is more popular amongst the educated and may be one reason for its less use in rural areas. The acceptance as far as educational status is concerned is as follows:

- No education: 1.5%
- Less than 8 years of study: 3.4%
- 8-9 years of study: 5.7%
- 10 years or more of study: 14.8%
- The method is more popular amongst the educated.

Unmet Need for Family Planning: Unmet need denotes that the client desires to use a certain method but due to its unavailability at the time to need the client fails to use it. This is generally the result of operational failure.

Total Unmet Need: It is heartening to note that the total unmet need is coming down over the years, as reflected in the figures given below:

- NFHS- 1:17.4%
- NFHS- 2: 11.8 %
- NFHS- 3: 8.8 %

As expected, the unmet need is more in the rural areas as compared to the urban areas, as reflected below:

- Urban: 6.0%
- Kolkata: 4.7%
- Rural: 10.0%

Surprisingly, contrary to the expectation, the percentage in unmet need increases from the illiterate to those who have studied for 8-9 years. However, the percentage is the lowest amongst those who have studied 10 years or more. The reading goes as follows:

- No education: 8.5%
- Less than 8 years: 9.9%
- 8-9 years: 9.6%
- 10 years or more: 6.5 %

Unmet Need for Spacing: The unmet need for spacing, as expected, is coming down over the years as reflected below:

- NFHS- 1: 9.4%
- NFHS- 2: 6.3%
- NFHS- 3: 4.4%

As in case of the total unmet need, the unmet need for spacing too is more in the rural areas as compared to the urban areas, as reflected below:

- Urban: 2.7%
- Kolkata: 2.5%
- Rural: 5.1%

As far as the educational status is concerned, the picture is similar to the total unmet need and is reflected below:

- No education: 3.6%
- Less than 8 years of education: 4.9%

- 8-9 years of study: 6.2%
- 10 years or more: 3.8%

Among well-educated people the unmet need for spacing is the least.

Unmet Need for Limiting Methods: The unmet need for limiting methods is coming down over the years as depicted below:

- NFHS- 1: 8.0%
- NFHS- 2: 5.5% and
- NFHS- 3: 4.4%

The unmet need for limiting methods is more in the rural areas as compared to the urban areas, as reflected below:

- Urban: 3.3%
- Kolkata: 2.3%
- Rural: 4.9%

Educational Status: There is a gradual decline in the unmet need for limiting methods as the educational level of the acceptors increases, which is as follows:

- No education: 4.9%
- Less than 8 years of education: 5.0% (slight aberration)
- 8-9 years of study: 3.4% and
- 10 years or more: 2.7 %

Thus the NFHS studies come out with results which could help the planners and implementers in developing operational plans and also in taking course corrective measures.

Basic Health Indicators (Latest available rates):

Indicators	*West Bengal*	*India*	*Major states better than West Bengal*
Birth Rate 2006	18.4	23.5	Kerala, 14.9,Tamil Nadu, 16.2, Punjab, 17.8
Death Rate 2006	6.2	7.5	Lowest
Infant Mortality Rate 2006	38	57	Kerala, 15,Maharashtra, 35, Tamil Nadu, 37
Maternal Mortality Ratio 2001-03	194	301	Kerala, 110,Tamil Nadu, 134,Maharashtra, 149, Haryana, 162,Gujrat, 172, Punjab, 178

Comparative Picture and Discussion

Indicators	*NFHS*			*Discussions*
	1992-93	*1998-99*	*2005-06*	
1	*2*	*3*	*4*	*5*
Women aged 20-24 married by age 18 (%)	56.4	45.9	53.3	The trend is not consistent. It is a matter of great concern that 53.3 % of women are getting married before they are 18 years old which leads to high maternal (194) and neonatal deaths.
Total fertility rate	2.92	2.29	2.27	There is marginal improvement over the years.
Median age at first birth for women (25-49)	18.6	19.2	19.9	There is hardly any improvement over the years.
Contraceptive prevalence rate any method (%)	57.7	66.6	71.2	This has improved a substantially over the years. The

(Contd...)

1	*2*	*3*	*4*	*5*
				difference between any method and the modern method is quite a lot (21.3 for NFHS-3) where couples are relying on methods like safe period, withdrawal etc.
Contraceptive prevalence rate for any modern method (%)	37.6	47.3	49.9	Improved over the years
Unmet need for family planning	17.4	11.8	8.8	There is a satisfactory reduction in the unmet need indicating an improvement in the provision of services.
Mothers who had at least 3 antenatal care visits for their last birth (%)	50.3	57.4	62.4	There is clear-cut improvement over the years. However, there scope for improvement as 100% of pregnant women needs to get the ANC. Decentralization and popularization of services is required.
Births attended by doctors/nurses/ LHV/health personnel	33.9	44.2	45.7	There is some improvement over the years. Several programmes have been launched under the national NRHM such as Janani Suraksha Yojana (JSY)/ supporting referral transport, delivery at headquarter sub-centre

(Contd...)

1	*2*	*3*	*4*	*5*
				etc., to improve institutional delivery. The programme needs to be further strengthened.
Children 12-23 months fully immunized (%)	34.2	43.8	64.3	There is improvement over the years. However there is much left to be done as at least 80% of children are to be immunized in order to ensure herd immunity.
Children under three years who are stunted (%)	Not available	41.5	33.0	There seems to be some improvement. However, it is disheartening to note that one-third of the children are stunted.
Children under three years who are wasted (%)	Not available	13.6	19.0	The situation has worsened over the years. Nutritional programmes needs revamping
Children under three years who are underweight (%)	58.4	48.7	43.5	Situation seems to be improving over the years. However a large chunk of the children are inadequately fed.
Women whose BMI is below normal (%)	Not available	43.7	37.7	Situation seems to be improving. However, a large section of the women are underfed.
Children age 3-35 months who are anaemic (%)	Not available	78.3	69.4	There is some improvement but a chunk of the population is anaemic.

(Contd...)

1	*2*	*3*	*4*	*5*
Ever married women aged 15-49 who are anaemic (%)	Not available	62.7	63.8	The situation has worsened over the survey periods.
Pregnant women age 15-49 who are anaemic	Not available	56.9	62.6	The situation has worsened over the years.
Women who have heard of AIDS (%)	9.8	26.4	50.2	There is a considerable improvement in the level of knowledge.

Conclusion and Recommendations

National Family Health Survey is an important tool to bring to the surface the performance of the Department of Health and Family Welfare. It also brings out indirectly the performance of the departments working on the nutritional front of the pregnant/lactating mothers and children up to 6 years.

The surveys clearly spells out that even though there has been some improvement in areas like acceptance of family planning and reduction in the unmet need for it attention needs to be given in the areas like age at marriage, total fertility rate, three antenatal check ups during pregnancy, institutional delivery, immunizati on of children, anaemia control amongst women and children and nutrition of mothers and children.

Table XIV.43: N F H S - 3 - Key Indicators, West Bengal (2005 - 06)

		Residence			Education					
	NFHS-3	*Urban*	*Rural*	*Kolkata*	*No. education*[2]	*< 8 years complete*[2]	*8-9 years complete*[2]	*10 years complete and above*[2]	*NFHS-2 (1998-99)*	*NFHS - (1992-93)*
Family Planning (currently married women age 15-49)										
Current use										
7. Any method (%)	71.2	75.5	69.5	77.0	70.2	71.8	71.7	72.0	66.6	57.7
8. Any modern method (%)	49.9	49.9	49.9	45.6	54.4	50.9	45.4	38.7	47.3	37.6
8a. Female sterilization (%)	32.2	28.8	33.5	24.6	42.4	31.9	22.8	12.0	32.0	26.5
8b. Male sterilization (%)	0.7	0.5	0.8	0.2	1.0	0.8	0.2	0.4	1.8	4.3
8c. IUD (%)	0.6	0.9	0.5	1.4	0.5	0.4	0.6	1.5	1.4	1.3
8d. Pill (%)	11.7	10.7	12.1	9.2	8.8	14.1	16.2	10.2	9.2	3.6
8e. Condom (%)	4.5	8.9	2.7	9.9	1.5	3.4	5.7	14.8	2.9	1.9
Unmet need for family planning										
9. Total unmet need (%)	8.8	6.0	10.0	4.7	8.5	9.9	9.6	6.5	11.8	17.4
9a. For spacing (%)	4.4	2.7	5.1	2.5	3.6	4.9	6.2	3.8	6.3	9.4
9b. For limiting (%)	4.4	3.3	4.9	2.3	4.9	5.0	3.4	2.7	5.5	8.0

REFERENCES

Census Publications, 2001.

Health on the March 2006-07, Department of Health and Family Welfare.

National Family Health Survey (NFHS-3) 2005-06 International Institute for Population Sciences, Mumbai.

Sample Registration System Statistical Report 2005, Register General, India.

SRS Bulletin, Sample Registration System, Register General, India (October 2007).

SRS Analytical Studies, Abridged Life Table (2000-04), Register General of India.

Website of Ministry of Health and Family Welfare, Government of India.

V. Miscellaneous

21

Health Insurance in India: An Overview

Dr. N. Devadasan

Summary

Health care in India is mainly funded by out of pocket expenses from individual households. The other main source of financing is through tax revenue. The government is interested in introducing health insurance as another mechanism of financing health care, so that the patients are protected from high medical expenses. This article gives an overview of health insurance in India and suggests ways to move forward for our country. Health insurance is defined as a mechanism where there are three basic elements, *pre-payment; risk pooling and guarantee of services.* The main pillars of any health insurance programme are the *Community, the Providers and the Organiser* of the scheme. All three are very essential for the success of any scheme. Other requirements for success are a *comprehensive benefit package and an affordable premium.* In India, there are examples of all the three types of health insurances. Mandatory social health insurance is represented by the Employees State Insurance Scheme (ESIS) and the Central Government

Health Scheme CGHS). There are a lot of private health insurance companies providing voluntary health insurance, targeted mainly for the middle and upper class. And finally there are more than 100 community health insurance schemes that provide protection for the people in the informal sector. The Government of India has also launched a series of schemes for the poor, the most recent among them being the Rashtriya Swasthya Bima Yojana. This is a heavily subsidised scheme for the BPL families in India and protects against hospitalisation expenses up to a maximum of Rs 30,000 per family per year. The author recommends that in the future, the government should encourage multiple risk pools, rather than having an uniform programme for the entire country; the IRDA should regulate both the insurance companies as well as the providers and finally, move gradually towards a social health insurance model.

Introduction

Health financing in India is unique in many ways. It has one of the highest out-of-pocket spending on health care. This spending by individual households has important consequences. For one, it reduces access to health care. A quarter of those who do access health care become impoverished by the high hospital expenses (Peters et al., 2002), (Sainath, 2004); labelled iatrogenic poverty (Meessen et al., 2003) by some authors.

Though the government has promised to increase the public spending, it is doubtful that there will be enough money to meet the needs of the billion Indians. One other option that is being suggested is to increase the insurance penetration from the current 3.0% to universal coverage. While this is an admirable recommendation, the current policy confusion regarding health insurance is not encouraging (The Economic Times, 2003;Viswanathan, 2003). It is clear that both the government and the insurance companies are approaching the problem from an economic perspective rather than a health systems perspective (Economic Bureau, 2004). This paper tries to undo this error by providing a brief overview of the health insurance schemes currently available and making recommendations on what is to be done to achieve universal coverage.

Health Insurance

The author defines health insurance as 'the reduction or elimination of the uncertain risk of loss for the individual or household by combining a larger number of similarly exposed individuals or households who are included in common fund that makes good the loss caused to any one member' (ILO - 1996) (Criel Bart, 1998). There are three basic elements in health insurance:

- Pre-payment, i.e. people pay money (also called premium) when they are healthy.
- Risk pooling, i.e. both healthy and ill people pay this premium, not just the patients
- Guarantee of services, i.e. in return for this premium, the individual is guaranteed definite benefits.

The last element makes it different from a tax-based economy, where there is pre-payment and risk pooling (taxes), but there is no legal binding on the State to guarantee health services.

A model for health insurance has been built, which describes the main pillars and their relationship to each other (Figure 1). The most important pillar is of course the community. Without a specific community, there is no insurance. Ideally this community should be a mixture of healthy and ill, rich and poor and employed and unemployed (e.g. retired, children) people. This is called true risk pooling. Unfortunately, in our country, risk pooling is largely limited to sharing between the healthy and ill.

The next pillar is the provider. Without providers, again there cannot be a health insurance programme. Providers can be hospitals, dispensaries, clinics, depending on the benefit package. Success of a health insurance programme largely depends on this pillar.

Tho third pillar is the organiser of the health insurance programme. Various institutions can organise the health insurance programme. For example, it could be an insurance company or a third party administrator (in private health insurance), or the government (in social health insurance) or an NGO (in community health insurance). There are many management roles that the organiser has to undertake and in that way, this is also a crucial pillar.

Each of these pillars is related to each other through intrinsic arrangements. For example, the community pays the premium to the organiser. This may be in cash or in kind, may be annually monthly, may be voluntary or mandatory. The premium is a sum of the cost of the benefit package, the administrative costs for running the programme and the cost of the reserves. The more affordable the premium, the greater the acceptability of the insurance programme. Also one has to remember that there is a cost in collecting premium, which adds to the administrative costs.

The benefit package is the cover that the insured gets for paying the premium. Usually this is limited to hospitalisation expenses, but there are schemes that have covered Outpatient care, travel costs and compensation for loss of wages. Acceptability of the scheme depends on how comprehensive the package is.

The providers are usually paid by the organiser. This may be an insurance company or a third party administrator (TPA) or an NGO. Earlier, the patients were reimbursed, but the current trend is to reimburse the hospitals. Usually the reimbursement is for the services provided, which is conducive for cost escalation. Gradually some insurance schemes are shifting to a case-based payment mechanism, which has the potential to reduce costs.

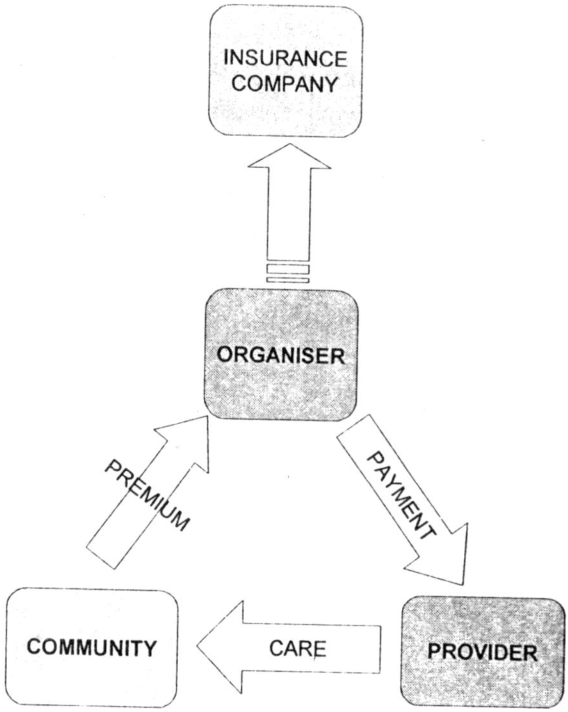

Figure 1: The Basic Health Insurance Model

Health Insurance in India

Social security in India for medical emergencies is as old as the Indian civilisation. Even today, it is a common practise for villagers to take a '*piruvu*' (a collection) to support a household with a sick patient. However, health insurance as we know it today was introduced only in 1912 when the first Insurance Act was passed. The current version of the Insurance Act was introduced in 1938, but since then there has been very little change till 1972 when the insurance industry was nationalised and the few hundred private insurance companies were brought under the umbrella of the General Insurance Company (GIC). The winds of liberalisation that blew across India in the 1990s affected the insurance industry also. Private and foreign entrepreneurs were allowed to enter the market in 1999 with the passage of the IRDA bill (Box 1).

There is very low penetration of health insurance in India. It is estimated that only about 3.0% of Indians are covered under any form of health insurance. The Indian health insurance scenario is a potpourri of mandatory social health insurance; voluntary private health insurance and community-based health insurance. In the next sections the author presents a brief overview of these schemes and their strengths and weaknesses. A section on the lessons learnt and the way forward follows.

Mandatory and Contributory Social Health Insurance:

There are two mandatory and contributory health insurance schemes in India – the CGHS for the government of India's civil servants and the ESIS for the low paid industrial workers. Here the eligible people contribute through a payroll tax towards a specific health fund. This fund then finances specific benefits for them.

The Central Government Health Scheme (CGHS)

The Central Government Health Scheme (CGHS) was introduced in 1954 as a contributory health scheme to provide comprehensive medical care to the central government employees and their families. The list of beneficiaries includes all categories of current as well as former central government employees, members of parliament, supreme court and high court judges (Ellis et al., 2000), (Gumber, 2002). In 1997, there were approximately 4.2 million beneficiaries (Gumber, 2002).The staff contributes a nominal amount (ranging from Rs 15 to Rs 150 per month) from their salaries.

The benefit package includes both outpatient (OP) care and hospitalisation. OP care is provided through its own dispensaries, 320 in 2002 in 17 major cities. It also uses the facilities of the government and approved private hospitals to provide inpatient care and reimburses the expenses to the patient.

The entire scheme is funded by the government of India and is administered by a separate directorate. Various evaluations have noted that while it has been effective in providing health security for more than 4 million people, there are certain problems in the scheme that needs to be addressed. These are:

- **Equity:** It in a country where the government spends less than 0.9% of the GDP on health care, it is unacceptable that a sizable amount of this goes to the better off section of the society.
- **Demand Side Moral Hazard:** It is noted that 83.0% of the hospitalised patients are self-referred. It appears that most patients prefer to bypass the dispensaries and directly avail of specialist services. The number of annual visits per beneficiary was 3.5 (1994-95).
- **Poor Quality Care:** There are regular complaints about long waiting periods, inadequate supply of medicines and equipment and unhygienic conditions.
- **High Out of Pocket Expenditure:** A study in 1994 documents that an average patient pays about Rs 1507 for the first treatment episode.

The Employees State Insurance Scheme (ESIS) (Ellis and Gupta, 2000), (Bhat and Mavalankar D 2000), (Government of India, 2003), (Subrahmanya, 1998)

Established in 1948, the Employees State Insurance Scheme (ESIS) is an insurance system, which provides both cash and medical benefits. It was conceived as a compulsory social security benefit for workers in the formal sector. The Employees State Insurance Corporation (ESIC) manages the scheme and is a corporate semi-government body headed by the Union Minister of Labour as Chairman and a Director General as the Chief Executive. Its members are representatives of central and state governments, employers, employees, medical profession and members of parliament.

The Act compulsorily covers: (a) all power using non-seasonal factories employing 10 or more persons; (b) all non-power using factories employing 20 or more employees and (c) service establishments like shops, hotels restaurants, cinema, road transport and news papers are covered. The plantation and mines sector or those institutions that provide similar or better benefits than the ESIS are exempt from joining the ESIS. In the eligible organisations, only those workers with a salary of less than Rs. 10,000 per month can join the ESIS. To avail of the sickness benefit, the employee has to have worked for 78 days prior to the sickness. Similarly, to avail of the maternity benefit, the woman has to have worked for 70 days prior.

Contributions are paid through a payroll tax of 4.6 levied on the employer and a tax of 1.6% levied on the employee. Workers earning less than Rs 40 a day are exempt from contributing. State Governments contributes 12.5% of total shareable expenditure worked out by prescribed ceiling on expenditure, which is Rs. 600 per insured person per annum, and expenditure incurred over and above the prescribed limit.

All workers and their dependent relatives are eligible for the benefits. These include health care at ESIS facilities, cash compensation for illness, maternity benefits, disability benefits, survivorship and funeral expenses in the event of death of the worker. Health care includes preventive, promotive, curative and rehabilitative services. ESIS has its own dispensaries, hospitals and medical staff. It also empanels select private practitioners to provide medical care. Patients requiring treatment from specialists not available at the ESIS hospitals can receive them at the speciality facilities, with the ESIS programme reimbursing the expenses. The details are given in Table 1. All ESIS facilities are managed by the State governments and financed by the ESIC.

Table 1
ESI Medical Infrastructure (As on 31.3.2001)
(Government of India, 2003)

ESI Hospitals (Nos.)	140
ESI Annexes (nos.)	43
Beds constructed in ESI Hospitals (nos.)	22620
Beds in ESI Annexes	867
Reserve Beds in State Govt. Hospitals	3443
Medical Officers	6542
ESI Dispensaries	1443

Presently the scheme is spread over 677 centres in 25 states and Union territories across India covering 8.4 million employees and more than 35 million beneficiaries[1]. In 1992, of a total expenditure of Rs. 3.8 billion, Rs. 2.2 billion was spent on health care. In 2001, the ESIC had surplus funds of Rs. 67 billion, invested mostly in government securities.

While the ESIS has managed to cover the low paid workers in many organizations and provided them with a degree of comprehensive health security, it has been criticized for the following reasons.

- Less than half the enrolees use the ESIS facilities because of the low quality of care (Gumber, 2002). This is further compounded by the rude and impudent behaviour of the ESIS staff, shortage of staff, inadequate drug and supplies and non-functional equipment.

- Many of the staffs are not aware of the benefits. The employers also do not disseminate the information to their staff. Further, some employers manipulate records to make the staff ineligible for the benefits. Also because of the salary limits on eligibility, some staff keep shifting in and out of the ESIS and they may not be aware of their eligibility status (Gumber, 2002).
- There is duality of control – with both the ESIC and the State governments trying to establish superiority. Also, there is conflict between the health department and the labour department for control of the ESIS.
- Poor penetration in rural areas.

Mandatory and Non-contributory Social Health Insurance

While these are not strictly health insurance schemes, we document them to demonstrate the wide variety of health security measures available in the country.

The Workmen's Compensation Act (1923) (Government of India, 2003), (Subrahmanya, 1998):

This is the beginning of social security legislation in India. It is based on the principle of employers' liability, whereby the liability for payment of the various benefit admissible under the Act is that of the employer. This act applies to railway servants and persons employed in any such capacity as is specified in Schedule II of the Act. Schedule II includes persons employed in factories, mines, plantations, mechanically propelled vehicles, construction works and certain other hazardous occupations. It is applicable only to employees engaged in hazardous employments.

The Act provides for payment of compensation to workmen and their dependants in case of injury and accident (including certain occupational disease) arising out of and in the course of employment and resulting in disablement or death. Minimum rates of compensation for permanent total disablement and death have been fixed at Rs 90,000 and Rs 80,000 respectively. Maximum amount for death and permanent total disablement can go up to Rs.4.56 lakhs and Rs.5.48 lakhs respectively depending on age and wages of workmen.

The Maternity Benefit Act (1961) (Government of India, 2003)

Introduced in 1961, the main object is to regulate the employment of women in certain establishments for certain periods before and after childbirth and to provide for maternity and certain other benefits. The Act is applicable to mines, factories, circus industry, plantation, shops and establishments employing ten or more persons. There is no wage limit for coverage under the Act. A woman must be an employee and must have worked for not less than 80 days, in the 12-month period preceding the date of her expected delivery, to be eligible for the maternity benefit. Workers covered under the ESIS are not covered by this act.

It is managed by the State Governments except for mines and circuses. The employer makes the contributions; there is no employee contribution.

Employer-Managed Facilities (Ellis and Gupta, 2000)

This form of health security is available in large public sector and private sector organisations, including railways, mines, plantations, universities and defence forces. They have their own health facilities and provide free health care to their staff and dependents.

It is estimated that about 50 million people benefit by this scheme.

Employer Reimbursement of Health Expenses (Ellis and Gupta 2000)

Many private sector employers as well as autonomous institutions (like commercial banks) reimburse their employees' medical bills. This may be in two forms – one is linked to the employees' wages. Thus an employee is reimbursed up to a maximum limit, depending on his/her wage. In the other form, the employee is reimbursed depending on the amount of contribution that the employee has made to the medical fund. This is akin to a medical savings account[2]. Unfortunately, there is no real estimate about how many employees (and beneficiaries) are covered under this scheme.

There is also anecdotal evidence that in the smaller establishments, where ESIS is not applicable, and employers would cover the medical expenses of their employees. This of course depends on various factors and invariably is an ad hoc arrangement.

Voluntary Health Insurance

Mediclaim

Health insurance in India is usually associated with the 'Mediclaim' policy of the GIC. Introduced in 1986, it is a voluntary health insurance scheme offered by the public sector (and since 1999 the private sector) health insurance companies.

Anybody (3 months to 80 years) who can afford the risk rated premium is eligible to join the scheme. The premium depends on the age; risk and the benefit package opted for. The minimum premium is Rs. 201 for < 25 years old for a maximum benefit of Rs. 15,000. Group membership allows for discounts in the premium. In 2001, there were 7.8 million persons covered under Mediclaim[3]. The subscribers are usually the middle and upper class, especially since there is a tax benefit in subscribing to Mediclaim (Bhat and Mavalankar, 2000).

The standard Mediclaim policy covers only hospital care and domiliciary hospitalisation benefits. Most medical conditions are reimbursed though there are important exclusions. These include – pre-existing diseases, pregnancy and child birth, HIV-AIDS, etc. Traditionally, only reimbursement insurance is provided, though the companies have tried a third payment system with TPAs. Hospitals with more than 15 beds and registered with a local authority can be identified as providers.

The insurance company (or the TPA where applicable) administers the scheme. Being an indemnity scheme, the patient pays the hospital bills and submits the necessary documents to the company. The company in turn reimburses the patient. A study done in Gujarat showed that the average time between submission of documents and reimbursement is 121 days (Bhat and Reuben, 2001). There is also uncertainty about the amount reimbursed, there are times when the patients are only reimbursed partially, and the usual reason provided is that the documentation is insufficient.

During 1994, 4.4% of insured persons made a claim, of which only 75.0% of claims were settled. The claims ratio was 45.0%. However, of late the claims ratio is growing at a fast rate, allegedly because of collusion between the patients, the insurance agents and the hospitals (Bhat and Mavalankar, 2000; Syed, 2004).

Some of the strengths of the Mediclaim policy are

- Currently, the only voluntary health insurance policy in the country, with about 8 million subscribers.
- Provides protection against catastrophic health expenditure

- Easily available in most insurance companies
- Is being modified to make it customer friendly

However there are some major weaknesses that need to be addressed.

- Most of the insurance companies are wary about selling health insurance as they do not have the data, the expertise and the power to regulate the providers
- There are a lot of problems in reimbursing the patients, ranging from long delays to partial reimbursements.
- There are also reported fraud and manipulation by clients and providers. The monitoring systems are weak.
- The benefit package needs to be modified to suit the needs of the customers. Exclusions go against the health system logic of covering risks.
- And, lastly, the reimbursement method of payment is highly unpopular among the customers. The experiment with TPAs appears to have been unsuccessful and the reasons for this needs to be studied.

These weaknesses have resulted in Mediclaim topping the number of grievances in the non-life insurance sector (2003).

Health Insurance Products for the Poor

(i) Universal Health Insurance Scheme (UHIS)

This was one of the first health insurance schemes introduced for the people live below the poverty line (BPL) in India. Family was the unit of enrolment and the premium of Rs. 248 (for a family of five) was subsidised by nearly 50.0% by the central government. The benefit package was Rs.

30,000 on a family floater basis. However, there were important exclusions that meant that many of the conditions were not covered. NGOs were expected to market this scheme in their catchment area and the insurance companies administered the scheme. While the intention was good, the scheme failed, as the insurance companies were not able to market it even in urban areas. This meant that very few people purchased the cover and even fewer availed of the benefits.

(ii) National Rural Health Mission (NRHM)

The NRHM is a new initiative, again by the government of India to introduce architectural changes within the public health services. This programme encourages state governments to support community health insurance programmes. This was supposed to be initiated by NGOs and the governments would subsidise the premium by a fixed amount e.g. Rs. 300 per family. The design and the implementation was the responsibility of NGOs. Unfortunately, there have not been too many takers for this programme also.

(iii) Rashtriya Swasthya Bima Yojana

This is the latest from the government of India stables. Anchored by the Ministry of Labour and Employment, it is supposed to provide protection against hospitalisation expenses for the families in the informal sector (mainly BPL households). The premium of Rs. 600 is heavily subsidised by the governments (centre and state) and the BPL household has to only pay a registration fee of Rs. 30. In return, they get a smart card that can be used in any of the empanelled hospitals in the country. The cover if for Rs. 30,000 per family per year and there are practically no exclusions. The entire programme is cashless, so the patient does not have to arrange for any money at the time of illness.

(iv) Others

Four GIC companies and eight Private general insurance companies have introduced 14 health insurance products for the poor (ILO, 2005). All of them cover hospitalisation expenses; only one also provides subsidised OP services. These are all variations of the Mediclaim policy, though some have included maternity benefits to make the package more acceptable. However, the premiums are usually fixed in the range of Rs 100+ for an individual and this may be the reason why they are not very popular.

Other than this, the Textile Ministry has introduced a subsidised scheme for handloom weavers, the Assam government introduced a critical illness cover for all its citizens and the Andhra Pradesh Government has also introduced a critical illness cover for the poor.

Community Health Insurance (CHI)

Community health insurance is defined as any not-for-profit insurance scheme that is aimed primarily at the informal sector and formed on the basis of a collective pooling of health risks. This definition includes mutual health organisations (MHOs), local health insurances and micro health insurances.

While the CHI movement is vibrant in Africa, it is slowly picking up momentum in India. Currently, there are about 100+ CBHIs in the country, many of which have begun operations in the past four years. Of this, 22-offer hospitalisation cover (Table 2), the rest only provide OP cover and cannot strictly be classified as a health insurance scheme.

There are 3 types of CHIs in the country (Devadasan et al., 2004b). The first and the oldest type is the 'provider' model, where a hospital has initiated a health insurance product. The hospital is both the provider of care as well as the insurer. The second type is the 'insurer' model, where the NGO organises and implements the insurance scheme and purchases care from various providers. There are very few examples of this, the most famous being the Yeshasvini model (Box 2). And, finally, the most common type is the 'linked' model, where the NGO collects premium from the community and purchases insurance from a formal insurance company and health care from providers (Box 3).

The membership to these CHIs varies from 1000+ to more than 2 million. Most of these schemes operate in rural areas and cover people from the informal sector. Enrolment is usually facilitated by membership organisations e.g. micro finance groups, cooperatives, trade unions etc. The premium ranges from Rs. 20 to Rs. 60 per individual per year. Only three schemes had premiums larger than Rs.100. At most of the schemes, the unit of enrolment is the individual and membership is voluntary.

All the 22 schemes offer hospitalisation; this ranges from the classical Mediclaim product to a very comprehensive cover including all conditions and no exclusions. It is clear that many of the NGOs have been successful in negotiating an appropriate insurance package for its community. Most of the providers are either NGO or private-for-profit providers. The utilisation rates range from 6 to more than 240 per 1000 insured. The latter obviously indicates extreme adverse selection.

All the CHIs have been initiated by NGOs, and they are the ones who administer the scheme. In many of the schemes, the community is also involved in various administrative activities e.g. in creating awareness, collecting premiums, processing claims and reimbursements and in the management of the scheme (deciding the benefit package, the premiums etc).

The main strengths of the CHIs are that they have been able to reach out to the weaker sections of society and have been able to provide some form of health security. Evidence from some CHIs indicate that they have been able to increase access to health care (Devadasan et al., 2004a) or protect the households from catastrophic health expenditure (Devadasan et al., 2007; Ranson, 2002). Community involvement increases the participation of the members in the scheme. The benefit packages are tailored to meet the community needs and so are more acceptable. Also these meet health system needs as compared to schemes designed by actuarial.

On the other hand, there are certain weaknesses, the main one being the lack of risk sharing. Usually the members are the poor and there is very little cross subsidy between the rich and the poor. The premiums are low and so the benefit packages are also small. This means that financial protection is also limited in many of the schemes. Some of the NGOs manage the scheme by themselves, which may be illegal within the current IRDA regulations. Also, some of the schemes cover very small numbers and so the potential for scaling up is restricted. And, finally, many of the schemes see health insurance as an end in itself. However, it must be remembered that health insurance is a means for a more equitable and functional health system.

Lessons Learnt

It is clear that the penetration of health insurance is very low, especially among the rural and informal sector. A summary of probable insured is given in Table 3. From this it appears that only 4.0% to 5.0% of Indians are covered under any form of health security. And most of this is from the better off formal sector. Given the high costs of health care in our country and the probability of it increasing (with the new patent regime); it is important for more people (especially the poor and vulnerable) to come under insurance cover.

Table 2
Summary of Insured Population In India

Category	*Approximate Numbers*	*Year Of Report*
CGHS	4.2 million	1997
ESIS	8 million	2004
Railways	?	
Plantation	?	
Mines	?	
Defence	?	
Public sector companies	?	
Private sector companies	?	
Private voluntary health insurance	18 million	2001
Community health insurance	13.5 million	2004
	Total	40+ million

India has two options. It could strengthen its current national health services to provide better care for its population. However, this would require more investment and major changes in the way health care is delivered. Or the government could be a purchaser of care. This would have the added advantage of targeting scarce resources for the weaker sections. It is in this context that health insurance could be a sensible option.

Health Insurance Needs To Meet Health Systems Goals

In the discussion on health insurance, too much emphasis has been paid to the financial and actuarial aspects. Unfortunately, the fact that health insurance is a financing tool to meet health systems goals has been forgotten. This needs to be placed back in the centre of the debate. While health insurance is seen as a panacea for all evils in the health services, it must be remembered that health insurance is simply a more equitable financing mechanism. And if used properly can increase access to health care and protect the households from catastrophic health expenditure at the time of illness (Kutzin, 1998). So, any deliberations on health insurance should look into these aspects principally. Financial goals of claims ratio etc are secondary.

In this context, it is important that India pursue the Bismarckian model of social health insurance rather than the private voluntary health insurance. The differences between the two are given in Table 3 and clearly demonstrate the benefits of the former.

Currently most policy makers and the insurance companies are in the 'voluntary, individual' health insurance mindset. They need to shift from this to the social health insurance mindset where large groups of populations need to be considered for insurance. Similar to the German / Canadian model, the government should pursue mechanisms to bring homogenous groups mandatory under coverage rather than introduce policies for individuals and wait for everybody to voluntarily join the scheme. We need to learn from the European example, where multiple small 'sickness funds' (akin to the currently defined community health insurances) were the predecessors of today's equitable social health insurance (Barnighausen and Sauerborn, 2002), (Ogawa et al., 2003). Once small risk pools (e.g. the farmers' cooperatives, the driver's union etc) are covered, with time they can coalesce to form a larger insurance pool.

Multiple Risk Pools

Given the varied nature of the Indian population, it would be utopian to consider a single national health insurance scheme for our country. Neither would it be possible, nor desirable. This is further compounded by the fact that Health is under the jurisdiction of the state governments.

One option would be to classify the population into various occupational groups – e.g. formal – informal sectors. And in the formal sector, the public – private sectors; while in the informal sector, the cooperative – union – informal groups etc. This would help in targeting health insurance interventions. One possibility is to expand the CGHS and the ESIS to rest of the formal sector. For example, the ESIS could be opened to all in the industrial sector, making it mandatory for everybody to contribute. Benefits can be made standard for everybody at the ESIS facilities and those desirous of availing extra benefits could use the private sector. This way, the rich would be sharing their risks with the poor – a true insurance mechanism. The same could be done for CGHS. Companies that have their own health facilities could continue, but others could be mandated to enrol their employees into a suitable health insurance scheme.

The informal sector could be tackled in a step-by-step manner. Organised sectors e.g. the cooperatives, the trade unions, the associations could be tackled first and health insurance are introduced through these vehicles. While initially voluntary insurance be allowed, once certain structures are in place, health insurance should be made mandatory.

During this phase voluntary health insurance could be provided for the unorganised informal sector. However, once the organised sector is covered, then they could extend coverage to the unorganised sector.

Legislation

If one takes the path of social health insurance, then it may be advisable to introduce legislation to make health insurance mandatory. This is a social security measure akin to vehicle insurance and is aimed at protecting the population from high medical costs. This would also help in reducing the premiums as these would no longer be risk rated but community rated.

If universal health insurance is the end point, then the current government health services need to be modified in a systematic manner. Government should withdraw funding to them and instead they should depend on their finances by attracting patients and receiving money from the insurance companies for services rendered.

There should also be supporting legislation introduced to make it mandatory for registering health care institutions, ensuring minimum quality and finally accreditating them.

Regulate the Providers

While it is important to make changes in the health insurance products etc, it is also very important that the government make other changes to support the move towards universal health insurance coverage. One of the most important steps is to regulate the health care providers. The Indian health care provider is not regulated at all (Bhat, 1999). The Government has failed to do so and it is unlikely to do so in the near future. On the other hand, health insurance is a good vehicle to introduce regulation among the providers. As the insurance companies become the financers of care, they will have the power to demand for acceptable quality of care at a particular cost. Thus the insurance companies should take the initiative in controlling costs (capitation methods, case based payments, use of generics etc) as well as introducing quality assurance mechanisms in the hospitals. This could include introducing standard treatment guidelines etc.

It must be remembered that quality of care can be improved without too much cost escalation. People put too much emphasis on structural quality and want more inputs. But more emphasis should be on the process of consultation

– on making diagnosis and treating rationally and in the outcomes in terms of morbidity and mortality after treatment.

The current mechanisms of provider payment – fee for service is a perfect stimulus for cost escalation when health insurance is introduced. This will affect not just the insured but also the non-insured – that is why it is important for introducing cost control measures.

Regulate the Insurance Companies

It is equally important to ensure that the insurance companies are oriented towards a social purpose rather than a totally profit oriented purpose. They should not end up insuring only the healthy population and leave the non-healthy and weaker sections of the society to the public sector health insurance companies. Legislation should ensure this in no uncertain terms.

An Appropriate Health Insurance Scheme

It is easy to blame the people, illiteracy, and poverty for the poor insurance penetration. However, one also needs to consider the inappropriately designed schemes currently existing. If these were modified then the chances of people accepting health insurance would increase. Some of the changes that need to be introduced are

- An affordable premium, in the range of about Rs. 200 – 250 for a family of 5 would be attractive for most of the poorer sections of the society. This could be a minimum premium for a basic package. The premium could be increased according to the benefits for the wealthier sections of the society. Have the family as the minimum enrolment unit with a floater clause that would reduce the premium considerably.
- A comprehensive coverage that takes care of most inpatient conditions is required. This could include

day procedures like POP for fractures, scopes etc, but for the time being one should exclude OP conditions. May be this could be introduced at a later date. Other than this, there should be minimal exclusions. This is in keeping with the health systems perspective, where the health insurance is aimed at covering illnesses rather than providing profits.

- The administrative procedures should be simplified as much as possible. So enrolment should be done through existing mechanisms, e.g. the cooperative societies for the cooperative sector etc. Similarly, control of fraud, processing claims and reimbursements can be minimised, if appropriate local mechanisms are used. Thus, the administrative load and cost on the insurance companies and the people would be reduced.

- Along with this, the IRDA/Insurance companies/ TPAs should regulate the providers and ensure cost control measures and quality of care is introduced. This has been discussed in detail earlier. This is the only way that the products will be attractive for the community and will also be sustainable for the insurance companies.

- For a health insurance product to be successful, the community should trust the stakeholders, principally the providers and the insurance company. The IRDA has a major role – to engender this trust.

The Way Forward

The Indian health system is at a crossroads. It has to choose to finance its health care either through more government funds or through an insurance mechanism. If it decides to go to the latter way, then the challenge is to see that it benefits the poor people in terms of better coverage and health services at lower costs without the negative aspects of cost increase and over use of procedures and technology in provision of health care. The experience from other places suggest that if health insurance is left to the private market it will only cover those which have substantial ability to pay leaving out the poor and making them more vulnerable. Hence, India should proactively make efforts to develop Social Health Insurance patterned after the German model where there is universal coverage, equal access to all and cost controlling measures such as prospective per capita payment to providers (Bhat and Mavalankar, 2000). Given that India does not have large organized sector employment, the only option for such social health insurance is to develop it through co-operatives, associations and unions. The existing health insurance programmes such as CGHS, ESIS and Mediclaim also need substantial reforms to make them more efficient and socially useful. And, finally, the health sector needs to be reformed and regulated, if health insurance has to be successful. Government should catalyze and guide development of such social health insurance in India. Towards this end, the Indian and state governments can learn important lessons from its neighbours like Thailand, Vietnam, Phillipines and Korea who have introduced health insurance with considerable success.

Table 1
Some Community Health Insurance Schemes in India

Name and Location of the Scheme	*Population Covered (Target Population 2003)*	*Premium Collected (Percent of Target Population Covered 2003).*	*Benefit Package*
1	*2*	*3*	*4*
ACCORD			
Gudalur, Nilgiris, Tamil Nadu	Tribals living in Gudalur Taluk and who are members of the AMS union (N= 13000).	Rs. 25 per person per year (36.0%).	Hospitalisation covers up to Rs. 1500 per person per year.
BAIF			
Urali Kanchan, Pune, Maharashtra	Women members (between 18 – 58 years) of the micro savings scheme in 22 villages (N=1500).	Rs. 105 per person per year (58.0%)	Hospitalisation cover up to Rs. 5000 per person per year.
BUCCS,			
Buldhana, Maharashtra.	Members of the Buldhana Urban Cooperative and Credit society (N=175,000).	Rs. 98 per person per year	Hospitalisation cover up to Rs. 5000 per person per year.
DHAN			
Foundation, Kadamalai Taluk, Theni	Women members of the micro finance scheme	Rs 100 per person per year	Hospitalisation covers up to Rs. 10,000 per person

(Contd...)

1	*2*	*3*	*4*
District, Tamil Nadu	and living in Mayiladumparai block (N= 19049).	(40.0%).	per year.
Karuna Trust			
T Narsipur Block, Mysore District, Karnataka	BPL families in T Narsipur block (N=278,156).	Rs. 30 per person per year. Fully subsidised for the SC/ST population. (31.0%).	Hospitalisation covers up to Rs. 2500 per person per year. Includes ambulance services and loss of wages
MGIMS Hospital			
Wardha, Maharashtra	The small farmers and landless labourers living in the 40 villages around Kasturba Hospital (N=30,000).	Rs 48 per family of four (in cash or kind) (90.0%).	Hospitalisation cover up to Rs. 1,500 per person per year.
Raigarh Ambikapur Health Association, (RAHA)			
Raigarh - Chattisgarh	Poor people living in the catchment area of the 92 rural health centres and hostel students (N=92,000 individuals).	Rs. 20 per person (58.0%).	Primary and secondary health care

(Contd...)

1	*2*	*3*	*4*
SEWA			
Ahmedabad - Gujarat	SEWA Union women members (urban and rural), plus their husbands living in 11 Districts of Gujarat (N= 1,067,348 individuals).	Rs. 22.50 per person or Rs 45 for a couple (10.0%)	Hospitalisation covers up to Rs. 2000 per person.
SHADE			
Kolencherry – Kerala	Members of the SHGs operating in Ernakulam district (N=9000)	The Universal Health Insurance Scheme (Rs. 548 for a family of 5) (20.0%)	Hospitalisation covers for family up to a maximum limit of Rs. 30,000 per family per year
Student's Health Home			
Kolkata – West Bengal	Full-time student in West Bengal State, from Class 5 to University level (N=5.6 million students).	Rs. 4 per student per year (23.0%)	Primary and secondary health care.
Voluntary Health Services			
Chennai - Tamil Nadu.	Total population of the catchment area of 14 mini-health centres (N= 104,247 individuals).	Rs. 250 per family of five (12.0%)	Hospital cover

(Contd...)

1	2	3	4
Yeshasvini			
Bangalore - Karnataka	Members of the District Farmer's cooperative societies and their families (N–8 million)	Rs. 60 per person (25.0%)	Cover for all surgeries up to Rs. 100,000

Box 1: The Insurance Regulatory and Development Act (IRDA) 1999 (Mahal 2002).

The IRDA Act was passed in Dec 1999 by parliament. The Act allows for the entry of private sector entities in the Indian insurance sector, including health insurance, and envisages the creation of a regulatory authority. The IRDA is supposed to protect the interests of the policyholders, promote efficiency in the conduct of insurance, regulate the rates and terms and conditions of policies offered by insurers and direct the maintenance of solvency margins.

The IRDA act provides sufficient protection for Capital and solvency margins. There is an entry requirement of a minimum capital of Rs. 100 crores. Then there is a minimum lower bound of Rs. 50 crores for the solvency margin along with a requirement of 20.0% of net premiums or a 30.0% of the average of net incurred claims in the 3 preceding years.

The IRDA has wide powers for accounting and auditing insurers.

The Insurance act does not allow the insurers to undertake additional business that is not directly linked to insurance.

The Insurance act discusses the liquidation of a company but does not talk of a Guarantee fund.

The IRDA specifies a code of conduct for the insurance agents and also allows for a tariff advisory committee to oversee premium rates, insurance plans and to prevent discrimination. However, there is no specific clause for the consumer, who has to use the CPA of 1986 to redress any complaints.

The IRDA does not have much to say about the relationship between the insurer and the provider.

The IRDA does not have much to say about rating the premium, though the Tariff advisory committee can make recommendations.

The IRDA does not also specify the benefit packages. It, however, allows for the entry of re-insurers in the market.

Its main two functions are - maintaining market standards and overseeing solvency and financial regulations.

Conclusion: The legislation concerning health insurance in India is fairly comprehensive even in comparison to a model set of regulations when focusing on auditing, financial controls, investment guidelines and licensing regulations. There is much less regulatory focus on the consumer of insurance products and the overall goals of health policy in the form of regulation that curbs risk selection, protects consumers, promotes HMOs and the like. It also cannot involve in the relationship between insurers and providers (which comes under the MRTP act) or the expansion of ESIS (which is the ESIS Act).

In India, health insurance is not given much importance. The IRDA bill itself contains no reference whatsoever to the health sector or to health insurance. Nor is health mentioned in the nearly 175 pages of the Insurance Act of 1938. This broadly reflects the policy environment in India, where health insurance continues to be neglected. Even in the GoI's report on Insurance reforms (1994), there was precisely one reference to health insurance.

Source: Ajay Mahal - Assessing Private Health Insurance in India: Potential impacts and Regulatory Issues. *Economic and Political Weekly* 2002: 559-71

Box 2: The Yeshasvini Co-operative Farmers' Health Care Scheme

The Yeshasvini scheme is operational in Karnataka and covers the members of the district cooperative societies and their families. At last count, there were more than 18 million members in these societies.

The collection of contributions has been channelled through the District Cooperative Societies. Members who wish to join fill in an application form and their premium is deducted at source at the village level itself. The premium is Rs 60 per person per year. The money is collected and is deposited in the Yeshasvini Trust's bank account.

The list of insured is handed over to the TPA who provides the insured with a photo identity card. If any of the insured members fall sick, they can go to any of 114 empanelled hospitals (private sector hospitals mostly). If the person needs surgery, then they are provided the necessary treatment and allowed to go home. The hospital then submits the bills to the TPA who in turn reimburses the hospitals.

In 2003-2004, 1.6 million had joined the scheme and there were 5.6 admissions per 1000 insured. In 2004 – 2005, 2.07 million have joined the scheme

Box 3: The Types of CHI in India

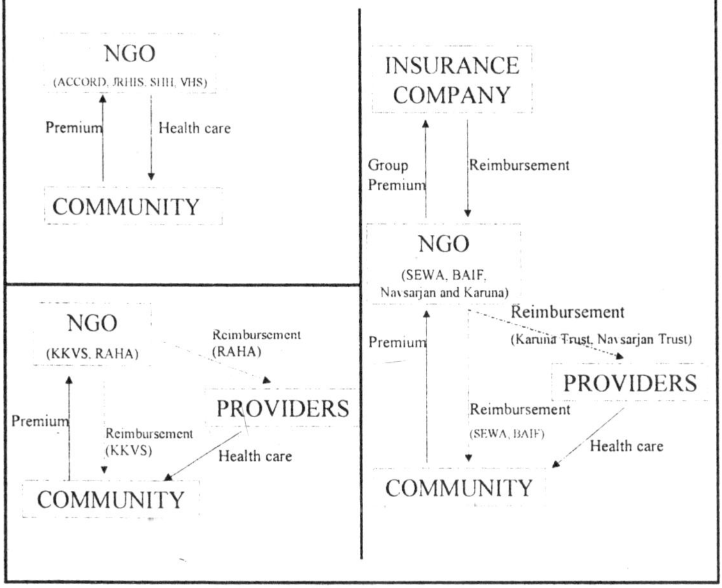

Table 3
Differences between the German and the American Health Insurance Schemes

Key Features	*American System*	*German System*
Owners of health insurance	Private companies	Sickness funds composed of enrolled members
Coverage, and access to health	70.0% of population covered and access	99.5% of population covered and access to

(Contd...)

Key Features	*American System*	*German System*
care	to health care is unequal	every one is equal
Premium based on	Actuarial risk (Age, sex, disease)	Income - % of pay roll. Shared equally by employer and employees.
Selection and refusals	Do occur	Not allowed by law
Reimbursement to providers	Based on costs and per cases/ procedure basis	Outpatient is on prospective per capita basis, in-patient per day, per case basis
Nature of risk pooling	From healthy to sick	Healthy to sick, high income to low income, young to old, small families to big families
Choice of providers	Yes	Yes
Coverage and co- payment	Limited to medical care and co- payment high	Coverage very wide and co-payments low
Nature of competition	Between companies	Not much
Nature of regulation	Minimal by government, mostly by market forces	Self-regulation by autonomous bodies under overall framework of social legislation
Effect of medical costs	Highly inflationary	Inflationary effect limited due to the prospective per capita payment

Modified from Ramesh Bhat, Dileep Mavalankar. Health Insurance in India: Opportunities and challenges.

REFERENCES

Barnighausen, T. and Sauerborn, R. (2002). One Hundred and Eighteen Years of The German Health Insurance System:

Are There Any Lessons For Middle- and Low-Income Countries? *Soc Sci. Med*, 54, 1559-1587.

Bhat, Ramesh (1999). Characteristics of Private Medical Practice In India: A Provider Perspective. *Health Policy and Planning*, 14, 26-37.

Bhat, Ramesh and Mavalankar, D. (2000). Health *Insurance in India. Opportunities, Challenges and Concerns*, 1-28.

Bhat, Ramesh and Reuben, E. (2001). Analysis of Claims and Reimbursements Made Under Mediclaim Policy of the General Insurance Corporation of India. 2001. Ref Type: Personal Communication

Criel Bart (1998). Insurance and Solidarity: Concepts and Typology,' in *District based health insurance in sub-Saharan Africa*, 1 edn, ITM, Antwerp, 59-82.

Devadasan, N., Criel, B., Van, Damme W., Ranson, M.K., and Van, der Stuyft, P. (2007). Indian Community Health Insurance Schemes Provide Partial Protection Against Catastrophic Health Expenditure. *BMC Health Services Research*, 7.

Devadasan, N., Manoharan, S., Menon, N., Menon, S., Thekaekara, M., Thekaekara, S., and AMS Team (2004a). Accord Community Health Insurance - Increasing Access To Hospital Care. *Economic and Political Weekly*, 39, 3189-3194.

Davidson, N., Ransom, M.K., Van, Dame W., and Criel, B. (2004b). Community Health Insurance In India: An Overview. *Economic and Political Weekly*, 39, 3179-3183.

Economic Bureau. Fin Min Rejects LIC IPO Plan, Rules Out Dilution In Banks. Financial Express Online. 10-20-2004. Indian Express Group. Ref Type: Newspaper

Ellis, R., Alam, M., and Gupta, I. (2000). Health Insurance in India: Prognosis and Prospectus. *Economic and Political Weekly*, 35, 207-217.

Government of India (2003). *Social Security*. Ministry of Labour, New Delhi, 43-51.

Gumber, A. (2002). *Health Insurance for the informal sector: Problems and prospects*. ICREAR, New Delhi, 1-49.

ILO (2005). *Insurance Products Provided By Insurance Companies To The Disadvantaged Groups In India*, 1 edn. ILO, Geneva, 1-211.

Kutzin, J. (1998). 'Enhancing the Insurance Function of Health Systems: A Proposed Conceptual Framework,' in *Achieving Universal Coverage of Health care*, 1 edn, Nitayarumphong Sanguan and Mills Anne, eds., MOH - Thailand, Bangkok, 27-101.

Mahal, A. (2002). Assessing Private Health Insurance in India: Potential Impacts and Regulatory Issues. *Economic and Political Weekly*, 559-571.

Mediclaims Top Non-Life Grievances. Business Standard. 2003. Ref Type: Magazine Article

Meessen, B., Zhenzhong, Z., Van Damme W., Devadasan, N., Criel B., and Bloom, G. (2003). Editorial: Iatrogenic Poverty. *Tropical Medicine and International Health*, 8, 581-584.

Ogawa, S., Hasegawa, T., Carrin, G., and Kawabata Kei (2003). Scaling up Community Health Insurance: Japan's experience with the 19th Century Jyorei Scheme. *Health Policy and Planning*, 18, 270-278.

Peters, D.H., Yazbeck, A.S., Sharma, R.S., Ramana, G.N.V., Pritchett, L.H., and Wagstaff, A. (2002). *Better Health Systems for India's Poor* World Bank. Washington, 1-347.

Ranson, M.K. (2002). Reduction of Catastrophic Health Care Expenditures By A Community-Based Health Insurance Scheme In Gujarat, India: Current Experiences and Challenges. *Bull World Health Organ*, 80, 613-621.

Sainath, P. (2004). Anatomy of a Health Disaster. The Hindu. 7-1-2004. Chennai. Ref Type: Newspaper

Subrahmanya, R.K.A. (1998). 'Extension of Social Insurance Schemes In The Formal Sector,' in *Social Security for all Indians*, 1 edn, van Ginneken W, ed., Oxford University Press, New Delhi, 23-56.

Syed, F. (2004). Inflated Bills Hit Mediclaim Schemes. Indian Express Online. 2004. Ref Type: Newspaper

The Economic Times (2003). Concern Over Low Rural, Health Insurance Focus. The Economic Times, 9. 12-9-2003. Bangalore, Times of India. Ref Type: Newspaper

Viswanathan S. (2003). IRDA to Establish Health Insurance Database. Express Health Care Management Online. 2003. Indian Express Group. Ref Type: Newspaper

NOTES

1. http://esic.nic.in/ accessed on 08.09.2004
2. Cynthia Ramsay. Medical Savings Accounts, Universal, Accessible, Portable, Comprehensive Health Care for Canadians. Fraser Institute, Vancouver. 1998.
3. Aloke Gupta. The Health Care continuum. IRDA Journal January 2003

22

Reproductive and Sexual Health Questionnaire (RASHQ)

Swarn Lata & Prof. Archana Shukla

Instructions: Read these questions carefully and respond by putting a tick mark on any one of the three options that best describes your opinion for each question/statement. Then, follow instructions at the end to figure out how well you understand the issues related to Reproductive and Sexual Health (RSH). Reproductive and Sexual Health is one vital aspect of our overall health. So, let us get concerned. And, get talking ...

Gender: Age: Education:

1. Which is a prominent physical change in boys during puberty?

    a. Appearance of facial hairs

    b. Increase in height

    c. Reduction in weight

2. Which is a prominent physical change in girls during puberty?

   a. Increase in weight

   b. Stoppage in increase in height

   c. Increase in the size of breast

3. What is the normal frequency of menstrual cycles?

   a. Twice a month

   b. Once a month

   c. Once in two- three months

4. How is menstrual period caused?

   a. Due to release of egg from the ovaries

   b. Excess collection of blood in the uterus

   c. Due to some complications in the uterus

5. At what age does a woman typically reach menopause?

   a. 30-40 yrs

   b. 45-55 yrs

   c. 20-30 yrs

6. What are the chances of a girl getting pregnant when she has sex during her period?

   a. 0%

   b. 50%

   c. 100%

7. What are the chances that a girl will become pregnant when she has sexual intercourse for the first time?

   a. low

b. high

c. moderate

8. Is infertility just a woman's problem?

a. Yes

b. No

c. May be

9. Sita has three daughters. She is constantly criticized by her in-laws for not bearing a son. Her husband is thinking of getting married again for this reason. Who do you think is responsible in determining the sex of the baby?

a. Father

b. God and fate.

c. Mother

10. How long after delivery must breastfeeding be initiated?

a. When the mother reaches home.

b. Within an hour of delivery.

c. Only when the proper white milk starts flowing from the breast.

11. How can breast engorgement be prevented?

a. Take medicines

b. Breast feed at every one and a half hour

c. Stop breast feeding

12. For a newly born child mothers' milk is

a. Completely sufficient.

b. Insufficient therefore supplement required.

c. Not at all sufficient, Lactogen is better.

13. How long can a woman continue working after she becomes pregnant?

a. Till the 7th month

b. Till the 4th month

c. Till the end of 9th month

14. Is it safe to have sexual intercourse during pregnancy?

a. Yes

b. No

c. Undecided

15. Is it desirable to drink fizzy drinks during pregnancy?

a. No

b. Yes

c. Don't know

16. What is the ideal weight gain for a woman during healthy pregnancy?

a. 5-6 kgs

b. 11-14 kgs

c. 15-20 kgs

17. How can one determine the due date of delivery?

a. By adding 40 weeks to the first day of your last menstrual period.

b. By adding 36 weeks to your last day of your last menstrual period.

c. By adding 40 weeks to the day you consult doctor.

18. What is a normal healthy weight for a newborn?
    a. 2-2.5 kg
    b. 1.5 kgs
    c. 2 kgs
19. Which is common deficiency in pregnant women?
    a. Iron
    b. Magnesium
    c. Vitamin C
20. Which is the minimum ideal age for the girl to conceive?
    a. 18 yrs
    b. 16 yrs
    c. 22yrs
21. Which of the following injections are given to a woman during her pregnancy?
    a. Tetanus
    b. Iron
    c. Glucose
22. Some fruits like papaya can lead to abortion.
    a. Yes, True
    b. No, Not true
    c. Don't know
23. Onset of Menstruation means that
    a. The girl is ready for marriage.
    b. Her reproductive system is developing.
    c. The girl is ready to conceive a child

24. During menstruation one should not take bath.

    a. Yes

    b. No

    c. Don't know

25. Masturbation and 'wet dreams' for boys is

    a. A normal activity

    b. An abnormal activity which can lead to ill health

    c. Immoral and undesirable

26. 'Orgasm' refers to

    a. Any sexual intercourse between a man and a woman

    b. Rhythmic pelvic thrusts with peak experience of satisfaction

    c. Sexual feelings of a prostitute

27. A woman who desires to experience orgasm during sexual activity is

    a. A normal woman

    b. An immoral woman

    c. A women with extreme sexual hunger

28. During a sexual intercourse most woman are able to experience orgasm.

    a. True

    b. False

    c. Undecided

29. 'Withdrawal Method' is

    a. No guarantee for prevention of pregnancy

b. Easy to practice for prevention of pregnancy

c. A safe and sure technique for not conceiving a child

30. How accurate is a home pregnancy test

a. 99%

b. 0%

c. 50%

Scoring Key

Transfer your responses to the table. Suppose your answer to Question 1 is 'a', then tick 'a' in front of the question no.1, similarly if your answer to Question no. 2 is 'b', tick 'b' in front of question no.2.

Next, under each column, count the number of tick marks in that column, and write it. Similarly, fill each of the other two column totals.

Examine the total number of your 'aaha', 'ouch' and 'hmm' responses with those given in the table. A big 'aaha' score means that you have good knowledge; a big 'hmm' score means you are quite off the target. A big 'ouch' score means you are unaware (and may be unconcerned) about reproductive and sexual health. In any case talk more often with persons who have authentic knowledge about RSH. Also please share your knowledge with your young ones.

Question No.	*Aaha*	*Hmm*	*Ouch*
1.	a	b	c
2.	c	a	b
3	b	a	c
4	a	b	c
5	b	a	c

(Contd...)